Impoliteness

When is language considered 'impolite'? Is impolite language only used for anti-social purposes? Can impolite language be creative? What is the difference between 'impoliteness' and 'rudeness'? Grounded in naturally occurring language data and drawing on findings from linguistic pragmatics and social psychology, Jonathan Culpeper provides a fascinating account of how impolite behaviour works. He examines not only its forms and functions but also people's understandings of it in both public and private contexts. He reveals, for example, the emotional consequences of impoliteness, how it shapes and is shaped by contexts, and how it is sometimes institutionalised. This book offers penetrating insights into a hitherto neglected and poorly understood phenomenon. It will be welcomed by students and researchers in linguistics and social psychology in particular.

JONATHAN CULPEPER is based in the Department of Linguistics and English Language at Lancaster University.

Studies in Interactional Sociolinguistics

EDITORS
Paul Drew, Marjorie Harness Goodwin, John J. Gumperz, Deborah Schiffrin

Impoliteness

Using Language to Cause Offence

Jonathan Culpeper

Lancaster University

CAMBRIDGE UNIVERSITY PRESS

CAMBRIDGE
UNIVERSITY PRESS

University Printing House, Cambridge CB2 8BS, United Kingdom

Cambridge University Press is part of the University of Cambridge.

It furthers the University's mission by disseminating knowledge in the pursuit of education, learning and research at the highest international levels of excellence.

www.cambridge.org
Information on this title: www.cambridge.org/9780521689779

© Jonathan Culpeper 2011

First published 2011
Reprinted 2012

A catalogue record for this publication is available from the British Library

Library of Congress Cataloguing in Publication data
Culpeper, Jonathan, 1966–
Impoliteness : using language to cause offence / Jonathan Culpeper.
    p.   cm. – (Studies in interactional sociolinguistics ; 28)
Includes bibliographical references and index.
ISBN 978-0-521-86967-6
1. Politeness (Linguistics)   2. English language – Honorific.
3. Power (Social sciences)   4. Interpersonal relations.   I. Title.
P299.H66C85   2011
306.44 – dc22   2010041665

ISBN 978-0-521-86967-6 Hardback
ISBN 978-0-521-68977-9 Paperback

I dedicate this book to my father,
who embodies everything this book is not about.

Contents

Figures and tables

Figures

Tables

Preface

Any research needs to justify its existence, because all research requires effort, time and money. Impoliteness is, in its modern incarnation, a new field of study, and any new field is prone to insecurity. More than this, impoliteness is up against prejudice. Embarrassed silence is a typical reaction when I declare what my research is, followed by a rapid change of topic. This is not quite the reaction one gets having declared one's research to be Shakespeare or the syntax of world languages. Impoliteness is assumed to be an unfortunate behavioural aberration, and, as far as language is concerned, it is the nasty scum on the margins. To be fair, this is not so often the reaction of people with more social interests. Impoliteness is, in fact, of great social importance. It is salient in the consciousness of the general public. In the guise of 'verbal abuse', 'threats', 'bullying' and so on, it is referred to and prohibited by public signs, charters, laws and documents relating to public places (especially in England); it is addressed by government (cf. Tony Blair's *Respect Agenda*); it is often reported in the media, particularly when it occurs in contexts where it seems 'abnormal' (e.g. verbal abuse directed at the elderly); and beamed into our living rooms usually as entertainment, as in the case of exploitative TV chat, quiz and talent shows (e.g. *Britain's Got Talent*). In fact, it is much more salient than politeness – in the UK, we almost never see signs urging positive verbal behaviour, such as 'Please use "please" to the staff' (though signs urging positive behaviours in general, such as 'Thank you for driving carefully', do sometimes appear). In private life, of course, we may well hear politeness rules being articulated and enforced, particularly in contexts such as parent–child discourse. And here we will also come across behaviours that break those politeness rules being condemned as impolite. Impoliteness has an intimate, though not straightforward, connection with politeness. Impoliteness is also of great interpersonal significance. Impoliteness is involved in aggression, abuse, bullying and harassment. Minimally, it results in emotional pain but can even end in suicide.

So, why do we need a linguist for this topic? Research suggests that the saying 'sticks and stones may break my bones, but words can never hurt me' is not always true. The sociologist and criminologist Michele Burman and her colleagues (e.g. Burman *et al.* 2002) found, for example, that teenage girls viewed non-physical or verbal behaviours as potentially more hurtful and damaging than physical violence. Greenwell and Dengerink (1973: 70), working in a very different psychological tradition of research on aggression, had arrived at a very similar conclusion: 'while attack is an important instigator of aggressive behaviour, it appears that the physical discomfort experienced by a person may be subordinate to the symbolic elements that are incorporated in that attack'. Symbolic violence is an important feature of much impolite language. One can get a sense of this by considering how words describing specific kinds of impoliteness have developed. For example, the word *insult* is derived from Latin *insulto*, which in the period of Classical Latin had two senses: (1) to leap or jump upon, and (2) to taunt, ridicule or insult. The original meaning of physical violence – jumping on one's victim – had developed a metaphorical symbolic violent meaning, and this is the one that survives today. However, neither sociologists nor psychologists investigate in any detail what those verbally impolite behaviours consist of or how they work. Enter the linguist! Indeed, there is much for the linguist to do. Verbal impoliteness is not simple (e.g. a mere reflex of anger). As I will demonstrate in this book, it can be elaborately creative. Moreover, the study of language and impoliteness is of value to the discipline of linguistics, despite the fact that it is rarely mentioned. Theories of linguistic interaction and communication developed in fields such as pragmatics, interactional sociolinguistics and communication studies are biased towards, and developed from, socially cooperative interactions. Consequently, they cannot adequately account for anti-social, impolite interactions. Yet, as I have noted, impoliteness is an important aspect of social life, and indeed plays a central role in many discourses (from military recruit training to exploitative TV shows), discourses which are rarely described in detail.

The writing of this book was made possible by a three-year Research Fellowship awarded to me by the UK's Economic and Social Research Council (ESRC) (RES-063–27-0015). Without this, it probably never would have happened. Along the way, I have accumulated a significant overdraft of favours. I would like to extend particular thanks to Leyla Marti (Boğaziçi University, Turkey), Meilian Mei (Zhejiang University of Technology, China), Minna Nevala (University of Helsinki) and Gila Schauer (Lancaster University) for letting me draw on some of their diary-report data for some sections of Chapter 2. Similarly, I have benefitted from the generosity of John Dixon (Lancaster University), for not only allowing me to report our pilot study in Section 5.5 but for undertaking it with me in the first place. I thank the many people who helped procure impoliteness diary-reports, including: Pu Bei (Zhejiang University of Technology); Martin Pütz (Universität Koblenz-Landau); Beatrix Busse (Universität Bern); Roland Kehrein (Philipps Universität Marburg); Tanja Giessler (Philippps Universität Marburg); Hans-Jörg Schmid

(Ludwig-Maximilians Universität München); Anke Lüdeling (Humboldt Universität zu Berlin); John Dixon, Andrew Wilson, Eivind Torgersen, Sebastian Hoffman, Kevin Watson, Veronika Koller, Pelham Gore (Lancaster University); Sara Mills (Sheffield Hallam University); Andrew Merrison (York St John University); and Amy Wang (Manchester Metropolitan University). I am very grateful to: Brian Walker, who saved me from the tedium of transcribing all the British data, and ran some data searches for me; Jane Demmen, who helped procure some of the literature I needed; and Claire Hardaker, who, with remarkable efficiency, helped lick the bibliography of this book into shape. Special gratitude is reserved for John Heywood who read the entire manuscript, saving me from many a howler and infelicity, and prepared the index. More generally, I am indebted to the very many people who have helped shape my thinking over the years, including the members of the Linguistic Politeness Research Group (LPRG). Finally, I owe apologies more than thanks to Elena, Emily and Natalie who have born the brunt of a stressed-out family member.

The figures and a small amount of text in Sections 4.5.3 and 5.3 are drawn from Culpeper (2005; an article which is available here: www.reference-global.com/toc/jplr/1/1) and printed here by kind permission of De Gruyter; some text in Sections 1.3.2, 1.4.3 and 1.5 is based on Culpeper et al. (forthcoming); the tables and some of the text in Sections 3.4 and 3.6 are drawn from Culpeper (2009); some text in Sections 4.3 and 4.4 is drawn from Culpeper (forthcoming a). Every effort has been made to secure necessary permissions to reproduce copyright material in this book, though in some cases it has proved impossible to trace or contact copyright holders. If any omissions are brought to our notice, we will be happy to include appropriate acknowledgements in reprinting and any subsequent edition.

Introducing impoliteness

Orientating to impoliteness

Let us begin by working through two brief examples. I will use these as a springboard for the array of impoliteness phenomena to be examined later in the book (I will not cite much supportive research here, but will do so in later chapters).

The first example is taken from my report data. It is a kind of diary report, with some reflective commentary, written by a British undergraduate (details of the methodology are given below). (Note: I make no attempt to 'clean-up' the data analysed in this book, and so there will be spelling errors and other infelicities.)

[1]

> I was in a taxi with 5 other girls, on our way into town. The taxi driver seemed nice at first, commenting on how pretty we looked etc. Then he turned quite nasty, making vulgar sexual innuendos, swearing a lot and laughing at us. He then insulted some of us, commenting on the clothes we were wearing and when we didn't laugh, he looked quite angry. He then asked where we were from, we told him, and then he started criticising and insulting us and our home towns. We mostly stayed quiet, giving non-committal, single word answers until we could leave.

My informant commented that the taxi driver's behaviour was 'sexist, rude, very offensive and inappropriate given the context'. Clearly, impoliteness behaviours are labelled in particular ways; impoliteness has its own metadiscourse. The behaviour is described as 'rude', a term that encompasses the semantic domain of impoliteness. It is also described as 'sexist', a notion that partially overlaps with impoliteness (for an excellent account of language and sexism, see Mills 2008). Impoliteness often involves seeking to damage and/or damaging a person's identity or identities. This behaviour had the particular negative effect of being 'very offensive'. Later in her commentary, the informant adds that they felt 'angry, disgusted, and upset'. These are typical emotions triggered by language considered impolite. The informant observes that the behaviour was 'inappropriate given the context'. Most impoliteness behaviours are inappropriate. This, of course, is a very broad observation; lots of things are considered inappropriate, but do not amount to impoliteness. I will need to be more specific in this book. In her commentary, the informant does in fact make more specific points: '[i]t made us feel bad because we had been insulted when we had done nothing to provoke it'. This reflects the fact that impoliteness as retaliation for impoliteness is considered justifiable and appropriate, and thus less impolite (Section 7.4 elaborates on this particular context). The report also alludes to a dynamic aspect of context: 'the taxi driver seemed nice at first... then he turned quite nasty'. Some research has suggested that negative violations of conversational expectations are particularly bad, if they occur after a positive beginning. Note also that the report is peppered with references to specific kinds of communicative behaviour produced by the taxi driver: 'commenting' (twice), 'innuendos', 'swearing', 'laughing', 'insulted/insulting' and 'criticising'. In addition, the informant observes that 'he looked quite angry', and in her commentary that 'his tone of voice and facial expressions also made us feel very uncomfortable'. Clearly, behaviours such as these will need careful examination.

It is not an unusual occurrence that people take offence at *how* someone says something rather than at *what* was said. Consider this exchange between two pre-teenage sisters:

[2]
    A: Do you know anything about yo-yos?
    B: That's mean.

On the face of it, speaker A's utterance is an innocent enquiry about speaker B's state of knowledge. But speaker B provides evidence of her negative emotional reaction in her response, a metapragmatic comment – 'That's mean.' The impoliteness is referred to by the metalinguistic label 'mean'. Clearly then, the communicative behaviour has evoked a negative attitude. One might infer that her wish to have her competence in yo-yos upheld, her expectation that it normally is upheld by others, and/or her belief that it should be upheld (in accord with family 'rules') has been infringed. Emotions relating to her perception of self, how her identity is seen by others and/or how her identity should be treated are triggered. How are they triggered? Speaker A heavily stressed the beginning of 'anything', and produced the remainder of the utterance with sharply falling intonation. This prosody is marked against the norm for yes-no questions, which usually have rising intonation (e.g. Quirk *et al.* 1985: 807). It signals to B that A's question is not straightforward or innocent. It triggers the recovery of implications that A is not asking a question but expressing both a belief that speaker B knows nothing about yo-yos and an attitude towards that belief, namely, incredulity that this is the case – something which itself implies that speaker B is deficient in some way. Without the prosody, there is no clear evidence of the interpersonal orientation of speaker A, whether positive, negative or somewhere in between. Why exactly does B take offence? She takes offence at the communicative behaviour because: it infringes expectations/beliefs that are strongly held and emotionally sensitive; its pragmatic meaning required a considerable amount of inferential work to recover; there are no obvious mitigating factors in the context (though the prior co-text provides evidence that speaker A is frustrated with her); on the contrary, there are interpretative factors that are likely to intensify the offence, namely that speaker B is likely to infer that speaker A intended it to happen.

These two examples give a sense of the range of phenomena that need to be addressed in a treatment of impoliteness, such as particular behavioural triggers, the communication and understanding of implicit and explicit meanings, emotions, norms, identities, contexts and metadiscourse.

The field of study

Impoliteness is a multidisciplinary field of study. It can be approached from within social psychology (especially verbal aggression), sociology (especially verbal abuse), conflict studies (especially the resolution of verbal conflict), media studies (especially exploitative TV and entertainment), business studies (especially interactions in the workplace), history (especially social history), literary studies, to name but a few. This is not to say that all the researchers from these various disciplines will use the label impoliteness. As I will show in Chapter 3, certain researchers gravitate towards certain labels, labels which reflect their particular interests and approach. Here, I will briefly elaborate on impoliteness issues in three disciplines outside the realms of linguistic pragmatics, and then within linguistic pragmatics.

Work in social psychology on aggression or aggressive behaviour constitutes a large literature (for useful overviews, see Baron and Richardson 1994; Geen 2001). From the outset, with classics such as Buss (1961), verbal acts of aggression were considered alongside physical acts. This has implications for how aggression is defined. An interesting definition is provided by Baron and Richardson (1994: 7): '[a]ggression is any form of behaviour directed toward the goal of harming or injuring another living being who is motivated to avoid such treatment'. Note the use of the word 'harming'. Baron and Richardson (1994: 9–10) go on to say:

The notion that aggression involves either *harm* or injury to the victim implies that *physical* damage to the recipient is not essential. So long as this person has experienced some type of aversive consequence, aggression has occurred. Thus, in addition to direct, physical assaults, such actions as causing others to 'lose face' or experience public embarrassment, depriving them of needed objects, and even withholding love or affection can, under appropriate circumstances, be aggressive in nature.

In Tedeschi and Felson's (1994) work on aggression, the notion of 'social harm' is central, and defined thus:

> Social harm involves damage to the social identity of target persons and a lowering of their power or status. Social harm may be imposed by insults, reproaches, sarcasm, and various types of impolite behaviour. (1994: 171)

This is where the connection with impoliteness is clearest. It should be acknowledged, however, that the bulk of work on aggression focuses on physical aggression (or does not distinguish verbal aggression in particular), and on aspects that are fairly remote from notions such as social identity and power, such as the acquisition of aggressive behaviours, broad determinants of aggression (e.g. emotional frustration, the ambient temperature, alcohol), aggressive personality dispositions and biological foundations.

Research which is anchored in the field of sociology (or anthropology) has focused on the social effects of verbal abuse. Many studies have considered verbal abuse in relation to, for example, gender, race, adolescents, crime, school bullying, marital breakdown, public employees and workplace harassment. As briefly noted in the preface of this book, the finding of the sociologist and criminologist Michele Burman and her colleagues (e.g. Batchelor *et al.* 2001; Burman *et al.* 2002) is that teenage girls viewed non-physical or verbal behaviours as potentially more hurtful and damaging than physical violence. Their impressive study of perceptions of violence amongst teenage girls deployed self-report questionnaires, focus group discussions and in-depth interviews. It shines light on the forms of violence, the contexts they take place in, their purposes and functions, and their impact on recipients. Regarding forms of violence, they state:

> The most common 'violent' encounter reported by girls of all ages and from all backgrounds and situations concerned their use and experience of (what we have called) 'verbal abuse'. Examples include threats (e.g. 'You're a lying cow and if you don't stop it I'm gonna hit you'), name-calling and insults (e.g. calling someone a 'lezzie', a 'ned' or a 'fat cow'), ridicule, and intimidation by shouting or swearing. Girls reported being singled out for their so-called undesirable physical attributes (such as being overweight or having red hair), their dress style (especially 'cheap', non-branded clothes) or suspect personal hygiene. Skin colour and regional accents were also identified as signifiers of difference and therefore ridicule, as were sexual reputation and sexual orientation. Insults were not solely directed at girls themselves, however. Like Campbell (1986) and Anderson (1997) we found that family members, particularly mothers, were also targets for derogatory and critical remarks. (Batchelor *et al.* 2001: 128)

Although they do not use the terms impoliteness or impolite, this fits the underlying notion of impoliteness. In fact, we will see in Chapter 4 that devices such as threats, name-calling and insults, ridicule and shouting are conventionalised impolite ways of achieving offence. Also, especially in Chapter 1, which draws upon a similar self-report methodology, we will see people taking offence when undesirable physical attributes, dress style, personal hygiene, regional accents and so on are flagged up by something that is said or done. However, these scholars do not investigate in any detail what verbal violence consists of or how it is said, or how different verbal expressions might interact with the co-text or context. It is also the case that this study is limited to one specific speech community.

Conflict studies is a wide-ranging multidisciplinary field, focusing in particular on conflicts of viewpoint, interest, goal, etc. and their resolution in relations of various sorts (e.g. amongst partners, family members, institutions, countries). There are two particular subfields that are relevant to my concerns. One is interpersonal conflict, focusing on relations between individuals. In this subfield '[c]onflict now refers to the general concept of any difference or incompatibility that exists between people' (Cahn 1997: 59); it is defined as 'interaction between parties expressing opposing interests' (Bell and Blakeney 1977: 850; see also Cahn 1997: 61). The other is conflict and discourse. Kakavá ([2001] 2003: 650) defines this as any 'type of verbal or non-verbal opposition ranging from disagreement to disputes, mostly in social interaction'. This subfield focuses on 'structural' patterns in conversational disputes, including such patterns as repetition, escalation and inversion (Brenneis and Lein 1977). I will discuss some of these patterns with respect to impoliteness in Chapters 6 and 7. If impoliteness involves using behaviours which attack or are perceived to attack positive identity values that people claim for themselves (cf. Goffman's 1967 notion of 'face') or norms about how people think people should be treated, as I will argue, then it involves 'incompatibility', 'expressing opposing interests, reviews, or opinions', 'verbal or non-verbal opposition' – it is intimately connected with conflict. However, there is little detailed work on language in social interactions being used for conflict. Moreover, we should remember that conflict is a broad category not solely restricted to cases involving positive identity values or social norms.

The main home for impoliteness studies is sociopragmatics, a branch of linguistic pragmatics and a field that blurs into several others, but most notably communication studies and interactional sociolinguistics. One reason why this is the best home for the study of impoliteness is that most work on politeness has been produced in this field, and so it seems natural that its apparent antithesis should be here too. A more substantial reason is that it fits the research agenda of sociopragmatics. Leech (2003: 104) states that politeness is situated in the field of sociopragmatics, because that research is geared towards 'explaining communicative behaviour'. Likewise, investigating impoliteness involves the study of particular communicative behaviours in social interaction. In the remainder of this section, I will overview the evolution of impoliteness in sociopragmatics.

One of the most enduring language-oriented lines of research feeding into the study of impoliteness must be the study – often philological in flavour – of swearing. The classic is Montagu's *Anatomy of Swearing* (2001 [1967]); and the most substantial work to-date is Hughes's mighty *An Encyclopaedia of Swearing* (2006). Moreover, perspectives on swearing have recently broadened to include both a sociolinguistic perspective (see McEnery 2006), and one that combines both social and cognitive issues (see Jay 2000). Nevertheless, whilst, unlike earlier studies such as Montagu's, these approaches focus on the use of swearing in context, it is obvious that there is more to being impolite than just swearing. Perhaps the first comprehensive and theoretically grounded paper on the topic is Lachenicht's (1980) 'Aggravating language: a study of abusive and insulting language'. Although there are problems with both the theory and methodology (see Culpeper *et al.* 2003: 1553–4), it is weighty and innovative. Surprisingly, far from being a catalyst for further research, it almost disappeared without trace.

In the interim, research into 'politeness' gathered momentum. The classic politeness theories, Brown and Levinson (hereafter B&L) (1987 [1978]) and Leech (1983), focused on harmonious interactions, and thus, quite understandably, ignored impoliteness. Moreover, as elaborated by Eelen (2001: 98–100), they are generally not well equipped, conceptually or descriptively, to account for impoliteness. In particular, they tend to give the impression that impoliteness is either some kind of pragmatic failure, a consequence of not doing something, or merely anomalous behaviour, not worthy of consideration. The revival of discussions of impoliteness, within pragmatics at least, seems to have come about partly as a reaction to this impression, and this book will further demonstrate how untrue this is. Lakoff (1989), Kasper (1990), Beebe (1995) and Kienpointner (1997) argue and demonstrate that impoliteness can be strategic, systematic and sophisticated. Culpeper *et al.* (2003) point out that impoliteness and conflictive interactions, far from being anomalous behaviour, are commonplace in a variety of different discourses. Locher and Bousfield (2008) go so far as to argue that impoliteness is ubiquitous. Interestingly, studies that embrace the whole of Goffman's (e.g. 1967) notion of facework, rather than just the face-saving aspect (as do B&L 1987), have not experienced difficulty in accommodating impoliteness, or (at least) phenomena related to it. Although Goffman (1967) briefly mentions 'aggressive facework', it is Craig *et al.* (1986: 456–61) who seem to have been the first to discuss face-attack or face aggravation in relation to politeness theory. They point out the consequences for B&L (1987) of failing to treat face-attack strategies systematically, demonstrating that descriptive holes will be left in the analysis of data. Scholars developing accounts of face-attack include Austin (1987, 1990), Penman (1990) and Tracy and Tracy (1998). More recently, relational approaches to politeness (e.g. Holmes and Schnurr 2005; Locher and Watts 2005; and Spencer-Oatey 2000, 2005) — which focus on the analysis of interpersonal relations and facework — have relatively unproblematically accommodated impoliteness-related phenomena.

Culpeper (1996) was specifically designed to answer Craig *et al.*'s (1986) call for a comprehensive treatment of face-attack strategies. To an extent, the framework developed here is the face-attack 'flip-side' of B&L (1987). As this is also true of Lachenicht (1980) and Austin (1987, 1990), Culpeper (1996) is not the first B&L inspired impoliteness model, though it should be noted that all these models differ considerably in theoretical slant and in the detail. A common weakness, however, is the very fact that they draw on B&L, and thus any weaknesses of that politeness model are (at least in part) carried over. Culpeper *et al.* (2003) remedied some of those weaknesses, specifically examining how impoliteness can be both deployed and countered over sections of discourse longer than a single speech act (this is discussed in considerably more length in Bousfield 2007a and 2007b). Culpeper *et al.* (2003) also began to consider how prosody can be used to communicate or augment impoliteness (this is further dealt with in detail in Culpeper 2005). Furthermore, Culpeper (2005) explicitly abandons B&L's (1987) distinction between positive and negative face, and assesses interactions within context. Indeed, a feature of most recent publications on impoliteness is their focus on the role of context (see, for example, the papers in Bousfield and Locher 2008).

However, researchers taking the discursive or postmodern approach to impoliteness, for example, Mills (2003), Watts (2003, 2008) and Locher and Watts (2008), would argue that this does not go far enough. They emphasise that the very concept of impoliteness itself and its definition are subject to discursive struggle, and that we should be focusing squarely on the articulation of that struggle in discourse; in other words, on how the lay person's (or member's own) conception of impoliteness is revealed in their discourse, and not on how the lay person's discourse fits a conception devised by academics. In some respects, this position is consistent with the approach taken by Conversation Analysts (see Piirainen-Marsh 2005; Hutchby 2008, for a Conversation Analytic approach to impoliteness).

The year 2008 was important for impoliteness scholarship. In this year, the field saw the arrival of its first monograph, Bousfield (2008), its first volume of papers, Bousfield and Locher (2008), and first journal special issue devoted to impoliteness: 'Impoliteness: Eclecticism and Diaspora' (*Journal of Politeness Research* 4 (2), edited by Bousfield and Culpeper).[1] As Locher and Bousfield (2008) have noted, work on impoliteness in recent years is perhaps moving towards a middle ground between the classic and the discursive approaches. However, whilst there has been something of a rapprochement between the two perspectives, there is still no agreement about some of the basics. One of the main aims of this book is to establish what those basics might be.

The data challenge

In order to avoid building a castle in the sky, it is essential that my work on impoliteness is grounded in data. This is not to say that my aim is simply to reveal the facts: there are no 'brute facts'; all facts are theory-laden, because they involve subjective interpretation, and this is especially true of social phenomena. Acquiring relevant data for impoliteness research is particularly difficult. Not all the traditional methodologies for collecting data for pragmatics research, particularly cross-cultural pragmatics research, are equally viable (for an overview, see Kasper 2008). Experimentally induced impoliteness is fraught with ethical problems. For example, older research (e.g. Brenneis and Lein 1977; Lein and Brenneis 1978) created situations in which participants might conflict with one another, but of course this would not be considered acceptable now. Role-play is also ruled out, partly because of ethical considerations, but also because it is difficult to imagine that participants could conduct such extreme behaviours in a natural way. This book is based on the following data sets:
* video recordings and written texts involving naturally occurring impoliteness;
* 100 informant reports containing a description of an impoliteness event, including what was said, contextual information, and the informant's reflections on that event (I also, at particular points in this book, deploy 400 other report forms, as I will explain below);
* corpus data; in particular, drawing on the two-billion word *Oxford English Corpus*; and
* an impoliteness perception questionnaire.
I will describe the first two datasets here, as they are used at various points throughout this book. The corpus data is heavily used in Chapter 3 and the impoliteness perception questionnaire forms a section at the end of Chapter 5, and so I will describe them in those chapters.

I have collected the following datasets (all already in the public domain) over the years:
1. *Tapped phone calls.* Available as part of courtroom transcripts in North America (e.g. www.courttv.com; some sound files are available), particularly those submitted as evidence because they are deemed threatening or abusive.
2. *Fly-on-the-wall documentaries.* Particularly, those relating to army recruit training. Approximately twenty hours from *Soldiers*, *Soldiers To Be*, *Soldier Girls* and *Red Caps*; approximately ten hours from programmes about traffic wardens (*Clampers* and *Car Wars*).

3. *Fly-on-the-wall pseudo-documentaries*. Fly-on-the-wall recording of contrived situations designed to spark conflict: approximately ten hours from *Wife Swap* and *Supernanny*.
4. *'Exploitative' TV shows*. Approximately twelve hours from *The Weakest Link* (a quiz show) and *Pop Idol* (a talent show).
5. *Graffiti dialogues*. Fifty-one graffiti dialogues collected from Lancaster University library desks by Chris Hayes (a former student).

In addition, I have sundry examples culled from various contexts. These data are largely drawn from UK-based cultures, and include a mix of genders, social classes and ages. Some data is North American. The data predominantly concern contexts where social conventions sustaining polite behaviours are flouted by those in power in order to coerce (as for example in threatening phone calls), where social conventions legitimise impolite behaviours (as for example in army training or exploitative TV shows), or where misunderstandings about what the social conventions are arise.

Whilst impoliteness plays a central role in a number of discourses such as those mentioned above (see also Culpeper *et al.* 2003: 1545–6), naturally occurring impoliteness is relatively rare in everyday contexts and thus difficult to collect for analysis. For this reason, I decided to use the diary or fieldnotes method. My inspiration here is Spencer-Oatey (2002), for which students were asked to record 'rapport sensitive' incidents, that is, 'incidents involving social interactions that they [the student informants] found to be particularly noticeable in some way, in terms of their relationship with the other person(s)' (2002: 533–4). Spencer-Oatey's analysis was based on 59 report forms. I collected 100. In addition, I contacted colleagues in other countries, in order to gather, using the same instrument, data from other cultural groups. Turkish data was gathered by Leyla Marti (Boğaziçi University, Turkey), Chinese data by Meilian Mei (Zhejiang University of Technology, China), Finnish data by Minna Nevala (University of Helsinki; with help from Johanna Tanner from the same institution) and German data by Gila Schauer (Lancaster University). The total dataset, then, was 500 report forms. The full dataset will be deployed in Chapters 2 and 3. Furthermore, I devised a report form that was more detailed and focused than Spencer-Oatey's. In particular, unlike Spencer-Oatey who focuses on events that have either a 'particularly positive effect' or a 'particularly negative effect', I sought to investigate only the latter. One aspect of my design was to avoid mentioning a label that described the kind of behaviour I am interested in – labels such as 'impolite', 'rude', 'abusive', 'aggressive' – because the choice of a particular label may have biased my results towards particular behaviours and, moreover, I wished to see what labels the informants would choose. Thus, I asked informants to report conversations that had a particular *effect* on them – conversations 'in which someone said something to you which made *you* feel bad (e.g. hurt, offended, embarrassed, humiliated,

Table 1 *The social profile of the report data*

		English	Chinese	Finish	German	Turkish
Age	*18–29*	98	100	99	99	100
	30–59	2	0	1	1	0
Gender	*Female*	79	67	89	73	64
	Male	21	33	11	27	36

threatened, put upon, obstructed, ostracised)'. A box extending a little less than half a page was provided for reports. In addition, and unlike Spencer-Oatey, I asked informants to reflect on their reported conversations in a number of specific ways:

• In order to gauge the gravity of the offence, I posed the question: 'How bad did the behaviour in the conversation make you feel at the time it occurred?' Responses were recorded on a 5-point Lickert scale.

• In order to gauge the degree of intentionality ascribed to the behaviour, I posed the question: 'Do you think that person *meant* to make you feel bad?' Responses were recorded on a 5-point Lickert scale.[2]

• In order to gain information about resultant emotions, I asked two questions: (1) 'We know you felt "bad", but describe your feelings?' and (2) 'Why did this particular behaviour make you feel bad?' Boxes allowing for a few lines of text were supplied for responses.

• In order to gain information about metalinguistic labels, I asked the question: 'How would you describe the behaviour of the person who made you feel bad (how would you label this kind of behaviour?)?' A box allowing for a few lines of text was supplied for responses.

I asked informants to supply information about their age and gender, and membership of each national dataset was determined by a question about the country the informant grew up in. Table 1 quantifies this information.

As can be seen, the profile of each national dataset is broadly similar. It should be noted that my results reported in this book from this report data are biased towards the perceptions not only of young students but also students who are female.

At no point were informants told that the research was related to anything to do with 'impoliteness'. Moreover, informants were not put under pressure to fill the form out on the spot. I thought that there would be no guarantee that at any particular moment an individual could remember a particular impoliteness event. A consequence of this is that huge numbers of report forms were administered, in order to achieve 100 complete forms, because students frequently forgot about the form altogether (and ignored reminders). In the case of the British data, well over 1,000 report forms were given out in order to achieve

100 completions. However, the positive side of this is that the completed forms I did receive contained very rich data which gave no indication of having been made up or embellished.

One summary point to bear in mind for the up-coming chapters is that my data largely reflect Anglo cultures, mainly British, and thus my conclusions regarding specific conventionalised pragmatic strategies and formulae are conclusions about impoliteness in those cultures.

Sources of evidence

How do I arrive at a decision that the data I am analysing is impolite? With regard to my report data, they have been reported because they elicited the kind of emotional reaction associated with impoliteness, and they are also labelled by reporters with the metalanguage associated with impoliteness, and so this provides some evidence that they can be taken as impolite. But what about the analysis of naturally occurring data? In fact, scholars in pragmatics are generally reticent to spell out the evidence used to support highly subjective interpretations. One of the few exceptions is Thomas (1995: 204–7), and my own evidence sources are similar to hers.

My sources, ordered in terms of their weight in guiding my interpretation, were as follows:

- co-text,
- retrospective comments,
- certain non-verbal reactions, and
- use of conventional impoliteness formulae.

The first three points capture the idea that people react to impoliteness in certain ways, not least of all through the articulation of an emotional response. Co-text is a hugely valuable source of participant understandings. Evaluating something as impolite, sometimes with explicit impoliteness metapragmatic comments and/or metalanguage (e.g. 'rude', 'abusive', 'insulting'), gives us good evidence that impoliteness was perceived. The second example of this introduction illustrates this. The first utterance 'do you know anything about yo-yos?' could be an entirely innocent question; it is the target's immediate response 'that's mean' that provides us with evidence that it was taken as impolite. The following two points are in some ways subcategories of the first. By 'retrospective comments', I am referring to comments made after the event in question. These often take the shape of long discussions by participants and/or observers about whether X counts as impolite. A particularly rich source for such discussions is weblogs, and indeed that will be a source of corpus-data in Chapter 3. Impoliteness is associated with certain emotional reactions, and sometimes those emotional reactions are evident in particular non-verbal actions, as I will explain in Chapter 2 (though we need to be wary of the fact that emotion displays can be strategically controlled to some extent). Finally, there is the use of conventionalised impoliteness formulae. The first example of this introduction above illustrates these. An insult, for example, is a conventionalised impoliteness formula. However, and this needs to be stressed, this can never be used as the sole source of evidence for impoliteness interpretation. A conventionalised impoliteness formula could be used in a context where it is interpreted as banter, and thus the ultimate interpretation of the communication is not that it is impolite. There is also the danger of circularity, at least at the micro level, as one of my research aims is to find out what the conventional impoliteness formulae are. Nevertheless, participants clearly orient to such formulae, as is evidenced by the fact that they are often a focal point of subsequent discussions. They can be taken as flagging the potential for impoliteness.

Background notions

This section briefly clarifies a number of important concepts to be used in this book.

Cultures and identities

Research on impoliteness needs some way of capturing the fact that different groups of people – different 'cultures' – have different norms and different values. Values and norms lie at the heart of impoliteness (see Mills 2009). Culture, of course, is a notoriously difficult notion to define. Classic definitions (e.g. Kroeber and Kluckhohn 1952: 181) often give the erroneous impression that culture consists of a relatively short list of stable features passed on from generation to generation – something that reflects an essentialist view. Cultures are multiple and constantly undergoing change, and people shift in and out of particular cultures (cf. Kachru 1999; Gudykunst and Kim 2003). Discourse plays an important role in shaping the cultural context, and is also shaped by it (cf. Gee 2008 [1999]). We need to be wary that the concentration in cross-cultural politeness research on the notion of 'national cultures' does not give the impression that this kind of group constitutes a culture; nations are made up of many cultures. In fact, research on cross-cultural communication has treated different language groups, nationalities, geographical communities, genders, ages, and academic disciplines as cultures, and there are other groups too. In this book, I will follow the definition of culture proposed by Spencer-Oatey (2000: 4):

Culture is a fuzzy set of attitudes, beliefs, behavioural conventions, and basic assumptions and values that are shared by a group of people, and that influence each member's behaviour and each member's interpretations of the 'meaning' of other people's behaviour.

Identities are connected to the notion of 'face', which can account for some important aspects of impoliteness (see Section 1.3). Being English, male, white, middle-class, and so on are features that are part of my identity; they are also cultural groups. Identity is connected with one's sense of self. The self can be seen as 'the person's mental representation of his or her own personality attributes, social roles, past experience, future goals, and the like' (Fiske and Taylor 1991: 181–2); it is a self-schema (schema theory will be explained below). Some researchers (e.g. Kihlstrom and Cantor 1984) have argued that a self-schema consists of multiple context-specific self-concepts (e.g. myself as an academic, myself as a classic car enthusiast). Others (e.g. Markus and Nurius 1986) have suggested that a self-schema also includes possible selves, for example the selves that people would like to become. Of particular relevance to this chapter, there are also selves we think we ought to be, or selves that we think other people should be, or even selves that we think that others ought to think that we are. Of course, not all of this information can be active at the same time: we would become mentally overloaded. Instead, as with cultures, the context and what we are doing – including, importantly, saying – play a role. Identities are selves enacted by behaviours in particular situations (cf. Alexander and Knight 1971). However, it should not be thought that identities are solely determined by situations; they can be strategically enacted to determine situations. Le Page and Tabouret-Keller (1985: 181), discussing Creole-speaking communities, propose the hypothesis that

the individual creates for himself [sic] the patterns of his linguistic behaviour so as to resemble those of the group or groups with which from time to time he wishes to be identified, or so as to be unlike those from whom he wishes to be distinguished.

In this book, I sometimes refer to 'national cultures'. Here the notion of culture is bound up with the equally problematic notion of national identity. A particular national cultural identity will not be equally relevant to all individuals, and may well have ideological implications that are rejected by some. It is also but one cultural layer amongst many (Hofstede 1994: 10). Perhaps the worst pitfall is ethnocentrism involving English; that is, to assume that what holds for some notion of English culture applies across all cultures (see Wierzbicka 2003: Chapter 2, for relevant discussion). Nevertheless, it is a notion regularly employed in everyday interpretation, and some academics acknowledge that there is a lack of a viable alternative, at least for some purposes (see, for example, Matthews 2000: 184). My diary report form data, which informs this book and particularly Chapters 2 and 3, is focused on groups of undergraduates from countries across the world, specifically China, England, Finland, Germany and Turkey. Involving just undergraduate students allowed me to conduct contrasts with students of a similar age and educational background in other countries.

Of course, my study does not contrast entire nations. It is centred in 'student culture', and student informant populations do not reflect the total cultural diversity of a particular nation. It is simply not possible, methodologically, to contrast all the cultures constituting a nation with all the cultures of another nation. However, the perceptions of specific student groups are also guided by their knowledge of experiences and interactions with *other* cultural groups particularly within their respective nations (e.g. families, shop assistants, bus drivers, people on television, and so on); that is, by their knowledge of when they are members of other cultural groups and enacting relevant identities. Indeed, the bulk of my data involves reports of impoliteness that are not in university contexts. No culture is an island unto itself. Consequently, it is highly likely that some of my conclusions about the characteristics of the groups do indeed reflect more general differences amongst national cultures. The bulk of the report data examples used in this book are from the England-based dataset for the simple reason that I was in charge of it (examples from other cultures can be found in Culpeper *et al.* forthcoming).

Schema, attitude and ideology

Impoliteness often involves a clash with expectations, particularly concerning behaviours associated with particular contexts. More specifically, expectations can partly account for people's sense of appropriacy, something which feeds into politeness. Schema theory explains such expectations and various other aspects of understanding. Although propounded by cognitive psychologists and researchers from other fields (e.g. Bartlett 1995 [1932]; Minsky 1975; Neisser 1976; Rumelhart 1984; Schank and Abelson 1977), schema theory was anticipated in early research in social cognition (e.g. Asch 1946), where it is often related to research on 'cognitive stereotypes' (e.g. Andersen *et al.* 1990: 192). According to Eysenck and Keane (2010: 401), schemata are 'well-integrated packets of knowledge about the world, events, people, and actions', and include 'what are often referred to as *scripts* and *frames*'. The various terms for schemata – 'frames', 'scripts', 'scenarios', etc. – each belong to a somewhat different tradition and have a somewhat different emphasis. A schema is a structured cluster of concepts containing relatively generic information derived from experience, and is stored in semantic long-term memory. A person's experiences are unique to them, and so it is no surprise that schemata are to an extent variable from person to person and unstable over time. Indeed, Fredric Bartlett's (1995 [1932]) early pioneering work in schema theory was partly designed to explore cultural differences in interpretation (see also the experiment by Steffenson *et al.* 1979). The important point for the understanding of impoliteness is that whilst people may have some schemata that overlap because they share cultural experiences, others may well differ, with the result that the same behaviour may be understood as impolite by some but less impolite or not impolite at all by others.

Schemata incorporate evaluative beliefs. Evaluative beliefs provide the foundation 'needed to assess the (inter)subjective "position" of social members' towards behaviours (van Dijk 1987: 189), and thus further enrich our understanding. For example, a defendant telling a judge to 'sit down', as they get up to leave the courtroom, could be considered as both inappropriate and as inflicting face damage on the judge (this would probably not be the case if a host said it to dinner guests at the beginning of the meal). Attitude schemata are made up of evaluative beliefs, which may be associated with emotive aspects (e.g. like or dislike) (1987: 188–9). Attitudes contain 'general, context-free information', are organised in 'schematic clusters' and located in 'social memory' (1987: 189–93). Social memory is van Dijk's term for semantic memory, a label which stresses the fact that social groups share to an extent particular social cognitions. Such attitude schemata are distinct from the personal opinions represented in episodic memory (episodes are personal experiences associated with a particular time and place rather than generic knowledge) (cf. Tulving 1972, for the semantic/episodic distinction). Thus, it is possible to express an opinion which is at odds with one's attitudes. To use one of van Dijk's examples, one might have a belief such as 'blacks are lazy', but for reasons of self-presentation (i.e. not to be seen as a racist) express a contrary opinion. As I will elaborate in Section 1.2, impoliteness can be considered a kind of attitude schema, comprised of certain evaluative beliefs concerning certain behaviours. Discourse about impoliteness, the topic of Chapter 4, involves the expression of opinions about impoliteness.

Ideology concerns the 'worldview or governing philosophy of a group or a discourse system' (Scollon and Scollon 2001: 108); ideologies can be seen as 'taken-for-granted interpretations of activities and events' (Verschueren 2004: 65); they refer to 'ideas, meaning and practices which, while they purport to be universal truths, are maps of meaning which support the power of particular social groups' (Barker 2000: 59). Given that I have described impoliteness as an attitude towards certain behaviours and given the sociocognitive thrust of this book, including more specifically its use in various places of schema theory, I will follow Teun van Dijk's (e.g. 1988a, 1990) particular understanding of ideology. Following on from the observation above concerning the variability of schemata, it follows that different groups will have different attitude schemata. These attitudes will influence the way associated schemata are employed in the interpretation and production of social discourse, which in turn would influence the development of the schemata. Moreover, it is clusters of attitudes shared amongst members of a social group which constitute ideologies (van Dijk 1988a, 1990), and could be labelled, for example, 'conservative', 'racist' or 'sexist'. Cultures not only involve particular norms of group behaviour but also the attitudes associated with those norms. These attitudes constitute 'impoliteness' ideologies. They play a role in determining what counts as impolite, and sustain and are sustained by those who dominate the particular group power structure (see Section 6.2, for more detail).

Politic behaviour and politeness

The distinction between politic behaviour and politeness, as proposed by Richard J. Watts (1989, 2003), is a useful one, partly because it relates to expectation and acceptability, and it is one which I will occasionally mention in this book. Politic behaviour is defined as '[l]inguistic behaviour which is perceived to be appropriate to the social constraints of the ongoing interaction, i.e. as non-salient, should be called *politic behaviour*' (Watts 2003: 19), and is illustrated by the following examples:

[3]
>   A: Would you like some more coffee?
>   B: Yes, *please.*
>
>   (Watts 2003: 186, emphasis as original)

[4]
>   M: *Hello*, Mr. Smith. *How are you?*
>   S: *Hello* David. Fine *thanks. How are you?*
>
>   (Watts 2003: 186, emphasis as original)

Politeness, on the other hand, is '[l]inguistic behaviour perceived to go beyond what is expectable, i.e. salient behaviour, should be called *polite* or *impolite* depending on whether the behaviour itself tends towards the negative or positive end of the spectrum of politeness' (Watts 2003: 19). We can re-work Watts's examples to provide an illustration:

[5]
>   A: Would you like some more coffee?
>   B: Yes, *please, that's very kind, coffee would be wonderful.*

[6]
>   M: *Hello*, Mr. Smith. *It's great to see you. We missed you. How are you?*
>   S: *Hello* David. *I'm fine thanks. It's great to see you too. How are you?*

One qualifying note is that, contrary to Watts, I think the distinction between politic behaviour and politeness is scalar (as does Leech 2007: 202–3).

The up-coming chapters

Chapters 1 and 2 address the understanding of impoliteness. In particular, they examine the various components that constitute or are connected with impoliteness attitudes. These include the notion of face, social norms, morality, interpretive heuristics and strategies (such as intentionality) and emotions. They also note the role of ideologies. These chapters also use cross-cultural data in order to probe the notions of face, social norms (particularly sociality rights) and intentionality. It needs to be stressed that the main aim here is not to draw conclusions about 'cultures', however defined, but to probe those notions with groups of people who are highly likely to have had differing experiences, which may shape their perceptions. These chapters culminate in a section which suggests, with reference to schema theory, how all these components are related and used in the understanding of impoliteness. Chapter 3 investigates the metadiscourse of impoliteness. It shows how the study of such metadiscourse affords insights into the concepts that lie behind it. In the first sections of this chapter, I explore the various metalinguistic terms used for impoliteness in the impoliteness literature, showing how they distribute across academic disciplines and also their currency in everyday usage. I focus particularly on the terms *impolite* and *rude*. In the remaining sections of this chapter, I explore impoliteness metapragmatic comments. In particular, I examine the notion of 'over politeness'. I also look at impoliteness 'rules', which I consider to be a kind of institutionally crystallised metapragmatic comment, both in the public domain and in the private. Chapter 4 begins by considering the idea that impoliteness can be inherent in language. Rather than rejecting this notion out of hand, it argues that there is a sense in which impoliteness can be inherent. It focuses on the notion of conventionalised impolite formulae, and identifies the conventionalised impolite formulae used in my data. Moreover, it discusses the important linguistic work undertaken to exacerbate offence, through either lexical or prosodic intensification. The focus of Chapter 5 is on behavioural triggers for implicational impoliteness, that is, an impoliteness understanding that does not match the surface form or semantics of the utterance or the symbolic meaning of the behaviour. It examines three types of trigger: form-driven, convention-driven and context-driven. This chapter concludes with an investigation of directness and impoliteness, and how they correlate with gravity of offence. Chapter 6 addresses co-text and context. It begins with a discussion of impoliteness events and context. Having noted contexts in which face or social norms are made salient, it considers cultures and institutional ideologies that normalise or legitimise impoliteness. It then focuses on norms created by the co-text, and the importance of what I shall term 'politeness thresholds'. It concludes with an examination of mock impoliteness, and the issue of the neutralization of impoliteness. Chapter 7 considers the functions of impoliteness events. I argue that there are three key functions: affective impoliteness, coercive impoliteness and entertaining impoliteness. The chapter concludes with a discussion of institutional impoliteness. Finally, in the concluding chapter, I draw some of the threads of the book together.

1 Understanding impoliteness I: Face and social norms

1.1 Introduction: Impoliteness definitions

Surveying a recent volume of papers on impoliteness, the editors conclude 'there is no solid agreement in the chapters as to what "impoliteness" actually is' (Locher and Bousfield 2008: 3). As the following quotations illustrate, there is no commonly accepted definition of impoliteness:

(1) The lowest common denominator [underlying definitions of impoliteness in Bousfield and Locher 2008] can be summarized like this: *Impoliteness is behaviour that is face-aggravating in a particular context.* (Locher and Bousfield 2008: 3)

(2) [rude behaviour] does not utilise politeness strategies where they would be expected, in such a way that the utterance can only almost plausibly be interpreted as intentionally and negatively confrontational. (Lakoff 1989: 103)

(3) ... rudeness is defined as a face threatening act (FTA) – or feature of an FTA such as intonation – which violates a socially sanctioned norm of interaction of the social context in which it occurs. (Beebe 1995: 159)

(4) ... impoliteness, communicative strategies designed to attack face, and thereby cause social conflict and disharmony ... (Culpeper *et al.* 2003: 1546)

(5) Impoliteness comes about when: (1) the speaker communicates face-attack intentionally, or (2) the hearer perceives and/or constructs behaviour as intentionally face-attacking, or a combination of (1) and (2). (Culpeper 2005a: 38)

(6) ... marked rudeness or rudeness proper occurs when the expression used is not conventionalised relative to the context of occurrence; following recognition of the speaker's face-threatening intention by the hearer, marked rudeness threatens the addressee's face ... impoliteness occurs when the expression used is not conventionalised relative to the context of occurrence; it threatens the addressee's face ... but no face-threatening intention is attributed to the speaker by the hearer. (Terkourafi 2008: 70)

(7) ... impoliteness constitutes the communication of intentionally gratuitous and conflictive verbal face-threatening acts (FTAs) which are purposefully delivered: (1) unmitigated, in contexts where mitigation is required, and/or, (2) with deliberate aggression, that is, with the face threat exacerbated, 'boosted', or maximised in some way to heighten the face damage inflicted. (Bousfield 2008: 72)

(8) ... verbal impoliteness [is] linguistic behaviour assessed by the hearer as threatening her or his face or social identity, and infringing the norms of appropriate behaviour that prevail in particular contexts and among particular interlocutors, whether intentionally or not. (Holmes *et al.* 2008: 196)

(9) Rudeness is a kind of prototypically non-cooperative or competitive communicative behaviour which destabilises the personal relationships of the interacting individuals ... creates or maintains an emotional atmosphere of mutual irreverence and antipathy, which primarily serves egocentric interests ... (Kienpointner 1997: 259; see also Kienpointner 2008)

These definitions appear in what can be considered the linguistic pragmatics literature. If we cast the net wider, other definitions referring to the same or closely related phenomena can be found. This is particularly true of work on anti-social interaction undertaken in social psychology or communication studies. Consider, for example:

(10) *Aggression* may be defined as any form of behaviour directed towards the goal of harming or injuring another living being who is motivated to avoid such treatment. (Baron and Richardson 1994: 37, original emphasis)

(11) *Communicative aggression* is defined as any recurring set of messages that function to impair a person's enduring preferred self image ... (Dailey *et al.* 2007: 303, original emphasis).

(12) People feel hurt when they believe someone said or did something that caused them emotional pain. (Vangelisti 2007: 122)

(13) [Social harm involves] damage to the social identity of target persons and a lowering of their power or status. Social harm may be imposed by insults, reproaches, sarcasm, and various types of impolite behaviour. (Tedeschi and Felson 1994: 171)

Whilst there are differences amongst these definitions, there are two notable commonalities. First, all but (2), (10) and (12) refer to the notion of 'face', 'preferred self-image' or 'social identity' (regarding (8), face is mentioned in the full definition). In fact, in all but (2), (9), (10) and (12) face, or a closely related concept, plays a central role. As Locher and Bousfield note in (1) the notion of 'face-aggravating' behaviour seems to be key. Indeed, Erving Goffman (1967) himself refers to 'aggressive facework', as more recently does Watts (2003). In my work (cf. (5)), I use the term 'face-attack' or 'face-attacking', and I take this to be synonymous with 'face-aggravation' or 'face-aggravating'. A justification as to why 'face-attack' is better than 'face-threat' is given in Section 4.3.1. However, the problem here, as I pointed out in Introducing impoliteness, is that the explanatory difficulties that surround impoliteness are simply transferred to another notion that is both itself controversial and, importantly, may well not cover all cases of impoliteness, or at least may not cover the central aspect of some cases of impoliteness. One aim in this chapter is to consider how central face is in accounting for impoliteness phenomena, what kinds of face are involved, and also whether other concepts are needed to account for it fully. An important framework in dealing with these issues, amongst others, will be that of 'rapport management' developed by Spencer-Oatey (e.g. 2000).

Second, some notion of intentionality is referred to in many definitions, all except (1), (3), (9), (11) and (12) (regarding (13), intention is mentioned in the full definition). Of course, intentionality is the subject of much debate, and I will need to consider what it means. The particular issues I address are (a) whether impoliteness can only be said to have taken place if the behaviour concerned was (or was perceived to be) intentional, and (b) how it interacts with perception of the degree of offence taken. Although other features in the definitions are not so consistent, it is worth drawing attention to two of them. Definitions (3) and (8) accord a central role to social norms, whilst some others stress (social) contexts (cf. (6) and (7)), expectations about contexts (cf. (2)), or more specifically relational contexts (cf. (9)). Definitions (9) and (12) emphasise emotional aspects, and this is indirectly alluded to in some others. Impoliteness always involves emotional consequences for the target (victim). This should be a central part of any definition of impoliteness. Interestingly, the legal definition of antisocial behaviour in the UK revolves around consequences for the target – antisocial behaviour involves somebody acting 'in a manner that caused or was likely to cause harassment, alarm or distress' (Crime and Disorder Act 1998, 1.1). In sum, the key notions under scrutiny are face, social norms, intentionality and emotions. I will elaborate on the first two in this chapter and the second two in the next. In the final section of the following chapter, I will draw the threads of both this chapter and that together by postulating a model for the understanding of impoliteness. The theoretical background here will be drawn from social cognition and discourse comprehension.

A feature of this chapter and the next will be that it also examines impoliteness perceptions in a cross-cultural perspective. A major impetus for new approaches to politeness, notably the 'postmodernist' or 'discursive' approaches (e.g. Watts 2003; Locher and Watts 2005; Locher 2006), has been the rejection of traditional approaches to politeness in the light of contrary evidence provided by cross-cultural studies. For instance, B&L's (1987) notion of face has been criticised for being biased towards an individualistic perspective, and one that cannot adequately account for the group dynamics of at least some 'non-western' cultures (cf. Matsumoto 1988; Gu 1990; Nwoye 1992; Mao 1994). It makes sense to put impoliteness notions to the cross-cultural test as a matter of priority, the objective being to accommodate variation within a definition of impoliteness, rather than let a definition of impoliteness obscure variation. However, the examples I present to illustrate the analyses are almost all from the British diary report-form data set, for the simple reason that I was in charge of it. Further examples from the other data sets can be found in Culpeper *et al.* (forthcoming). That paper also pays much more attention to exploring 'cultures', whereas the focus in this chapter is on using data from different groups with different experiences to probe notions related to impoliteness. It must be stressed that the use of labels for countries – England, China, etc. – are labels for datasets, datasets which may provide evidence of cultural variation in perceptions at some level. They are not to be taken as labels for unproblematic, monolithic national cultures.

Given that I have dwelt on the impoliteness definitions of others in this section, it is appropriate that I spell out what I take impoliteness to be. This is the task of the next section.

1.2   The notion of impoliteness

Defining impoliteness is a real challenge. An important reason for this is that although some verbal behaviours are typically impolite, they will not always be impolite – it depends on the situation. To take an extreme example, shouting and using potentially offensive language to an older person living in a quiet cul-de-sac might be taken as extremely impolite, but the same behaviour in the midst of a football crowd might not be taken as impolite at all. Impoliteness is very much in the eye of the beholder, that is, the mind's eye. It depends on how you perceive what is said and done and how that relates to the situation.

Impoliteness involves (a) a mental attitude held by a participant and comprised of negative evaluative beliefs about particular behaviours in particular social contexts, and (b) the activation of that attitude by those particular in-context behaviours. The notion of an attitude is, of course, well established in social psychology, and especially language attitude research. It involves a favourable or unfavourable reaction to stimuli, and has cognitive, affective and behavioural elements (see Bradac *et al.* 2001, and references therein). With regard to politeness, the idea that it is subjective and evaluative is fairly frequently stated (e.g. Eelen 2001; Watts 2003; Spencer-Oatey 2005; Ruhi 2008). Haugh (2007: 91) refers to it more specifically as an 'interpersonal attitude', noting also that that attitude can be expressed (attitudes can be represented in discourse). Ruhi (2008: 305) proposes that 'politeness is a "optional" meta-representation of (non-)verbal acts, which concern people's representations of others' words, attitudes, beliefs, actions and relational and/or transactional goals'. She sees the issue of attribution as key: 'politeness phenomena may

be better investigated as attributions directed towards "linguistics" behaviour'
(Ruhi 2008: 290). I would see impoliteness phenomena in a similar way. It
follows then that my approach will be socio-cognitive in thrust. With respect to
pragmatic theory, Bruce Fraser introduced the idea that politeness is a matter
of perlocutionary effects (Fraser and Nolen 1981: 96; Fraser 1999). However,
this idea is first thoroughly articulated in Terkourafi (2001: 120–7). She argues
that politeness 'is more adequately viewed as a perlocutionary effect' because
it 'may, but need not, rely on recognising the speaker's intention' (2001: 122).
I would see impoliteness in the same way. Indeed, in Section 2.1.2 I will give
evidence of the fact that an understanding of impoliteness does not depend on
the recognition of intentions.

My own definitions of impoliteness have evolved over the last dozen years,
the last being:

> Impoliteness comes about when: (1) the speaker communicates face-attack intentionally,
> or (2) the hearer perceives and/or constructs behaviour as intentionally face-attacking,
> or a combination of (1) and (2). (Culpeper 2005a: 38)

This is not the definition that I will be using in this book. Whilst it has the merit
of emphasising that impoliteness arises in social interaction (it is not simply
something the speaker does), it nevertheless tacks the notion of impoliteness on
to the notion of 'face-attack'.[1] That simply transfers the explanatory load on to
another notion that is itself controversial (see, for example, Bargiela-Chiappini
2003) and may well not cover all cases of impoliteness (see Spencer-Oatey
2002; and Chapter 2). Below I give the definition of impoliteness that reflects
my current thinking. It will be elaborated throughout this book.

> Impoliteness is a negative attitude towards specific behaviours occurring in specific
> contexts. It is sustained by expectations, desires and /or beliefs about social organisation,
> including, in particular, how one person's or a group's identities are mediated by others
> in interaction. Situated behaviours are viewed negatively – considered 'impolite' – when
> they conflict with how one expects them to be, how one wants them to be and/or how
> one thinks they ought to be. Such behaviours always have or are presumed to have
> emotional consequences for at least one participant, that is, they cause or are presumed
> to cause offence. Various factors can exacerbate how offensive an impolite behaviour is
> taken to be, including for example whether one understands a behaviour to be strongly
> intentional or not.

I label the language attitude described above 'impoliteness' (and I will also
occasionally use the adjective 'impolite' for elements that involve it). This
is a technical usage of that term, rather than how that term might be used
in everyday English. In fact, there are other labels relating to the notion of
impoliteness which I could have chosen. Here is a very short list of English
synonyms of the term *impoliteness*:

bad manners, boldness, boorishness, brusqueness, coarseness, contempt, contumely, discourtesy, discourteousness, dishonour, disrespect, flippancy, hardihood, impertinence, impiety, impudence, incivility, inurbanity, inconsideration, insolence, insolency, insolentness, irreverence, lack of respect, profanation, rudeness, sacrilege, unmannerliness (http://thesaurus.reference.com/)

As Locher and Watts (2008: 29) note, each of such terms evokes a particular kind of negative evaluation of behaviour. Just like the other terms listed above, *impoliteness* (or *impolite*) relate to a specific domain of negatively evaluated behaviours. Moreover, all these labels are shaped by English-speaking cultures, especially the dominant ones. Thus, letting the meaning of any particular label determine the underlying notion of impoliteness would lead to an exceedingly narrow focus of study. Of course, this is not to deny that much is to be gained from studying all such metalinguistic labels, as indeed I will do in Chapter 3, given that each reflects an understanding of some aspect of the notion of impoliteness. There are two reasons why I chose the term impoliteness to denote the underlying concept: (1) it provides an obvious counterpoint to the field of politeness studies, and (2) it has almost no currency in the English language, and thus is ripe for appropriation as a technical term (see Chapter 3).

1.3   Face and offence

1.3.1   Face

What is face? Notions such as reputation, prestige and self-esteem, all involve an element of face. In English, the term is perhaps most commonly used in the idiom 'losing face', meaning that one's public image suffers some damage, often resulting in emotional reactions, such as embarrassment. Although the concept of face seems to hail from China (cf. Hu 1944; Ho 1976), much modern writing on face draws upon the work of Goffman (e.g. 1967). Goffman (1967: 5) defines face as:

the positive social value a person effectively claims for himself by the line others assume he has taken during a particular contact. Face is an image of self delineated in terms of approved social attributes.

B&L (1987: 61) claim that their notion of face is 'derived from that of Goffman and from the English folk term', and consists of two related components, which they assume are universal, that 'every member wants to claim for himself' (1987: 61). One component is labelled 'positive face', and appears to be close in some respects to Goffman's definition of face. It is defined as: 'the want of every member that his wants be desirable to at least some others ... in particular, it includes the desire to be ratified, understood, approved of, liked or admired' (1987: 62). The other component, 'negative face', is defined as: 'the want of every "competent adult member" that his [sic] actions be unimpeded by others' (1987: 62). Recent discussion has focussed on the precise definition of face (see in particular Bargiela-Chiappini 2003). Much of this has been a reaction to B&L's (1987) idea that face can be described in terms of universal individualistic psychological 'wants'. Compare the definitions above; that of B&L is very reductive in comparison with Goffman's. With Goffman, it is not just the positive values that you yourself want, but what you can claim about yourself from what *others* assume about you. The point is that how you feel about your 'self' is dependent on how others feel about that 'self'. Hence, when you lose face you feel bad about how you are seen in other people's eyes. This social interdependence has been stripped out of B&L's definition.

As is clear from Goffman's definition and emphasised by Spencer-Oatey (2007: 643), face is comprised of 'positive' attributes. However, attributes can be evaluated differently by different people. To cite Spencer-Oatey's (2007: 644) example:

many secondary school children in England feel they will lose face among their peers if they appear to be too clever and/or studious, because they value the attribute 'cool' more highly than clever or hardworking.

In fact, this is a crucial point for potentially impolite behaviours: what might be evaluated negatively for some might not be by others, or even might be considered positive. Some youth cultures define themselves in terms of an oppositional stance to the value systems that are upheld by the adult, public world: it is not cool to be polite, but it is cool to be impolite (the example discussed in Section 4.2 illustrates this). I will pursue the idea of different value systems and ideologies in more detail in Section 6.2.2.

Face is not confined to the immediate aspects of an individual's self (e.g. abilities, disposition, appearance), but includes all that the self identifies with (e.g. family, school, possessions). This is touched on by B&L (1987: 62–4), but is more neatly conceptualised by Liu (1986) and later by Scollon and Scollon (2000: 144–7). Liu argues that '[w]e can hypothesize a prototypical diagram of the self as consisting of layers of components with the most face-laden closest to the ego' (1986: 30). Thus an insult directed at the colour of my shoes will, theoretically, hurt less than one levelled at this book, as I have invested much more of myself in the latter and see it as a reflection of my abilities as an academic. Face claims vary from person to person. It is not difficult to imagine that some colour could be an important aspect of self for someone more fashion conscious than I am. However, what makes components closest to the centre of the self, the so-called 'ego', so 'face-laden'? I will follow work on self in social cognition. As described in Introducing Impoliteness, a person's self is a mental representation, a self-schema, of their physical features, traits, social roles, goals, their selves in particular contexts, and so on. A distinguishing feature of knowledge about the self compared with knowledge about others is its degree of emotional importance (e.g. Bargh 1982; Ferguson *et al.* 1983). So, we can extend this idea and revise Liu's statement thus: we can hypothesise the self as a schema consisting of layers of components varying in emotional importance with the most highly charged closest to the centre, and this is thus where potentially the most face-sensitive components lie. With respect to cultures and identities, it is context that primes a particular component of face. I will have more to say about contexts and face in Section 6.3.

1.3.2   Types of face and offence

Some researchers have criticised the individualism reflected in B&L's definitions of face, particularly in negative face. Positive face is about what you as an individual find positive; negative face is about being imposed upon as an individual. This seems to ignore cases where the positive attributes apply to a group of people (e.g. a winning team), or where an imposition on yourself is not the main concern, but rather it is how you stand in relation to a group (e.g. whether you are afforded the respect associated with your position in the team). As I noted in Section 1.1, politeness researchers have argued that B&L's emphasis on the individual is a reflection of Anglo-Saxon culture, and not at all a universal feature. Here, we are tapping into a distinction between 'individualist' cultures, which emphasise the individual over the group, "collectivist" cultures, which emphasise the opposite (Hofstede 1991), and the way in which these types of culture correlate with types of facework (Ting-Toomey 1985, 1988a, 1988b; Ting-Toomey and Kurogi 1998). Of course, there is no clear separation between individualist and collectivist cultures but rather a continuum between the two. Moreover, even within a generally individualist culture some people may want to be strongly linked and dependent rather than autonomous and independent, or are caught in tension between the two (Tracy 1990: 21) (and one can imagine the converse situation).

Clearly, we need something rather more complex than what B&L proposed. The analytical framework I have chosen for analysing the types of offence involving face described within my data is that of 'rapport management' developed by Spencer-Oatey (e.g. 2000, 2002, 2005, 2007, 2008). I chose this framework because it is broad, has been successfully deployed in empirical research involving various cultures, reflects research in social psychology, and has been successfully applied to impoliteness (for the final point, see Culpeper 2005a, and Cashman 2006). However, Spencer-Oatey's definitions of the various categories of her framework tend to be somewhat brief, and not always quite up to capturing the kind of variety one finds in a large dataset or solidly guiding the analyst. Also, the literature in social psychology underpinning these categories, though receiving some elaboration in Spencer-Oatey (2007), needs to be reinforced. Thus, I will add some clarifications and refinements to Spencer-Oatey's definitions where necessary, largely derived from data analyses, but also from referring back to the social psychology literature. One feature of my elaboration here is that for each category I will suggest a summary question (given in italics) which a researcher can ask in order to assess whether that category is an issue for a particular interaction.

Spencer-Oatey's rapport management framework consists of five categories. There are three types of face: 'quality', 'relational' and 'social identity'.[2] I will introduce these in the following paragraphs. There are also two types of 'sociality rights', which I will deal with in Section 1.4.3, after I have first discussed social norms and morality. Spencer-Oatey's (e.g. 2008: 13–14) understanding of face is that of Goffman, as given above. When deciding whether face is involved in a potentially impolite interaction the question to be asked is: *does the interaction evoke an understanding that something counters a positive attribute (or attributes) which a participant claims not only to have but to be assumed by other participant(s) as having?* Note that this question has a negative counterpart. In the case of the question above it would be: *does the interaction evoke an understanding that something affirms a negative attribute (or attributes) which a participant claims not only not to have but to be assumed by other participant(s) as not having?* This is also the case with the other such category-assigning questions given below, although I will not supply negative counterparts.

A fairly distinctive feature of Spencer-Oatey's account of face is that she proposes three sub categories (three categories of very similar definition can also be found in Domenici and Littlejohn 2006: 6, 13). The inspiration for this comes from work on identities in social psychology and communication studies. More specifically, Spencer-Oatey (2007: 641) cites Brewer and Gardner (1996: 84), who distinguish (1) an individual level of self-representation where we find the 'personal self', (2) an interpersonal level where we find the 'relational self' and (3) a group level where we find the 'collective self'. Spencer-Oatey also notes that the communication studies scholar Michael Hecht (1993; Hecht *et al.* 2005) makes similar distinctions. In fact, an increasing number of studies have elaborated these distinctions. Sedikides and Brewer (2001), for example, is an entire edited collection devoted to distinctions amongst these levels of self-representation. Some distinctions will emerge in my discussion below of Spencer-Oatey's categories of face. One point to remember here is that the notion of identity is not the same as that of face. Arundale (2006: 202) argues that face is both relational and interactional:

...face is an interpreting [sic] that a participant forms regarding 'persons-in-relationship-to-other-persons'. Face meanings and actions arise, and are maintained and change in relationships, as those relationships are conjointly co-constituted within and socially constructed across communication events. . . . Face is also not equivalent with identity . . . both relationships and identity arise, and are maintained and changed in communication, but a relationship, and hence face, is a dyadic phenomenon, whereas identity is an individual (a much broader) phenomenon.

Spencer-Oatey (2007: 642–4) also highlights differences: identity is more situated within an individual, whereas face is more relational; face is not associated with negative attributes; and face is affectively sensitive. These three points have already been discussed in the previous section. The final point here is an important one which I will address in Section 2.3.2. Below I introduce each of Spencer-Oatey's types of face.

Quality face   Spencer-Oatey (2002: 540) defines quality face as follows:

We have a fundamental desire for people to evaluate us positively in terms of our personal qualities; e.g. our competence, abilities, appearance etc. Quality face is concerned with the value that we effectively claim for ourselves in terms of such personal qualities as these, and so is closely associated with our sense of personal self-esteem.

She makes it clear that these values are individually based (cf. Spencer-Oatey 2005: 106–7; 2008: 14). When deciding whether quality face is involved in a potentially impolite interaction the question to be asked is: *does the interaction evoke an understanding that something counters positive values which a participant claims not only to have as a specific individual but to be assumed by other participant(s) as having?* Below is an example (recollect that all quotations from my data are given as they were written, with no attempt to 'tidy' spelling, punctuation, etc.):

[1]
>   I walked into my male flatmates room just before going out.
>   Matt: your not going out in that are you?
>   Me: [embarrassingly] yer, shut up you! [in a joke like way]

Social identity face   Spencer-Oatey (2002: 540) defines social identity face as follows:

We have a fundamental desire for people to acknowledge and uphold our social identities or roles, e.g. as group leader, valued customer, close friend. Social identity face is concerned with the value that we effectively claim for ourselves in terms of social or group roles, and is closely associated with our sense of public worth.

In contrast with quality face, social identity face is based on the group or the collective (cf. Spencer-Oatey 2005: 106–7; 2008: 14). Spencer-Oatey's examples in her 2002 quotation above emphasise membership of roles. A problem with this is overlap with relational face, a subcategory of face which Spencer-Oatey added in later publications (e.g. 2007, 2008) (see below). Role relationships are relational. They seem to be downplayed in later publications when exemplifying social identity face:

> [social identity face involves] any group that a person is a member of and is concerned about. This can include small groups like one's family, and larger groups like one's ethnic group, religious group or nationality group. (2005: 106).

> The attributes that people are face-sensitive about can apply to the person as an individual and also to the group or community that the person belongs to and/or identifies with. . . . A person could regard him/herself as a talented individual (e.g. a talented artist), and s/he could regard the small group or community that s/he belongs to as being talented (e.g. a talented family or a talented work team or sports team). (2008: 15)

Actually, roles can span both social identity face and relational face or be more focused on one type. For example, if a teacher says that they get offended by comments about teachers having a soft life because they supposedly get such long holidays, that would be a critical comment about all members of the group – an issue of social identity face. However, if a teacher says that they get offended by comments that they are not sympathetic to the needs of their own students, that would be a critical comment about a role relationship – an issue of relational face.

When deciding whether social identity face is involved in a potentially impolite interaction the question to be asked is: *does the interaction evoke an understanding that something counters positive values which a participant claims not only to have in common with all other members in a particular group, but to be assumed by other participant(s) as having?* Here is an example from the report data:

[2]

> We were playing American football and one of my teammates went to tackle whoever had the ball. The person with the ball dived to the ground to avoid taking the hit. My teammate then returned to me to moan about him. 'it's because he's a vegetarian, fucking veggie', he said. I then replied 'I'm a vegetarian'. He then started to apologise prefucely, but I told him to get out of my face! … Obviously I was insulted as he stereotyped all vegetarians as being wimps.

The negative counterpart of this question was evoked with some frequency in my data, involving cases where offence is induced by a claim that somebody is not part of a group that they would wish to be part of or claiming that they are part of a group that they would not wish to be part of.

Relational face   As I pointed out above, Spencer-Oatey's addition of this subcategory reflects the three levels of representation argued for in relatively recent social psychological work. Of relational face, Spencer-Oatey writes: '[s]ometimes there can also be a relational application; for example, being a talented leader and/or a kind-hearted teacher *entails a relational component that is intrinsic to the evaluation*' (2008: 15, my emphasis). In fact, following on from the point raised above, both examples here, leader and teacher, are clear examples of roles. Social roles entail relationships. Of course, all social phenomena are relational in a general sense. Spencer-Oatey (2007: 647) clarifies what she specifically means by relational:

the relationship between the participants (e.g. distance – closeness, equality-inequality, perceptions of role rights and obligations), and the ways in which this relationship is managed or negotiated.

However, where I disagree with the above definition is in the inclusion of the words 'rights and obligations'. Including these words invites unwanted, at least from a methodological point of view, overlap with the categories of sociality rights which I will discuss below. For further clarification of this category, it is worth considering the social psychological literature.

In a comprehensive review article, Chen *et al.* (2006: 153) states that 'the relational self reflects who a person is in relation to his or her significant others'. The inclusion of 'significant others' – referring not merely to partners, but to any person or group of people in a relationship considered significant (e.g. partners, family, friends) – in a definition of relational face is a useful way of distinguishing it from social identity face. (Spencer-Oatey 2007: 641 does mention 'significant others' when discussing the 'relational self' as distinguished by Brewer and Gardner 1996: 84.) Chen *et al.* (2006: 160) elaborate on the distinction:

Like relational selves, then, collective selves entail some degree of connection with others. However, whereas relational selves involve a connection with a known, identifiable significant other or group of significant others, collective selves designate connections with individuals whose identities may not be known . . .

Collective selves generally involve shared features amongst in-group members, rather than unique relations between individuals (Chen *et al.* 2006: 161). When deciding whether relational face is involved in a potentially impolite interaction the question to be asked is: *does the interaction evoke an understanding that something counters positive values about the relations which a participant claims not only to have with a significant other or others but to be assumed by that/ those significant other(s) and/ or other participant(s) as having?* Examples would include someone being thought of as a good friend, a valued family member or a popular teacher. Rather tellingly with regard to cross-cultural variation, there were no clear examples of this subcategory in my English report data, so here I cite an example from the Chinese data set (in translation):

[3]

> Lunch time, I saw her immediately after I went to the cafeteria. I told her ideas for some activities for our class. I intended to collect some suggestions from my classmates by telling them the activities ahead of the schedule. I was shocked at her answer. She rejected the ideas loudly with a tone of ordering in front of all the people in the cafeteria. Despite explaining to her softly and humbly, she rejected them more disrespectfully than before, paying no attention to my good manner. I was greatly annoyed because my classmates all respected me and I had never come across situations like that before.

This informant comments thus on this interaction: 'My good intention was rejected coldly and rudely. That was a great threat and puzzle to a *leader of a class*' (my emphasis). What troubled this informant is that her relational value as a leader of her classmates had been threatened.

1.4   Social norms and offence

1.4.1   Defining social norms

Face is not at the heart of all interactions that can be considered impolite. Often, the central issue seems to be one of breaches of social norms and conventions. As preliminaries to outlining sociality rights, the notion Spencer-Oatey proposes to cover cases where face is less central, I will discuss social norms and morality. What counts as a social norm or convention, how they are motivated, how people orientate to them, and so on are complex and controversial issues. The various definitions of social norms can be distinguished by their emphasis on one (or more) of the following three aspects.

Rationality and self-interest   For Lewis (1969), following the spirit of the British philosopher Douglas Hume, convention is a matter of rational choice: convention is driven by conformity and people conform for reasons of self-interest (e.g. to avoid sanctions), and out of this conformity norms evolve. His definition of convention is socially neutral (cf. 1969: 76). Note that Gricean pragmatics, and the politeness theories fed by it, such as Leech (1983) and B&L (1987), similarly emphasise rationality and self-interest. People are assumed to be motivated to avoid face-threatening acts and are willing to incur costs in order to save face (Brown 1970). Brown and Levinson make the assumption that it is of 'mutual interest' (1987: 60) for interactants to cooperate by supporting each other's face. A threat would lead to a counter-threat, and thus the speaker has a vested interest in maintaining the hearer's face, since this will enhance the probability of reciprocal facework. However, there are two major problems.

First, rationality and self-interest do not motivate social conventions/norms in the first place – they are assumed to be there already for people to negotiate via rationality. Second, if rationality is the guide for human behaviour, then human beings are conspicuous in their failure to be guided by it. As Anderson (2000: 173), discussing rational choice and self-interest as an explanation for human behaviour, points out (providing many supporting references in a footnote):

We are not very good at judging probabilities; we do not think about risks in the way decision theorists think we ought; we do not order our preferences consistently; we care about sunk costs; and we systematically violate just about every logical implication of decision theory. There is probably no other hypothesis about human behaviour so thoroughly discredited on empirical grounds that still operates as a standard working assumption in any discipline.

Regarding self-interest specifically, experimental work has shown that people are willing to expend effort in upholding a social norm – to cooperate in solving problems that require collective action or to enforce others to uphold a social norm – despite that very effort conflicting with (at least a restrictive definition of) the individual's self-interests (see Fehr *et al.* 2002; Sunstein 1995: 31–32, and also the references given there).

People do make considered, rational decisions about choices that will achieve goals that are of benefit to them. However, that rationality and self-interest do not operate in a vacuum. They operate in the context of social norms and the value systems that underpin them: what counts as rational or in one's self-interest will be determined in the light of social norms. As Sunstein (1995: 7) forcefully argues in his paper, '[i]ndividual choices are a function of social norms, social meanings, and social roles, which individual agents may deploy, and over which individual agents have little or no control'. Moreover, Terkourafi (2005a: 249) points out that a speaker's options are constrained by assumptions about what the addressee can recognise and ratify, in other words: 'the speaker's *individual* rationality is constrained on this occasion by a *societal* rationality which has pre-cast, so to speak, for him/her the universe of possibilities into a range of concrete choices (cf. Mey 1993: 263)'. As Terkourafi illustrates,

[t]o choose to be rude to you by using an offensive gesture, I must think that you are familiar with this gesture, and that you attribute to it the same negative value. In other words, I can only be rude to you in a way that you recognize as being rude. Otherwise, no matter how rude I think I am being, unless you concur with this evaluation I have not been rude to you. (2005a: 249)

Impoliteness is a case where the balance of costs/benefits often suggests an 'irrational' choice is taken, particularly in the context of the emotions of hate, anger or simply frustration. A particular consideration is that expressing impoliteness may, depending on the context, lead to the speaker who expressed it being characterised as impolite, an attribution that can often be taken as face-damaging (see also the discussion of procedural values in Section 7.3). In his essay 'Embarrassment and Social Organisation' (1967: 97–112), Goffman (1967: 105–6) makes a similar point:

> During interaction the individual is expected to possess certain attributes, capacities, and information which, taken together, fit together into a self that is at once coherently unified and appropriate for the occasion.... When an event throws doubt upon or discredits these claims, then the encounter finds itself lodged in assumptions which no longer hold.... By the standards of the wider society, perhaps only the discredited individual ought to feel ashamed; but, by the standards of the little social system maintained through the interaction, the discreditor is just as guilty as the person he discredits – sometimes more so, for, if he has been posing as a tactful man, in destroying another's image it destroys his own.

Habits   Regularities of behaviour can become social norms. Consider this event. When I was last in Budapest, I joined a tour bus. The bus made frequent stops at particular sites at each of which we would all get off, and then, having looked around, get back on. Each time we boarded the bus we sat in the same places, even though nobody had articulated a rule that we should do so. Towards the end of the tour, a colleague wished to speak to me about a future collaboration, and suggested that I sat next to him. I did so, but this meant breaking the routine which had established the seat next to my colleague as somebody else's. Hence, I had to apologise to that person and offer them my seat as an alternative. Of course, not every regularity of behaviour becomes a social norm. During the day of the tour, it became very hot and so I took off my coat. People regularly divest themselves when the temperature goes up, but this is not a *social* norm. What characterised the seating arrangement as a social norm is that choosing one's usual seat had become the 'right' thing to do (in contrast, failing to take my coat off when the temperature went up would have led to people thinking I was odd and no apology would be expected). Why is it that regular, usual behaviour can become the right thing to do? Opp (1982) argues that regular behaviours develop into expectations, those expectations give people a sense of certainty, and it is this certainty that has value. People generally like to know what will happen next – a point made forcefully in social cognition in relation to schema theory (see Fiske and Taylor 1984: chapter 5, and Fiske and Taylor 1991: 97). Additionally, in the area of human relations, Kellerman and Reynolds (1990: 14), investigating the link between expectancy violations and attraction, state that deviations from expectations are 'generally judged negatively'. It is important to note, however, that we have in focus a de-contextualised claim about *general* expectations. In interactional contexts, things are much more complicated as we will see in Chapter 6. Furthermore, it is clearly not the case that all violations of expectations are negative: one can be pleasantly surprised! The point is that social choices have social implications:

choosing a different seat on the tour bus was not simply breaking a routine but it also impacted on the choices others could make. I will discuss this kind of issue below, under the heading social 'oughts'.

Interestingly, Marina Terkourafi places statistical behavioural regularities at the heart of her frame-based politeness approach: 'politeness is a matter not of rational calculation, but of habit' (2005a: 250). Moreover, '[i]t is the regular co-occurrence of particular types of context and particular linguistic expressions as the unchallenged realisations of particular acts that create the perception of politeness' (2005a: 248; see also 2005b: 213). This captures an important aspect of politeness, particularly the aspect that Watts (e.g. 2003) would label 'politic behaviour', relating to social routines. Terkourafi suggests that it is through that regularity of co-occurrence that we acquire 'a knowledge of which expressions to use in which situations' (2002: 197), that is, 'experientially acquired structures of anticipated "default" behaviour' (2002: 197). She also points out that formulae are more easily processed by both speaker and hearer, when juggling face concerns, goals, and so on, and that using them demonstrates a knowledge of community norms (2002: 196). Thus, 'formulaic speech carries the burden of polite discourse' (2002: 197; see also references given in 2005b: 213). The fact that this is so accounts for the observation that politeness often passes unnoticed (Kasper 1990: 193).

However, whilst behavioural regularities do play a major role in politeness, not all behavioural regularities are linked to politeness, just as I argued that not all behavioural regularities are linked to social norms. One important factor is the 'valence' of the behaviour itself, that is, whether the behaviour is judged to be socially positive or negative. A regularity could consist of a string of behaviours perceived as socially negative; this is hardly likely to be judged as polite! Importantly, Terkourafi's (2005a: 248, my emphasis) definition of politeness accommodates valence: it is 'the regular co-occurrence of particular types of context and particular linguistic expressions as *unchallenged realisations* of particular acts that creates the perception of politeness'. Thus, it is, one assumes, behaviours judged to be negatively valenced that are challenged. As I noted above, it is irregularities that are predisposed towards negative judgement. Of course, we are dealing with generalisations here. For example, it is not entirely clear how Terkourafi's definition would accommodate contexts, such as army recruit training, where impoliteness is institutionalised (see Section 7.6). There, behaviours are regular and also unchallenged for reasons of the power structure, but are often negatively valenced.

If impoliteness is merely an irregularity, a deviation from a norm, then impoliteness can never be conventional. And yet, as I shall elaborate in Chapter 4, it is evident that there are normal or conventional ways of achieving impoliteness. So, where do these conventions come from, if not (entirely) the regularity of experience? I will pick this issue up in Chapter 4.

Social 'oughts'   As a preliminary, it should be noted that the term social norm overlaps with the term social convention. Lewis (1969: 99) comments: '[a]ny convention is, by definition, a norm which there is some presumption that one ought to conform to'. This is precisely the kind of norm I will refer to as a *social* norm (for the purposes of this section, I take the term (social) convention to be synonymous with social norm). Anderson (2000: 17) defines a social norm as 'a standard of behaviour shared by a social group, commonly understood by its members as authoritative or obligatory for them'. The key work articulating this view is probably Margaret Gilbert's (1989) book *On Social Facts*. She proposes that:

our everyday concept of a social convention is that of a jointly accepted principle of action, a group fiat with respect to how one is to act in certain situations. . . . Further, each party to the convention will accept that each one personally ought to conform, other things being equal, where the 'ought' is understood to be based on the fact that together they jointly accepted the principle. (1989: 377)

Note that the focus here is not on the individual but on the group. If social choices have social implications, then this focus is correct. Her argument is that belonging to a social group is part and parcel of accepting the norms that constitute it, and adopting a group's fiat is a matter of making manifest one's willingness to do so. People are not fundamentally driven by self-interest or the fear of sanctions, but by the stake they have in galvanising that social convention in the first place. That stake is to do with group membership, with people's sense of identity with various groups. Gilbert (1989: 377) notes that nonconforming behaviour, as indeed impoliteness usually is, provokes strong reactions – discourse about impoliteness, which is the topic of Chapter 3 – because it raises questions of relationships to others and also what kind of behaviour is appropriate given those relationships. In this view, the social convention itself is not driven by sanctions but by the group's willingness to uphold the convention, by their acceptance and internalisation of them as authoritative principles of action (see also Anderson 2000). A good illustration of this can be seen in the car parking practices of the cul-de-sac where I live. Parking space is extremely limited. A social norm has developed whereby nobody parks in the space in front of somebody else's house. Even when a particular household is known to be away on holiday, the space is left empty. This is clearly not a rational, self-interested way of maximising parking space. But the point is that neighbours make manifest the fact that they are complying with the group convention. The act of parking a car, perhaps belonging to an unknowing visitor, in the 'wrong' place is viewed with morally tinged opprobrium and the owner (if the car is not recognised) is considered an outsider. Where Gilbert's account has something of a deficit is that it does not address the fact that social norms are ideological: social groups (and individuals in social groups) do not have equal influence in reproducing and imposing social norms. I will pursue this particular point in Section 6.2.2.

The social-norm view of politeness is neatly summed up by Fraser (1990: 220):

> Briefly stated, [the social-norm view] assumes that each society has a particular set of social norms consisting of more or less explicit rules that prescribe a certain behavior, a state of affairs, or a way of thinking in context. A positive evaluation (politeness) arises when an action is in congruence with the norm, a negative evaluation (impoliteness = rudeness) when action is to the contrary.

Politeness, in this sense, subsumes notions such as 'good manners', 'social etiquette', 'social graces' and 'minding your Ps and Qs'. Parents teaching their children to say *please* typically proscribe requests that are not accompanied by that word. It is worth noting here that the Conversational-Contract view of politeness, briefly articulated in Fraser and Nolan (1981) and Fraser (1990: 232–4), also bears some affinity with the kind of social conventions articulated by Gilbert, although these authors do not eschew rationality. More particularly, the 'sociality rights' of Spencer-Oatey's (e.g. 2000) scheme clearly fit here, and I will illustrate how they relate to impoliteness later in this chapter.

In this book, the term social norms will primarily refer to the notion outlined under the heading 'social "oughts"' above. Such norms relate to authoritative standards of behaviour, and entail positive or negative evaluations of behaviour as being consistent or otherwise with those standards. The term experiential norms will primarily refer to the notion outlined under the heading 'habits'. Such norms are related to the regularity or typicality of behaviour, and may acquire positive value through their aura of certainty. However, it needs to be stressed that absolute separation of the two is not possible. Any neutral social habit has the theoretical potential to develop a positive value through the certainty of regularity; conversely, any social norm develops regularity as group members make manifest that they value and have a stake in the norm. In fact, my tour bus example would have involved a social norm in the context of an equal number of bus seats and people, as seating choices would rely on a complementary distribution of one person choosing a seat and the others not, that is, people arriving at a jointly accepted principle for the overall seating arrangement (in fact, there were some spare seats on the bus, so the issue was more one of regularity). When it is not necessary to emphasise either social norms or experiential norms, I will simply use the term 'norms'.

1.4.2   *Social norms: Fairness, morality and the moral order*

The social psychology literature, particularly that pertaining to aggression or cooperative/competitive interactions, has focused on social norms relating to the distribution of resources or rewards (including, of course, things that have symbolic value). Three kinds of social norm have received particular attention:

> *The equity social norm.* Adams (1965) put forward the idea that each member of a community is entitled to a quantity of resources or rewards that are in proportion to his or her investment or contribution. (This overlaps to an extent with the notion of 'distributive justice'; see Tedeschi and Felson 1994: 218–9.)

> *The reciprocity social norm.* Gouldner (1960) put forward the idea that behaviour, prosocial, antisocial or of some other kind, should be matched.

> *The social responsibility social norm.* Deutsch (1975) put forward the idea that the more needy should be allocated a greater proportion of the resources or rewards. (The same idea is captured by Lerner's (1980) concept of the 'just-world belief'.)

These social norms infuse a wide variety of social contexts. Consider the notion of 'speaking rights'. At a meeting, there may be a sense that the person who invested the most time in writing a report should be given the most time to talk about it (the equity social norm), that discourse perceived to be polite should be met with polite discourse (e.g. the person who is thanked for writing the report may thank the committee for giving them the opportunity to write it) (the reciprocity social norm), and that those who have the greatest need to speak (e.g. the report affects them the most) are granted a greater proportion of the speaking time compared with others (the social responsibility social norm). All three of these social norms underpin people's sense of fairness.

There is an important connection here with morality. Violating fairness is a matter of being immoral. Interestingly, the word *morals* is derived from the Latin *mores*, meaning customs. It is the obligations associated with social norms that underlie their morality. Such obligations can be articulated in rules of conduct. Goffman (1967: 49) makes the link with morality clear:

Rules of conduct impinge upon the individual in two general ways: directly, as obligations establishing how he is morally constrained to conduct himself; indirectly, as expectations, establishing how others are morally bound to act in regard to him.

The violation of the social norms of behaviour leads to the attribution of immorality. Impoliteness can involve such violations. Interestingly, people's perceptions of fairness are not determined solely by whether people comply with the above three social norms or not. What also matters is procedural justice: that the procedure for distribution is perceived to be just (Thibaut and Walker 1975). In fact, when procedures are perceived to be fair, a violation of these norms is far less important (Brockner *et al.* 1995). Spencer-Oatey (e.g. 2000) adopts the term 'equity' for one of her two categories of sociality rights. Within this category, she also briefly mentions reciprocity. I will discuss these aspects of her work in more detail later in this chapter.

It should not be thought that morality has nothing to do with face. There are social norms to do with how face is managed in interaction. One can see reciprocity in B&L's assumption that it is of 'mutual interest' (1987: 60) for interactants to cooperate by supporting each other's face: '[i]n general, people cooperate (and assume each other's cooperation) in maintaining face, such cooperation being based on the mutual vulnerability of face' (1987: 61) (see also Goffman 1967: 29). A threat would lead to a reciprocal counter-threat, and thus the speaker has a vested interest in maintaining the hearer's face, since this will enhance the probability of reciprocal supportive facework. Note that if someone fails to reciprocate politeness work, it is likely that their actions will be perceived as breaking some implicit social norm, thus giving rise to a sense of unfairness. In fact, reciprocity also has a negative side, as work on aggression has shown the importance of reciprocity in fuelling a conflict spiral. If somebody is verbally attacked (or even if somebody just thinks they have been verbally attacked), people feel justified in retaliating. Moreover, although they may retaliate in kind, that retaliation is perceived to be less aggressive, a matter of fair defence (Brown and Tedeschi 1976). Reciprocity is a key principle in the contextual dynamics of impoliteness, and politeness for that matter, where its general neglect is a major deficit. I will discuss this further in Section 6.4.

Moral standards arise from internalised social norms. They primarily involve behaviours which have negative consequences for others and about which there is a broad social consensus that they are 'wrong' (Tangney *et al.* 2007: 346). They are linked to moral intentions, moral emotions and moral behaviours (Tangney *et al.* 2007: 346–7). For example, a child may violate a moral standard in failing to thank somebody for an expensive gift. A parent may experience a tinge of anger or annoyance (a moral emotion), decide to act to rectify the situation (a moral intention), and prod or whisper to the child to remind them (a moral, pro-social behaviour). Moral emotions 'may be critically important in understanding people's behavioural adherence (or lack of adherence) to their moral standards' (Tangney *et al.* 2007: 347), and this is why I discuss them in Section 2.3.2. Perceptions of fairness, and thus morality, are moulded not only by social norms but by broader belief systems or ideologies concerning social organisation (ideologies will be discussed further in Section 6.2.2). Following Pearce (1989: 104), we can refer to our understandings of morality as a 'moral order'. This notion is clearly elaborated by Domenici and Littlejohn (2006: 7, original emphasis):

The moral order is a socially constructed set of understandings we carry with us from situation to situation. It is *moral* because it guides our sense of right and wrong, good and bad. It is an order because it is reflected in a patterned set of personal actions. The moral order is a tradition of thought worked out over time within a community. It is normally implicit and sub-conscious, but it is powerful in driving human action. The moral order guides our sense of how the world is divided up into categories; it establishes the place of humanity in the larger scheme of the universe; it delineates individual rights, roles, and responsibilities; it provides a set of values characterising the worlds of people and things; it creates a logic of relations among things, or a sense of how things work together; and the moral order provides notions of how groups and individuals should act or respond to the conditions of life (Pearce and Littlejohn 1997).

1.4.3   Types of sociality rights and offence

Spencer-Oatey (2008: 13–14) defines 'sociality rights' thus:

The management of sociality rights and obligations... involves the management of social expectancies, which I define as 'fundamental social *entitlements* that a person effectively claims for him/herself in his/her interactions with others'. In other words, face is associated with personal/relational/social value, and is concerned with people's sense of worth, dignity, honour, reputation, competence and so on. Sociality rights and obligations, on the other hand, are concerned with social expectancies, and reflect people's concerns over fairness, consideration and behavioural appropriateness.

The essence of sociality rights (and obligations) is that people expect that others should do or not do certain things in certain contexts (cf. Spencer-Oatey 2005: 98–100; 2007: 651–3). The basis of these expectations could be semi-legal, associated with a particular role, or simply just a social convention that has developed on the basis of what normally happens (Spencer-Oatey 2008: 15). In other words, their basis is in both experiential and social norms. As discussed in Section 1.4.2, when people conflict with such rights, there is often a sense of injustice or lack of fairness. Sociality rights are not considered face issues, 'in that an infringement of sociality rights may simply lead to annoyance or irritation, rather than to a sense of face threat or loss (although it is possible, of course, that both will occur)' (2002: 541). However, Spencer-Oatey (e.g. 2007: 652) emphasises that the two can be closely connected. Indeed, Domenici and Littlejohn (2006: 153) comment that reciprocity, briefly touched on by Spencer-Oatey as a sociality right (see below), 'constitutes a kind of face work'. Spencer-Oatey (2007) provides the following illustration of the close connection: a friend who tries to force one to do something or who ignores you, may make you feel irritated or annoyed, but such treatment could also make you feel that you are not valued by your friend, and hence your face is threatened. In my data, often the issue was one of primary versus secondary effects (see Section 1.4.4).

When deciding whether sociality rights are involved in a potentially impolite interaction the question to be asked is: *does the interaction evoke an understanding that something counters a state of affairs which a participant considers to be considerate and fair?* Sociality rights are in fact indirectly alluded to in some of the definitions of impoliteness given in Section 1.1. Definitions (2), (3) and (8) all explicitly mention either expectations or social norms. Social norms, rights and obligations are discussed in the social psychology literature, and often in reference to aggression or competitive social interactions (see, for example, Mummendey and Otten 2001: 334). This is particularly true of notions subsumed within Spencer-Oatey's subcategory 'equity rights'. In the remainder of this section, I focus on Spencer-Oatey's two subcategories, first equity rights and then association rights, and then I briefly consider any data that does not fit one of the offence types mentioned in this chapter thus far.

Sociality rights: Equity   Although both the subcategories equity and association rights are defined in some detail in Spencer-Oatey (2002: 540–1), some refinements were added in later work. Further, in that later work, Spencer-Oatey refers to equity and association as 'interactional principles' from which behavioural expectations flow (see Spencer-Oatey and Jiang 2003). Here, I will continue to refer to them as 'rights'. Spencer-Oatey (2005: 100) defines equity as follows:

> . . . people have a fundamental belief that they are entitled to personal consideration from others and to be treated fairly; in other words, that they are not unduly imposed upon, that they are not unfairly ordered about, and that they are not taken advantage of or exploited. This principle . . . seems to have three components: cost-benefit considerations (the principle that people should not be exploited or disadvantaged), fairness and reciprocity (the belief that costs and benefits should be 'fair' and kept roughly in balance), and autonomy-control (the belief that people should not be unduly controlled or imposed upon).

There are obvious overlaps here with the social norms discussed in Section 1.4.1 and 1.4.2, norms which contribute to people's sense of fairness. When deciding whether equity rights are involved in a potentially impolite interaction the question to be asked is: *does the interaction evoke an understanding that something counters a state of affairs in which a participant considers that they are not unduly exploited, disadvantaged, unfairly dealt with, controlled or imposed upon?* Below is an example from my data:

[4]
    At a bar:
    Me: Can I have a glass of tap water please?
    Staff: No, it's not my job to walk up and down getting you *points* water.
    Me: But it's illegal not to serve water when you work behind a bar
    Staff: Says who? You don't pay my wages to walk and get you lot water.
    Me: I just want tap water please.
    Staff: I'm not fucking doing it. If you want a drink, you pay for one. You can get tap water from the ladies toilet. *leaves*

This informant commented thus on this interaction: 'She was denying me a basic human right and was talking down to me. She questioned my knowledge when I said it was illegal, and made me feel like I was impinging on her when it was actually her job to serve drinks.'

Sociality rights: Association Spencer-Oatey (2005: 100) defines association as follows:

... people have a fundamental belief that they are entitled to an association with others that is in keeping with the type of relationship that they have with them. This principle ... seems to have three components: involvement (the principle that people should have appropriate amount and types of 'activity' involvement with others), empathy (the belief that people should share appropriate concerns, feelings and interests with others), and respect (the belief that people should show appropriate amounts of respectfulness for others).

Although Spencer-Oatey does not make the connection, there are obvious overlaps here with Goffman's discussion of 'involvement obligations' in his essay 'Alienation from interaction' (1967: 113–36). Consider for example:

There are many occasions when the individual participant in conversation finds that he and the others are locked together by involvement obligations with respect to it. He comes to feel it is defined as appropriate (and hence even desirable in itself or prudent) to give his main focus of attention to the talk, and to become spontaneously involved in it, while the same time he feels that each of the other participants has the same obligation. Due to the ceremonial order in which his actions are embedded, he may find that any alternate allocation of involvement on his part will be taken as a discourtesy and cast an uncalled-for reflection upon the others, the setting, or himself. (1967: 115)

When deciding whether association rights are involved in a potentially impolite interaction the question to be asked is: *does the interaction evoke an understanding that something counters a state of affairs in which a participant considers that they have an appropriate level of behavioural involvement and sharing of concerns, feelings and interests with others, and are accorded an appropriate level of respect?* Below is an example from my data:

[5]
Conversation occurred on a bus
P1(me): Yeah, I occasionally zone out of a conversation by accident, and just have to nod or something. I feel terrible about it.
P2: I do that when [friend's name] talks.
P1: Yeah, me too (both chuckle)
P2: Actually, no offense, but sometimes I do that when you talk.
P1: (is very shocked)
P2: ... that's why I sometimes don't remember things you've said, because –
P1: – because you weren't listening in the first place (appears offended)
(An awkward silence followed, where I must have looked quite upset,) (and so P2 apologised greatly)

Clearly, P1 assumes a right to a certain level of attention from P2, a right which is violated.

The five categories above accommodated the bulk of my data. However, a handful of cases did not fit quite so easily, and so I created two additional categories. One area that did not obviously fit concerns conversations in which offence was taken mainly because of the use of taboo words or topics, as illustrated by the following example:

[6]

> On the beach in the South of England with my family. My dad has bought me a snorkel set but the sea is freezing and I don't use it.
> 'Come on son, be brave.' <said quite jokingly>
> 'I am'.
> 'your not gonna do much snorkelling there'. <said quite jokingly>
> (After attempting to get in the sea).
> 'Dad its freezing . . . I don't want to!' <being stubburn>
> 'Oh don't be a wimp'.
> 'No dad I'm not going in'. <being stuburn> (said as I walked up the beach).
> 'Well we might as well throw it in the f**king sea then'! <stress on f**king>

The informant comments: 'I wasn't used to my dad swearing so I was quite shocked. . . . Maybe he could have refrained from swearing but his behaviour, looking back, was expected.' Brown and Levinson (1987: 67) treat 'irreverence' and the 'mention of taboos' as a positive face issue, on the basis that 'S indicates that he doesn't value H's values and doesn't fear H's fears.' It is not clear, however, that using taboo words/topics is primarily an issue of face. Taboos are less a matter of mediating an individual's self and more a matter of social conventions. This would suggest sociality rights. Although not explicitly accommodated within equity rights, one can construct an argument that the producer of something taboo shows lack of consideration for the perceiver by introducing something with strong negative emotions (i.e. it causes them emotional cost). However, I wished to track taboo language separately, so I created a specific taboo category as a subcategory of sociality rights. I will return to the topic of taboo words in Section 4.5.2.

Some of my examples involve intimidation – not mild intimidation where someone might not feel confident, but intimidation where they feel frightened. Consider the first example given in Introducing impoliteness. The informant comments: 'We felt angry, disgusted, and upset. We [felt] quite threatened by this man, he seemed scary and dangerous. . . . His behaviour was sexist, rude, very offensive and inappropriate given the context.' None of my examples were reported solely because they involved such intimidation; as here, it accompanied other aspects of offence. There is a sense in which intimidation does involve an aspect of self: it is one's concept of one's own physical self. I thus added an additional category, physical self, to cover cases where something a participant does leads the target to feel that their physical self is threatened or in danger.

1.5   Cross-cultural variation in offence type

My aim here is to consider the impoliteness events reported by students in five geographically separated cultures and consider whether there is variation in offence type; in other words, whether there is cultural variation in the ways in which people get under each other's skin. Given that differences have been found for politeness (see section 1.3.2), I expect to see differences for impoliteness. As mentioned in Introducing impoliteness, I am greatly indebted to colleagues for collecting parallel data sets in China, Finland, Germany and Turkey, and allowing me to report results based on their analyses.

We applied codes to the reported impoliteness events, each representing an offence type (Spencer-Oatey's 5 fives, plus the addtional two categories mentioned at the end fo the previous section). Two particular difficulties confronted us, and were handled methodologically in the following way:

(1) *Primary and secondary types.* As I have already mentioned, one type of offence can have secondary effects for another. For example, someone who doesn't pay you the attention you expect given the relationship (association rights) may imply also that they have a low value of your opinions (quality face). These multiple meanings were accommodated in the classification scheme by assigning '2' to the primary offence type and '1' to any secondary offence types (N.B. these do not represent numeric values; they are just symbols that could easily be assigned to the data and counted up).

(2) *Ambiguities.* In coding the data, we were greatly assisted – indeed, guided – by the informants' own reflective comments. Nevertheless, there were very rare cases where no primary category emerged. Such events would receive '1' for any relevant offence type.

All codes were assigned by the researcher responsible for that (national) culture, and then checked by the author of this book. Problematic cases were discussed; coding decisions that had general implications were recorded in a 'coding guide' and then circulated to all members of the team. In compiling descriptive statistics, 1s and 2s were not summed for each offence type, as these numbers indicate the primary and secondary offence types. There is no suggestion that 2 represents an offence that is exactly twice as grave as one given 1. Also, different principles guided their application (only one 2 could be supplied for a single impoliteness event, whereas any number of 1s could be supplied, though in practice this was usually one or two). We conducted two kinds of analysis: in one counting any value awarded to an offence type whether 1 or 2 (i.e. combining the counts for 1s and 2s), and in the other just counting 2s. The first analysis allows us to see if there are differences in terms of *what offence*

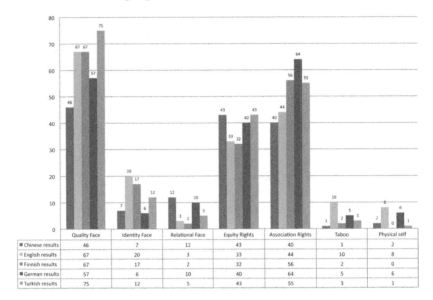

	Quality Face	Identity Face	Relational Face	Equity Rights	Association Rights	Taboo	Physical self
■ Chinese results	46	7	12	43	40	1	2
▨ English results	67	20	3	33	44	10	8
■ Finnish results	67	17	2	32	56	2	0
■ German results	57	6	10	40	64	5	6
▨ Turkish results	75	12	5	43	55	3	1

Figure 1.1 Cross-cultural variation in the types of offence in impoliteness events

type is involved, and the second allows us to see if there are differences in terms of *what primary offence type is involved*. The results of these analyses are presented in Figures 1.1 and 1.2.

I would make the following observations:

- Except German for any type of offence and Chinese for primary offence, all the cultures for both any and primary offence feature Quality Face – the aspect of face most in tune with Goffman's original definition – as the most important.
- However, face is far from being the only source of offence, whether primary or secondary; Equity and Association Rights clearly play an important role. Together, Quality Face, Equity Rights and Association Rights constitute the three big categories.
- There appears to be a pattern of complementary distribution in the primary offence results (and to a lesser extent the any offence results) for the English and Turkish cultures, such that when Quality Face is high, Sociality Rights (i.e. Equity and Association Rights summed) are low, and vice versa for Chinese and German (with Finnish bucking the trend with a more balanced weighting).
- Regarding Quality Face, for primary offence there are significant differences amongst the values (X^2 17.5; d.f. 4; $p < 0.002$). The Turkish data had the most instances (followed by English), and the Chinese the least (preceded by Finnish).

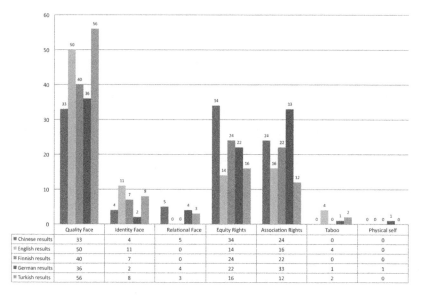

	Quality Face	Identity Face	Relational Face	Equity Rights	Association Rights	Taboo	Physical self
▣ Chinese results	33	4	5	34	24	0	0
▤ English results	50	11	0	14	16	4	0
▥ Finnish results	40	7	0	24	22	0	0
▦ German results	36	2	4	22	33	1	1
▧ Turkish results	56	8	3	16	12	2	0

Figure 1.2 Cross-cultural variation in the primary types of offence in impoliteness events

- Regarding Equity Rights, for primary offence there are significant differences amongst the values (X^2 13.4; d.f. 4; $p < 0.01$). The Chinese data had the most instances (followed by Finnish), and the English the least (preceded by Turkish).
- Regarding Association Rights, for primary offence there are significant differences amongst the values (X^2 14.5; d.f. 4; $p < 0.006$). The German data had the most instances (followed by Chinese), and the Turkish the least (preceded by English).
- Other categories are of minor consequence, though it is interesting to note that Social Identity Face and Taboo are more important in the English data, and Relation Face is more important in the Chinese and German data.

Of course, all of these results need replication and validation from further studies, ideally deploying different yet complementary methodologies. On the face of it, they offer some intriguing hypotheses and puzzles. Finding Quality Face to be an important category for the English data was not a surprise, given that that concept (very closely matching Goffman's definition) has been central in Anglo-Saxon politeness research. But why is it the most important category of all for the Turkish data? Looking at the detail of the reports, one difference that emerged concerned the circumstances in which Quality Face was lost. The Turkish informants often reported that what hurt was the public loss of Quality

Face; this was not a feature of the English data.[3] This points to the importance of interactions between face and context.

The importance of Equity Rights for the Chinese data can be explained in two ways.[4] One is the long-standing influence of Confucianism in Chinese culture. *Liji* 'Book of Ritual', a collection of ideas of Confucianism, says that *li shang wang lai, wang er bu lai, fei li ye; lai er bu wang, yi fei li ye* 'Propriety suggests reciprocity. It is not propriety not to give out but to receive, or vice versa' (Shisanjing zhushu, *Explanations of the Thirteen Lections*: 1231c). Chinese culture advocates a reciprocity principle (Hwang 1987; Gu 1990; Spencer-Oatey 2002). This is shown in Chinese expressions like *tou tao bao li* 'if one gives you a peach, you should requite his favour with a plum' and *di shui zhi en yong yuan xiang bao* 'If you have received a drop of beneficence from other people, you should return to them a fountain of beneficence.' The other explanation is by referring to Chinese family planning policy, according to which families can only have one child. The only child in a family would be regarded as a great treasure by his/her parents and grandparents, and be the centre of attention, accustomed to having his/her desires satisfied. University students, most of whom are the only child in their families, experience a radical change in their set of Equity entitlements: they easily get hurt as they experience new group norms.

The importance of Association Rights for the German data was something we did not expect. One possibility is that this arises because the quality and quantity of friendship relationships tends to be different. Bruckner and Knaup (1993: 250) summarise relevant findings of research on friendship relations in a national cross-cultural perspective thus:

> While Americans tend to enter into many informal associations of a friendly character, in Germany 'private' activities are limited to a small group of 'selected' and long-standing 'real' friends. Corresponding differences in the average number of friends have been corroborated by Pappi and Melbeck (1988) in their empirical study on core discussion networks in the United States and Germany.

Association violations in the context of friends may have been perceived particularly strongly in such networks. And finally, the Finnish data is notable for the fact it generally steers a middle course, particularly as far as primary offence is concerned.

Finally, it is intriguing to observe that Social Identity Face and the category Taboo is so important for the English data. This correlates with my informal observations that public notices and signs, not to mention policy documents and charters, prohibiting 'swearing', 'offensive language' and 'derogatory remarks' (often specifically remarks pertaining to gender, ethnicity or age) are particularly frequent in England (see Section 3.9). A possible interpretation is that in the non-English cultures the strength of taboo is so strong that such items are rarely used, whereas in British cultures there is more ambiguity about when and where taboo language can be used.

1.6   Conclusion

Definitions of impoliteness tend to lean either towards the notion of face or the notion of social norms. Spencer-Oatey's framework incorporates both, and accounting for my data needed both (they are not, of course, entirely separate, for example there are social norms concerning the management of face). Although the bulk of my data was neatly accounted for by Spencer-Oatey's categories, I suggested two further but admittedly rather minor categories, one relating to Taboo words or topics, and the other relating to the Physical self. With regard to face, Quality Face turned out to be overwhelmingly the most important type of face relating to impoliteness. I also clarified the nature of Spencer-Oatey's categories, particularly the category of relational face, emphasising the role of 'significant others', and also the background to sociality rights. Regarding cross-cultural variation, I observed, and offered explanations for, the importance of: Quality Face for the English data and also the Turkish data; Equity Rights for the Chinese data; Association Rights for the German data; and Social Identity Face and Taboo for the English data. Of course, as has been emphasised previously, these are conclusions about differences that emerged amongst the datasets produced by groups of undergraduates in various countries. The extent to which we can generalise these conclusions to the whole 'national' cultures is questionable; it certainly would require further research.

I devoted particular space to the discussion of norms. Traditional politeness theory emphasises rationality and self-interest, and would predict that politeness is a rational choice, given that reciprocality would promote further politeness. Impoliteness has high costs, given that people, depending on the context/culture, generally do not like to be seen to be impolite. For this reason, in some cases impoliteness can be considered irrational. Generally, violations of expectations are judged negatively, perhaps because they instil a sense of uncertainty. Impoliteness can involve an unpleasant shock as we realise what we expected is not the case. However, there are contexts where impoliteness is highly regular (see Chapters 4, 6 and particularly 7). Social norms as authoritative standards of behaviour are the basis of sociality rights. These rights relate to morality, a sense of fairness in social organisation – an important feature of impoliteness.

2 Understanding impoliteness II: Intentionality and emotions

2.1 Introduction

This chapter continues the investigation of key concepts constituting the notion of impoliteness. More specifically, it focuses on the concepts of intentionality and emotion, both of which have been utilised in definitions of impoliteness (see Section 1.1). Unlike the previous chapter, the two concepts in focus here are not closely related. I will first discuss intentionality and then emotions. In both, I will start by considering what the concept is, then move to the relationship with impoliteness, and finally deploy my diary report data. The final section of this chapter proposes a socio-cognitive model for understanding impoliteness in which the concepts discussed in this chapter and the previous are located.

2.2 Intentionality and offence

2.2.1 The notion of intentionality

Intentions and intentionality have become a battleground of much scholarly debate. As far as the field of pragmatics is concerned, this debate about intentions is usefully reviewed in Haugh (2008), a paper that acts as an introduction to a 2008 special issue (edited by Michael Haugh) of the journal *Intercultural Pragmatics* (8:2) on this topic. Traditional approaches to politeness, in particular B&L (1987) and Leech (1983), are underpinned by the Gricean notion that intentions exist *a priori* in the minds of speakers and that it is the recovery of a speaker's 'polite' intentions by hearers that leads to the understanding of politeness (see also Brown 1995). But this Gricean (e.g. 1989 [1957]) model of communication has been challenged in various respects, including its emphasis on the reflexivity of (communicative) intentions, the relative neglect of conventionality and the fact that it ignores collective or 'we-intentions' (Haugh 2008: 101, where many supporting references can be found). An alternative to this kind of philosophical or cognitive communicative model has been emerging in work that is more social, cultural and interactional in thrust. This alternative approach accords a much reduced role to intentions in communication – for example, equating it simply with the 'directionality' or even just the 'about-ness' of communicative action (e.g. Duranti 2006) – or rejects it altogether. The emphasis is on intention as a '*post-facto* construct that is explicitly topicalized in accounting for actions including violations of norms or other interactional troubles explicitly invoked in other subtle ways through interaction' (Haugh 2008: 101). This is in accord with my own view, shaped not least by the evidence I will cite below concerning intention and impoliteness. Moreover, methodologically, *post facto* notions of intention clearly have the upper hand over *a priori* notions, as participants in communication (very often) display their understandings in talk, using the notion of intention as an explanatory and evaluative tool. Those displays are available for analysis. Having said that, it is completely counterintuitive to suggest that people do things without any intention-like notions in their heads. Although my focus is on intentionality as a *post-facto* construct, not least for methodological reasons, I align myself more closely with views of communication that involve the *joint* construction of meaning by participants in an interaction (e.g. Pearce and Cronen 1980; Clark 1996; Arundale 1999).

Having considered intentions, we can now more easily appreciate the notion of intentionality. Perhaps the only study to have thoroughly investigated people's 'folk' notions of intentionality and intention, as opposed to those of scholars, is Malle and Knobe (1997). They conclude that

In people's folk concept of intentionality, performing an action intentionally requires the presence of five components: a desire for an outcome; beliefs about an action that leads to that outcome; an intention to perform the action; skill to perform the action; and awareness of fulfilling the intention while performing the action. For example, we are hereby intentionally writing a self-referential example to illustrate our model – that is, we wanted to provide a vivid illustration (desire); we thought that a self-referential example might be vivid (belief); we therefore decided to write such an example (intention); we had the skill to do so (skill); and we were aware of fulfilling our intention (awareness) while writing the example.

In talking about 'people's folk concept of intentionality' they explicitly follow Gibbs's (1999: 22) assertion that '[i]ntentionality is a social judgement, not an objective fact about the world'. Malle and Knobe (1997) also reveal that the concept is hierarchical, and this sheds light on the distinction between intention and intentionality. An intention is an attribution that links desire (for an outcome) and belief (about a plan by which an action can achieve a certain outcome) to an action; it requires desire and belief as necessary conditions. Intentionality is an attribution that requires intention and also both skill (i.e. the actor's ability to bring about the outcome) and awareness (at least a minimal conscious awareness). My focus will be on intentionality.

2.2.2   *Intentionality and impoliteness*

As we saw in Section 1.1, intentionality is common to a number of definitions of impoliteness, where it often seems to be criterial (see in particular definitions (5) and (7)). The same emphasis is also the case for definitions of aggression. Carlson *et al.* (1989) suggest that the intent to cause harm is a commonality among such definitions. Moreover, studies in social psychology have repeatedly shown that aggressive behaviours perceived to be intentional are considered more severe and are likely to receive a strong response (e.g. Ohbuchi and Kambara 1985). Studies in the area of social communication have found that hurtful verbal behaviours and messages are considered more hurtful, malicious, immoral, etc., if they are considered intentional (e.g. Leary *et al.* 1998; Stamp and Knapp 1990; Vangelisti and Young 2000).

Within politeness or impoliteness studies more generally, intentionality is associated with (im)politeness2 approaches (the so-called pseudo-scientific approaches) and resisted by, backgrounded or qualified by (im)politeness1 approaches (reflecting the lay person's understandings) (for example, intentionality is mentioned once briefly in Eelen's 2001 book on politeness, and not at all in Watts' 2008 article on impoliteness) (see Sections 3.1 and 4.3.2, for further discussion of these approaches). However, this is not to say that intentionality is eschewed in the latter. Consider the following statement by Locher and Watts (2008: 80):

In a first order approach to impoliteness, it is the interactants' *perceptions* of communicators' intentions rather than the intentions themselves that determine whether a communicative act is taken t be impolite or not. In other words, the uptake of the message is as important if not more important than the uttterer's original intention.

I would agree with this. I follow Gibbs (1999: 17) in viewing intentions as 'dynamic, emergent properties of interactive social/cultural/historical moments within which people create and make sense of different human artifacts'. People make use of understandings of intentions and intentionality in their judgements, including their judgements of potentially impolite behaviour. It is a commonplace observation that people orientate to some notion of intentionality in their everyday discussions and evaluations of impoliteness events. By way of illustration, consider these quotations from the weblogs:

[1]

> Will, a lesson I learned when I was a little kid was that if you think someone's saying something that's offensive, shocking, or out of character, have the decency and respect to ask him if he meant it.

[2]

> 'Yes, my best friend. . . anyway, he kept talking about her when I was there with him. It was kind of rude.'
>
> 'Perhaps he didn't mean it that way.'

In Culpeper *et al.* (2003), we approached impoliteness and intention by deploying Goffman's (1967: 14) categories of action which constitute a threat to face.
One category is when 'the offending person may appear to have acted mali-
ciously and spitefully, with the intention of causing open insult' (Goffman
1967: 14). We saw this as impoliteness. Goffman's other categories concern
incidental offence (i.e. not done out of spite, but as a by-product of something
else) or accidental offence (including *faux pas*, gaffes, etc.). For example, tutors
regularly give students critical comments which may have potentially offensive
consequences, but this is a by-product of helping the students to improve, not
the primary goal – the tutor is not (usually!) seeking to offend the student.
Incidental face threat is at the heart of politeness theories. A sub-type of accidental offence is 'failed politeness'. An interactant might misjudge how much
politeness work is required in a particular situation and thus cause offence, or
simply make incorrect assumptions. Consider this interaction:

[3]

> [Former Vice-Chancellor of Lancaster University (V-C) in the UK speaking to
> the woman (W) sitting next to him at a classical music concert during the interval]
>
> V-C: When's it due?
> W: [*pause*] I'm not pregnant.

Here, the Vice-Chancellor assumed that woman sitting next to him was pregnant, presumably on the basis that she looked physically larger than usual.
Given that she is not pregnant, the utterance exposes a potentially impolite
assumption, namely, that she looks unusually big or fat. However, it is unlikely
that he intended to cause offence, and hence this case would not have been
classified as impoliteness in my older work.

Indeed, the key intentionality problem posed by Malle and Knobe (1997) for
the field of social perception is: 'How do they ['lay people'] distinguish between
intentional and accidental rudeness?' However, I am not now convinced that
(full) intentionality is an essential condition for impoliteness. Maybe the woman
mentioned in the above example was offended despite knowing that it was not
an intentional implication, and blamed the Vice-Chancellor for not having been
more careful in what he said. My data shows that people can, at least in some
contexts, still take serious offence in the absence of intention. Consider this
example:

[4]

> Went to meet a friend who I hadn't seen for a long time, the first thing he said
> was: 'you've got more "curves" than you used to have! Have you put some weight
> on? You've got a right J-Lo bum now' – implying I was now fat!
>
> I replied by saying 'thanks' sarcastically

This informant comments: 'I felt embarrassed and fat! Because no-one has ever
said it to me before, I took it as a huge insult and he wasn't joking when he

said it to me. He wasn't malicious.' On the 5-point rating scales of my report form she gave this '4' for gravity of offence, but only '1' for intentionality. This finding, that (full) intentionality is not an essential condition for impoliteness, is also reflected in (Gabriel 1998), a study of workplace impoliteness events that deployed a very similar methodology to my own. Furthermore, it is in tune with Vaillancourt *et al.* (2008) who found that students, whilst agreeing that bullying involves verbal aggression, did not see intentionality as a necessary component, and with Heisel (2010: 29–30), working on the neurobiological aspects of verbal aggression, who points out that people experience psychological pain regardless of intentionality.

One way of accommodating such examples is to consider intentionality as a scalar concept. Weaker positions on the scale would involve such notions as responsibility for or control over an act, or, at an even further remove, the foreseeability of an act. In the example above, whilst the offensive consequences of the utterance might not have been considered intentional, the informant may well have considered them foreseeable, and thus consequences that should have been prevented by a friend. This is in tune with a study by Ferguson and Rule (1983), which showed that failure to avoid doing unintended yet foreseen harm tended to result in judgements of moral culpability. One might predict that judgements of impoliteness based on foreseeability are more likely in contexts involving salient relationships, where transgressions have clearer consequences, and/or close relationships, where the participants know each other well and thus are in a position to make stronger assumptions about foreseeability. The 'J-Lo bum' example would fit this, as would the 'when's it due' example, as in that case the woman (who did not know the Vice-Chancellor) in fact reported to me that she had not been offended (merely amused).

The thrust of all this is that definitions of impoliteness that say it must be intentional to count as such gloss over some complexities. Intentionality is a scalar concept, comprised of various components, not all of which may be in focus. In the following section, I will consider whether intentionality exacerbates impoliteness effects in my data, and whether intentionality is culture specific.

2.2.3   Cross-cultural variation in the correlation between intentionality and gravity of offence

In Section 1.4.1, I made the point that rationality and self-interest do not operate in a vacuum but in the context of social norms and values. I noted Terkourafi's (2005a) observations on societal rationality. Terkourafi also argues that intentions are socially influenced (e.g. 2005a: 249). Malle and Knobe (1997: 116) point out that '[p]eople may differ in their response thresholds of

Table 2.1 *The correlation of intentionality and gravity of offence*

	Pearson correlation coefficients (1= a perfect positive correlation)	Significance of correlation (probability values from a one-tailed t-test)
English	0.15	0.07
Finnish	0.15	0.07
German	0.08	0.21
Turkish	0.16	0.07
Chinese	0.07	0.24

judging a behaviour intentional, and different cultures may impose different social consequences for intentional behaviour'.

The key issue I will address in this section is whether there is any kind of correlation in our report data between the culturally diverse informants' perceptions of gravity of offence and the intentionality of the act. The former was elicited through the question 'How bad did the behaviour in the conversation make you feel at the time it occurred?', and the latter through the question 'Do you think that person meant to make you feel bad?' Responses were recorded on a five-point Likert scale. I expected to see differences, given the culturally influenced nature of intentionality. Table 2.1 presents the strengths of the correlations.

Analysing correlation is not easy from a statistical point of view, largely on account of 'outliers' which can skew the results. On the face of it, no culture exhibits a significant correlation between intentionality and gravity. I conducted a X^2 statistical test in order to explore the heterogeneity of the correlation coefficients, and the result was: X^2 2.99; d.f. 4; $p < 0.56$. The absence of a strongly statistically significant X^2 value suggests that the coefficient values are relatively homogeneous. In other words, although we can see that there are two somewhat distinct groups – English, Finnish and Turkish have lower coefficients than German and Chinese – overall the differences are barely significant. Differences amongst correlations for intentionality and gravity of offence for English, Finnish and Turkish are weak, but at a seven per cent probability level only just outside the usual level for significance. It is intriguing to recollect that these datasets have in common the fact that they are stronger for impoliteness involving Quality face as opposed to Sociality rights. This raises the possibility that intentionality is sensitive to the kind of offence.

2.2.4   Beyond intentionality: Other interpretative heuristics and strategies

Whilst intentions and intentionality have gained much attention in the literature, they are certainly not the only notions that we deploy in making sense of things. Here, I will briefly touch on stereotyping, perceptual salience and perspective in the understanding of impoliteness.

Impoliteness depends on contextual judgements. However, it is not realistic to assume that on every occasion people put in a large amount of effort to work out how a particular behaviour stands in any particular context. As Fiske and Taylor (1984) put it, people are 'cognitive misers'. We simply get by with inferences based on limited information and on our past experience. In attribution theory, a theory about how people infer connections between causes and effects, Kelley (1973) suggests that 'causal schemas', knowledge about the regular associations between causes and effects, allow people to short-circuit inferencing, simply relying on prior knowledge, causal schemata, about what normally causes what. Here, we are tapping into the notion of stereotyping, something that can be approached through schema theory. If stereotypes are 'highly organised social categories that have the properties of schemata' (Andersen *et al.* 1990: 192), they 'can then influence subsequent perceptions of, and behaviors toward, that group and its members' (Hamilton and Sherman, 1994: 15).

The kind of person you perceive to be saying something will affect your evaluation of what they say. Knowledge about people can be grouped, following research in social cognition (see Culpeper 2001: 75–6, for references), into three areas:

- Personality norms (concerning preferences, interests, traits, goals, etc.).
- Social relation and role norms (concerning kinship roles, occupational roles, relational roles, etc.).
- Group membership norms (concerning gender, race, class, age, nationality, religion, etc.).

Let me briefly illustrate the implications these have for impoliteness. Regarding personal norms, it has been proposed that Type-A personalities are characterised by competitiveness, being in a hurry and being aggressive (Rosenbaum and Friedman 1974). The connection between Type-A and aggression has been confirmed in a number of studies (e.g. Carver and Glass 1978; Strube *et al.* 1984). One might reasonably expect Type-A personalities to be more likely to engage in impolite behaviour and be more expected to do so. Regarding social role norms, in the context of North America, Ainsworth (2008: 7) highlights the fact that is common for police officers to swear at criminal suspects in street-level interactions. In this context then, someone identified as a suspect might expect impoliteness from somebody performing the role of police officer. Regarding group membership norms, gender has received most attention in studies on aggression. For example, in Mary Harris's (1993) study of anger women were found to be more angered than men by insensitive and condescending behaviour from men, whereas men were more angered than women by physical attack from another man or by a physically aggressive female. Clearly, perceptions of gender colour impoliteness evaluations of behaviour. Also, note that there are schematic associations between the three above groups. For example, the social role of 'rugby player' is schematically associated with aggressive (personality norm) males (group membership norm).

There is evidence for the age-old adage that we believe what we see, and a key driving force for this is perceptual salience. The idea is that we have a tendency to attribute causes for a person's behaviour to their character, and attach rather less weight to the situation. Hence, we theoretically have a tendency to jump to the conclusion that impolite behaviour is the result of a habitually impolite person. Ross termed this the *fundamental attribution error*: 'the tendency to underestimate the impact of situational factors and to overestimate the role of dispositional factors in controlling behaviour' (Ross 1977: 183). Although this tendency has caused controversy, a good deal of research has substantiated it (Jones 1990: 164). One contributory factor, as Heider (1958: 54) noted, is that behaviour tends to be more salient than situational factors:

it tends to engulf the field rather than be confined to its proper position as a local stimulus whose interpretation requires the additional data of the surrounding field – the situation in social perception.

The salience of behaviour often leads to it acting as an attributional anchorage point from which we can make adjustments according to the situation. The problem is that we often make insufficient adjustment (Tversky and Kahneman 1974; Gilbert and Jones 1986). One issue here of relevance and importance is the neutralisation of impoliteness (or rather the lack thereof), and I will elaborate this in Section 6.6.

Heider (1958: 157) also notes that perceivers tend to make different kinds of attributions according to whether they take the role of 'actor' or 'observer'. Jones and Nisbett (1972) label this the 'actor–observer effect' and describe it thus: 'There is a pervasive tendency for actors to attribute their actions to situational requirements, whereas observers tend to attribute the same actions to stable personal dispositions' (1972: 80). Again, this tendency has caused controversy. However, an interesting group of studies (e.g. Storms 1973; Taylor and Fiske 1975) attempt to explain the actor–observer bias in terms of differences of perspective. Again, perceptual salience is key. The argument is neatly put by Augoustinos and Walker (1995: 82) (see also, Fiske and Taylor 1991: 73):

Observers see the actor acting, but don't see a situation. The actor is salient; the situation is not. Actors, though, don't see themselves acting. They see the situation around them, and are aware of responding to invisible situational forces. Thus, when actors and observers are asked to explain the same event, they give different accounts because different facets of the same event are salient to them.

In fact, research on the interpretation of behaviours as aggressive have considered perspective, and arrived at the conclusion that actors typically have a more positive evaluation of their behaviours compared with their targets or even observers (see references in Mummendey and Otten 2001: 331). The same is likely to apply to the interpretation of impoliteness. Part of what is going on here may be differences in perceptual salience, but there are also differences in knowledge (e.g. a speaker may know that their plan is not to be offensive, but the hearer does not).

2.3   Emotion and offence

2.3.1   Emotion, cognition and aggression

The traditional approach to human emotion considered emotional displays as a reflex of a physiological state (e.g. Darwin 1872). Traditional research on aggression with a biological emphasis proceeded with not dissimilar assumptions. Aggression was viewed as a basic human instinct, with genetically predetermined expressions of emotion, as one would find with animals (e.g. growling as a threatening gesture) (e.g. Lorenz 1966; Morris 1967). More recently, evolutionary social psychology, developed from Darwinian theory, argues that there is a biological basis for all social behaviour, and that aggression is adaptive – it can be used to ward off threats and can increase access to resources (Buss 1990, 1999; Simpson and Kenrick 1997). Of particular note is Beatty and Pence's (2010) review of studies pointing to biological causes of verbal aggression and those pointing to social causes. Whilst they acknowledge that the evidence for biological factors is suggestive, they conclude that by the highest standards of scientific rigour 'verbal aggression is best accounted for by biological factors rather than variables in the social environment' (2010: 21) (see also Heisel 2010, on prefrontal cortex asymmetry). However, whilst biological theories clearly play a part, biological theories are not sufficient as full explanations of (verbal) aggression. For example, people can be angry, yet control that anger and not display aggression. Increasingly, approaches to aggression have paid attention to the role of cognition. Recent work has suggested that aggressive behavioural routines in particular situations – scripts – can be learnt and enacted (e.g. Perry, Perry and Boldizar 1990) (for more on scripts and schema theory generally, see Sections 1.7, 2.6 and 6.2). Berkowitz's (1993) cognitive-neoassociationist model is even more explicit about linkages between emotions and cognitions. More recently, Anderson and Bushman (2002; see also Anderson *et al.* 1995) have developed a 'general aggression model', which can be seen as a development of Berkowitz's model. They focus on three internal states, cognitions (including aggressive scripts), affect and arousal (whether physical or perceived). These states are triggered not just by a stimulus, such as a gun (one stimulus used in Berkowitz's research), but also by a person with specific characteristics in a particular context. Importantly, once one or more of the three internal states are primed by the stimuli, there is not a hotwired link to behavioural actions. The internal states go through a process of appraisal, whereby the person judges what happened, why it happened, how angry he or she feels, and so on. That appraisal may also include consideration of various courses of action, and it can be more thoughtful or more impulsive. Such a model better accounts for the complexities of social encounters. The model for the understanding of impoliteness I am proposing (see especially, Section 2.4) is consistent with theirs. A model of impoliteness needs to link, minimally, language, situations, judgements of impoliteness and the specific emotions associated with impoliteness. Appraisal, that is, interpretation, is crucial: how else will banter be recognised as banter?

The cognitive models mentioned above assume that emotions can be represented in our minds. This is now a fairly established idea. Ortony *et al.* (1988) associate emotions with certain cognitions, and this association is a result of the way in which a perceiver cognitively constructed the situation that gave rise to the emotion. There is empirical evidence that emotions are represented in schema-like structures (e.g. Conway and Bekerian 1987). Understanding emotion concepts as schema-like helps us to accommodate complex intuitions about emotions, account for borderline cases, and to explain how we make assumptions and arrive at understandings. Russell (1991: 39) comments:

Although we often speak of an emotion as a thing, a more apt description is a sequence of subevents. In other words, the features that constitute emotion concepts describe the subevents that make up the emotion: causes, beliefs, feelings, the physiological changes, desires, and overt actions, and vocal and facial expressions. These subevents, described by the concept features, are ordered in a casual sequence – in much the same way that actions are ordered in a playwright's script. To know the sense of a term like anger, fear or jealousy is to know a script for that emotion. . . . Few or no features of the script are necessary; rather, the more features present, the closer the resemblance and the more appropriate the script label.

For example, merely seeing somebody looking angry may lead to assumptions that something has made them angry, that they feel tense and agitated, that they wish for retribution, that they may lose control and strike out, and so on. It is important to remember that emotions interact with information about situations and their norms, information that is represented in the emotion schema. People have prescriptive norms about the appropriateness of emotions in particular situations. For example, laughing and smiling as displays of happiness are not appropriate at a funeral. People appraise the situation and regulate their emotion displays accordingly. Not only are people aware of prescriptive emotion norms for particular situations, but they also have experiential norms for particular situations. Heise and Calhan (1995: 237) found that 'particular social circumstances tend to produce specific emotions', something which is consistent with the idea that there is some kind of automatic link between them. Failure to abide by emotion-situation norms leads to one kind of affective impoliteness, as I will elaborate in Section 7.2.

What kind of emotion schemata exist in our heads? I will not attempt a complete review of this area, but instead focus on aspects pertinent to impoliteness. Shaver et al. (1987) compiled a list of 135 emotion names and then asked 100 subjects to sort them into groups on the basis of similarity. The results were then put through a cluster analysis. What emerged is a tree-like hierarchy of groups, with a basic level in the middle and superordinate categories above and subordinate categories below. This is not an unexpected finding, as early work on prototype theory (Rosch 1973, 1978; Rosch et al. 1976) also found three levels for categories of things, superordinate (e.g. furniture), basic (e.g. chair) and subordinate (e.g. kitchen chair). The basic level is named that by Rosch because it strikes the best balance between informativeness and cognitive economy: categories are sufficiently distinguished but not overwhelmingly rich in attributes. Consequently 'people seem naturally to prefer basic-level categorisation for much of the everyday conversation and thought' (Shaver et al. 1987: 1062). At the highest superordinate level, the only distinction that emerged was a very generic – though important – one between positive and negative emotions. Obviously, impoliteness is associated with the latter. The basic level was comprised of five emotions: love, joy, anger, sadness and fear (and, more weakly, surprise). Interestingly, Shaver et al. (1987: 1069) comment that subordinate-level distinctions are mainly to do with differences in intensity and with differences in the context in which the emotion arose – two important dimensions that I will use to help organise impoliteness metalinguistic labels in Section 3.7. In the following section, I will consider the emotion labels reported for my impoliteness data. For now, it is worth briefly noting that sadness and anger appear to be particularly relevant to impoliteness events, and in particular the subordinate categories neglect and suffering, and disgust, rage, exasperation and irritation.

In a further study, Shaver et al. (1987) attempted to reveal a wider prototype or schema of which the emotion concepts are a part. This they did by listing 120 accounts of emotional experiences, and then using six coders to identify features of these accounts. Some of the accounts clearly involved impoliteness, as this sample illustrates:

I called him a jerk. I yelled at him. I said (excuse me, please) 'fuck you' and called him 'shit head.' I also try to tell him he was wrong to act the way he was over no big deal. I hit and kicked and cursed him repeatedly. (Shaver et al. 1987: 1073)

The schemata for all five emotions contained three features: situational antecedents, behavioural responses and self-control procedures. It is situational antecedents that are particularly important to impoliteness, as impoliteness is an emotionally charged attitude towards behaviours. Fear antecedents relate to the individual's lack of power or control, particularly in certain situations. Sadness antecedents relate to the realisation that an undesirable outcome has occurred, which may include, similar to fear, the discovery that one is relatively powerless (e.g. 'an undesirable outcome; getting what was not wanted: a negative surprise', 'loss of a valued relationship; separation', 'rejection, exclusion, disapproval', 'not getting what was wanted, wished for, striven for, etc.'). Anger antecedents involve the judgement that something/someone has interfered with one's plans or goals by reducing power, violating expectations, interrupting, etc., and that interference is illegitimate (e.g. 'reversal or sudden loss of power, status, or respect; insult', 'violation of an expectation; things not working out as planned', 'frustration or interruption of a goal-directed activity', 'real or threatened physical or psychological pain', 'judgement that the situation is illegitimate, wrong, unfair, contrary to what ought to be'). There are obvious echoes here with the emotional consequences of face damage and/or the violation of norms. Before leaving this section we should remember that there is no guarantee that emotion names and accounts of emotional events are an exact mirror for what goes on emotionally. Also, we should be mindful that the contents of emotions elaborated above are culturally sensitive, particularly at the subordinate-level (Shaver *et al.* 1987: 1083).

2.3.2   (Im)politeness, emotion and morality

Approaches to politeness have generally not placed emotion at the centre of things. The single exception of note is the work of Arndt and Janney (e.g. 1985, 1987), whose notion of politeness involves emotional support conveyed multimodally through verbal, vocal and kinesic cues. Emotion has been a little more prominent in research on impoliteness. As indicated in Section 1.1, emotions are clearly part of the impoliteness definitions (9) and (12) and other definitions allude to emotion aspects. More specifically, Kasper (1990) and Beebe (1995) both discuss a type of impoliteness which is characterised by the fact that it is emotionally driven; I will label this type of impoliteness 'affective impoliteness' and discuss it in Section 7.2. Regarding impoliteness generally, I proposed in Section 1.2 that impoliteness is an attitude that is activated by specific kinds of behaviours in specific contexts. More specifically, I suggested that that attitude could be conceptualised as a kind of attitude schema. Attitude schemata are comprised of evaluative beliefs. Van Dijk (1987: 188–9) suggests that evaluative beliefs may be associated with emotive aspects, such as like and dislike. I would suggest that attitude schemata are associated with an array of emotion schemata; in other words, they are associated with an array of features that comprise the emotion schema, including contextualised antecedents, behavioural responses (i.e. emotional displays) and self-control procedures. Certain contextualised antecedents will be linguistic behaviours in situations where they are considered impolite by perceivers (i.e. evoke impoliteness attitude schemata), and produce particular behavioural responses and particular self-control procedures (e.g. suppression of the emotion) and other actions addressing the situation. Behaviours that evoke impoliteness attitudes are also likely simultaneously to prime emotions in producers, because such attitudes are schematically associated with emotion schemata. Displaying emotions such as contempt or anger has nothing in itself to do with impoliteness. However, somebody displaying great contempt for and anger at someone and doing so publicly may be judged (via an appraisal of behaviour in context) to have acted in an inappropriately and unfairly hurtful way (activation of impoliteness attitude schemata), causing an emotional reaction such as embarrassment or anger (activation of impoliteness-related emotion schemata). Emotions are evoked for both the producer and target of impoliteness, though in this section I will generally focus on the target. Of particular interest in this section is what kind (or kinds) of emotion impoliteness is associated with, and whether different kinds of impoliteness are associated with different kinds of emotion. To begin to answer this, we need to consider moral emotions. First I will briefly touch on the connection between face and emotion, and from there proceed to social norms, morality and moral emotions.

I have already highlighted the emotional sensitivity of face in Section 1.3. Goffman noted the emotional consequences of face loss:

If events establish a face for him [sic] that is better than he might have expected, he is likely to 'feel good'; if his ordinary expectations are not filled, one expects that he will 'feel bad' or 'feel hurt'. (1967: 6)

He may become embarrassed and chagrined; he may become shamefaced. (1967: 8)

Goffman pursued the topic of embarrassment in his essay 'Embarrassment and social organisation' (1967: 97–112). He comments:

Whatever else, embarrassment has to do with the figure the individual cuts before others felt to be there at the time. The crucial concern is the impression one makes on others in the present... (Goffman 1967: 98)

Cupach and Metts's (1994) book on facework contains a chapter on 'embarrassing predicaments', triggered by such events that figure impropriety, lack of competence, conspicuousness, breach of privacy or overpraise (this typology is derived from Buss 1980). Goffman also notes the kind of behavioural display caused by embarrassment:

An individual may recognise extreme embarrassment in others and even in himself by the objective signs of emotional disturbance: blushing, fumbling, stuttering, and unusually low- or high-pitched voice, quavering speech or breaking of the voice, sweating, blanching, blinking, tremor of the hand, hesitating or vacillating movement, absent-mindedness, and malapropisms. (1967: 97)

More recent research follows similar lines. According to Harris (2001: 886), the most commonly reported non-verbal behaviours associated with embarrassment include 'blushing, smiling, avoiding eye contact, and self touching'. Signs of embarrassment can be symptoms of face loss, as observed by both Goffman (1967: 8) and B&L (1987: 61), and thus will be touched on in the analyses in later chapters.

In Section 1.4, I elaborated on the idea that norms are a key notion related to (im)politeness, and I discussed morality in the context of social norms. I pointed out that the management of face also involves norms (especially reciprocity) and matters of morality, and I briefly noted the idea of moral emotions. Haidt (2003: 853) defines moral emotions as 'those emotions that are linked to the interests or welfare either of society as a whole or at least of persons other than the judge or agent'. Typical moral emotions do not have direct benefits for the self. By this token, one might assume that face-related actions do not involve moral emotions. For example, if one loses face and experiences the emotion of embarrassment, actions taken to alleviate that embarrassment clearly benefit the person who is experiencing it. However, emotions like embarrassment promote actions which 'generally make people conform to rules and uphold the social order' (Haidt 2003: 861). We collectively try to avoid embarrassment, because we collectively experience it. This idea is not lost on Goffman (1967: 99–100), who points out that we get embarrassed at other people's embarrassment, or even get embarrassed at other people who ought to be embarrassed though they show no signs of being so.

Moral emotions can be positively or negatively valenced (gratitude would be an example of a positively valenced moral emotion), but I will only focus on negatively valenced moral emotions here. Haidt (2003: 854) suggests two dimensions for identifying typical moral emotions: (1) the extent to which emotions are self-interested or disinterested, and (2) the extent to which they result in moral, prosocial actions. An emotion such as sadness is low on both counts, as sadness involves self-concern and results in lethargy or actions to help the self. Fear also involves self-concern, but is somewhat higher on moral actions, as fear of punishment may drive people to conform to social norms. The more moral negatively valenced emotions are: anger, disgust, contempt, embarrassment, shame and guilt. Haidt (2003: 855; see also Rozin *et al.* 1999) divides these into two groups: anger, disgust and contempt which consist of 'other-condemning' emotions, and embarrassment, shame and guilt which consist of 'self-conscious' emotions. Consider Aristotle's definition of anger:

An impulse, accompanied by pain, to a conspicuous revenge for a conspicuous slight directed without justification towards what concerns oneself or toward what concerns one's friends. (Rhetoric, Book 2, Chapter 2, cited in Haidt 2003: 856)

Haidt (2003: 856) notes of Aristotle's remark that

anger is not just a response to insult, in which case it would be just a guardian of self-esteem. Anger is a response to unjustified insults, and anger can be triggered on behalf of one's friends as well as oneself.

The key to anger here is that the action was unjustified, not just that face was involved. Compare this with Haidt's (2003) comments on shame and embarrassment (emotions that are closely linked, the border between them being particularly sensitive to cultural variation). Haidt (2003: 860) summarises research thus:

In Western cultures, shame is elicited by the appraisal that there is something wrong or defective with one's core self, generally due to a failure to measure up to standards of morality, aesthetics, or competence . . . Embarrassment, in contrast, is said to be elicited by appraisals that one's social identity or persona within an interaction is damaged or threatened, most commonly because one has violated a social-conventional rule but also at times because of events beyond one's control . . . In many non-Western societies, however, any appraisal that one has violated cultural standards of behaviour in front of other people or that one is at high risk of such violations (as when one is around one's superiors) triggers a self-conscious emotion that combines shame and embarrassment.

What is key to these emotions, specifically in a Western cultural context, is the involvement of the self – the loss of face that accompanies these emotions. This contrasts with anger at the unjustified nature of the insult in the previous example. So, my prediction is that impoliteness resulting from violations of sociality rights is more likely to be accompanied by other-condemning emotions (e.g. anger, disgust and contempt), whilst violations of face are more likely to be accompanied by self-conscious emotions (e.g. embarrassment and shame), though face-violations could additionally involve other-condemning emotions if the face-attack is considered unfair. It may be remembered that this is in tune with Spencer-Oatey's (2002: 541) claim that sociality rights are not considered face issues, 'in that an infringement of sociality rights may simply lead to annoyance or irritation, rather than to a sense of face threat or loss (although it is possible, of course, that both will occur)'. This is essentially an argument about different emotional responses. In the following section, I will examine whether this is supported by my report data.

2.3.3   Impoliteness and emotional reactions

My report data was specifically designed to capture conversations that make one 'feel bad', or indeed feel other negative feelings that constitute the offensive

Table 2.2 *Emotions associated with offences involving Quality face (in brackets, raw frequencies are given, followed by percentages)*

Superordinate	Basic	Subordinate	Emotion names (n = 140)
Negative	Fear (4/2.9)	Horror (4/2.9)	shocked (4/2.9), scared
	Sadness (98/70.0)	Neglect (76/54.3)	embarrassed (23/16.4), humiliated (12/8.6), stupid (6/4.3), self-conscious (4/2.9), belittled (3/2.1), inadequate (2/1.4), insecure (2/1.4), small (2/1.4), uncomfortable (2/1.4), useless (2/1.4), cheap, disrespected, rejected, insignificant, insulted, losing face, shown-up, substandard, unintelligent, ostracised, fat, ugly, unappreciated, like an idiot, like a child, judged, let down, lonely, misunderstood, self-critical, shy, singled out, undermined
		Shame (3/2.1)	ashamed (2/1.4), guilty
		Sadness (1/0.7)	sad
		Suffering (18/12.8)	hurt (10/7.4), upset (8/5.7)
	Anger (20/14.3)	Rage (12/8.6)	angry (10/7.4), indignant, resentful
		Exasperation (1/0.7)	frustrated
		Irritation (7/5.0)	annoyed (7/5.0)
	Unclassified (12/8.6)		bad (4/2.9), patronised (3/2.1), offended (2/1.4), weird, put upon, not fair

effects of impoliteness. More specifically, the declared aim of the report form was as follows:

To collect records of conversations in which someone said something to you which made *you* feel bad (e.g. hurt, offended, embarrassed, humiliated, threatened, put upon, obstructed, ostracised).

The point behind using a long string of example emotions was to avoid eliciting conversational antecedents of a particular type because they are connected to a particular emotion type. What was wanted was *any* conversation that resulted in a negatively valenced emotion or emotions. 'Feel bad' was placed in a key position because it seems to be broad. Nevertheless, it is conceivable that 'bad' and the list of examples could have biased the informants in some way, so what is reported here will certainly need further validation.

In one box on the questionnaire, I asked informants to describe their feelings, using the instruction 'We know you felt "bad", but describe your feelings.' In order to get a sense of whether those emotion descriptions varied according to the nature of the offence reported, Table 2.2 displays the emotion labels that

Table 2.3 *Emotions associated with offences involving Equity rights (in brackets, raw frequencies are given, followed by percentages)*

Superordinate	Basic	Subordinate	Emotion names (n = 37)
Negative	Fear (1/2.7)	Horror (1/2.7)	scared
	Sadness (18/48.6)	Neglect (10/27)	humiliated (3/8.1), embarrassed (3/8.1), disrespected, ignorant, ridiculed, small made me feel like I was impinging on her
		Shame (1/2.7)	
		Suffering (7/18.9)	hurt (4/10.8), upset (2/5.4), traumatised
	Anger (10/27.0)	Rage (5/13.5)	angry (2/5.4), fed-up, makes me mad, unfair
		Irritation (5/13.5)	annoyed (4/10.8), irritating
	Unclassified (8/21.6)		threatened (3/8.1), intimidated (2/5.4), offended (2/5.4), bad

accompanied Quality face being identified as the primary mechanism for the offence.

The results of Table 2.2 concerning Quality face neatly fit the prediction at the end of Section 2.3.2. The bulk of the items, 70%, belong to the category 'sadness', a self-conscious emotion. Within that category, 54.3% belong to the category 'neglect', containing labels such as *embarrassed, humiliated* and *stupid*, and 12.8% belong to the category suffering, containing such labels as *hurt* and *upset*. 'Anger' is the next most important category, but accounts for only 14.3% of the descriptor labels used in my report data. Its most important subcategories are 'rage' (7%; mostly the label *angry*) and 'irritation' (5%; containing the label *annoyed*).

Table 2.3 displays the emotion labels that accompanied Equity rights being identified as the primary mechanism for the offence. Equity rights flow from social norms, and the prediction at the end of Section 2.3.2 would suggest other-condemning emotions are dominant. This is not supported by Table 2.3, where we still see 'sadness' as the most densely populated category, accounting for 48.6%. However, the dominance of this category is much less, and we see a dramatic increase in 'anger', which now accounts for 27%.

Table 2.4 displays the emotion labels that accompanied Association rights being identified as the primary mechanism for the offence. Association rights flow from social norms in the context of personal relationships. We might expect something of an emotional mix, given that the category Association rights deals with both rights and relations close to the self. This is not supported by Table 2.4, where we still see 'sadness' as the most densely populated category, accounting for 68% and 'anger' far behind, accounting for 12.8%. In fact, we can see here

Table 2.4 *Emotions associated with offences involving Association rights*

Superordinate	Basic	Subordinate	Emotion names (n = 47)
Negative	Fear (4/8.5)	Nervousness (1/2.1) Horror (3/6.4)	paranoid shocked (2/4.3), speechless
	Sadness (32/68.0)	Neglect (15/32.0)	embarrassed (3/6.4), betrayed (2/4.3), let down (2/4.3), humiliated, inferior, secluded, stupid, uncomfortable, under appreciated, unloved, withdrawn
		Shame (4/8.5) Disappointment (1/2.1) Suffering (12/25.5)	ashamed, guilty, regretful, remorseful disappointed hurt (9/19.1), upset (3/6.4)
	Anger (6/12.8)	Rage (4/8.5) Exasperation (1/2.1) Irritation (1/2.1) Unclassified (5/10.6)	angry (4/8.5) frustrating annoyed intimidated, offended, spoken down to, unexpected, wasn't expecting it

a balance between these two categories that is quite similar to that for Quality face in Table 2.2.

Overall, it seems to be the case that self-conscious emotions dominate my report data. However, this is most true of the categories Quality face followed by Association rights, and least true of Equity rights, where 'anger', an other-condemning emotion, takes on increased importance. Equity rights have more to do with injustices being done that involve others and have weaker implications for the self. Furthermore, the fact that Equity rights were not more strongly associated with anger may well be a function of the methodology. The informant instruction flagged up the word 'bad', which may have encouraged the report of bad self-conscious emotions rather than other-condemning emotions. We also need to remember that we are dealing with data that is not hotwired to the emotions experienced at the time of the impoliteness event.

2.4 Understanding impoliteness: An integrated socio-cognitive model

Impoliteness exists in the mind. Although I believe this statement to be true, it is also trite. For humans, and indeed many other species, everything that 'is' exists in the mind, including language. What we need to know are the mental concepts that are involved and the role they play. Of course, establishing these things is not at all easy. We can look at behaviours which are experimentally induced or observed in their natural contexts. We can look at what people say about behaviours. We can even measure galvanic skin responses or conduct MRI scans. But all of these things require additional interpretation from the analyst. Cognitive concepts are interpretive constructs, postulating connections amongst things in the world. Notions such as 'schema', 'mental models', 'attribution' and 'goals' are metaphors about how the mind tackles experience. Notions like 'schema' make palatable the actual neural networks and chemical actions that constitute the workings of the mind as it deals with experience. But why does an account of impoliteness need to bother with this cognitive stuff? The answer to this applies to any account of language in its social contexts. Van Dijk (pers. com.) argues that the social context is not linked in some direct fashion to language: it is linked via the mind. The mind is a necessary buffer because it accounts for subjectivity and variability. In his recent book, van Dijk (2008: 59–60) states:

[mental models] do not objectively represent the event discourses are about, but rather the way language users variably interpret or construct such events, for instance, as a function of different personal aims, knowledge or previous experiences – or other aspects of the 'context' . . .

Impoliteness is conspicuously a subjective and variable notion involving understandings of behaviours in context. This line of argument is consistent with the points made in Section 2.3.1 that emotions, including emotions linked to impoliteness, are not simply biological reflexes, but involve cognitive appraisal.

My proposal for the understanding of impolite language is loosely based on the model of text comprehension described in van Dijk and Kintsch (1983).[1] Their model has stayed the course of time. Furthermore, van Dijk (e.g. 1987) showed how this model could be used in the study of social interaction, notably, the communication of ethnic prejudices and racism. Indeed, Ruth Wodak's more recent work (e.g. 1996) in the area of critical linguistics and understanding is based on van Dijk and Kintsch (1983). At the heart of this model lies the 'situation model'. This is the 'representation of events, actions, persons, and in general the situation a text is about' (van Dijk and Kintsch 1983: 11–12).[2] It is created through the integration of new information, derived in a bottom-up fashion from the discourse (or indeed from any information extracted from visual or aural stimuli), and of old information from memory (e.g. schemata). Being able to create a situation model is, in van Dijk and Kintsch's view, the major goal in understanding the text: '[i]f we are unable to imagine a situation in which certain individuals have the properties or relations indicated by the text, we fail to understand the text itself' (1983: 337). Two features of the situation model need to be stressed. Firstly, the situation model is dynamic, constantly being updated in the light of in-coming information. Secondly, the situation model is not just a representation of the discourse in the current situation, but will also include assumptions about what others are thinking, what might happen next, and so on. In fact, van Dijk's (2008) most recent work on context stresses the dynamic, flexible and complex nature of what amounts to the situation (or, to use his recent term, context) model.

Figure 2.1 maps out the key concepts, associations and processes involved in the understanding of impoliteness. Each of the three large rectangular boxes represents an important and identifiable component in the process of understanding. The line arrows show some of the linkages between these components. Moreover, they show that understanding is a combination of both top-down processes (i.e. determined by knowledge in memory) and bottom-up processes (i.e. determined by visual/aural stimuli) and that comprehension is cyclic (i.e. what you see influences what you know, and what you know influences what you see) (Neisser 1976: 20–1; Rumelhart 1984: 179–80). Diagrams, unfortunately, are fraught with danger. They are two-dimensional and static. This is quite unlike the human mind which processes things in parallel (i.e. it is multi-dimensional) and is dynamic. There are also limits to the amount of information that can be captured in a diagram. In fact, in the schematic knowledge box, the thick bold lines connecting the items around the edge to those more in the centre are best conceived of as multiple and diffuse (two-way) connections of varying strengths to all other concepts in the box (think in terms of three-dimensional networks). Thus, what I present here is both idealised and simplified.

Below I list some important notes and caveats:

- The diagram is a snapshot of an individual's cognitions.
- One kind of schema relates to attitudes. The label 'Attitudes/Ideologies' is given because a subset of attitudes relates to ideologies (see the explanation in Introducing impoliteness). Strictly speaking, another circle within the Attitudes circle would have been the best way of representing this, but I have not done this in order to keep the diagram from becoming more complex.
- The differences in relative sizes of the circles and boxes should not be taken to indicate the size of differences in importance.
- The diagram does not attempt to represent every possibly relevant concept. Instead, it focuses on key concepts, as discussed in this and the previous chapters.
- The diagram does not indicate:
  ○ the fact that one's understanding is dynamic and also includes one's dynamic understanding of one's interlocutor's understanding, etc.;
  ○ the role of episodic memory (i.e. autobiographical memories);
  ○ how different types of memory and discourse/context are integrated to form an (im)politeness judgement;

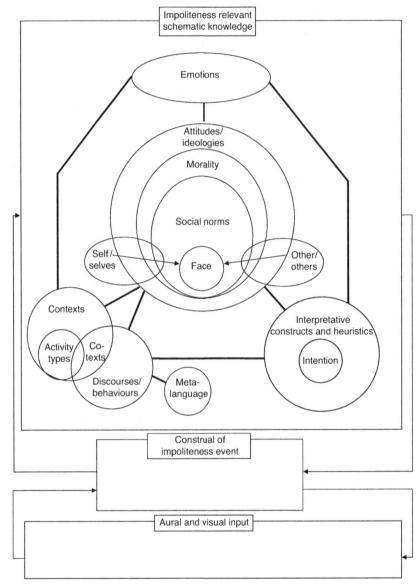

Figure 2.1 Components and processes in the understanding of impoliteness

○ that understanding is strategic (in the van Dijk and Kintsch (1983) model, the reader is an active comprehender, allocating varying amounts of scarce mental resources, depending on 'the goals of the language user, the amount of available knowledge from text and context, [and] the level of processing or the degree of coherence needed for comprehension' (1983: 13)).

2.5   Conclusion

This chapter, building on the last, has examined the concepts involved in the understanding of impoliteness. For some definitions of impoliteness, intentionality is criterial. However, people take offence even if they know that the behaviour that caused it was not fully intentional. We can accommodate this by taking intentionality to be a scalar concept comprised of various components, not all of which may be in focus. People can still take offence if they know intentionality to be only weakly involved, that is, somebody was merely responsible for an act and/or could foresee its offensive effects. I hypothesised that weaker forms of intentionality, such as foreseeability, were likely to be an issue in the context of salient and/or close relationships with highly predictable norms and rights. Of course, all this is not to deny that perceiving strong intentionality *can* reinforce the offence taken. However, there is no generally strong connection between intentionality and the degree of offence taken: it is not automatically the case that X on a scale of intentionality equals Y on a scale of gravity of offence. In what circumstances intentionality is evoked and how it interacts with the social context is something that future research could usefully address, though I noted that in cultures, as far as they can be surmised from my student data, that gravitated rather more towards impoliteness caused by violations of face, as opposed to rights, intentionality seemed to play a somewhat stronger role. In fact, generally we should not get carried away with intentionality – it is but one notion by which people try to understand things. In Section 2.2.4 I noted people's reliance on stereotyping, perceptual salience and perspective in their understandings.

Emotions are of key importance to impoliteness. Some scholars have discussed the affective aspects of impoliteness (see Section 7.2). In the context of schema theory, I noted that van Dijk (1987: 188–9) claims that evaluative beliefs, which constitute attitude schemata, may be associated with emotive aspects, such as like and dislike. Behaviour evoking an impoliteness attitude schema on the part of either the producer or the target is highly likely to trigger semi-automatically associated emotions. The emotional consequences of face loss were noted by Goffman (1967), particularly with regard to embarrassment, a self-conscious emotion. However, emotions flowing from the violation of sociality rights are particularly oriented to moral emotions, including anger and contempt. As Haidt (2003) points out, the former are self-conscious emotions, whilst the latter are other-condemning emotions. My report data broadly supported these tendencies.

In the final section of this chapter, I integrated the various components of impoliteness and showed how they can come together in a model for the understanding of impoliteness. Of course, such two-dimensional models have their limitations, not least of all the fact that they do not explicitly represent the dynamic nature of impoliteness understanding over time.

3　Impoliteness metadiscourse

3.1　Introduction

One way in which the impoliteness definitions given in Section 1.1 vary is in the label they use to refer to impoliteness phenomena. The studies pertaining to definitions (2), (3) and (9) use *rude/rudeness* rather than *impolite/impoliteness*. Furthermore, as can be seen from quotations (10) to (13), outside linguistic pragmatics other terms are used, such as *communicative aggression*. Indeed, in everyday life a myriad of terms are encountered, including *bitchy, mean, uncivil, disrespectful, ill-mannered, cheeky, brusque* and *discourteous*. Clearly, all these terms refer to behaviours that are antisocial in some way, but equally clearly there are nuances of difference amongst them. A particular aim of this chapter is to understand the meanings of such terms, and thereby gain some insight into impoliteness, its characteristics and dimensions. This approach to understanding the meaning of impoliteness by examining terms referring to it echoes the agenda of the 'post-modern' or 'discursive' approach. Studies espousing this approach criticise classic politeness theories for articulating a pseudo-scientific theory of particular social behaviours and labelling it polite-ness (so-called politeness2), whilst ignoring the lay person's conception of politeness as, for example, revealed through their use of terms such as *polite* and *politeness* to refer to particular social behaviours (so-called politeness1) (e.g. Eelen 2001; Locher and Watts 2005; Watts 2003). Politeness, they argue, is a notion that is constructed and contested in discourse, and looking at those constructions and contexts will provide a firmer ontological basis for politeness studies than has been the case hitherto. Moreover, whatever one's approach, all politeness or impoliteness studies need to adopt a metalanguage to describe the linguistic phenomena that relate to politeness (or impoliteness). In fact, Tracy (2008: 173) argues that the term *impolite* is not the best metalinguistic label for the phenomena that are the focus of this book:

Face-attack is a better way to label communicative acts that are (or are seen as) inten-tionally rude, disrespectful, and insulting. 'Impolite' is too tame a descriptor for serious acts of face threat; moreover, to call such acts '(im)polite', whether that definition is an everyday one or researcher-stipulated, leaves unexamined whether acts that insult should be conceptualised in the same discourse family as those that smooth interaction and display considerateness.

There are two issues here. First, Tracy's intuitions are that the term *impolite* is too 'tame' for 'serious acts of face threat'. This is exactly the kind of issue this chapter will be addressing – is it the case that in general usage *impolite* is not used for serious acts of face threat? Second, Tracy makes the point that by using the term *impolite* one involves the term *polite*, presumably via an antonymic relationship, but that this has a consequence that the phenomena those terms refer to are brought together, without any consideration as to whether they should be. My decision in this book has been to use the label *impoliteness* (and to a lesser extent *impolite*) as a blanket-term for the various kinds of phenomena referred to therein. One reason I do this is because the term impoliteness, as we shall see, is so rarely used that the issue of its lay usage does not arise. Further, I am not averse to the idea that the term *impoliteness* primes phenomena referred to by the term *politeness*: impoliteness and politeness phenomena can and do interact, as I will elaborate in Section 6.4.

Despite the call to arms, researchers have generally not scrutinised the usage of such terms. A notable exception is Haugh and Hinze (2003), which discussed the notion of metalanguage in relation to 'face' and 'politeness', and conducted a few collocational analyses ('face' in English, for example, is largely restricted to the contexts 'losing face' and 'saving face'). Another is Ide *et al.* (1992), who found that for American informants the adjectives *respectful, considerate, pleasant, friendly* and *appropriate* correlated with the concept of 'polite', whereas the adjectives *conceited, offensive* and *rude* correlated with the concept of 'impolite'. However, it should be noted that informants in this study were supplied with adjectives to rate – we do not know whether the informants would actually have used these adjectives if they had been free to choose them. Also, the informants were directed to consider their 'feelings' rather than how they would describe or label the language that caused those feelings. No study has attended to politeness or impoliteness related terms in a comprehensive and systematic fashion, and certainly not using the full armoury of the lexicographical methodology of choice, the corpus-based approach. Corpus linguistics is the main methodology of this chapter. In particular, I interrogate the huge *Oxford English Corpus*. I will also report an analysis of the metalinguistic labels used for impoliteness events described in my report data.

Impoliteness metalanguage is not confined to the labels used for impoliteness phenomena, which is why the title of this chapter contains the broader label metadiscourse. When people express opinions about language they consider impolite, they use what I will refer to as impoliteness metapragmatic comments. I will show how these comments can shed light on specific aspects of impoliteness. Many impoliteness metapragmatic comments are articulations of prescriptive rules concerning behaviours in the light of particular social norms. I will consider both impoliteness rules that are publically displayed and those that are not.

I shall begin with a general discussion of the notion of metalanguage/ metadiscourse and impoliteness. The following sections present analyses, largely corpus-based, of the items *impolite, rude, verbally aggressive* and *verbally abusive*. In Section 3.6 I examine the metalinguistic items which my informants supplied when asked to label the behaviour they had described in their reports. Section 3.7 then pulls together the threads and suggests how some of the items I have been investigating might map in conceptual space. I then turn to metapragmatic comments. In Section 3.8 I conduct a case study of metapragmatic comments concerning 'over politeness'. The remaining sections investigate prescriptive rules, a special kind of metapragmatic comment.

3.2   Metalanguage/metadiscourse and impoliteness

I use the terms 'metalanguage' or 'metadiscourse' in the broad sense of language which focuses on language itself (see Jakobson's 1960 definition of the metalingual function). The study of metalanguage is of general importance in sociolinguistics. The reason for this is neatly put by Jaworski *et al.* (2004b: 3):

> How people represent language and communication processes is, at one level, important data for understanding how social groups value and orient to language and communication (varieties, processes, effects). This approach includes the study of folk beliefs about language, language attitudes and language awareness, and these overlapping perspectives have established histories within sociolinguistics. Metalinguistic representations may enter public consciousness and come to constitute structured understandings, perhaps even 'common sense' understandings – of how language works, what it is usually like, what certain ways of speaking connote and imply, what they *ought* to be like.

The role of these metalinguistic representations is seen as twofold: on the one hand they are data for understandings, and on the other hand they become structured understandings. In other words, they both reflect thought and influence it. This assumes at least a weak version of the Sapir–Whorf hypothesis. Indeed, John A. Lucy, an important figure in the study of metalanguage (see, for example, Lucy 1993), supports a form of linguistic relativism (see Lucy 1992). The hot debate about whether or not language influences thought is not key to the arguments in this chapter; what is key is the less controversial idea that language is connected to thought, and thus affords insight into it. I view an individual's impoliteness metalanguage as representations of evaluations that certain behaviours count as impolite, and those evaluations are based on beliefs about the mediation of face and social norms – about what counts as 'correct', 'normal', 'appropriate', etc. behaviour. Moreover, Cameron (2004: 313) points out that morality is an important theme in studies of metalanguage: '[m]etalinguistic resources seem very often to be deployed to connect various aspects of linguistic behaviour to a larger moral order'. This is particularly pertinent to impoliteness, as it is intimately connected to moral order, i.e. beliefs about how things ought to be (see Section 1.4.2). As I described in Introducing impoliteness and Section 2.3.2, all these beliefs are stored in memory, either as part of attitude schemata represented in social (semantic) or as part of personal opinion represented in personal (episodic) memory. By analysing the metalanguage relating to a particular linguistic or communicative area, we have a way of tapping into impoliteness-related attitude schemata. Of course, any particular instance of metalanguage is subject to its own context. It could have local strategic purposes and meanings (e.g. telling somebody that they are 'polite' could be a strategy to ingratiate, or telling them that they are 'impolite' could be a strategy to antagonise), and those purposes and meanings could be disputed. Verschueren (2004: 65, my emphasis) points out that it is when we see '*persistent* frames of interpretation related to the nature and social functioning of language which are no longer subject to doubt or questioning' that we can talk about ideologies of language, those taken-for-granted interpretations (the link between metalinguistic representations and ideologies is also pointed out by Coupland and Jaworski 2004: 36–7 and Verschueren 2004: 65–7; see also Jaworski *et al.* 2004a: 105–62). Regularly occurring metalanguage acts as a window on those persistent 'frames of interpretation', including impoliteness schemata.

In this chapter, I will make a distinction between metapragmatic comments and metalinguistic expressions. A metapragmatic comment is an opinion about the pragmatic implications of utterances, their functions, indexical relations, social implications, and so on (cf. Silverstein 1993; Verschueren 2004). Impoliteness metapragmatic comments are simply a specific kind of metapragmatic comment. Impoliteness metapragmatic comments (e.g. 'That's rude') may involve expressions conventionally understood within a speech community to refer to an evaluation of certain behaviour-in-context as impolite. These expressions (e.g. 'rude') are impoliteness metalinguistic labels (I use the term metalinguistic for labels rather than metadiscoursal because these items are constituted by short, usually one-word, linguistic expressions rather than the whole utterance, though of course they are also part of the metadiscourse). Such labels are subject to normal processes of variation and change, and consequent instability of meaning; as what counts as impolite changes so will the meanings of the metalinguistic expression.

3.3 The corpus-methodology and impoliteness metalanguage/metadiscourse

Consider this quotation:

Any natural corpus will be skewed. Some sentences won't occur because they are obvious, others because they are false, still others because they are *impolite*. The corpus, if natural, will be so wildly skewed that the description would be no more than a mere list. (Chomsky 1962: 159, a conference paper delivered in 1958, my emphasis)

Chomsky's solution of using constructed data is hardly likely to be less skewed than a corpus of naturally occurring data. My main point is that Chomsky made this statement in a period when corpora were small and biased towards scholarly or literary texts, but that is not the case now. Of course, Chomsky is talking about language or behaviour that can be labelled impolite and not the labels – the metalinguistic expresssions – themselves. But, as I argued in the previous section, the two things are linked: behaviours that are interpreted as impolite drive the labelling (although a metadiscoursal comment following impolite behaviour can be delayed or fail to appear). One needs huge corpora to pursue the study of either impoliteness devices or impoliteness metalinguistic expressions, and this fact partly explains the dearth of previous studies deploying this methodology.

The corpus I will use for the investigations in Sections 3.4 and 3.6 is the *Oxford English Corpus* (hereafter *OEC*) (I will also use it as a source of additional evidence elsewhere, particularly Chapter 4). With the benefits of both size and structure, this makes it an ideal resource to use. To be precise, the version of the *OEC* used in my studies has 1,889,417,697 words (figure given by the program *Sketch Engine*). The *OEC* is comprised of material largely collected from the web, with some supplements drawn from printed texts for certain subject areas (e.g. academic journals).[1] The *OEC* is structured according to subject domain, text type, variety of (world) English and date. There are twenty subject domains or areas, each divided into more specific categories. These are displayed in Figure 3.1.

The *OEC* is weighted towards British and US English, which together account for 80 per cent. Regarding period, the *OEC* spans 2000 to 2006. The *OEC* is accessed and manipulated via *Sketch Engine*, software developed by Lexical Computing Ltd (see www.sketchengine.co.uk) (see Kilgarriff *et al.* 2004). *Sketch Engine* is a tool that can produce 'word sketches' for particular words, 'sketch differences' for two (usually semantically related) words, a corpus-based thesaurus, as well as more familiar corpus query functions (e.g. a KWIC concordance). Much more detail on the methodology used to derive the results given in Sections 3.4 and 3.6 is given in Culpeper (2009).

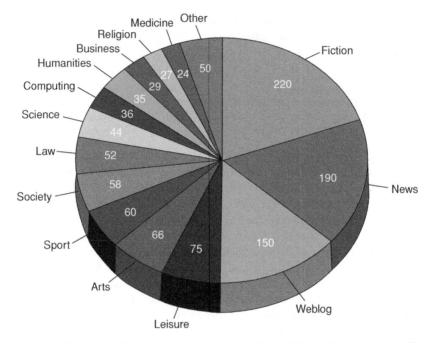

Figure 3.1 The twenty subject domains of the *OEC* (raw frequencies in millions of words) (Figure sourced from www.askoxford.com/oec/mainpage/oec01/?view=uk)

3.4   The frequencies of impoliteness metalinguistic labels: Academia and general usage compared

The point of this section is to provide the grounds for a contrast between what is happening in academia and what the 'lay person' is doing. Below I give a list of labels used in the linguistic pragmatics literature for impoliteness-related phenomena. In order to make sure that these labels were fulfilling a metalinguistic function, I only included labels that were used in indexes, figures, titles and sub-titles, and abstracts.

- *Impolite(ness)* (e.g. Leech 1983; Blum-Kulka 1987; Culpeper 1996; Kien-pointner 1997; Spencer-Oatey 2000; Harris 2001; Eelen 2001; Watts 2003; Mills 2003; Locher 2004; Bousfield and Locher 2008)
- *Rude(ness)* (e.g. B&L 1987; Spencer-Oatey 2000; Lakoff 1989; Tracy and Tracy 1998; Kasper 1990; Beebe 1995; Kienpointner 1997)
- *Aggravation, aggravated/aggravating language/facework* (e.g. Blum-Kulka 1987, 1990; Lachenicht 1980; Craig *et al.* 1986) (also *aggravated impoliteness*, Rudanko 2006)

Table 3.1 *Frequency and distribution of hits for IMPOLITENESS-related nominal expressions in the Social Sciences Citation Index and the Arts and Humanities Citation Index (searched 1 February 2008)*[2]

Search item	*Verbal aggression*	*Verbal abuse*	*Rudeness*	*Impoliteness*
Top five subject categories	Psychology, multidisciplinary (155) Psychiatry (151) Psychology, clinical (129) Psychology, developmental (107) Family Studies (98)	Psychiatry (158) Psychology, clinical (116) Family studies (115) Psychology, multidisciplinary (59) Psychology, social (55)	History (8) Humanities, multidisciplinary (5) Sociology (4) Psychology, social (3) Architecture (2)	Language and Linguistics (12) Linguistics (10) Acoustics (1) Asian Studies (1) Communication (1)
Overall total	874	705	37	17

- *Aggressive facework* (e.g. Goffman 1967; Watts 2003)
- *Face-attack* (e.g. Tracy and Tracy 1998)
- *Verbal aggression* (e.g. Archer 2008)
- *Abusive language* (e.g. Lachenicht 1980)

I have not attempted a precise quantification of how frequently these labels are used, my main aim being to discover the range of different labels that were used. However, by any estimation, the labels *impolite(ness)* and *rude(ness)*, either in their nominal or adjectival forms, emerge as vastly more frequent than the other labels. Interestingly, some authors use both of these labels interchangeably (Spencer-Oatey 2000, for example, explicitly states that they are nearly synonymous). And we should note the absence of other possible labels used in other disciplines (e.g. psychology, sociology), particularly the label *verbal abuse* (rather than *abusive language*), which I will include in up-coming analyses.

My next step was to consider the usage of the above set of labels in various academic fields. To do this, I used the Social Sciences Citation Index combined with the Arts and Humanities Citation Index, performing a search on each item and recording both its frequency and the field of study in which it appeared. The results are displayed in Table 3.1, for nominal expressions, and Table 3.2, for adjectival expressions. My search expressions also include *verbally aggressive* and *verbally abusive*. However, my search expressions did not include *aggravating language* or *aggravating behaviour*, because only three instances arose in the *OEC* in total; in other words, those expressions are very much researcher

Table 3.2 *Frequency and distribution of hits for IMPOLITENESS-related adjectival expressions in the Social Sciences Citation Index and the Arts and Humanities Citation Index (searched 1 February 2008)*

Search item	*Rude*	*Verbally aggressive*	*Impolite*	*Verbally abusive*
Top five subject categories	History (113) Humanities, multidisciplinary (39) Political Science (24) Sociology (18) Literature (16)	Psychiatry (27) Gerontology (21) Geriatrics and Gerontology (18) Psychology, clinical (17) Psychology, multidisciplinary (14)	History (10) Linguistics (8) Language and Linguistics (7) Communication (5) Psychology, social (5)	Family Studies (3) Psychology, clinical (3) Psychology, developmental (3) Communication (2) Law (2)
Overall total	384	101	48	23

terms as opposed to lay person's. It should be remembered that these search terms do not constitute an entirely level playing field with respect to their focus on verbal behaviour: *rude(ness)* and *impolite(ness)* can apply to any kind of behaviour, not just verbal, but this is not true of the other expressions.[3]

Comparing the two tables, it is clear that adjectival forms of the pairs *rude/rudeness* and *impolite/impoliteness* tend to occur more frequently than the nominal forms, but that the opposite is true for *verbal aggression/verbally aggressive* and *verbal abuse/verbally abusive*. In all cases it is the more complex form that is used less (something that is, incidentally, consistent with George Zipf's law of abbreviation; cf. *The Psycho-Biology of Language* 1935: 38). There are differences in the frequency ranking of the items in the tables, most notably in the positioning of *rude* relative to the much less frequent *rudeness*. This is possibly evidence that *rudeness* is not so often theorised and researched as a concept in itself. Turning to the distribution of subject categories in the tables, nominal and adjectival variants of particular pairs distribute across subject categories in broadly similar ways. The top-five subject categories for *verbal aggression* reveal a heavy emphasis on psychology and psychiatry. In these disciplines, aggression is considered a feature of personality, a cognitive disposition, and is often related to personality disorders and mental illnesses. This is particularly transparent in the subject areas for *verbally aggressive*, where we see gerontology and geriatrics, that is, subject areas that cover mental illnesses associated with ageing processes. *Verbal abuse* bears

Table 3.3 *Frequency of IMPOLITENESS-related expressions in the* OEC
(accessed 5 February 2008)

Search item	Rude	Rudeness	Verbal abuse	Impolite	Not polite	Verbally abusive	Verbal aggression	Verbally aggressive	Impoliteness
Total	18,387	1,546	1,522	871	473	201	164	64	30

some similarities to *verbal aggression*, but there is a difference of emphasis: *verbal abuse* is used in disciplines where there is a greater concern with the social context, with the effects of the abuse, hence family studies appears higher in the list and we also see social psychology. This is also reflected in *verbally abusive*. *Rude* is distinctly different, having a strong humanities profile, with a particular emphasis on history, as does *rudeness*. Generally, these terms refer to the social, cultural or historical aspects of offensive behaviour. *Impoliteness* is strongly related to linguistics and communication, and this pattern can also be seen in *impolite*. The reason for this may be due to the monumental success of B&L's (1987) book labelled *politeness*. Subsequent publications in the area of pragmatics may have selected *impoliteness* partly as a way of positioning themselves in relation to this major work, as well as the many other works that use the label *politeness* (there is also now a journal that uses this label). Regarding overall frequency in these tables, it is clear that just two terms, *verbal aggression* and *verbal abuse*, account for the bulk of the metalanguage in academia. *Impolite/impoliteness* occur much less frequently than *rude/rudeness*. In particular, *impoliteness* emerges as a highly specialised term used in a particular academic niche – linguistics and communication.

To get a sense of the more general currency of the metalinguistic items for impoliteness used in academia, I searched for each one in the *OEC*. In addition, I added one further item. The word *impolite* has evolved through *polite* plus a negative prefix. My concern is that that is not the only way in which *polite* can be negated and thereby refer to impoliteness. Consequently, I have added *not polite*.[4] To retrieve instances, I used the following search query: "not" [tag != 'VB.*']{0,1}"polite". Table 3.3 displays the raw frequency counts in the *OEC* for the metalinguistic items in focus.

Rude is outstandingly the impoliteness-metalinguistic expression of general currency. In contrast, in academia *rude*, though the most frequent adjectival expression, ranks well behind *verbal aggression* and *verbal abuse* (see Tables 3.1 and 3.2). *Rudeness* is in second position in Table 3.3, but *rudeness* in academia is much lower relatively. Close behind *rudeness*, *verbal abuse* emerges near the top of this frequency list, as it did with that for academia.

This is despite the fact that *abuse* is constrained by the modifier *verbal*, unlike some other items in the list. For the sociologically and humanities-oriented disciplines, then, there seems to be a reasonable match between their metalanguage and that of the lay person, at least as far as currency relative to the other metalinguistic items considered is concerned. *Verbal aggression*, the most frequent term in academia, emerges near the bottom of this frequency list, with a mere 164 instances.[5] It is in mainstream psychology and psychiatry that there seems to be a dramatic mismatch between the academic metalanguage and that of the lay person. *Impolite* appears roughly in the middle of the frequency list, and interestingly somewhat higher than *not polite*. *Impoliteness*, the term used in linguistics and communication, appears at the bottom of our frequency list here, as it did for academia. Thirty instances out of almost 2 billion is, of course, an exceedingly small number: *impoliteness* has no general currency – it is very much an academic metalinguistic term. My view is that its lack of general currency makes it an ideal candidate as a blanket-term for the semantic areas covered by all the other terms. Each of these terms has a particular identity, encompassing a particular domain of impoliteness, as I will show below.

3.5   Impoliteness metalinguistic labels and their semantic domains

In this section my objective is to see what extant resources can offer with regard to identifying the semantic domains of impoliteness metalinguistic labels. By extant resources I am primarily referring to thesauri, as it is here that attempts have been made to group words into semantic domains. I concentrated mainly (though not exclusively) on British sources, and used both hardcopy and online thesauri. The limitations of the sources should be noted. Hardcopy thesauri rapidly become dated; online versions use much more flexible formats (and some allow for user feedback and input, and offer links to other sites for information about word meanings). However, the editorial/authorial input of the hardcopy versions is clearer than for the online versions. All thesauri are subject to the prejudices of the editors, editorial policy and also assumptions about readership. Generally, the suggested synonyms, antonyms and examples of use seem to be based on an assumed, homogenous group of speakers. The hardcopy of *The Oxford Thesaurus*, for example, features examples of a man not getting up when a woman enters, and conversation with a hotel chambermaid, suggesting perhaps usage of upper middle-class British English speakers from a bygone era.

Table 3.4 below displays frequent synonyms for the items *rude*, *impolite*, *offensive*, *aggressive* and *abusive* (there were no entries for *verbally aggressive* or *verbally abusive*; I added *offensive* as an item that would furnish interesting comparisons).

Table 3.4 *Synonyms for* rude, impolite, aggressive, abusive *and* offensive *given in seven different thesauri (the numbers refer to the thesauri listed below the table; to appear in this table, synonyms needs to be listed in at least four thesauri, the only exception to this being (verbally) abusive, where – for reasons of scarcity – all items were included)*

Rude	Impolite	(Verbally) aggressive	(Verbally) abusive	Offensive
impertinent	discourteous	assertive	scurrilous	revolting
(1, 3, 4, 5, 6, 7)	(1, 2, 3, 4, 5, 6, 7)	(2, 3, 5, 6, 7)	(1, 3, 6, 7)	(1, 2, 3, 5, 6, 7)
crude	ill-bred	enterprising	vituperative	foul
(1, 2, 3, 5, 6, 7)	(1, 2, 3, 4, 6, 7)	(1, 2, 3, 5)	(1, 3, 6, 7)	(1, 2, 3, 6, 7)
disrespectful	disrespectful	militant	contumelious	horrible
(1, 3, 4, 6, 7)	(1, 3, 4, 6, 7)	(1, 2, 3, 6)	(1, 6, 7)	(1, 2, 3, 6, 7)
impolite	ill-mannered	offensive	defamatory	nauseating
(1, 2, 5, 6, 7)	(1, 2, 3, 6, 7)	(1, 3, 5, 7)	(1, 7)	(1, 2, 5, 6, 7)
rough	impertinent	pushy	invective	repellent
(1, 2, 3, 6, 7)	(2, 4, 5, 6, 7)	(1, 3, 6, 7)	(1, 6)	(1, 2, 3, 6, 7)
uncivil	uncivil	pugnacious	libellous	repugnant
(1, 3, 5, 6, 7)	(1, 2, 3, 5, 6, 7)	(1, 3, 5, 7)	(1, 7)	(1, 2, 3, 6, 7)
unmannerly	ungracious	vigorous	offensive	disagreeable
(1, 3, 5, 6, 7)	(1, 2, 3, 6, 7)	(1, 4, 5, 7)	(1, 6)	(1, 3, 5, 7)
coarse	rude	warlike	opprobrious	disgusting
(1, 3, 5, 7)	(1, 2, 3, 5)	(1, 3, 4, 7)	(1, 6)	(3, 5, 6, 7)
discourteous			rude	horrid
(1, 4, 6, 7)			(1, 7)	(1, 2, 6, 7)
ill-bred			slanderous	loathsome
(1, 3, 4, 6)			(1, 7)	(2, 3, 6, 7)
ill-mannered				nasty
(1, 3, 6, 7)				(2, 3, 6, 7)
impudent				obnoxious
(1, 3, 5, 7)				(1, 2, 3, 7)
rough-hewn				sickening
(1, 2, 3, 6)				(2, 5, 6, 7)
uncouth				
(1, 3, 6, 7)				
unrefined				
(1, 2, 3, 7)				

Key to publications (by number)
1. *Roget's 21st Century Thesaurus, Third Edition* (online version of *Roget's Thesaurus*; part of Ask.com at http://thesaurus.reference.com/)
2. *Merriam-Webster's Online Thesaurus*, www.merriam-webster.com/
3. *The Oxford Thesaurus* (Urdang 1991)
4. *Roget's Thesaurus* (Kirkpatrick 1998)
5. *The Macmillan Dictionary of Synonyms & Antonyms* (Urdang 1995)
6. *The Merriam-Webster Thesaurus* (1991)
7. *The Oxford Paperback Thesaurus* (Waite 2001)

This analysis provides some evidence that the words included in Table 3.4 represent a cohesive semantic set. At their centre lies the word *rude*. *Rude* appears in the *impolite* list, in the *(verbally) abusive* list and also in the *offensive* list, although in this case just outside criterion of appearance in Table 3.4 of four sources, having only three sources. It does not appear in the *(verbally) aggressive* list, but we can see *offensive* there, so it is connected at one remove. *Rude* and *impolite* are almost entirely overlapping. *Ungracious*, as a synonym for *impolite*, does not appear in Table 3.4 as a synonym for *rude*, but it does appear outside the criterion for the table, having three sources. The semantic trend that characterises *rude* but not *impolite* is a sense of roughness: *crude, rough, coarse* and *rough-hewn* (a sense that used to be the dominant meaning of *rude*). It is also worth noting that for *impolite* there is a greater emphasis on negating an element more associated with politeness, as we have: *dis-courteous, dis-respectful, ill-mannered, im-pertinent, un-civil* and *un-gracious*. The synonyms for *(verbally) aggressive* all have a sense of forcefulness and in some cases violence. The final two items, *(verbally) abusive* and *offensive*, both relates to effects. A semantic trend for *(verbally) abusive* is damage to someone's reputation: *scurrilous, defamatory, libellous* and *slanderous*. The *Collins Cobuild Dictionary* (1987) defines *scurrilous* as behaviour which 'uses lies, unfair criticism, and insulting language, usually in order to damage someone's reputation'. The synonyms for *offensive* all relate to emotional or physical reactions to something which is extremely unpleasant. Unlike *(verbally) abusive*, *offensive* it is only used to describe effects.

In sum, the key things to take forward are the ideas that these items represent a relatively cohesive set, although the connection with *(verbally) aggressive* is somewhat weaker; that *rude* and *impolite* overlap a great deal; and that *(verbally) abusive* and *offensive* relate to effects, the former having more to do with the effects on one's reputation and the latter being a general term for any extremely unpleasant effects. Incidentally, this analysis justifies my decision to use *offensive* specifically as a term for the effects of impoliteness.

3.6   Metalinguistic labels and their domains of usage: Corpus and report data findings

3.6.1   Rude and impolite compared via the Word Engine usage thesaurus

As noted in Section 3.4, the fact that *rude* and *impolite* are the most frequent items used in studies in the area of linguistic pragmatics makes them obvious candidates for further investigation. I also noted that some scholars use them interchangeably, assuming them to be synonymous. We can investigate the extent to which this is true.

Table 3.5 Rude *and* impolite*: Words sharing the same corpus-based thesaurus category (top thirty in order of statistical significance) (accessed 6 February 2008)*

Rude	Impolite
arrogant, selfish, obnoxious, cruel, sarcastic, stupid, ignorant, nasty, insensitive, disrespectful, abusive, cynical, ugly, vulgar, foolish, lazy, silly, unpleasant, angry, harsh, violent, funny, pathetic, offensive, irresponsible, ridiculous, stubborn, dumb, boring, inappropriate	discourteous, presumptuous, hurtful, demeaning, insulting, flippant, bossy, unprofessional, unappreciative, overbearing, impertinent, insolent, disrespectful, distasteful, pushy, disloyal, nosy, illmannered, unbecoming, inconsiderate, unladylike, tactless, ungenerous, unsportsmanlike, blasphemous, thoughtless, boorish, derogatory, flirtatious, uncalled [for]

The *Thesaurus* facility within the program *Sketch Engine* considers whether a word shares collocational relations with another word in the same grammatical relationship (the statistical operations follow Lin 1998). Thus, *beer* might be grammatically related to *drink* as an object, as might *wine*, and so both *beer* and *wine* can be allotted to the same thesaurus category. Of course, the advantage of this approach is that similarities are revealed through actual usage and not the vagaries of editorial research and practice, as in the previous section. Table 3.5 displays items associated with *rude*, and items with *impolite*.

Not surprisingly, for both *rude* and *impolite*, the thesaurus companions are all adjectives, and all attribute negative qualities (with the possible exception of *funny*). All of the items of both *rude* and *impolite* can describe language; that is, they could fit the frame 'that was a(n) X thing to say'. For *rude*, the following items could happily describe the social and personality characteristics of an individual without reference to either communicative or relational behaviour: *stupid, ignorant, vulgar, foolish, lazy, silly, angry, pathetic* and *dumb*. For *impolite*, it is difficult to find the same kind of item; a possibility is *boorish*, or the more questionable *unprofessional, unladylike* and *unsportsmanlike*. These thesaurus words help reveal those 'structured understandings' of the social world. The tendency is that *rude* belongs to a set of items that links speakers and their talk (i.e. rude speakers doing rude talk); *impolite* belongs to a set of items that link hearers, someone else's talk and contexts (i.e. hearers perceiving impolite talk). This supports Gorji's (2007) (unsubstantiated) observation that although the dominant sense of the word '"rude" describes behaviour or language which causes offence', additionally it is used as a 'term of social description' (p. 3) for the uneducated, the uncultured, the unintelligent – those perceived to be of low social class. To conclude this section, we can also briefly note that a difference between the items for *rude* and those for *impolite* is length: items associated with *impolite* tend to be longer. This hints that *impolite* has a more formal, more high-brow flavour.

3.6.2   Rude *and* impolite *compared via* Word Sketch

A *Word Sketch* is defined as a one-page automatic, corpus-based summary of a word's grammatical and collocational behaviour. Rather than searching some possibly arbitrary window of text surrounding a particular word for collocates, each grammatical relation a word participates in is searched for collocates, and then those collocates are presented in separate lists according to statistical salience (the statistic is logDice, based on the Dice coefficient). For example, if our target word were a verb, its collocates are considered and presented according to the grammatical relations of which it is a part, including, in this case, the subject, the objects, conjoined verbs, modifying adverbs, prepositions and prepositional objects. For English, *Sketch Engine* uses a repertoire of 27 grammatical relations. *Word Sketch* analysis can only be applied to single-word items like *rude* and *impolite*, which means, unfortunately, it cannot be applied to expressions like *verbal abuse* or *verbal aggression*. I shall undertake a comparison of *rude* and *impolite* (including their comparative and superlative forms), using *Sketch Differences*, which performs a statistical comparison of two *Word Sketches*. A slight limitation of this comparison is that the number of instances of *impolite*, 871 instances compared with 18,387 for *rude*, is somewhat low for achieving rich Word Sketches. For this reason, I adopted a relatively low cut-off point of five for any collocate of *impolite/rude* to be taken into consideration. This, of course, increases the danger of idiosyncratic results creeping in, for which reason, I closely scrutinised concordances of all resulting collocates.

In Tables 3.6, 3.7 and 3.8 collocates are ordered in terms of the density with which they occur within a particular grammatical relation. Where two frequencies are given in round brackets, the first refers to the grammatical relation with *rude* and the second the same relation with *impolite*. All results in this section were produced on 6 February 2008. Results that are errors, usually tagging errors, are enclosed within square brackets.[6] (*Sketch Engine* operates on lemmatised forms; for example, *awakening*, listed in Table 3.8 below, also includes instances of the plural form *awakenings*.)

I do not have space to comment in detail on the tables, but will make the following observations:

- Both *impolite* and *rude* share the following prototypical linguistic context: '[It / that] [is / [considered] [terribly / rather] *impolite* / *rude* [and disrespectful] [to stare / refuse / ask]'. This then is the prototypical impoliteness metapragmatic comment, at least as far as metapragmatic comments using

Table 3.6 Rude *and* impolite*: Lexico-grammatical patterns in common*

Grammatical pattern plus its frequency in brackets (first for impolite, *then* rude*); an example of the pattern with* impolite*; an example of the pattern with* rude	*Collocates of* impolite *and* rude *appearing in that grammatical relation, and their frequencies (first for* impolite, *then* rude*)*
Adjectival complement (6625/380) It is <u>considered</u> *impolite* to visit someone's home unannounced ... avoid pointing as well as it is <u>considered</u> *rude*.	consider (133/49)
Infinitival complement (871/224) It's *impolite* to <u>stare</u>. It's *rude* to <u>stare</u>.	stare (74/10), refuse (26/6), ask (69/19)
And/or (3564/195) I believe that you were *impolite* and <u>disrespectful</u> to your host Such conduct is *rude* and <u>disrespectful</u>.	disrespectful (44/5), rude (33/27), polite (9/[7])
Modifies (5726/144) The manager, in a very *impolite* <u>manner</u>, told them to leave the bar. ... the fellow brushed past me in a *rude* <u>manner</u>	manner (67/6)
Modifier (5073/202) It would be <u>terribly</u> *impolite* to impinge upon another chap like that Not only was it <u>terribly</u> *rude* to discuss such matters generally	terribly (50/6), [something (113/5)], rather (184/8)

Table 3.7 *Lexico-grammatical patterns peculiar to* impolite

Grammatical pattern plus its frequency for impolite *in brackets; an example of the pattern with* impolite	*Collocates of* impolite *in that grammatical relation, and its frequency*
Infinitival complement (224) Some worry that it is somehow undiplomatic or *impolite* to <u>speak</u> the language of right and wrong.	[speak (14)], discuss (6), eat (6)
And/or (195) [see example above]	undiplomatic (8)

Table 3.8 *Lexico-grammatical patterns peculiar to* rude

Grammatical pattern plus its frequency for rude *in brackets; an example of the pattern with* rude	*Collocates of* rude *in that grammatical relation, and its frequency*
Adjectival complement (6625) I knew it <u>sounded</u> *rude*, but I was curious.	sound (187), [damn (25)], seem (168), be (3030), [bite (16)], realize (23), appear (46), [care (6)], act (15), [mention (13)], is (2626), feel (32)
NP adjectival complement (445) Some cultures <u>consider</u> it *rude* for students to question a teacher.	consider (22), [sound (6)], think (28), find (40)
Adjectival subject (1114) <u>Doormen</u> are so *rude* to some customers.	doorman (8), bouncer (7), staring (10), bartender (5), [tad (5)], waitress (6), waiter (5), [bit (138)], yorker (5), staff (78), french (5), [stop (7)]
Infinitival complement (871) Julius knew that it was *rude* to <u>eavesdrop</u> on conversations.	eavesdrop (6), interrupt (25), [staff (8)], point (17), print (5), ignore (15), decline (5), invite (7), smoke (5), listen (6), refer (6), laugh (6)
'to' PP (429) A person who is nice to you, but *rude* to the <u>waiter</u>, is not a nice person.	waiter (8), stranger (12), guest (16), customer (17), host (6), reporter (5), journalist ([5])
And/or (3564) I don't much care for kids; they're loud, *rude*, and usually <u>obnoxious</u>.	obnoxious (93), arrogant (151), inconsiderate (38), impolite (27), crude (93), [awakening (17)], discourteous (16), sarcastic (42), unhelpful (22), dismissive (24), lewd (18), pushy (15)
Modifies (5726) She experiences a series of extremely *rude* <u>awakenings</u>.	awakening (672), bwoy (132), yute (21), gesture (171), remark (140), boyz (13), mechanical (16), bwoys (10), interruption (23), shock (156), comment (266), jolt (10)
Modifier (5073) Beyond ignoring the widely posted 'no cell phone' signs, this just seemed <u>downright</u> *rude*.	downright (117), plain (69), fucking (28), awfully (34), incredibly (106), unspeakably (12), [sound (25)], unnecessarily (17), unbelievably (12), outright (11), horribly (17), little (96)
PP of-i (36) Tretiak delivered the *rudest* of <u>awakenings</u> to the North American hockey.	awakening (5)

one or both *impolite* and *rude* to evaluate certain behaviours (verbal or non-verbal) are concerned.

- Both *rude* and *impolite* vary in offensiveness (see 'terribly'/'rather'). However, for *rude*, even allowing for the mis-tagged items 'a little bit rude' or 'a tad rude', the bulk of modifiers indicate a generally high degree of impoliteness.
- Considering that the contents of Table 3.7 are so scant as to be discounted, we can say that *impolite* has no real identity separate from *rude*; its usages overlap with a subset of the usages of *rude*. Although the following three bullet points below describe usages relating to *rude*, the item for which we have most evidence on account of its frequency, we have no counter evidence that *impolite* follows different paths but at least some evidence that it shares them.
- Subjects regularly described as *rude* include: 'doorman', 'bouncer', 'bartender', 'waitress', 'waiter', 'yorker', 'staff' and 'french'. 'Doorman', 'bouncer', 'staring', 'bartender', 'waitress', 'waiter' and 'staff' nearly all relate to public service contexts, where people have expectations of 'service' entitlements, which are not always met or are disputed. In addition, we find 'yorker' (as in 'New Yorker') and 'french', suggesting that people evaluate national or place stereotypes as impolite (remember that the bulk of the OEC emanates from North America).
- Actions regularly described as *rude* include: 'eavesdropping', 'interrupting', 'pointing', 'ignoring', 'declining', 'inviting', 'smoking', 'listening' and 'laughing'. These actions give particular insight into the social underpinnings of behaviours regularly evaluated as impolite. Note, in brief, that 'eavesdropping', 'pointing' and 'listening' relate to unwarranted intrusions; 'interrupting' and 'declining' relate to unwarranted impositions; 'ignoring' relates to unwarranted exclusion; 'laughing' relates to devaluing somebody; and 'smoking' relates to what is allowed in a particular context (i.e. they all violate social norms).
- Similar to subjects regularly described as *rude*, *rude* is often applied to people inhabiting particular social roles: 'waiter', 'guest', 'customer', 'reporter' and 'journalist'. 'Waiter' and 'customer' again relate to contexts where people have expectations of 'service' entitlements, which are not always met or are disputed. Similarly, a 'guest' might be thought to have a claim to special treatment, a claim which might not be met or could be disputed. Those scenarios could lead to the use of *rude*. 'Reporters' and 'journalists' presumably attract the use of *rude* because they are regularly involved in conflictual situations. We should also note the collocate 'stranger'. Interestingly, B&L's (1987) politeness framework predicts that strangers attract more politeness work. As with 'waiter', 'customer' and 'guest', it is perhaps situations of assumed special entitlement that, if a rupture occurs, attract evaluation as impolite.

Table 3.9 *The distribution of* rude *and* impolite *over text-type (up to the most frequent ten)*

	Rude			Impolite	
Text type	Freq.	Rel. freq.	Text type	Freq.	Rel. freq.
fiction	7,814	268.9	fiction	340	198.7
weblog	3,650	211.5	humanities	50	168.4
life and leisure	1,791	130.6	weblog	149	146.7
transport	92	85.3	life and leisure	65	80.5
arts	964	78.2	society	41	57.1
paranormal	42	69.7	arts	36	49.6
humanities	293	58.1	news	102	39.9
religion	250	55.7	–	–	–
news	2,250	51.8	–	–	–
computing	263	50.7	–	–	–

- The items that are regularly coordinated with *rude* include: 'obnoxious', 'arrogant', 'inconsiderate', 'impolite', 'crude', 'discourteous', 'sarcastic', 'unhelpful', 'dismissive', 'lewd' and 'pushy'. It is no surprise to see the item 'impolite', given that I have claimed above that the usages of *impolite* are subsumed within *rude* – using them both reinforces the point being made.
- *Rude* differs from *impolite* in its wider array of usages. It has the following usages that are not shared with *impolite*: (1) It has potentially positive uses, notably, 'rude boyz', 'rude yute', 'rude bwoys', reflecting a usage of rude that originated about 50 years ago in Jamaica, but is now also current in the UK, and has the sense of being loud, sexy and fashionable (this also relates to the distinct popularity of *rude* in the language use of Caribbean men; see Culpeper 2009). (2) It is used to describe sex and nudity taboos. Note that it coordinates with the item 'lewd'. (3) It is part of the frequent collocation 'rude awakening(s)'. This is similar to 'rude shock' and 'rude jolt'. All of them relate to unexpected and unpleasant change. (4) Unlike *impolite*, it also has a clear connection with social description usages (e.g. 'rude mechanicals', a usage that originated in Shakespeare's *Midsummer Night's Dream*, meaning rough and unsophisticated).

3.6.3   An examination of verbally aggressive *and* verbally abusive

Given that a *Word Sketch* can only be created for single-word expressions, other techniques must be used to examine *verbally aggressive* and *verbally abusive*. As a starting point, let us consider the distribution of the items across text types. Table 3.9 displays the distributions of *rude* and *impolite*, and Table 3.10 displays the distributions of *verbally aggressive* and *verbally abusive* over the

Table 3.10 *The distribution of* verbally aggressive *and* verbally abusive *over text-type (up to the most frequent ten)*

Verbally aggressive			Verbally abusive		
Text type	Freq.	Rel. freq.	Text type	Freq.	Rel. freq.
medicine	21	756.3	law	26	471.6
law	3	155.4	medicine	27	340.5
society	5	113.2	life and leisure	27	190.4
life and leisure	5	100.7	sport	12	107.7
news	15	95.4	news	47	104.7
arts	3	67.2	weblog	12	67.2
weblog	4	64.0	religion	3	64.7
humanities	1	54.7	fiction	18	59.9
science	2	47.4	humanities	3	57.5
sport	1	25.6	computing	3	55.9

various text types of the *OEC* (strictly speaking, what the *OEC* refers to as domains) (given that the *OEC* contains different quantities of the various text types, the relative frequencies are more meaningful, and the items are ordered accordingly).

Table 3.9, displaying results for *rude* and *impolite*, contains no surprises. Both items occur in very similar text types, and those text types reflect social and humanistic concerns. The fact that fiction is the highest listed for both *rude* and *impolite* may be because impoliteness-related behaviours can be entertaining and make for high-drama (see Sections 7.4 and 7.5), and the appearance of weblogs fairly high in each list might be explained by the fact that it is in weblogs that many people discuss salient events, most notably impoliteness events. Table 3.10 provides a striking contrast: medicine and law, text types that did not feature at all in relation to *rude* or *impolite*, appear in the top two items for both *verbally aggressive* and *verbally abusive*. Similar text types to *rude* and *impolite* – fiction, weblog, life and leisure, etc. – do appear, but lower in the list. This points to *verbally aggressive* and *verbally abusive* having a particular institutionalised usage. There are differences between them: *verbally aggressive* is very closely associated with medicine, its raw frequency in law being very small; *verbally abusive* is more closely associated with law, although it appears with equal frequency in law and medicine, its relative frequency in law is much higher. We shall see from the examples below, the associations *verbally aggressive* has with the medical register and *verbally abusive* with the legal register are broader than the figures in Table 3.10 suggest, as they are used in other text types because of their medical or legal associations (e.g. using *verbally aggressive* in 'news' can give a report an air of medical authority).

Table 3.11 *The collocates of* impolite *and* rude *(the top-ten rank ordered according to MI score)*

Impolite			Rude		
Collocate	Freq.	MI score	Collocate	Freq.	MI score
undiplomatic	8	16.919	bwoys	11	16.147
disrespectful	6	12.327	bwoy	164	15.570
rude	31	11.930	awakening	676	13.837
insensitive	6	11.272	yute	22	12.992
polite	13	10.830	mechanicals	13	12.880
improper	5	10.611	discourteous	18	12.852
downright	5	10.555	awakenings	24	12.789
stare	11	9.821	boyz	13	12.469
terribly	6	9.417	inexcusably	8	12.357
considered	62	9.383	self-seeking	14	12.335

In order to examine more closely the meanings and usage of *verbally aggressive* and *verbally abusive*, I will investigate their collocates and scrutinise the contexts of those collocates. 'Eyeballing' a lengthy concordance to identify collocates with a particularly strong association is not a reliable methodology, even if the concordance is sorted in various ways. Using the relevant facility within *Sketch Engine*, I calculated the strength of collocates in a five-word window to the left and right of the target item using Mutual Information (MI) scores. The remaining tables in this section are rank-ordered according to those scores. Let us start with a very swift glance at *impolite* and *rude* in Table 3.11. The point of doing this is to show that this methodology reveals the similar conclusions to those arrived at through Word Sketches, albeit in a less sophisticated manner. (The analysis in Table 3.11 has a frequency cut-off point of five, a cut-off point that matches that used for Word Sketches.)

The collocates for *impolite* are exactly what we would expect, given what we saw in the Word Sketch analysis. For *rude*, things seem a little different. But remember that these results are for the strength of collocation only, they are not crosscut by grammatical relationship. We see here evidence that, for example, 'rude bwoys/bwoy/boyz' (associated with Caribbean English) or 'rude awakening/awakenings' occur as particularly strongly associated word units. If we consider items ranked in the top twenty, we find collocates such as 'inconsiderate', 'impolite', 'unspeakably', 'doormen', 'obnoxious' and 'disrespectful' – all of which were revealed in the Word Sketch analysis.

Table 3.12 shows the top-ten rank ordered collocates for verbally aggressive and verbally abusive. (A raw frequency cut-off point of five was used for

Table 3.12 *The collocates of* verbally aggressive *and* verbally abusive *(the top-ten rank ordered according to MI score)*

Verbally aggressive			Verbally abusive		
Collocate	Freq.	MI score	Collocate	Freq.	MI score
abusive	4	13.549	physically	14	11.939
prone	3	12.638	threatening	5	10.468
physically	6	12.371	episode	6	10.463
hostile	3	11.997	aggressive	5	10.113
statements	4	11.135	violent	6	10.106
angry	3	10.204	became	19	9.318
girls	3	9.009	behavior	6	9.272
became	4	8.725	towards	17	9.218
=	3	8.349	staff	8	8.268
patients	3	8.254	father	9	8.210
often	4	8.012	toward	5	8.155

verbally abusive, but of three for *verbally aggressive* on account of its much smaller frequency of occurrence; see Table 3.3).

As a preliminary, note that 'abusive' appears as the strongest collocate for *verbally aggressive*, whilst 'aggressive' appears as a strong collocate of *verbally abusive*. An example of each is as follows:

[1]

> *news* 'I think his recent outburst was so incredibly <u>abusive</u> and **verbally aggressive**, hostile and foul-mouthed,' said Byrne, who was accused by Dunphy of getting paid for 'sitting on his arse'.

[2]

> *law* 'We were of the opinion that Sergeant Eastwood was acting in the execution of his duty in that he was faced with a situation that threatened the operation of the custody suite, namely the appellant and her mother being **verbally abusive** and <u>aggressive</u> while he was dealing with another prisoner.'

Clearly, just as the meanings of *impolite* and *rude* overlap, so do the meanings of *verbally aggressive* and *verbally abusive*. Note that these items seem to stand apart from *impolite* and *rude*, which failed to occur even in the top fifty rank ordered collocates (recall the separation of these pairs of labels noted in Section 3.4). Let us scrutinise *verbally aggressive* and *verbally abusive* in more detail.

Some collocates of *verbally aggressive* suggest that it has a visceral quality ('physically'), that it is driven by a specific emotion ('anger') and is socially negative ('hostile'), as illustrated by the following examples:

[3]

    society Is there anything that could be done without being <u>physically</u>/**verbally aggressive**?

[4]

    science In their study, they found there were no correlations between finger lengths and males who are prone to exhibit **verbally aggressive**, <u>angry</u>, or <u>hostile</u> behaviours, but there was to physically aggressive behaviour.

Other collocates show a clear link with *verbally aggressive* as a symptom of a medical condition. The collocate 'statements' always occurs in medical texts. The equals sign '=' appears in the context of medical research papers reporting quantitative results. Those results often involve sex as a variable, hence the occurrence of 'girls'. And of course the connection with 'patients' is clear. Examples of these collocates are given below:

[5]

    medicine Rejected children ($M = .18$) made more verbally aggressive statements than average children ($M = .04$), and boys ($M = 1.16$) made more **verbally aggressive** <u>statements</u> than <u>girls</u> ($M = .04$).

[6]

    medicine On both male acute wards <u>patients</u> were **verbally aggressive** towards staff approximately <u>four times as often</u> as they were physically aggressive (Argyle 77 and 22; Atherton 40 and 14).

The medicalisation of *verbally aggressive* is also clear in other collocates. In example [7], from a radio programme, 'often' and 'prone' are words that characterise *verbally aggressive* as one of the regular symptoms of a particular state:

[7]

    society After years of physical, sexual and emotional trauma at home, they're <u>often</u> **verbally aggressive**, violent, <u>prone</u> to self-mutilation, cruel to animals and intellectually disabled.

Like *verbally aggressive*, *verbally abusive* also has a visceral quality ('physically'), but seems to have a more destructive edge, moving beyond mere hostility, as is evidenced by 'threatening' and 'violent':

[8]

    humanities The mother charges the father with being <u>physically</u> and **verbally abusive**?

[9]

    news It was a woman being **verbally abusive** to the staff and <u>threatening</u> them.

[10]

    society At home, he is likely to become <u>violent</u> and **verbally abusive** towards his wife.

Note that these examples also illustrate a contrast with *verbally aggressive*: *verbally abusive* is not a symptom of a medical condition, it is a description of behaviour directed towards individuals (cf. the collocates 'towards' and 'toward'). 'Staff' appear as a particular target of *verbally abusive* behaviour, as illustrated below:

[11]

> *news* They have been **verbally abusive** to staff and students and challenging in their manner

This is not to say that the producer of *verbally abusive* behaviour is ignored. In fact, that turned out to be strongly associated with 'father'. However, even here the focus is on the producer of behaviour that caused negative effects in others (cf. 'hurt me', 'toward his mother'). This tendency to be concerned with negative effects is consistent with the findings of Section 3.4 and 3.5. Generally, note that, apart from examples involving 'staff', the context of usage is strongly weighted towards the in-group.

One aspect that *verbally abusive* shares with *verbally aggressive* is its tendency, though a lesser one, to belong to the medical register. The collocate 'episode', denoting events where somebody's behaviour caused negative effects for somebody else, is exclusively used in medical texts, as illustrated below:

[12]

> *medicine* In addition, participants were asked to write in any other emotional feelings encountered during a **verbally abusive** episode.

However, as pointed out earlier, it is in legal texts that *verbally abusive* comes into its own, for example:

[13]

> *law* She alleges that she saw the applicant at the door and, in response to his greeting, was **verbally abusive** to him.

And the legal register infuses other discourses too:

[14]

> *news* Fox was allegedly uncooperative and became **verbally abusive**, allegedly using foul 4 – letter words and obscene hand gestures.

The use of this expression in legal contexts is not surprising, given that it is concerned with the antisocial effects of behaviours, something that is at least partly within the remit of the law (see Section 3.9).

3.6.4 Metalinguistic labels and their domains of usage: Report data findings

One problem with the analyses conducted thus far is that the set of search terms were selected on the basis that they appear in the academic literature. Perhaps the lay person would not use such terms at all. In my report data, I asked

Table 3.13 *Metalinguistic labels provided for 100 reported impoliteness events*

Semantic domain	Metalinguistic label
PATRONISING (×32)	patronising/patronised (×5), arrogant (4), condescending (×3), put down (×3), snobby (×2), mocking (×3), degrading (×2), disregarding, belittling, disrespectful, abuse of power, bossy, authoritarian, superiority, showing off authority, take the piss, showing off
INCONSIDERATE (×28)	inconsiderate (×4), insensitive (×4), unthoughtful (×3), thoughtless (2), indifferent, unfeeling, unhelpful, spoke without thinking, offhand, offish, careless, uncaring, tactful (not), unsubtle, jumping to conclusion, impatient, harsh, blunt, abrupt
RUDE (×23)	rude (×22), impolite
AGGRESSIVE (×18)	aggressive/aggression (×6), bullying (×5), intimidating/intimidation (×4), violent, threatening, confrontational
INAPPROPRIATE (×16)	inappropriate (×4), unnecessary/not necessary (×5), unacceptable/not acceptable (×2), over-the-top (×2), over-familiar, make something into a big deal
HURTFUL (×16)	hurtful (×16), insult/insulting (×3), mean (×2), nasty, not very nice, spiteful, cruel, heartless, unkind, bitter
JOKING (×7)	joking, banter, teasing, possible joke, harsh joke, humour, joking
CHILDISH (×6)	childish (×3), ignorant (×2), immature
TABOO (×6)	swearing (×2), taboo, toilet humour, bad taste, non-PC
OTHER GROUPS AND ITEMS (×44)	offensive (×3), selfish (×3), sarcasm (×2), sarcastic, sexist (×2), unfair, unprofessional, unreasonable, anger, judgemental, shown up, urging me, angry, annoying, irritating, bitchy, common, laddish, confused, defensive, ganging up, grumpy, horrible, idiotic, impersonal, intrusive, judgmental, mooching, moody, obnoxious, out of character, petty, scheming

informants to provide labels for the conversations they had reported making them feel bad, etc. This provided me with 200 labels contained in 100 reports. I sifted through the metalinguistic labels and formed groups on the basis of semantic similarity. Semantic relations between items were verified by using a series of fairly recent (often corpus-based) dictionaries (notably, the *Collins Cobuild English Language Dictionary* 1987). Items where there was any doubt were not included in the groupings. Table 3.13 displays our results.

There is not a single instance of *abusive* or *abuse* (except in the rather different context of 'abuses of power'). This does not mean, of course, that (*verbally*) *abusive* is never used to describe everyday interactions, but it does seem to indicate that it is not a common expression. As we saw in Section 3.6.3, it seems to be primarily a legalistic term. There is but a single usage of the label *impolite*, which has been subsumed within the category rude. Similarly, there are but three instances of *offensive*, an item that was investigated by Ide *et al.* (1992) (see Section 3.1). There are six main groups: PATRONISING, RUDE, INCONSIDERATE, AGGRESSIVE, INAPPROPRIATE and HURTFUL. I will make a few remarks about each of the six major groups:

- The dominant semantic group is PATRONISING, a group that captures reactions to the face-damaging acts produced in a context in which the 'patroniser' is perceived to act in a way which presumes a superiority that they are not considered to have; in other words, there is a perceived abuse of power. There is some literature on the patronising aspects of communication, particularly concerning intergenerational interactions (see Hummert and Ryan 2001, for an overview). Interestingly, although impoliteness studies in linguistic pragmatics include only brief mentions of patronising acts if at all, the connection with impoliteness is explicitly made in this literature: 'the topic of patronising could be seen as a focus on strategies of impoliteness' (Hummert and Ryan 2001: 264). Patronising labels were used to describe 24 impoliteness events (out of 100). Scrutinising the type of offence involved, the strongest pattern is Quality face (14 primarily; 5 secondarily), and the next strongest Association rights (4 primarily; 12 secondarily). Being patronised involves a kind of 'double whammy': your face is devalued in some way, but it is also devalued in a particular relational context that does not licence the 'patroniser' to do so. This is not to say that the result is double the overall offence. In fact, on the five-point scale of gravity the average is 2.7 (n = 24). Being patronised seems to involve a range of minor face-related offences which might well have been overlooked had they not implied a power relationship that the target objected to. Of course, these findings are culture-specific. One might think that a group of a hundred university students on the cusp of adulthood would be particularly sensitive to any actions that could be construed as an exercise of power over them. However, this would be a more convincing hypothesis if the evidence showed that those exercising power were older adults. This is not the case: more than half of the impoliteness events involving patronising descriptions took place amongst student peers. It is quite possible then that this is a feature of a broader cultural group, although of course this needs further investigation.

- The notion of consideration is not unknown to politeness researchers (see, for example, Watts 2003: 14, and also references therein), so the presence of the group INCONSIDERATE is perhaps not a surprise. The labels constituting the INCONSIDERATE group populate the reflections on 21 impoliteness events. All but 4 involve interactions between family members or close friends. In such contexts there are stronger expectations of consideration, given that the interactants know each other well, and, most clearly in the case of friends, like each other. Consideration seems to involve a stronger emphasis on sociality rights. This is perhaps reflected in the type of offence involved in the

21 events: 9 involved Quality face and 9 involved Sociality rights (4 Equity rights; 5 Association rights). The INCONSIDERATE group is also associated with stronger assessments of gravity of offence: the average was 3.1 on the five-point scale (n = 21).

- It is surprising to see the RUDE group ranking merely third in terms of frequency. Looking more closely at the RUDE group, it is interesting to note the kind of contexts to which the expressions *rude* or (the single case of) *impolite* are applied. Fourteen were applied to contexts involving interactions between strangers, specifically in public service contexts (e.g. bars, cafes, shops). Only five took place between friends or family members, and a further two took place between acquaintances and two between teachers and pupils. Overwhelmingly then rudeness is associated with interactions between out-group members, one of which (the offender) is assumed to be obliged to perform certain tasks for the other (the person who is offended). Although the methodology was completely different, this is precisely the conclusion arrived at in the corpus-based analysis of *rude* and *impolite* in section 3.6.2. In terms of gravity of offence, RUDE has an average of 3.1 (n = 23) on the five-point scale, exactly the same as for the INCONSIDERATE group.

- Turning to the AGGRESSIVE group, it is interesting to note that *aggressive/aggression* is the label for an emotion, and the same can be said for other items in this group, such as *intimidating/intimidation* and *threatening* (see the discussion of emotions in Section 2.3). There clearly is a very close connection between the emotions produced in participants and the behaviours that cause them. This supports one of the claims I will make about impolite language in Chapter 4, specifically, that it has a particularly close association with emotion and varies along some of the same dimensions. The fact that this group appears here, and indeed fairly strongly, acts as a corrective to a possible impression gained from earlier analyses of *verbally aggressive* in this chapter. Whilst it is an academic, medicalised term used in a fairly specialist, technical way, expressions relating to aggression are also part of the general metalinguistic currency for everyday impoliteness. The AGGRESSIVE group is associated with an average of 3.6 (n = 16) on the five-point gravity of offence scale.

- Turning to the INAPPROPRIATE group, some researchers see politeness as a matter of doing what is appropriate (e.g. Meier 1995). The notion of appropriate behaviour looms large in the relational approach espoused by Richard Watts and Miriam Locher. Relational work is considered to cover 'the entire continuum from polite and appropriate to impolite and inappropriate behaviour' (Locher 2004: 51; see also Locher and Watts 2005: 11; Watts 2003: 19; Watts 2005: xliii). Note in this quotation that inappropriate behaviour is stated to be a feature of impolite behaviour. My findings here support this view, though, as I will argue in Sections 6.2 and 6.4, being inappropriate is not an essential feature of impoliteness, especially in contexts where it is in some sense legitimised.

- The HURTFUL group, like the AGGRESSIVE group, is connected with a particular emotion (see Section 2.5). We can note that the link between the label for an emotion and the label for the behaviour-in-context that caused it is strong. Hurtful communication has been the subject of research (e.g. Feeney 2004; Leary *et al.* 1998; Vangelisti 1994, 2001, 2007). In this research it is generally understood that '[p]eople feel hurt when someone else says or does something that they perceive emotionally injured them or when they perceive someone's failure to say or do something emotionally injures them' (Vangelisti 2007: 139). Clearly, there are strong overlaps here with the way I have been describing impoliteness. An important finding of hurtful communication research is the 'broad agreement that hurt is bound to be part of any close relationship' (Vangelisti 2007: 121). Given the low number of impoliteness events, I cannot verify this in my data, but I can note that the HURTFUL group is associated with an average of 3.6 (n = 14) on the five-point gravity of offence scale, that is, exactly the same as the average for the AGGRESSIVE group.

It is difficult to arrive at firm conclusions, largely because the low numbers of descriptors preclude any kind of statistical analysis, especially for different types of context (readers will note that I only gave offence-type frequencies relating to context for the three most dominant groups). Nevertheless, the findings do provide some insights, some confirmation or disconfirmation of previous research, and some pointers for future research. In the following section, I will synthesise the findings of this and the corpus-based label research thus far.

3.7   Mapping impoliteness metalinguistic labels in conceptual space

In this section I am concerned with how the metalinguistic labels discussed thus far relate not just to each other but to different behaviours in different contexts. What I am interested in is revealing those understandings that lie behind the labels. Figure 3.2 maps the key metalinguistic labels onto a conceptual background.

In Figure 3.2, the use of small capitals indicates metalinguistic groups of impoliteness labels, and these groups of labels are plotted to reflect broadly my corpus-analyses and diary report data, including, in particular, informants' ratings of gravity of offence (brackets surround groups of labels for which data is patchy). The word 'impoliteness', labelling the inner-circle, is in italics because it is not the name of a group of labels, but simply reflects my usage of the term as a cover-term in this book. Words in bold are labels for the dimensions along which I argue the groups of labels vary. As has been pointed out,

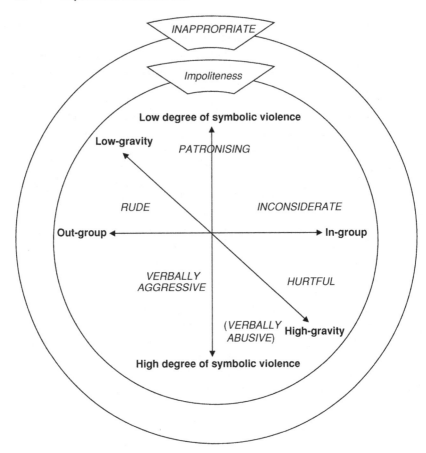

Figure 3.2 A mapping of impoliteness metalinguistic labels in conceptual space

there is a close connection between the labels for impoliteness behaviours-in-context and labels for emotions. It is not surprising then that the dimensions of variation noted by emotion researchers (see Section 2.3), particularly intensity and differences in context (see, for example, Shaver *et al.* 1987, and references therein), are similar, in my view, to the ways in which impoliteness metalinguistic labels vary. A problem with the notion of dimensions is that they are highly abstract. So, what comprises these dimensions and how one might operationalise them is fraught with difficulty. Nevertheless, they can help reveal the broader conceptual picture, and can be given more definition if viewed in a specific context.

INAPPROPRIATE labels are conceptually superordinate, because all of the other groups concern behaviours that can be considered inappropriate in some way (excluding contexts where the behaviours are legitimated in some way, cf. Sections 6.2 and 6.4). In fact, inappropriateness is a much broader notion than impoliteness. Impoliteness is an attitude towards communicative behaviours; those behaviours involve negatively evaluated implications for perceptions of a self (or selves) in a social organisation and simultaneously instil certain emotional reactions. Some examples of inappropriate but not necessarily impolite behaviour are: (1) wearing a thick coat in hot weather, (2) hitting somebody and (3) saying 'good morning' when it is the afternoon. These examples fall short of impoliteness in at least one of the following ways: they are not communicative, they cause actual physical pain rather than (or in addition to) emotional pain, they do not instil relevant negative emotions such as sadness and anger, and/or they are the result of obvious misunderstandings of the situation (for further examples of this issue, see the discussion of over-politeness in Section 3.8).

The vertical dimension captures the degree of symbolic violence or intensity, encompassing activity and power. Although used in the emotion literature (e.g. Shaver *et al.* 1987), this dimension can be related to the work of Charles Osgood and his colleagues on dimensions in semantic space. Intensity can be considered an amalgam of two dimensions identified as power potency and activity (e.g. Osgood *et al.* 1957). Osgood defined potency in terms of antonyms like *strong-weak, heavy-light*, and *hard-soft*, and activity in terms of antonyms like *fast-slow, active-passive* and *excitable-calm*. But he does not offer definitions of his dimensions. The fact that I am bringing together two of Osgood's dimensions does not run counter to his findings, as he notes 'significant interaction' between dimensions (Osgood 1962: 24). What we are dealing with here is symbolic visceral power or violence. Regarding the groups of labels, this is a pertinent dimension. Consider the evidence I have presented of, for example, the symbolic violence of VERBALLY AGGRESSIVE and, slightly more so, of VERBALLY ABUSIVE, as well as the fact that they involve sufficiently grave offences to be recruited into legal and medical discourses. Recollect also the collocates such as *angry, threatening, violent* and *physically* associated with *verbally aggressive* and *verbally abusive* suggesting high symbolic violence (though crucially the remit of impoliteness of any kind stops short of actual physical violence), whereas collocates such as *eavesdropping, ignoring* and *listening* associated with RUDE suggest low symbolic violence.[7]

Regarding context, emotion scholars note contextual variation but have not formed a consensus about the dimensions of that variation. A key dimension to emerge in my data is in-group versus out-group. This is in tune with the literature on hurtful communication. Vangelisti (2007: 121) notes that 'there is broad agreement that hurt is bound to be a part of any close relationship', and observes that 'some researchers argue that hurt and intimacy are intrinsically linked (L'Abate 1977, 1999) – that intimacy requires a degree of vulnerability and that the vulnerability associated with intimacy leads people open to being hurt'. This dimension captures differences between, for example, the RUDE and VERBALLY AGGRESSIVE groups, which comprise labels that are typically used of interactions between strangers in public situations, and the INCONSID-ERATE and HURTFUL groups, which comprise labels that are typically used of interactions between friends or family members in private situations.

The third dimension plotted in Figure 3.2 as a diagonal line is a hypothesis about the gravity of offence, that is, the degree of offence that an impoliteness behaviour causes in a particular context. In the report data it was operationalised through the question 'How bad did the behaviour in the conversation make you feel at the time it occurred?' The idea is that the more symbolically violent an utterance is and the more closely knit the social group within which it takes place, the more serious the offence taken, and vice versa. But it must be stressed that this is a hypothesis.

Some caveats are in order:

- Figure 3.2 represents the prototypical kind of impoliteness events referred to by the labels. There is absolutely no claim that any one label is necessarily restricted to a particular kind of impoliteness event.
- Figure 3.2 is biased towards the cultural and ideological viewpoint of, in particular, my informants, that is, young English UK university students (and is weighted somewhat towards a female perspective).
- The evidence, and thus the placing, is not consistently strong for all groups of labels.
- As I remarked earlier, metalinguistic labels can serve local strategic pur-poses. These purposes are not reflected in Figure 3.2. For example, *verbally abusive* typically serves institutional functions, that is, to enforce the law (it is frequently displayed on public notices in the UK). But the kind of impolite-ness events it refers to are quite often associated with close relationships (for instance, note the collocate *father*). Hence it is placed towards the in-group pole-end rather than they out-group pole-end of the contextual dimension.

3.8   Impoliteness metapragmatic comments and the case of 'over-politeness'

As explained in Section 3.2, metalinguistic impoliteness labels are embedded in metapragmatic impoliteness comments. However, metapragmatic impoliteness comments need not contain a conventional metalinguistic impoliteness label. Indeed, in analyses of extended examples in Chapters 5 and especially 7 we will see many such cases (an example is: 'how could you say that!'). Here, I want to extend my focus to metapragmatic impoliteness comments that do have metalinguistic impoliteness labels comprised of short expressions (single words or very short phrases) embedded within them. One advantage of maintaining the presence of a metalinguistic label is that it helps keep the focus on a specific impoliteness aspect. The specific impoliteness aspect I will address, by way of a brief case study, is 'over-politeness'. Methodologically, I use corpus-based techniques to realise examples, but a more qualitative approach to analyse them.

Watts (2005: xliv), commenting on a figure displaying relationships between politeness/impoliteness and marked/non-marked behaviour, includes some observations on over-politeness:

[Marked behaviour] may be perceived as negative either if it is open to an interpretation as impolite (or as downright rude), or if it is perceived as over-polite, i.e. those kinds of negatively marked non-politic behaviour tend towards similar kinds of affective reaction on the part of co-participants. Certain speakers consistently evaluate polite behaviour as unnecessary and offensive. The figure is thus meant to represent situations in which the communicative effects of over-polite behaviour may seem remarkably similar to those of downright rude behaviour, which is why the two ends of the spectrum are shown as turning in upon themselves.

Similarly, Locher (2004: 90) remarks: '[o]ver-politeness is often perceived as negative exactly because it exceeds the boundary between appropriateness and inappropriateness'. However, no data are presented or research cited in support of these claims, something which partly reflects the fact that there is no obvious research on the perceptions of over-politeness to cite – this is relatively unexplored territory.

The question as to whether over-politeness is taken positively or negatively by interactants can be explored empirically. I investigated people's metapragmatic comments in which the expressions *over-polite* and *too polite* are embedded, using WebCorp (available at www.webcorp.org.uk; all examples reported here were retrieved in September 2006). WebCorp treats the language on the World Wide Web as a (non-prototypical) corpus. It has two advantages for my purposes: (1) the vast size of the language sources it draws upon (much more than all the corpora created by linguists put together), and (2) the fact that its language sources are relatively 'unstandardised' and colloquial (compared with extant corpora which tend to include relatively 'standardised' material drawn from printed publications). Of course, in common with the *OEC* which largely draws its sources from the web, it has disadvantages too: 80 per cent of the language on the World Wide Web is in English, and the bulk of that emanates from North America.[8] It is thus linguistically and culturally biased. Nevertheless, it provides a starting point.

Examples such as [15] suggest that over-politeness need not be taken negatively:[9]

[15]

> Strolling along the streets you are bound to discover something, friendly invited by over polite personnel willing to see you as a respected guest.

However, such potentially positive usages are in a very small minority. The strongest pattern consisted of examples like the following:

[16]

> When I am performing . . . I find people are too polite to say anything which they think might offend. Usually people are complimentry about a performance to your face regardless how they actually feel. This does not help you as a performer to get a true measure of your performance.

Generally, these usages seem to be reactions to cases where, in Leech's (1983) terms, the speaker maintains the Politeness Principle as opposed to the Cooperative Principle; or, in B&L's (1987) terms, the speaker performs the strategy 'Don't do the FTA.' But there is more to it than this: they are reactions to what might be called relational mismanagement; in cases such as these a speaker's assessment that the interlocutor's need to maintain face would be in excess of the interlocutor's need for truth in the pursuit of a particular interactional goal turns out to be incorrect. There is no implication here that all cases of relational mismanagement involve the producer 'slipping up'; it is simply a matter of participants having differential perceptions resulting in the communicative behaviour chosen being negatively evaluated from at least one perspective. Note that the negative evaluation here is driven by facework in relation to somebody's 'interactional wants', something which Spencer-Oatey (2005) explicitly incorporates into her Rapport Management scheme. Such usages are indeed negative in the general sense of attracting a negative evaluation; more specifically, they are negative in the sense of 'misjudged' (hence attributions such as 'stupid'). However, they do not suggest the kind of negative behaviour by which over-politeness can be equated with 'downright rude behaviour' (Watts 2005: xliv).

There is yet, however, a further pattern, though much weaker than that above, which does support a version of negativity that is somewhat closer to 'downright rude behaviour'. Consider examples [17] to [19]:

[17]

> Come to the Emirates Palace Homer – you won't be able to walk 10 feet without someone calling you sir. . . . they were too polite as well. Polite in an irritatingly fussy and obsequious way.

[18]

> Job interview. * DO act polite but not over polite. 'Yes Sir,' 'No Sir,' and 'Thank You' can appear to insincere if used too frequently.

[19]

> The skeptics range from the oily, over-polite professionals who discreetly drop hints of the heresy of universalism, to the Bible thumper . . .

Interestingly, a strong characteristic of negatively marked over-politeness, as illustrated by the first two examples, is that being over-polite is a matter – at least in this cultural context – of doing politeness too *frequently*, or, more precisely, doing politeness too frequently with respect to what is appropriate in the situation, i.e. politic. Leech (1983: 147) comments: 'hyperbole suffers from diminishing returns because of incredulity'. Similarly, I would argue that a negative perception of communicative behaviour (cf. 'fussy and obsequious', 'insincere', 'oily') – that is, impoliteness – can come about through overuse of otherwise politic items, because overuse makes salient the fact that those items are merely politic, a situational norm, and not a sincere personal expression (cf. example [18]: '"Yes Sir," "No Sir," and "Thank You" can appear to [sic] insincere if used too frequently').

In sum, we need to: consider what *over*-politeness might mean in context (the use of language that is too polite for the situation, whatever that might mean? the over-use of otherwise politic language?); accommodate a range of evaluations (positive to negative); and also pay attention to communicative dynamics (e.g. the (mis)management of interpersonal relationships and interactional goals). Locher and Watts (2005: 30) acknowledge in a footnote that their hypothesis that over-politeness and rudeness/impoliteness will have similar effects needs to be investigated empirically, but predict that 'it is almost certain that they will both be negative'. They do indeed both have negative effects, but those effects are very different in type. The strongest pattern for over-politeness consists of cases which are negative because they reflect relational mismanagement. This has more to do with 'failed politeness' than impoliteness. It is not obvious that many examples of over-politeness involve a violation of face or social norms, or trigger the kind of emotions associated with such violations. Apart from examples [17] to [19], which I claim to be closest to impoliteness, the kinds of impoliteness metalinguistic labels discussed in previous sections of this chapter are not used here. But even these could involve issues of mismanagement. In fact, Kienpointner's (1997: 257) description of over-politeness turns out to be generally accurate: 'overpolite behaviour is not a case of rudeness, but a less than optimal application of politeness patterns which in principle are perfectly acceptable in a given language or culture'. However, it is worth remembering that there is a kind of over-politeness (in whatever way 'over' is defined) which can be used and/or perceived to create a negative effect, and often intentionally, but which is not clearly of the kind illustrated by the examples in this section. 'Sarcasm' involves, at least in British cultural contexts, a kind of over-politeness whereby the trappings of politeness are used in a context where they *cannot conceivably* sincerely apply – it is a kind of impolite 'mock-politeness'. I will discuss this in Section 5.3.

3.9 Impoliteness metapragmatic rules

A particularly important strand of impoliteness metadiscourse concerns 'rules'. Impoliteness rules are a particular type of metapragmatic comment. They are an opinion, almost always expressed in imperative form or with authoritative modality, about what should – or more often should not – happen in a particular social context. They are driven by social norms and conventions. In fact, Lewis (1969: 104) notes that most conventions can be referred to as rules: 'it is hard to show that there is any regularity that could not be called a rule in some contexts'. Rules, according to Lewis (1969: 103), 'codify regularities' – those social norms. But it is also quite possible to have rules that people habitually ignore. Rules are part of the moral order of societies (see Section 1.4.2). In the following two sections, I will first consider rules associated with public contexts and then rules associated with a variety of contexts but particularly private.

3.9.1   Institutional and public

Rules proscribing behaviours considered impolite draw authority from institutions (e.g. schools, the workplace, public service entities, government agencies), and are imposed through systems of rewards and penalties by the more powerful on the less. Even in the less public context of the family, rules for 'good behaviour' (a list of behaviours that are prohibited) are often drafted, stuck on the refrigerator and subject to rewards and penalties. Such rules are typically explicit, that is, they are on public display or at least are available for public scrutiny. They are usually couched as statements deploying modal elements expressing obligation and/or authority, and often threaten penalties for the transgression of rules. The rules are enshrined in laws, policy documents and charters, and public notices. Below, I will first briefly look at public notices and then policy documents and charters. In each case, my aim is to give the flavour of these rules and point out aspects of interest to impoliteness. A more comprehensive study awaits future research.

The British cultural context seems to be unusually replete with notices publicly displaying such rules, as exemplified by the following:

[20]

> The Airport Community Charter is here to help you but we will not tolerate . . .
> * Drunkenness
> * Insulting Words or Behaviour
> * Threats or Actual Physical Violence
> * Abusive Language
>
> *Essex Police/BAA London Stansted*, 2008

[21]

> ASSAULTS
> We take extremely seriously any attempt to intimidate our staff either by threats or assault.
>
> Offenders are liable to prosecution and may be imprisoned or fined.
>
> *Home Office. Border & Immigration Agency*, 2008

[22]

Royal Mail employees are expected to treat customers with respect.

In return you don't expect our people to tolerate abuse and bullying from customers.

We will challenge customers who verbally abuse, bully or threaten our people.

We will take the strongest legal action possible against anyone who physically attacks our people while they are trying to do their jobs.

Royal Mail, Lancaster Sorting Office, 2004

A common thread through these notices is a concern with bodily harm: *physical violence, assault* and *physically attacks*. This clearly lies outside the remit of impoliteness. But these notices also accommodate verbal harm, either explicitly or implicitly: *insulting words or behaviour, threats, abusive language, threats, abuse and bullying,* and *verbally abuse, bully or threaten*. Generally, these seem to reflect items high on a scale of symbolic violence, as proposed in Figure 3.2. More specifically, *insulting words or behaviour* is subsumed within HURTFUL, a group that is placed towards the higher end of the gravity of offence scale. Similarly, *abusive language* and *abuse*, subsumed within the VERBALLY ABUSIVE group, is high on the gravity of offence scale. In other words, these items refer to intense (potent and active) behaviours – the stuff of verbal violence – associated with maximal offensiveness of the kind that can be achieved in in-group contexts. These notices do not, of course, pertain to in-group contexts, but, as I pointed out earlier, my work in Section 3.7 was mapping out prototypes; people can enact a behaviour associated with one context in another. We might expect such semi-legal notices to target areas of maximal offensiveness. Recollect the legalistic contextual characteristics of *verbally abusive* identified in Section 3.6.3. It seems reasonable to suppose that *threats, bullying* and *bully* also fall high on the scale of symbolic violence, in such areas as VERBALLY ABUSIVE or VERBALLY AGGRESSIVE. Note that two notices are explicit about the legal power behind them ('liable to prosecution and may be imprisoned or fined', 'strongest legal action possible'). Only one sign articulates a positive expectation ('are expected to treat customers with respect'); the rest identify negative behaviours for prohibition.

Charters and policy documents are exemplified by the following:

[23]

Observing courtesies
Many passengers travel by rail to work, socialise, relax or have meetings. While many appreciate the ability to stay in touch, mobile phones, audio equipment, personal computers and loud talking can be irritating to others. We ask all passengers to be sympathetic to the needs and comfort of others, particularly with the use of mobile phones and personal stereos.

Coach A on Midland Mainline High Speed Trains is designated a mobile free zone and seats can be reserved in this area. In all other areas mobile phones and audio equipment should be used with consideration for other passengers.

Aggressive behaviour
We want to create an environment that is welcoming, safe and friendly. We will not tolerate aggressive or abusive behaviour towards either staff or customers.

Midland Mainline Passenger's Charter, January 2005, p. 11

[24]

Dignity at Work
All employees are entitled:
* To be treated with dignity, respect and courtesy.
* To a workplace free from bullying, harassment or victimisation.
* To experience no form of discrimination.
* To be valued for their skills and abilities.
... These standards of behaviour cover relationships between a manager and staff they manage ... Behaviour that is unwanted, unwelcome and undermines a person's dignity at work is unacceptable behaviour.... Behaviour may be perceived as unacceptable, even if there was no intent to cause offence. Behaviour may have overtones that a member of staff finds offensive, even if it was not directed at them.... Unacceptable behaviour can take many forms and can range from physical attack to more subtle conduct. It can include actions, jokes or suggestions that might create a stressful working environment.

The Crown Prosecution Service. Dignity at Work – Standards
of behaviour in the Crown Prosecution Service;
www.cps.gov.uk/Publications/equality/dignitywork.html;
accessed 15 May 2009

[25]

Harassment is difficult to define because it may take many different forms. It may consist of behaviour taking place over a period of time or a single incident. A general definition of harassment is that it is *verbal or physical conduct that denigrates or shows hostility or aversion toward an individual because of a specific characteristic of that person such as their race, skin colour, religion, gender, sexual orientation, national origin, age or disability.*

www.lancs.ac.uk/depts/hr/equality-diversity/files/harpol.html#Law

Charters and policy documents clearly have more space within which to articulate details. They often contain both prescribed and proscribed behaviours, and are couched both as advisory statements and behavioural rules. The first part of the Passenger Charter, Observing Courtesies, warns of negative effects ('loud talking can be irritating') requests consideration ('We ask all passengers to be sympathetic to the needs and comfort of others') or advises it ('mobile phones and audio equipment should be used with consideration for other passengers'). Consideration, as captured in Figure 3.2, is not associated with strong symbolic violence of grave offence, though it is more typical of close-knit groups, something that is perhaps relevant to passengers on over-crowded trains spending long journeys together. The modality of the Charter changes for 'aggressive or abusive behaviour', exerting authority: 'we will not tolerate'. This is similar to the notices [20] to [22].

The Crown Prosecution Service workplace policy document attempts to spell out in some detail 'standards of behaviour', which of course are closely linked to social norms. It orientates to prescriptions for politeness ('be treated with dignity, respect and courtesy', 'be valued for their skills and abilities') and proscriptions for impoliteness ('bullying, harassment or victimisation', 'discrimination'). The prescriptions for politeness are clearly relevant to face, as are the proscriptions for impoliteness. However, 'bullying, harassment or victimisation' are marked out, like *verbally abusive*, by a closer association with symbolic violence. Also 'discrimination' is not simply devaluing an individual; discrimination involves a judgement that the offence was unfair, breaking a moral social norm. More specifically, it involves a relative judgement. Consider the definition of discrimination given in the UK's Disability Discrimination Act 1995 (Part 2.5)

... an employer discriminates against a disabled person if –

(a) for a reason which relates to the disabled person's disability, he treats him less favourably than he treats or would treat others to whom that reason does not or would not apply; and

(b) he cannot show that the treatment in question is justified.

Note that the document says 'unfair and discriminatory behaviour'. Such behaviour conflicts with the social norms elaborated in Section 2.4, norms relating to social responsibility and also to distributive justice. Interestingly, the document goes to great lengths to define 'unacceptable behaviour'. It is behaviour that is 'unwanted' or 'unwelcome', a broad definition that captures any undesired behaviour. Moreover, it is noted that behaviour may still be perceived as unacceptable 'even if there was no intent to cause offence' or 'even if it was not directed at' the perceiver. Cutting intentionality out of the definition is consistent with the line I took in Section 2.2. Finally examples of unacceptable behaviour are given, and it is noted that it can include 'subtle conduct' and 'actions, jokes or suggestions that might create a stressful working environment'. It is not just about symbolic violence or high gravity of offence.

The Crown Prosecution Service policy document mentions both discrimination and harassment. In fact, institutions in the UK have a legal responsibility to tackle any form of discrimination or harassment (cf. Sex Discrimination Act 1975, Race Relations Act 1976, Disability Discrimination Act 1995, Protection from Harassment Act 1997, Human Rights Act 1998, Race Relations (Amendment) Act 2000, Employment Equality Regulations on Religion or Belief and Sexual Orientation 2003 and Gender Recognition Act 2004). Example [25] is the harassment policy statement formulated for Lancaster University. The point made at the beginning of this example, that harassment takes many different forms, is one of the things that has proved particularly difficult for its definition. As has been noted for impoliteness, the problem is that judgements of harassment are culturally and contextually determined. Interestingly, the Protection from Harassment Act 1997 (40.1) avoids definition altogether, instead opting for inter-subjective validity:

> For the purposes of this section, the person whose course of conduct is in question ought to know that it amounts to harassment of another if a reasonable person in possession of the same information would think the course of conduct amounted to harassment of the other.

Whilst it is good that this acknowledges a perceptual concern, the solution is fraught with its own difficulties (who counts as 'a reasonable person'?). Consequently, harassment policies in institutions, as illustrated by the Lancaster University document, have attempted to flesh out the notion. Interestingly, all of the examples given in the Lancaster document – 'race, skin colour, religion, gender, sexual orientation, national origin, age or disability' – concern social identity face.

3.9.2   General and private

General impoliteness rules apply to a variety of contexts, but in particular they are the stuff of everyday interactions. They are often articulated in private contexts, that is, in-group contexts involving, for example, friends or family. Unlike public rules, they are often made explicit in talk. This makes it methodologically more difficult to achieve my aim of surveying a range of such rules. I have opted to survey two rudeness 'manuals' designed for everyday contexts, including private. Both relate to the North American cultural context.

Jill A. Montry's (2002) *How To Be Rude! A Training Manual for Mastering the Art of Rudeness* is a humorous parody of etiquette manuals. Instead of training the reader in polite behaviours, it trains them in impolite behaviours. Each page contains an imperative statement. The book is a list of 'dos' rather than 'don'ts' (the stuff of politeness manuals). Of course, one might be concerned that these are not 'real' rules. However, the success of the humour depends on the reader recognising the rule that has been recommended for breaking – they must ring true. The following items are quoted from the chapter 'General Rudeness' (pp. 1–50). I have not included items which overlap with others or which could be non-communicative behaviours (e.g. sneezing without covering your mouth).[10] The groupings of the items are mine.

Insults (including derogatory statements and implications): Producing or perceiving a display of low values for some target (cf. Face (any type))
- Make derogatory statements about people of another race, religion, or lifestyle, preferably when those people are within earshot. (p. 6)
- Ask an overweight woman when she is 'due'. (p. 28)
- Ask any stay-at-home Mom what she does all day. (p. 29)

Pointed criticism/complaint (including expressions of disapproval and statements of fault, weakness or disadvantage): Producing or perceiving a display of low values for some target (cf. Face (any type))
- Criticise: earn extra points if you make someone cry. (p. 33)

Exclusion (including failure to include and disassociation): Producing or perceiving a display of infringement of inclusion (cf. Association rights)
- Talk about people in the third person while they're standing next to you. (p. 3)

Patronising behaviour (including condescending, belittling, ridiculing and demeaning behaviours): Producing or perceiving a display of power that infringes an understood power hierarchy (cf. Equity rights)
- Be really condescending; example: 'What would YOU know about that?' (p. 2)
- Treat people in a service capacity as if they are beneath you; whenever possible, use terms like 'the little people' or 'the help'. (p. 40)
- When dining in a restaurant, snap your fingers at the waiter when you want something. (p. 41)
- Make fun of people: laugh loudly and point. (p. 4)
- Talk loudly and slowly to people who speak a different language; use exaggerated hand gestures. (p. 7)

Failure to reciprocate: Producing or perceiving a display of infringement of the reciprocity norm (cf. Equity rights)
- NEVER write a thank-you note. (p. 23)

Encroachment: Producing or perceiving a display of infringement of personal space (literal or metaphorical) (cf. Equity rights)
- Encroach on someone's personal space; remember, the minimum radius is two feet. (p. 8)
- Eavesdrop then turn around and add your opinion to the conversation. (p. 9)
- Snoop: anything that you have no business looking into would be appropriate. (p. 24)
- Ask people how much they've paid for stuff; be persistent. (p. 14)
- Call people before 8:00 a.m. on a Saturday or Sunday morning. (p. 15)

Even from my British cultural perspective, I have no difficulty at all in recognising these rules. Interestingly, all of the items can be accommodated within my earlier work (e.g. 1996) which proposed a taxonomy of impoliteness strategies.

The second rudeness manual I will briefly look at is Catherine Rondina and Dan Workman's (2005) *Rudeness: Deal With It If You Please*. It is a serious manual, being part of a series that 'helps adolescents cope with conflicts in everyday life and aims to promote peaceful homes, schools, and communities' (backcover). The aim of the book is to show the reader 'how to deal with rudeness whether you're the offender, the offended or the witness' (backcover). The remit of the book is, like this book, not restricted to narrow matters of etiquette:

Demonstrating good manners goes way beyond not talking with your mouth full. Rudeness can lead to hurt feelings, misunderstanding, and ultimately conflict. (backcover)

Two lists of 'don'ts' are given within the book (p. 4 and p. 19). As these are stated very briefly, the full lists are given below:

[Good manners means no]
- forgetting to say 'please' or 'thank you.'
- belching, burping, fasting, or spitting in front of others.
- talking with your mouth full of food.
- letting the door slam in someone's face.
- keeping your seat instead of giving it to an elderly or disabled person.
- talking back to your parents or teachers.
- grabbing or pushing.
- insulting someone to their face.
- avoiding or ignoring someone.
  (2005: 4)

- Don't use crude language.
- Don't associate bad manners with being cool.
- Don't interrupt when someone is speaking.
- Don't embarrass or insult others.
- Don't forget to always say 'please' and 'thank you.'
- Don't act up in public places.
- Don't let your rudeness make you a bully.
- Don't think that someone being rude to you makes it okay to be rude back.
  (2005: 19)

Some of these are geared towards consequences of rudeness ('Don't let your rudeness make you a bully') or motivations to rudeness ('Don't associate bad manners with being cool'). The latter relates to an issue broached in Section 1.3.1 (see also Section 6.2.2), namely, that in some youth cultures certain behaviours have a positive value whereas outside those cultures they are more likely to have negative value. Some do not so clearly relate to communicative behaviours: 'letting the door slam in someone's face', and 'keeping your seat instead of giving it to an elderly or disabled person'. The latter example relates to the social responsibility social norm discussed in Section 1.4.2. Some allude to mechanisms that have been mentioned in discussion. 'Don't think that someone being rude to you makes it okay to be rude back' relates to the mechanism of reciprocity, also discussed in Section 1.4.2. In fact, as pointed out there but more substantially in Section 6.4, research is consistent with the idea that people do think it is relatively okay to be rude back to somebody who is rude to you. The other items fall into the following groups:

Insults (including derogatory statements and implications): Producing or perceiving a display of low values for some target (I) (cf. Face (any type))
- Insulting someone to their face.
- Embarrass or insult others.

Exclusion (including failure to include and disassociation): Producing or perceiving a display of infringement of inclusion (cf. Association rights)
• Avoiding or ignoring someone.

Patronising behaviour (including condescending, belittling, ridiculing and demeaning behaviours): Producing or perceiving a display of power that infringes an understood power hierarchy (cf. Equity rights)
• Talking back to your parents or teachers.[11]

Failure to reciprocate: Producing or perceiving a display of infringement of the reciprocity norm (cf. Equity rights)
• Forgetting to say 'please' or 'thank you.'
• Forget to always say 'please' and 'thank you.'

Encroachment: Producing or perceiving a display of infringement of personal space (literal or metaphorical) (cf. Equity rights)
• Interrupt when someone is speaking.
• Grabbing or pushing.

Taboo behaviours (including actions, signs and words): Producing or perceiving a display of behaviours considered emotionally repugnant (cf. Equity rights)
• Belching, burping, fasting, or spitting in front of others.
• Talking with your mouth full of food.
• Don't use crude language.

These of course are the same groups that emerged for the first manual, with the exception of the addition of Taboo behaviours.

3.10   Conclusion

Metalanguage/metadiscourse can reveal people's understandings of impoliteness. Impoliteness metalanguage is part of a schematic network linked to impoliteness attitudes (see Section 2.4). I showed that *verbal aggression* is outstandingly frequent as an academic term, and that particular terms tend to cluster in particular disciplines (*verbal aggression* in psychology; *rude* in history; etc.). *Rude* is outstanding as the term of general usage, whereas the usage of *impoliteness* is negligible. Using traditional thesauri, I noted that the items *impolite*, *rude*, *(verbally) abusive*, *offensive* and, to a slightly lesser extent, *(verbally) aggressive* form a cohesive semantic set with some specific semantic characteristics. Using corpus-based analyses, I revealed that *impolite* is not synonymous with *rude* but more precisely matches a subset of its meanings (in addition, *rude* is more 'low-style' and readily used as a term of social/personal description, for sex or nudity taboos, and postively). Note that impoliteness was found to be a scalar notion, though phenomena described as *rude* or *impolite* are generally weighted towards the more offensive end, a point that I will develop in the next chapter where I examine how conventionally impolite formulae are intensified so that they reflect extreme attitudes.

The items investigated in my corpus analyses were selected by me on the basis of their currency in the literature. How do we know that these are the ones that non-academics would use? I grouped the 200 metalinguistic labels of my report form data into semantic domains. The most frequent were: PATRONISING, INCONSIDERATE, RUDE, AGGRESSIVE, INAPPROPRIATE and HURTFUL. Whilst there is some overlap with the labels used in academia, there are some striking differences, most notably, the appearance of PATRONISING. Using metalinguistic data from my report forms, along with insights afforded by my corpus analyses, I plotted these domains in semantic space. I organised the semantic domains along two dimensions, symbolic violence and out-group versus in-group, and hypothesized a third dimension, gravity of offence.

The remaining sections of this chapter focused on metapragmatic comments. Specifically, I examined metapragmatic comments relating to the notion of 'over politeness'. These showed that over politeness is rarely taken offensively. Instead, it mostly seems to be a matter of miscommunication. I then turned my attention to a particular kind of metapragmatic comment, namely, prescriptive rules – metapragmatic comments that attempt to enforce how things should be, that codify social norms. I examined rules in institutional and public contexts, displayed in notices, set out in charters and policies and so on, showing that the connection with impoliteness is clear, particularly with respect to insulting, verbally abusive and/or threatening behaviours. In order to tap into the more implicit rules that infuse our everyday and also more private lives, I examined manuals that prescribed rules for such situations. Such rules in fact often capture what would seem to be conventional pragmatic impoliteness strategies, in which conventional impoliteness formulae may be embedded. It is to these that I turn next.

4 Conventionalised formulaic impoliteness and its intensification

4.1 Introduction

Goffman (1967: 89) discusses 'ritual affronts' or 'profanations' performed by patients in psychiatric wards, varying from hurling abuse to hurling faeces, and notes that these acts are, 'from the point of view of society at large and its cere-monial idiom', 'calculated to convey complete disrespect and contempt through symbolic means'. This chapter focusses on the symbolic linguistic means for conveying impoliteness. It is not, of course, the case that any particular linguis-tic form guarantees an evaluation of impoliteness in all contexts; moreover, people may disagree about how impolite a linguistic form is. However, the cur-rent tendency in the (im)politeness literature of emphasising the context rather than linguistic form risks throwing the baby out with the bath water. Virtually no study has attempted to understand how the notion of conventionality might be linked to politeness or impoliteness. The notable exception is Terkourafi's (e.g. 2001, 2002, 2005a, 2005b) work on a frame-based approach to polite-ness, and this will provide the basis for my own discussion of conventionalised impoliteness. Moreover, the importance of accounting for conventionalised impoliteness formulae is even greater than accounting for politeness formulae, as I will argue in this chapter and in Section 6.6, because the negative effects of impoliteness formulae and behaviours, especially when highly offensive and thus salient, are not easy to eliminate by means of the context (e.g. understand-ing them to be part of friendly banter between friends). Such conventionalised behaviours/formulae must be a focal point of study. Although only a rough indicator, I note that 41 of my 100 reported impoliteness events involved at least one of the conventional impoliteness formulae discussed in this chapter and often several.

This chapter begins by looking at facework, and in particular aggressive facework and context. The following section considers the idea that impo-liteness is inherent in language. In Section 4.4, I outline Terkourafi's (e.g. 2001, 2002, 2005a, 2005b) approach to conventionalised politeness formu-lae. Then I argue that impoliteness, whilst it has some similarities, draws upon different kinds of experiences. In Section 4.3, having identified some methodological options, I explain the basis of and identify the conventionalised impoliteness formulae in my naturally occurring data sets. In Section 4.4, I offer a brief illustration of a particular conventionalised impoliteness formula in context. Section 4.5 is devoted to the exacerbation of impoliteness formulae through either lexico-grammatical or non-verbal, especially prosodic, intensification.

4.2   Face-attack strategies and context

Goffman defines facework as 'the actions taken by a person to make whatever he [sic] is doing consistent with face' (1967: 12). He notes that they 'often become habitual and standardised practices' and that 'each person, subculture, and society seems to have its own characteristic repertoire of face-saving practices' (1967: 13). But this diversity does not imply a random set of practices: 'the particular set of practices stressed by particular persons or groups seems to be drawn from a single logically coherent framework of possible practices'; there is a 'single matrix of possibilities' (1967: 13). He adds a reason as to why practices must be limited to a particular set:

If a person is to employ his [sic] repertoire of face-saving practices, obviously he must first become aware of the interpretations that others may have placed upon his acts and interpretations that he ought perhaps to place upon theirs. (1967: 13)

This point, incidentally, is reflected in Terkourafi's (2005a: 249) arguments for societal rationality, namely, that it is 'pre-cast' in 'a range of concrete choices', and that one can only be rude to someone in a way that they recognise as being rude (see Section 1.4.1). Brown and Levinson's (1987) work on politeness is very much geared towards spelling out that single matrix of possibilities and listing sets of practices.

As for sets of practices for conveying impoliteness, Goffman does discuss the 'aggressive use' of facework, though he devotes barely more than two sides to the issue (1967: 24–6). The 'general method' for this is for 'the person to introduce favourable facts about himself and unfavourable facts about the others' (1967: 25) (something which is echoed in Leech 2007). But Goffman does not mention how these 'facts' are couched, and whether there is a single matrix of possibilities with various sets of practices for unfavourable facts. This neglect is not unique to Goffman. Cupach and Metts (1994: 13–14), an important book on facework, has two paragraphs in which they refer to an 'aggravation-mitigation continuum', and suggest that aggravating behaviours are 'aggressive, challenging, inflammatory, and generally escalate or exacerbate face threat' (1994: 14). Domenici and Littlejohn (2006), in their otherwise illuminating discussion of facework, devote but one paragraph to facework that 'threatens' others in their 204 pages of text (see pp. 73–4). However, there have been calls for a more comprehensive treatment. Craig *et al.* (1986) and Tracy (1990) argue that an adequate account of the dynamics of interpersonal communication should consider hostile as well as cooperative communication. Penman's (1990) model of facework as applied to courtroom discourse encompasses face-attack, and Tracy and Tracy (1998) focuses solely on face-attack. Other studies, notably Lachenicht (1980), Austin (1987, 1990), Culpeper (1996) and Bousfield (2008), not only focus on face-attack but also develop taxonomies of face-attacking strategies, or what we might consider sets of practices for pursuing face-attack.

The studies mentioned in the previous sentence have adduced increasingly robust evidence for their taxonomies (for a critique of the earlier works, see section Introducing impoliteness, and Culpeper *et al.* 2003, especially pages 1553–5). However, significant problems remain. The key problem for taxonomies of face-attack strategies is how to deal with context. Simply saying that some linguistic form or pragmatic strategy has negative implications for face is fraught with difficulty, as Cupach and Metts (1994: 13) note:

> to say that messages are aggravating or mitigating is misleading unless it is noted that such a statement is a shorthand way of saying that in certain situations certain messages are interpreted as aggravating or as mitigating.

With the possible exception of Lachenicht (1980), most taxonomies of face-attack or impoliteness are careful to supply cautionary notes such as the following from my own early work: '[i]t must be stressed that this list is not exhaustive and that the strategies depend upon an appropriate context to be impolite' (Culpeper 1996: 357). Of course, critics can easily overlook such brief notes. More fundamentally, an explanatory hole is left: if strategies depend upon a particular context in order to be considered impolite, what is the nature of that dependence? Why is it that when I say 'don't eat with your mouth open' to one of my daughters at the dinner table nobody gets offended (as far as I can tell!), but I wouldn't dare say this to my own father for fear of giving him offence? We need to account for that potential contextual relationship, if we are to proceed.

Intuition is too blunt a tool to reliably pinpoint conventionalised impolite formulae. At an impoliteness conference, I suggested that speakers had been throwing the baby out with the bathwater with their constant refrain that everything was so contextually determined. I argued that it was difficult to think of contexts which would neutralise extremely impolite linguistic formulae, such as the use of the word *cunt* to cause offence, a word which is generally considered the most offensive word in British English (see Section 4.5.2). But consider this report in my data collection:

[1]

> A close friend of mine from Norway was eating with myself and my parents. They asked about our shared friends and my friend (Eddie) began to tell anecdotes about them. Throughout this point he used the word 'cunt' repeatedly. I felt very embarrassed as I knew that Eddie uses this word in the place of words like 'guy' and 'dude'. In our circle of friends "Hi cunt" was a friendly greeting.
>
> However, my parents weren't to know this and I didn't want them to get the wrong impression. Similarly, I didn't want Eddie to think I wanted to be 'clean' in front of my family. So I couldn't say anything except nod and laugh. I felt very obstructed in my speech, restricted even.

The informant comments:

> My parents are OK with swearing but 'cunt' is a taboo. To hear it used so flagrantly brings my parents disapproval to a great height. I wanted everyone to get along but difference in their language use was causing offence... Enthusiastic, eager, friendly. Utterly oblivious to the offence he was causing. I would label this as unaware and well-meant offensive conversation.

As I pointed out in Section 1.2 (and will elaborate in Section 6.2.2), different groups have different value systems. Within the context of these friends, *cunt* can be used in a positive way. However, there is more to this. 'Hi cunt' counts as a 'friendly greeting': *cunt* is embedded in the frame of a friendly greeting, i.e.'Hi X'. Of course, the net effect of this could be offensive, if the usage of the friendly greeting frame is taken as mixed message sarcasm (see Section 5.3). But this is used in the context of a 'circle of friends', and here it seems less likely that sarcastic impoliteness is intended. In fact, I suspect that the parents would have been aware that this is some kind of miscommunication. Being '[e]nthusiastic, eager, friendly' suggests the use of particular prosodies and non-verbal actions that are not consistent with straightforward impoliteness (sarcasm is again a possibility, though remote in this context). This is not to say that the parents would not have been offended to some degree. As I argued in Section 2.2, offence is not dependent upon them interpreting the behaviour as intentional. But at least it is not exacerbated by a construal of intentionality, and moreover can be mitigated by an understanding that it is miscommunication.

In retrospect, I do not think my general comment at the conference was entirely wrong. Repeated calls for attention to context are a necessary corrective to some older models of communication, but they give the erroneous impression that it does not matter what you say. Recollect my general point about the salience of negative behaviours/formulae and the difficulty of eliminating negative effects in the first section of this chapter. This does not apply to all formulae equally. Some strategies or formulae that may appear impolite can in fact be neutralised or even made positive in many contexts, but with other strategies or formulae this is only possible in a highly restricted number of contexts. The distinction I am making here is described in Tracy and Tracy (1998) as:

subtle, context-tied strategies and blatant, context-spanning strategies. Context-spanning strategies are ones likely to be seen as face-attacking in many different situations. Context-tied strategies are ones that in other conversational situations . . . could be neutral or even face enhancing. (1998: 231)

This chapter is primarily focused on context-spanning strategies; the following three chapters focus more closely on context-tied strategies. Where I do think my conference comment was wrong – or at least not precise enough – was in supplying one highly taboo word as an example. Taboo language *per se* is used in a host of non-face-attacking contexts, and is not uncommon as an expression of solidarity (see Daly *et al.* 2004). It is much less context-spanning than the impression I gave. However, taboo language combined with certain other linguistic elements can result in relatively conventional context-spanning strategies. Consider, for example, *cunt* dropped into the frame of *you X*, delivered with sharply falling intonation and stress on *cunt*, and an expression of disgust. I would suggest that this is unlikely to be taken as neutral in many different situations. This is the kind of conventionalised formula I will be discussing in this chapter.

4.3 Is (im)politeness inherent in language?

The discussion of face-attacking strategies and the role of context leads naturally into the debate within work on impoliteness about whether impoliteness is inherent in language, that is, whether impoliteness is simply part of the conventional symbolic meaning of a particular linguistic form. Although I am particularly interested in impoliteness, the arguments in this section apply equally to politeness. Papers which take a position on whether (im)politeness is inherent or not do not actually define what inherent meaning is (citations for those papers are given below). Furthermore, the literature varies amongst talking about meanings inherent in (1) speech acts, (2) discourse/communicative/pragmatic strategies, and (3) linguistic forms or expressions. In Austinian (1962) terms, (1) refers to illocutions and (3) to locutions; (2), concerning strategies, is some kind of intermediary category, consisting of the kind of practices discussed in the previous section. Like Terkourafi (e.g. 2001) my point of entry for the identification of conventionalised impoliteness is not framed by the notion of 'strategy' or the dimensions, such as directness, along which strategies are purported to vary (for directness, see Section 5.5). Not only are these difficult to define but they are also fraught with methodological problems (they rely heavily on intuition). My point of entry will be (3), linguistic forms or expressions. In the next section, I will consider the proposal that (im)politeness is inherent in speech acts. I do this briefly, largely because it can easily be rejected. I then move to linguistic forms/expressions. I devote more space to this, because I will argue that there is a sense in which impoliteness can be inherent in such forms/expressions, and these arguments will help set up the following sections.

4.3.1   Speech acts and impoliteness

Brown and Levinson (1987: 65–8) discuss 'intrinsic FTAs'. By face-threatening *acts*, B&L (1987: 65) mean 'what is intended to be done by a verbal or non-verbal communication, just as one or more "speech acts" can be assigned to an utterance'. They classify intrinsic FTAs according to the kind of face threatened and whether the threat is geared towards the hearer's face or the speaker's (cf. 1987: 65–8). For example, orders and requests threaten the negative face of the hearer. What critiques of B&L's position neglect is that they talk about acts that 'primarily' (1987: 65, 67) or 'mainly' (1987: 68) perform such face threat. In other words, the notion of inherent or, to use their term, intrinsic face-threatening acts is fuzzy, not absolute. Thus, for instance, counter-examples such as orders which are beneficial to the hearer (e.g. 'Tuck in!', said to encourage the guest to begin a delightful feast) are not a problem. Similarly, cases of banter do not challenge the basic claim; in fact, they can be taken as exceptions that prove the rule (cf. Christie 2005: 5–6). However, there are still three problems.

Firstly, there is a terminological issue. To talk of 'threatening' face or face 'threat' in reference to impoliteness phenomena, as some works on politeness, facework and even impoliteness do, is problematic. Tracy (1990) points out that any interaction is potentially face threatening. In fact, politeness theory is based on the idea of potential face-threat. According to B&L (1987: 1), politeness comes about through one's orientation towards what Goffman called the 'virtual offense' (Goffman, 1971: 138ff.). In other words, by demonstrating concern for the face-threatening potential of an act, one shows that one has the other's interests at heart. Politeness work, as conceived by B&L, is about acknowledging the face-threatening potential of an act through redressive actions. Impoliteness is rather different: it is constituted by words and actions which themselves are taken as damaging face. The semantics of 'threat' herald future damage; this sense is not appropriate here. It is better to recognise the difference with different terminology, and thus with respect to face I prefer 'face-attack'.

Secondly, what happens if there are so many exceptions to a claim that an act is inherently face 'threatening' that the exceptions become primary? Pertinent examples are provided in work on a variety of cultures. Take, for example, Nwoye's (1992) exploration of the egalitarian Igbo society of Nigeria. He concludes that:

...very few actions are regarded as impositions. Requests, criticisms, thanks, and offers have been examined and have been found not to be generally considered as imposing. Rather, they are seen as a type of social insurance from which members of the group draw benefits by virtue of a reciprocal social contract according to which, for example, they can ask for (and get) a small quantity of salt when/if they run out of salt because they expect others to ask for (and obtain) it if they are in need. As speech acts, such requests are not in themselves inherently polite or impolite; rather, they are appropriate performances and attributes of good behavior inherent in good upbringing. (1992: 327)

Clearly, then, B&L's generalisation should have been made culture-specific (it would generally hold for stereotypical middle-class British culture, for instance).

Thirdly, meanings can only be inherent in speech acts if speech acts themselves have a degree of determinacy and stability. Unlike the linguistic form of an utterance, a speech act depends on a considerable amount of interpretive work *in context*. This point is neatly illustrated by Leech (1983: 23–4):

The indeterminacy of conversational utterances... shows itself in the NEGOTIABIL-ITY of pragmatic factors; that is, by leaving the force unclear, S may leave H the opportunity to choose between one force and another, and thus leaves part of the responsibility of the meaning to H. For instance,

'If I were you I'd leave town straight away'

can be interpreted according to the context as a piece of advice, a warning, or a threat. Here H, knowing something about S's likely intentions, may interpret it as a threat, and act on it as such; but S will always be able to claim that it was a piece of advice, given from the friendliest of motives.

Speech acts, as envisaged in the classic works, are a theoretical nonstarter for an argument that (im)politeness or face threat is inherent. In fact, B&L themselves acknowledge this in their second edition: 'speech act theory forces a sentence-based, speaker-oriented mode of analysis, requiring attribution of speech act categories where our own thesis requires that utterances are often equivocal in force' (1987: 10).

4.3.2   Linguistic expressions and impoliteness

The line between illocutions, as discussed in the previous section, and locutions, as discussed in this section, is not always held fast in discussions of inherent (im)politeness. Some discussions (e.g. O'Driscoll, 2007) encompass both locutions and illocutions, and sometimes drift from one to the other without spelling out the implications of doing so. Also, it should be noted here that some researchers refer to 'linguistic behaviour' or 'forms of behaviour' rather than 'linguistic forms'. The term 'behaviour' is better able to accommodate non-verbal forms and non-contrastive aspects of language, and it has a closer relation with social action (see, for example, Verschueren 1999: 6–7). Nevertheless, behaviour is still used to refer to forms of behaviour – relatively discrete oral or visual physical phenomena which encode aspects of meaning and constitute a participant's communicative repertoire. In this book I regularly use the term behaviour, and with respect to conventionalised behaviours I use the term conventional formulae to refer to behaviours consisting of conventionalised linguistic or verbal expressions. In this section, I will focus on what I will term linguistic expressions, a term that more accurately reflects my focus of discussion (word forms and grammatical structures). For the purposes of this section and in tune with the literature discussed therein, I will take a traditional view of inherent meaning that is, viewing it as formal semantic meaning which is more a matter of truth conditions than felicity conditions, more conventional than non-conventional, and more non-contextual (and thus non-relative) than contextual (such a view is espoused in, for example, the writings of Gottlob Frege). In Gricean terms, the focus is on what is said, which is 'closely related to the conventional meaning of the words (the sentence)' uttered, along with their syntax (Grice 1989: 25; see also Grice 1989: 87), as opposed to what is implicated, whether conventionally or non-conventionally. Of course, the line between semantic meaning (encompassing what is sometimes referred to as encoded, literal or explicit meaning) and pragmatic meaning is highly controversial, and has been a topic of hot debate in recent years.[1] With respect to the question posed by the title of Section 4.3, 'Is (im)politeness inherent in language?', I first consider two opposed mono views, one arguing for a positive answer and the other a negative answer. Then I consider two variants of a dual view, arguing for both a positive and a negative answer.

Yes, impoliteness is inherent in linguistic expressions It is not at all easy to find any mainstream (im)politeness theorist explicitly arguing that either politeness or impoliteness is wholly inherent in linguistic expressions. However, the focus on linguistic expressions in earlier works may have given the impression that context was somehow less important. Furthermore, this impression has been articulated and perhaps hardened in the work of scholars in other fields. Cruse (2000: 362, original emphasis), for example, comments:

Politeness is, first and foremost, a matter of what is said, and not a matter of what is thought or believed. Leech expresses the politeness principle thus:
(I) Minimise the expression of impolite beliefs.
     This is not an ideal formulation, as politeness does not essentially concern beliefs. However, it does have the merit of throwing the weight onto the *expression*. Let us rephrase the principle as follows:
(II) Choose expressions which minimally belittle the hearer's status.

In fact, it is precisely Leech's (1983) inclusion of the term 'belief' that incorporates the perception of participants. In the absence of this, there is no explicit acknowledgement that the definition of politeness or impoliteness has anything to do with what participants mean and understand by an expression. Without this aspect, it is difficult to account for how the same expression can have different politeness values when perceived by different people, in different situations, cultures, and so on, or even how an apparently polite expression can be used for sarcasm. Of course, Alan Cruse is a semanticist, and so it is not surprising that he views politeness through the prism of semantics. As we will see in the following section, much scholarship has been taken up with refuting this position. However, as I will argue, I am not convinced that it necessarily follows that politeness or impoliteness lies *entirely* outside the scope of semantics.

Given the fact that my definition of impoliteness in Section 1.2 is pitched as a subjective interpretative construct with various contextual factors playing a role, it would seem to be a foregone conclusion that impoliteness is not inherent in linguistic expressions. However, we should note that my definition of inherent meaning above articulated a notion that even many semanticists would not recognise as tenable. Some accounts of semantics are relatively restrictive. Kempson (e.g. 1977: 8) is knowingly polemic in her restriction of semantics to a truth-based account and a theory of semantic competence. Other key works on semantics from the same period take a very different line. Leech (1981 [1974]: 86) argues that a theory for 'an ideal semantic description' 'must also relate meaning to pragmatics – the way in which sentences are actually used and interpreted in speaker-hearer communication'. Palmer (1981 [1976]) argues that a restricted, non-contextual semantics, whilst justifiable on methodological grounds or as a terminological issue regarding the label semantics, should not be a form of semantics treated as 'more central to the study of language', because 'only a small part of meaning will ever be captured' (1981: 50) and 'it is not possible to draw a clear theoretical division between what is in the world and what is in the language' (1981: 51).

No, impoliteness is not inherent in linguistic expressions   Given the fact that, as pointed out in the previous paragraphs, it is difficult to find mainstream supporters of the wholly inherent view, scholars who argue against politeness or impoliteness being inherent in linguistic expressions are shooting at a straw – or at least partially straw – target. The earliest and clearest exponent of this view is perhaps Bruce Fraser:

... no sentence is inherently polite or impolite. We often take certain expressions to be impolite, but it is not the expressions themselves but the conditions under which they are used that determines the judgment of politeness. (Fraser and Nolen 1981: 96)

Sentences are not ipso facto polite ... (Fraser 1990: 233)

More recent statements include the following:

My aim will be to demonstrate that, at least in English, linguistic structures do not in themselves denote politeness, but rather that they lend themselves to individual interpretation as 'polite' in instances of ongoing verbal interaction. (Watts 2003: 168)

What is perceived to be (im)polite will thus ultimately rely on interactants' assessments of social norms of appropriateness that have been previously acquired in the speech events in question.... As a result, we claim – with many others – that no utterance is inherently polite. (Locher 2006: 250–1)

There is... no linguistic behaviour that is inherently polite or impolite. (Locher and Watts 2008: 78)

There are in fact different shades of strength in the 'no' camp, and also some lack of clarity about the particular positions taken. For example, Richard Watts writes that expressions '*lend* themselves to individual interpretation' (2003: 168, my emphasis), which suggests that they play some part in determining the interpretation of politeness, and indeed he describes in his book how some expressions constrain interpretation by virtue of the fact that they are encoded procedural meaning (Blakemore 1987). On the other hand, earlier in the book one finds this statement '(im)politeness does not reside in the language or in the individual structures of language', though to be fair that statement is part of a rhetorical strategy critiquing B&L (1987).

Approaches to politeness that emphasise the role of context are sometimes referred to as 'post-modern' or 'discursive' (e.g. Eelen 2001; Locher 2006; Mills 2003; Watts 2003). As far as the label post-modern signals a concern with cultural and individual relativism and a dislike of universalising generalisations it is accurate, but it brings some unwanted baggage with it, and so I will deploy the label discursive. The general focus of the discursive approach is on the micro, that is, on participants' situated and dynamic evaluations of politeness, not shared conventionalised politeness forms or strategies. As an antidote to the overly form-focused and speaker-centred classic politeness theories (and, in the case of B&L (1987), overly based on assumptions about politeness universals), discursive politeness work has been effective. However, one consequence of focusing on the dynamic and situated characteristics of politeness is that politeness is declared not to be a predictive theory (Watts 2003: 25), or even a post-hoc descriptive one (Watts 2003: 142). As Terkourafi comments (2005a: 245), '[w]hat we are then left with are minute descriptions of individual encounters, but these do not in any way add up to an explanatory theory of the phenomena under study'. Holmes (2005: 115) even suggests that the analyst is redundant if we take the discursive line to its logical conclusion: 'if everything is relative... the analyst cannot legitimately attribute meaning, one wonders what, then, *does* constitute a legitimate role for the analyst'. However, there is a tendency in critical reactions to discursive approaches to target extreme, even somewhat caricatured, interpretations of them, whilst ignoring the totality of what they are saying. Discursive politeness approaches are not in fact fully discursive in the manner of, for example, the discursive approach in social psychology (e.g. Edwards and Potter 1992) (see also Haugh's 2007 critique, arguing that the discursive approach to politeness in incoherent). For example, Watts (e.g. 2003) and Locher (e.g. Locher 2004; Locher and Watts 2005) both embrace the notion of a (cognitive) 'frame', a notion that has much in common with schema (and even could be considered a particular kind of schema; see Introducing impoliteness). By this, they account for how people make judgements about situations they have never before experienced: they draw on frame-based knowledge about situational norms and accompanying evaluations.

Indeed, it is difficult to see how communication could proceed without some shared conventions of meaning. Both Lewis (1969), the seminal work on convention, and Clark (1996), a comprehensive treatment of interactional pragmatics, argue that such conventions enable participants to coordinate their thoughts and actions. In contrast, discursive studies downplay, partly for rhetorical reasons, shared conventions of meaning, instead emphasising that meanings are very unstable, negotiable and fuzzy and that communication is a very uncertain business. In fact, shared conventions of meaning mediated by multiple modalities, each of which may and often do act to reinforce each other, make for much more stability and certainty than one might expect from reading discursive studies. Archer and Akert (1980) conducted three extensive empirical tests, involving around 1,000 informants and their unstructured comments on twenty thirty-second video-taped sequences of naturalistic face-to-face interaction. The tests exposed the informants to just a segment of the interaction, whether temporal segments of the interactions or a particular channel (a verbal transcript, transcript plus audio, etc.), after which they were asked interpretative questions concerning what was happening in the interaction. They found:

that most or even all pieces of an interaction can contain the information necessary for interpretation, and (2) that interpretations based on a very small piece of an interaction can be virtually as accurate as interpretations based on the whole interaction. (1980: 413)

They point out that perfect conditions for reception rarely obtain in real life, and yet 'we frequently are able to interpret an act sequence of behaviour *even if we have not observed it perfectly*' (1980: 414, original emphasis). Social interaction, they say, contains an 'extraordinary degree of informational redundancy' (1980: 414). They argue that their research shows that 'people encode meaningful, appropriate behaviours into each of a bewildering number of pieces – some of them very small – of an interaction' (1980: 415), and they do this unconsciously, as to do otherwise would be overwhelming. Archer and Akert (1980), of course, is not the only study to have investigated multimodal redundancy. For example, Bavelas and Chovil (2000: 186–7) report two studies which both suggest that redundancy is at least 60 per cent (i.e. there is a 60 per cent overlap between what non-verbal signals are conveying and what the words convey).

Furthermore, perhaps the most compelling evidence requiring us to re-think (at least an extreme version) of the discursive approach is intuitive – the commonplace fact that people have opinions about how different expressions relate to different degrees of politeness or impoliteness *out of context*, and often opinions which are similar to others sharing their communities. They must have some kind of semantic knowledge; or, to put it another way, the pragmatics of these expressions must be semantically encoded in some way.

Yes and no, impoliteness is partly inherent in linguistic expressions
Perhaps the clearest statement of the dual view appears in Leech (1983). Leech distinguishes between 'absolute politeness' and 'relative politeness'. Absolute politeness is 'a scale, or rather a set of scales . . . , having a negative and positive pole. Some illocutions (e.g. orders) are inherently impolite, and others (e.g. offers) are inherently polite' (1983: 83). Relative politeness is 'politeness relative to context or situation' (1983: 102), 'to some norm of behaviour which, for a particular setting, [people] regard as typical' (1983: 84). Leech (1983: 102) provides the following illustration:

In an absolute sense, [1] *Just be quiet* is less polite than [2] *Would you please be quiet for a moment?* But there are occasions where [1] could be too polite, and other occasions where [2] would not be polite enough. There are even some cases where [2] would strike one as less polite than [1]; where, for example, [1] was interpreted as a form of banter, and where [2] was used ironically.

Leech's examples include cross-cultural politeness variation. One might quibble that Leech seems to be focusing on illocutions, not locution. However, more recently, Leech (2007) changed the labels of these two types of politeness to a 'semantic politeness scale' and a 'pragmatic politeness scale', thereby making it clear that the first encompasses formal aspects. He also clarifies that these are 'two ways of looking at politeness' (2007: 174); that is, there is no claim that there are two discrete types of politeness.

Leech is not the only person to argue for dualism. Craig, Tracy and Spisak (1986: 456, original emphasis) put it this way:

The difficulty of rating politeness independently of appropriateness suggests that a distinction should be made between politeness as a system of *message strategies* and politeness as a *social judgment*. Politeness strategies can be identified in messages, albeit often with some difficulty, with limited use of context. Politeness judgments, on the other hand, are highly context-dependent, perhaps highly variable social-cognitive phenomena. Politeness judgments, although influenced by politeness strategies, are far from wholly determined by them.

Note the acknowledgement that there is some 'difficulty' in maintaining the distinction. Indeed, in the years following the 1980s research cited here, there was a shift in the way language and context are conceptualised. The papers in Duranti and Goodwin (1992), for example, emphasised that context is dynamic and constructed *in situ*, and that language and context are not two separate entities but rather held in a mutually dependent relationship. In fact, the role of language in constructing context had been clearly flagged for many years in Gumperz's (e.g. 1982a) work on 'contextualisation cues'. Studies involving politeness have been generally rather slow to grasp this.

My own position is dualist in the sense that I see semantic (im)politeness and pragmatic (im)politeness as inter-dependent opposites on a scale. (Im)politeness can be more determined by a linguistic expression or can be more determined by context, but neither the expression nor the context guarantee an interpretation of (im)politeness: it is the interaction between the two that counts. What is different about semantic (im)politeness from, say, the semantics of the noun 'table' is that it is the interaction between the expression and its interpersonal contextual effects that must be the central semanticised component for it to exist. If (im)politeness is defined as a negative evaluative attitude evoked by certain situated communicative behaviours, then an expression that did not in some way link itself to interpersonal context could hardly be inherently (im)polite. Expressions can be semanticised for (im)politeness effects to varying degrees. This is spelt out and illustrated by Terkourafi (2008: 74, footnote 27) discussing swearwords:

Paralleling what happens with face-constituting expressions that may be conventionalised to a higher or lower degree, swear words may semantically encode face-threat, but other constructions may simply pragmatically implicate face-threat in a generalised manner on a par with generalised conversational implicatures of politeness (Terkourafi, 2003, 2005).

In my view, it is helpful to see the kind of semantic knowledge being discussed here as schematic knowledge. Impoliteness expressions can be viewed as part of a schematic network relevant to the impoliteness attitude schema, a network including schemata relating to emotions and metalanguage (see Section 2.4). This is in line with the position articulated by Holtgraves (2005: 89): 'people possess a schematic knowledge regarding language and its social implications, knowledge that exists independent of any occasion of use'. Note the specific wording here: the claim is that it is 'independent of any occasion of use' and not that it is independent of context. The typical links between certain formulae and certain contexts have become part of the generic schema. Moreover, Holtgraves

(1997) provides empirical evidence that people 'encode a general impression of the politeness of the speaker's remarks', even if sometimes they do not remember the exact wording. It seems reasonable to suppose that the same will be true of impoliteness. In the following sections, I will consider the nature of conventionalisation and the process leading to the semanticization of (im)politeness more closely.

4.4   From conventionalised politeness to conventionalised impoliteness

4.4.1   Conventionalised polite formulae

Terkourafi's (e.g. 2001, 2002, 2005a) frame-based approach to politeness argues that we should analyse the *concrete linguistic realisations* (i.e. linguistic expressions) and *particular contexts of use* which co-constitute 'frames'. Moreover, '[i]t is the regular co-occurrence of particular types of context and particular linguistic expressions as the *unchallenged* realisations of particular acts that create the perception of politeness' (2005a: 248; see also 2005b: 213; my emphasis). The fact that the formulae are not only associated with a particular context but go unchallenged is an important point. This feature seems to be similar to Haugh's (2007: 312) claim that evidence of politeness can be found in, amongst other things, 'the reciprocation of concern evident in the adjacent placement of expressions of concern relevant to the norms invoked in that particular interaction'. Terkourafi suggests that it is through that regularity of co-occurrence that we acquire 'a knowledge of which expressions to use in which situations' (2002: 197), that is, 'experientially acquired structures of anticipated "default" behaviour' (2002: 197). She also points out that formulae are more easily processed by both speaker and hearer, when juggling face concerns, goals, and so on, and also that using them demonstrates a knowledge of community norms (2002: 196). Thus, 'formulaic speech carries the burden of polite discourse' (2002: 197; see also references given in 2005b: 213). The fact that this is so accounts for the observation that politeness often passes unnoticed (e.g. Kasper 1990: 193).

Terkourafi (2005b: 213; see also 2001: 130) offers the following definition of conventionalisation:

a relationship holding between utterances and context, which is a correlate of the (statistical) frequency with which an expression used in one's experience of a particular context. Conventionalisation is thus a matter of degree, and may well vary in different speakers, as well as for the same speaker over time. This does not preclude the possibility that a particular expression may be conventionalised in a particular context for virtually all speakers of a particular language, thereby appearing to be a convention of that language.

The general idea here of co-occurrence regularities between language forms and specific contexts is of course a familiar one in the world of sociolinguistics. It is out of these regularities that sociolinguistic resources develop. Consider, for example, how Bakhtin's (1986: 60, original emphasis) notion of 'speech genres' captures such regularities: 'Each separate utterance is individual, of course, but each sphere in which language is used develops its own *relatively stable types* of these utterances'.

Terkourafi (2001: 130–1) observes that her notion of conventionalisation bears some similarity to the notion of 'standardisation', as discussed by Kent Bach and Robert Harnish (e.g. Bach and Harnish 1979; Bach 1995, 1998). Standardisation captures the idea that one can short-circuit the inferencing normally required to derive pragmatic meanings: the 'hearer's inference is compressed by precedent' (Bach 1995: 678). Furthermore, discussing performatives, Bach comments that the success of the utterance would be 'vitiated if any of the steps of the [original, uncompressed] inference were blocked' (Bach 1975: 235, cited in Bach 1995: 683). Thus, for (im)politeness, an inappropriate contextual relation can block the inference. For example, 'thank you' may *appear* to be an English expression that is inherently polite, but in suitable contexts it could be interpreted as, for instance, sarcastic. The usual standardised inferencing leading to politeness (the conventionalised meaning) is blocked, but other pragmatic meanings (sarcasm) are derivable in context. As Terkourafi (2005b: 226) points out, even 'if an inference is compressed by precedent, it may still be learnt by an individual speaker' (i.e. learnt as a convention). Note that there is a scale of conventionalisation: pragmatic meanings can become more semanticised (i.e. conventional for the majority of the speakers of the language). Terkourafi argues that it is the 'potential for variation [which] keeps conventionalised inferences apart from conventional ones (Strawson 1964)' (2005c: 298). Whilst impoliteness formulae can be highly conventionalised, it is not so clear, in my view, that generally they can ever be as fully conventional as non-politeness related concepts, such as land, water, sky, etc. For example, *cunt* was generally viewed as the most offensive word in British English in the year 2000 (Millwood-Hargrave 2000). But we saw an example in Section 4.2 in which it was not used for impoliteness.

What I have been referring to as conventionalised meaning (as opposed to conventional meaning) sits midway between semantics and pragmatics, between fully conventionalised and non-conventionalised meanings (Levinson 2000: 25). The process by which expressions become semantically imbued with their politeness or impoliteness contexts assumes that some expressions have a more stable relationship with (im)politeness contexts and effects than others, and that over time those expressions begin to acquire conventional associations of the (im)politeness contexts in which they are regularly used – they become conventionalised. This process fits the broader historical processes of semanticisation, which has been described within historical pragmatics, a field which often focuses on the development of pragmatic markers and their highly context-sensitive meanings (see, for example, Traugott 1999, 2004).

An elegant Neo-Gricean account of the pragmatic inferencing of conventionalised polite expressions is given in Terkourafi (e.g. 2001, 2005b). The background to this lies in Grice's (1989) distinction between particularised and generalised implicatures, and its elaboration by Levinson (1992 [1979], 1995, 2000). Particularised implicatures are worked out from scratch on the basis of the particular context the utterance appears in; generalised implicatures have a more stable association with particular linguistic forms (cf. Grice 1989: 37). Scalar implicatures are an example of the latter: *hot* allows the generalised implicatures *not cold*, *not warm*, etc., and does so regardless of the context in which it is used. However, as with all implicatures, it is defeasible (e.g. 'it's hot today . . . actually with that breeze just warm'). Levinson's particular contribution was to characterise generalised implicatures as a level of meaning between particularised implicatures and fully conventionalised (nondefeasible) implicatures (1979b: 216). Terkourafi's contribution was to split generalised implicatures into two, a division based on the relationship with context. The first captures situations where the implicature is weakly context-dependent, requiring a minimal amount of contextual information relating to the social context of use in which the utterance was routinised and thus conventionalised to some degree; the second, as described by Levinson, captures situations where the implicature is even more weakly context-dependent – its meaning is presumed in a variety of contexts. The two clines described in this and the previous paragraph, one relating to the conventionalisation of meaning and the other relating to the kinds of meaning that feed conventionalisation, can be displayed as follows (the bottom cline is given in Terkourafi 2005b: 211–2).

Non-conventional pragmatic	$\longrightarrow$	Conventionalised pragmatic	$\longrightarrow$	Conventional semantic
Particularised implicature (utterance-token meaning derived in nonce context)	$\longrightarrow$ Generalised implicature I (utterance-type meaning presumed in minimal context)	$\longrightarrow$ Generalised implicature II (utterance-type meaning presumed in all contexts *ceteris paribus*)	$\longrightarrow$	Coded meaning (sentence meaning)

Hitherto, standard, classical Gricean accounts of politeness (e.g. Leech 1983) have made no explicit connection with generalised implicatures, instead discussing politeness in terms of the recovery of the speaker's intentions in deviating from Gricean cooperativeness on a particular occasion (i.e. in terms of particularised implicatures). In the introduction to their second edition, B&L (1987: 6–7) admitted that they may have underplayed the role of generalised conversational implicatures. Terkourafi, however, positions such implicatures at the heart of her scheme. Relating to the cline outlined above, she argues that, whilst politeness can involve full inferencing in a nonce context, what lies at its heart is a generalised implicature of the first type given above. Her argument is neatly summarised here (Terkourafi 2005a: 251, original emphasis):

> Politeness is achieved on the basis of a generalised implicature when an expression x is uttered in a context with which – based on the addressee's previous experience of similar contexts – expression x regularly co-occurs. In this case, rather than engaging in full-blown inferencing about the speaker's intention, the addressee draws on that previous experience (represented holistically as a frame) to derive the proposition that 'in offering an expression x the speaker is being polite' as a generalised implicature of the speaker's utterance. On the basis of this generalised implicature, the addressee may then come to hold the further belief that the speaker *is* polite.

One might note here that the idea of context-dependent versus context-spanning strategies as a cline parallels the two clines presented above.

The basic idea that particular expressions are associated in one's mind with particular contexts resonates with other work, notably Gumperz's notion of *contextualisation cues* (1982a, 1992a, 1992b). Gumperz (1982b: 162) elaborates:

> The identification of specific conversational exchanges as representative of socio-culturally familiar activities is the process I have called 'contextualisation' . . . . It is the process by which we evaluate message meaning and sequencing patterns in relation to aspects of the surface structure of the message, called 'contextualisation cues'. The linguistic basis for this matching procedure resides in 'cooccurrence expectations,' which are learned in the course of previous interactive experience and form part of our habitual and instinctive linguistic knowledge. *Cooccurrence expectations enable us to associate styles in speaking with contextual presuppositions.* We regularly rely upon these matching processes in everyday conversation. Although they are rarely talked about and tend to be noticed only when things go wrong, without them we would be unable to relate what we hear to previous experience.

Of course, it should be stressed that a conventionalised (im)polite expression does not guarantee an interpretation of (im)politeness (it can be cancelled by a contextual feature), and (im)politeness can be achieved in other ways apart from using such expressions. This will be illustrated at a number of points in the upcoming chapters.

4.4.2   Conventionalised impolite formulae

Not surprisingly, given the focus on politeness, Terkourafi concentrates on statistical regularities of usage: 'politeness is not a matter of rational calculation, but of habits' (2005a: 250); 'Empirically, frames take the form of observable regularities of usage' (2001: 185). Could conventionalised impoliteness formulae have the same basis as that argued for politeness formulae? Are they conventionalised frequency correlations between forms and particular contexts? My argument is that impoliteness cannot be adequately treated thus.

An apparent problem is that impoliteness formulae are much less frequent than politeness formulae. Leech (1983: 105) states that 'conflictive illocutions tend, thankfully, to be rather marginal to human linguistic behaviour in normal circumstances'. It is difficult to see how society would function if people were impolite (and perceived to be so) most of the time. This is a reason why Leech's statement is likely to be correct. Finding solid empirical evidence to support it is more difficult. In my own 'everyday' interactions (e.g. interacting with my family, buying a ticket for the bus, talking to colleagues at work), examples of impoliteness are relatively rare. I have some evidence that they are similarly rare for others. Although the 100 students who supplied me with diary-type reports of impoliteness events were given a week or more in which to report such events, many told me that they failed to find one to report (despite there being a financial incentive to do so!). That is why I ended up administering, with the help of colleagues, report-forms to well over 1,000 students in order to gain 100 completions. Further evidence may also be in the fact that the icons of English politeness *please* and *thank you* occur so much more frequently than possible icons of impoliteness such as *cunt* and *motherfucker* (the two British English lexical items considered most offensive in the year 2000, according to Millwood-Hargrave 2000). In the two-billion word *OEC* the frequencies are: *please* (14,627), *thank you* (5,533), *cunt* (157) and *motherfucker* (88). Of course, there is no guarantee that all these instances of usage actually involved politeness or impoliteness (some might have been, for example, sarcasm or banter), but, given the huge frequency differentials, there seems to be support for the idea that verbal impoliteness is relatively rare in terms of its general frequency.

Impoliteness, however, does play a central role and is relatively frequent in specific discourses, such as army recruit training, interactions between car owners and traffic wardens, exploitative TV, and so on (see, for example, Culpeper *et al.* 2003: 1545–6; Bousfield 2008) – contexts which perhaps my students and I are not party to very often and which are often less well represented in corpus data (although the *OEC* is admittedly vast). The crucial point about conventionality discussed in the previous section is that it relates to specific contexts of use. For impoliteness formulae, these 'abnormal' circumstances are indeed such specific contexts. Conventionalised impoliteness formulae can and do develop here, and I will pursue this avenue in Section 4.4.3. Where there is an interesting point of difference with politeness formulae is that people acquire a knowledge of impoliteness formulae that far exceeds *their own direct experience of usage* of formulae associated with impolite effects in such contexts. This, I argue, is because they also draw upon indirect experience, and in particular metadiscourse.

Indirect experiences of impoliteness formulae include mentions rather than uses, that is, discourse about impoliteness discourse – impoliteness metadiscourse (see Chapter 3). Indirect experience is accommodated within Terkourafi's framework. She notes:

> In acquiring language both by hearing it and by actively producing it, speakers develop repertoires of frames which include frames of which they only have a 'passive' knowledge. For example, in sexually segregated societies, men will be aware of women's 'ways of speaking', although they themselves will not use them. (2001: 182)

However, Terkourafi does not dwell on indirect experience or metadiscourse, and her analyses are focused squarely on direct experience – none of which is surprising, given that she focuses on politeness. Impoliteness, in contrast, casts a much larger shadow than its frequency of usage would suggest. Behaviours and expressions considered impolite are more noticed and discussed than politeness (cf. Watts 2003: 5). Impoliteness formulae are far from marginal in terms of their psychological salience, because their very abnormality (relative to their general frequency of use) attracts attention – they are foregrounded against the generally expected state for conversation, namely, politeness (Fraser 1990: 233). Not surprisingly, then, they are commented on and debated in all types of media, in official documents and in everyday chat, and so on. However, psychological salience is only part of what is going on here. Metadiscourse plays a role in the group dynamic that gives rise to a behaviour being evaluated as impolite in the first place.

Whilst any specific usage of impoliteness can be described in terms of face damage to individuals (as demonstrated in, for example, Bousfield 2008), those usages often have reverberations – some of which are articulated in impoliteness metadiscourse – for the broader community in which they take place. Recollect Jaworski, Coupland and Galasiński's (2004b: 3, original emphasis) comment on the general role of metadiscourse quoted in Section 3.2:

> Metalinguistic representations may enter public consciousness and come to constitute structured understandings, perhaps even 'common sense' understandings – of how language works, what it is usually like, what certain ways of speaking connote and imply, what they *ought* to be like.

The important point here is that we gain 'understandings' of what language is 'usually like' and 'what certain ways of speaking connote and imply' without recourse to the frequency of direct experience. Note that the argument is not merely that metadiscourse is a reflex of behaviours, but that metadiscourse comes to 'constitute structured understandings', including, in particular, understandings about what 'certain ways of speaking' '*ought* to be like'. A case where impoliteness is clearly linked to the 'social oughts' of metadiscourse concerns rules, as elaborated in Section 3.9. However, it is also possible to have rules that people regularly ignore. Rules do not depend on regularities, but arise from *social* norms. As I pointed out in Section 1.4.1, Gilbert's (1989) argument is that belonging to a social group is part and parcel of accepting the norms that constitute it, and adopting a group's fiat is a matter of making manifest one's willingness to do so. Impoliteness metadiscourse (e.g. condemning an impoliteness behaviour, upholding a rule) can be driven by the need to demonstrate one's orientation to a group and the norms by which it is constituted. We should note here, as I will elaborate in Section 6.2.2, that social norms are embedded in ideologies. Dominant ideologies, belief systems, can sustain and normalise the social conventions that serve power hierarchies. Silverstein (1998) stresses the importance of ideology in relation to indexical processes, indexicals, as Silverstein defines them, having a strong affinity with Gumperz's (e.g. 1982a) notion of contextualisation cues (cf. Mertz 1998: 152) and thus also my understanding of conventionalised impoliteness. He writes:

ideologies present invokable schemata in which to explain/interpret the meaningful flow of indexicals. As such, they are necessary to and drive default modes of the gelling of this flow into textlike chunks. Ideologies are, thus, conceptualized as relatively perduring with respect to the indexicals-in-context that they construe. And we recognise such schemata characteristically by the way that they constitute rationalizing, systematizing, and, indeed most importantly, *naturalizing* schemata: schemata that 'explain' the indexical value of signs in terms of some order(s) of phenomena stipulatively presupposable by – hence, in context, autonomous of – the indexical phenomena to be understood. (1998: 129, original emphasis)

Note that such ideologies echo Jaworski, Coupland and Galasiński's '"common sense" understandings' (2004: 3). Ideologies are involved in explaining/interpreting what counts as conventionalised impoliteness in particular contexts. They are evaluative and prescriptive assumptions about: 'what is "correct", "normal", "appropriate", "well-formed", "worth saying", "permissible", and so on, but also about what indexical expression x has as its default meaning (Silverstein 1998)' (Coupland and Jaworski 2004: 36–7). For example, a five-year old boy in a swimming pool changing room in the UK said to his father: 'I want my Kinder chocolate right now'. To which, his father replied: 'You're not getting anything if you're being rude'. The boy's use of a relatively direct request ('I want X') coupled with the aggravator 'right now' transgressed the ideologically natural, non-negotiable order whereby in the interpersonal context of the family certain members are accorded certain forms of language with certain indexical values, and transgressions count as rude, impolite, etc., evidence for which is displayed in the father's metadiscourse.

Although Terkourafi does not deploy the label ideology, I note that her framework encompasses the evaluative beliefs a community has that something is (un)acceptable in a particular context. Learning that an expression is conventionally polite entails learning the evaluative judgement in the community that it is so in the relevant context (cf. Terkourafi 2001: 142–3). More specifically, she deploys the notion of 'frame' (as we saw do other researchers, e.g. Locher and Watts 2005, albeit with perhaps a slightly different understanding of it) to help capture this evaluative link between language and context. There clearly is some overlap here with the notion of ideology.

4.4.3 Conventionalised impolite formulae in English

Following on from the arguments presented thus far, two (inter-connected) methods for identifying conventionalised impoliteness formulae present themselves:
1. Study those specific contexts in which participant(s) regularly display an understanding that something impolite was expressed (what expressions were used, if any?).
2. Study the metadiscourse concerning behaviours understood to be impolite (what expressions are they talking about, if any?).

The first method is akin to that adopted by Terkourafi (e.g. 2001) for politeness formulae. With regard to the second method, this is precisely what I did in Chapter 3, particularly Sections 3.9.1 and especially 3.9.2, which examined two rudeness training manuals. As I observed there, this method is good at capturing conventionalised pragmatic strategies. Indeed, this tallies with Tracy and Tracy's (1998: 242) observation that '[c]ontext-spanning strategies are those that could be and usually are identified in institutional training manuals; context-tied strategies rarely are'. However, a limitation of this method is that whilst good at revealing pragmatic strategies those strategies may or may not have specific linguistic expressions embedded within them. An enormous quantity of data would be required to see but a few trends regarding impoliteness formulae. Consequently, I shall pursue the first method here.

As I pointed out above, impoliteness is 'rather marginal to human linguistic behaviour in normal circumstances' (Leech 1983: 105). Having said that, I also noted that it is central to particular discourses (e.g. army training, exploitative TV shows). Those discourses can be studied quantitatively and/or qualitatively with a view to identifying conventional impoliteness formulae. The limitation of these contexts is that they reflect specific contexts which are either institutional or often at least partly contrived. Hence, I have also used my 100 diary-reports for more 'everyday' interactions considered impolite (for a full list of relevant datasets used in this study, see Introducing Impoliteness). The procedure I adopted for identifying candidates for conventionalised impoliteness formulae begins by collecting specific utterances within the above data to which somebody, typically the target, displayed evidence that they took the utterance as impolite (for details about what that evidence consisted of, see Introducing Impoliteness). As I accumulated candidates for impoliteness formulae, I grouped them according to structural commonalities. What I have in mind here is the Pattern Grammar of Gill Francis and Susan Hunston (Francis *et al.* 1996, 1998; Hunston and Francis 2000). Hunston and Francis define a pattern as:

a phraseology frequently associated with (a sense of) a word, particularly in terms of the prepositions, groups, and clauses that follow the word. Patterns and lexis are mutually dependent, in that each pattern occurs with a restricted set of lexical items, and each lexical item occurs with a restricted set of patterns. (2000: 3)

The pattern of a word can be defined as all the words and structures which are regularly associated with the word and which contribute to its meaning. A pattern can be identified if a combination of words occurs relatively frequently, if it is dependent on a particular word choice, and if there is a clear meaning associated with it. (2000: 37)

Patterns are sets of words which are semantically congruent in some way and which have grammatically patterned co-texts. As a whole they create specific meanings. Meaning is understood to include pragmatic meanings (see in particular Stubbs 2001). In this approach to grammar, there is no clear borderline between syntactic and lexical structures, something which echoes other approaches including, for example, Construction Grammar (e.g. Goldberg 1995).

I have also checked the robustness of all impoliteness formulae I derived in the *Oxford English Corpus* (*OEC*), with the exception of the category involving questions or presuppositions. I operated a criterion that at least 50 per cent of any one formula's variants had to involve impoliteness in more than 50 per cent of the *OEC*'s instances, that is, those instances had to be accompanied by evidence that they were interpreted as impoliteness (where the number of *OEC* instances was overwhelming, I analysed the first 100). For example, for the formula *shut up*, only one other variant emerged, namely, *shut the fuck up* (see Section 4.5.2, for a fuller discussion of this formula). *Shut up* has a strong correlation with impoliteness events in the *OEC* data, but does not clearly exceed the 50 per cent level (it can express, for instance, solidarity). In contrast, *shut the fuck up*, has a stronger correlation, clearly exceeding 50 per cent. Hence, this formula type is listed. The conventionalised impoliteness formulae identified thus are as follows. Square brackets are designed to give an indication of some of the structural characteristics of the formulae (finer grained structural analyses are possible, including a consideration of the degree of optionality each element has). Alternatives are indicated with slashes.

Insults
1. Personalized negative vocatives
   - [you] [fucking/rotten/dirty/fat/little/etc.] [moron/fuck/plonker/dickhead/
     berk/pig/shit/bastard/loser/liar/minx/brat/slut/squirt/sod/bugger/etc.]
     [you]
2. Personalized negative assertions
   - [you] [are] [so/such a] [shit/stink/thick/stupid/bitchy/bitch/hypocrite/
     disappointment/gay/nuts/nuttier than a fruit cake/hopeless/pathetic/
     fussy/terrible/fat/ugly/etc.]
   - [you] [can't do] [anything right/basic arithmetic/etc.]
   - [you] [disgust me] / [make me] [sick/etc.]
3. Personalized negative references
   - [your] [stinking/little] [mouth/act/arse/body/corpse/hands/guts/trap/
     breath/etc.]
4. Personalized third-person negative references (in the hearing of the target)
   - [the] [daft] [bimbo]
   - [she]['s] [nutzo]

Pointed criticisms/complaints
- [that/this/it] [is/was] [absolutely/extraordinarily/unspeakably/etc.]
  [bad/rubbish/crap/horrible/terrible/etc.]

Unpalatable questions and/or presuppositions
- why do you make my life impossible?
- which lie are you telling me?
- what's gone wrong now?
- you want to argue with me or you want to go to jail?
- I am not going to exploit for political purposes my opponent's youth and
  inexperience.

Condescensions (see also the use of 'little' in Insults)
- [that] ['s/ is being] [babyish/childish/etc.]

Message enforcers
- listen here (preface)
- you got [it/that]? (tag)
- do you understand [me]? (tag)

Dismissals
- [go] [away]
- [get] [lost/out]
- [fuck/piss/shove] [off]

Silencers
- [shut] [it] / [your] [stinking/fucking/etc.] [mouth/face/trap/etc.]
- shut [the fuck] up

Threats
- [I'll/I'm/we're] [gonna] [smash your face in/beat the shit out of you/box your ears/bust your fucking head off/straighten you out/etc.] [if you don't] [X]
- [you'd better be ready Friday the 20th to meet with me/do it] [or] [else] [I'll] [X]
- [X] [before I] [hit you/strangle you]

Negative expressives (e.g. curses, ill-wishes)
- [go] [to hell/hang yourself/fuck yourself]
- [damn/fuck] [you]

Of course, this list reflects regularities in my data; it is not a list of all English conventionalised impoliteness formulae. Having said that, I would be surprised if this list did not include many very generally used English conventionalised impoliteness formulae. Conversely, some items that one might expect to be included are not, simply because they did not occur frequently enough. For example, taboo words or behaviours can trigger a judgement of impoliteness, but they seem to do this *per se* extremely rarely – a mere two cases occurred in 100 diary reports. In most cases taboo words operate in conjunction with impoliteness formulae such as those above (see the discussion in Section 4.5.2). One way in which the above list is indeed incomplete is that it is mainly restricted to formulae that are defined by lexis and grammar. What about paralinguistic aspects? The following might be considered conventionalised non-verbal visual impoliteness behaviours in British culture, although they rarely occurred in my data (a more extensive list of gestural emblems perceived by North American undergraduates to be hurtful is given in Rancer *et al.* 2010):
- spitting
- sticking one's tongue out at somebody
- giving someone a two fingered (or one fingered) gesture
- rolling one's eyes
- leering
- turning one's back on someone

What about vocal aspects? In fact, vocal aspects, like taboo words, hardly ever are enough *per se* (i.e. without words) to be associated with impoliteness. Screaming or yelling at someone without recognisable words may be a possible case. Actually, the fact that non-verbal vocal aspects do not in themselves become conventional impoliteness behaviours is not surprising, given that the main role of such aspects is to help convey meanings. They have a rhetorical function. As Knowles (1984: 227) remarks:

The speaker has not only to decide what to say, but how to convey it effectively to the addressee. He [*sic*] has several channels at his disposal – verbal, intonational, paralinguistic – and employs communicative strategies to combine the signals sent on each channel so that the total effect will be correctly interpreted by the hearer. Conventional linguistics concentrates on the content of the message that is conveyed: intonation is part of rhetoric, or the strategies employed to get that message across.

The same point can be made of many non-verbal behaviours, an important example being pointing. They are also rhetorical strategies for securing an impoliteness effect. Some of the conventional impoliteness formulae listed above may look quite innocuous, that is, relatively context-dependent for their impoliteness effects. But they are generally conventionalised in spoken inter-action and thus will have conventional supporting prosodic and non-verbal aspects, such as sharply falling intonation, tense voice quality, increased loud-ness, frowning and pointing. I shall have more to say about non-verbal aspects in Section 4.5.3. In contrast, inconsistent accompanying prosodic and non-verbal signals may risk suggesting that the impoliteness is non-genuine, that it is, for example, banter, something which would have been excluded from the items brought into consideration here.

It is important to remember – to use the words of Gumperz on contextualisa-tion cues – that the formulae here are 'basically gradual or scalar; they do not take the form of discrete quantitative contrast' (1982a: 132). I would suggest that they vary according to three scales. One, most obviously, is the scale of conventionalisation discussed above. Another is the degree to which they are impoliteness context-spanning (i.e. taken as impolite in a range of contexts). And the third is the degree of gravity of offence they are associated with. It is likely that there are particular interactions between the scales. I hypothesise that formulae associated with higher offence are less easy to neutralise in a wider variety of contexts, and thus are more context-spanning. And, if they are more context-spanning, they are likely to be more conventionalised. Indeed, in Section 4.5.1 I will cite research which supports this hypothesis.

4.4.4 An illustration of a conventionalised impoliteness formula used in context

In the following chapter, I will touch on a number of ways in which convention-alised impolite expressions can be both contextualising and contextualised, and the implications this has for both their functions and effects. Here, I will supply a brief illustration of a conventionalised formula used in a matching context, or, in other words, in the kind of context which gave rise to its conventional contextual associations.

Consider example [2]:

[2]

> [*'Dog' Chapman, a bounty hunter in the USA, talks about taking a fugitive into custody*]
>
> It's important to make a scary first impression. 'I know Christians get upset because I say "Freeze, motherf***er!" but I told them that "Freeze in Jesus's name" doesn't work.'
>
> *Daily Telegraph*, reported in *The Week*, 5/10/06

The insulting vocative 'motherf***er' is conventionally associated with the particular contexts in which impolite effects occur. It should be remembered that we are dealing with a North American cultural context here. Jay (1992: 178) remarks: '[t]his word stands alone as the most offensive in American English', and this applies to both men and women. It marks strong negative attitudes – a person's anger at someone for being annoying, uncooperative, stupid, etc. It is also typically used between males but not females (Jay 1992: 178). Jay (1992: 205) reports that in 1985 the Nebraska Supreme Court declared *motherfucker* a 'fighting word'. The doctrine of fighting words is enshrined in North American law; they are outlawed by the dominant ideology. Jay (1992: 200–1) summarises Gard (1980) who concludes that there are four key elements to fighting words:

1. 'the utterance must constitute an extremely provocative personal insult',
2. 'the words must have a direct tendency to cause immediate violent response by the average recipient',
3. 'the words must be uttered face-to-face to the addressee', and
4. 'the utterance must be directed to an individual and not to a group of people'.

In the situation confronting Chapman, the fugitive can be predicted to resist, perhaps violently, and hence maximum coercion could be viewed as appropriate, even expected. Impoliteness is often deployed to facilitate coercion by doing symbolic violence. Chapman has legal powers of arrest, and is in some respects a pseudo-police officer. Ainsworth (2008: 7) highlights the fact that swearing at criminal suspects is a common occurrence in street-level policing interactions. She argues that it is a form of coercion and a demonstration of masculinity that is in tune with the norms and values of police culture. She adds that most police departments in fact have a formal rule that swearing by officers is forbidden, but transgressing such rules actually helps fuel the intimidation, giving the recipient the impression that 'an officer who is willing to be transgressive about language norms may also be willing to violate other norms, such as the norm against gratuitous physical abuse of citizens' (2008: 11). The insulting vocative *motherfucker* is context-spanning, being conventionally (schematically) associated with violent contexts, contexts characterised by anger, strong provocation, face-to-face interaction between males, coercion, and so on. Chapman's usage of 'motherfucker', then, is consistent with police cultural norms, it is consistent with its context of use. The same cannot be said of Chapman's alternative 'in Jesus's name'. This expression, though occasionally marking expressions of surprise or anger, has conventional associations with religious Christian contexts, and more particularly with the context of baptism and all its associations of solemn ceremony. Evidence of this is in the fact that the strongest collocates of this expression in the *OEC* are *amen*, *bapitized*, *pray*, *baptism*, *glory* and *Lord* (fifty-six instances of this expression in total; the strength of collocates was ranked by MI scores). This provides a contrast with the potentially violent situation, and the unconventional, creative mismatch adds a note of humour.

4.5 Exacerbating the offensiveness of impoliteness formulae

Using various means – the addition of modifiers, taboo words, particular prosodies, non-verbal features, and so on – to exacerbate the offensiveness of an impoliteness formula is not simply an optional extra that calibrates where exactly on a scale of impoliteness the item falls. A formula, such as those in the list given in Section 4.4.3, might not be considered impolite at all, were it not for the fact that it is intensified. Impoliteness is very much about signalling behaviours that are attitudinally extreme or understanding them to be so. Intensifying an impoliteness formula makes it less ambiguous, less equivocal – it helps secure an impoliteness uptake.

In this chapter, I am concerned solely with behavioural choices expressed as part of (in synchrony with) and in harmony with (contributing to the same meaning and effects as) conventional impoliteness formulae. The following chapters, especially Chapter 5, will be devoted to ways in which formulae can be pitched against the co-text or against the context, in order to achieve their offensiveness. I should add here that although intensification is most common in relation to conventionalised impoliteness formulae, it can also be used in the context of non-conventionalised impoliteness, as I will illustrate in Chapter 5.

4.5.1 Message intensity

The key notion is intensity. We have already encountered this notion in Section 3.7, where I labelled it symbolic violence and deployed it in the organisation of metalinguistic labels in conceptual space. The notion of intensity is also deployed by social psychologists, but, importantly, has a rather different meaning. The classic definition is provided by Bowers (1963: 345) who defines language intensity as 'the quality of language which indicates the degree to which the speaker's attitude toward a concept deviates from neutrality'. In the context of communication studies, which are more relevant to my own study, the notion of 'message intensity' has been defined thus: 'the strength or degree of emphasis with which a source states his attitudinal position towards a topic' (McEwen and Greenberg 1970: 340). Language or message intensity involves attitudinal intensity, and is closely connected to emotions. It is much narrower than symbolic violence, which involves not only a non-neutral attitude but also power and (physical) dynamism.

All conventionalised impoliteness formulae are non-neutral by definition; they involve a degree of language intensity. However, as already observed, the variants of each formula type vary in terms of how offensive they are. The intensity of an impoliteness formula plays a key role in determining how offensive it is perceived to be: I propose that a more intensely expressed formula will generally lead to more impoliteness being taken. Of course, as I have pointed out on a number of occasions, there are co-textual and contextual factors that contribute to the perception of impoliteness – they can mitigate or exacerbate effects. But there is evidence that the intensity of the message is key. For example, Young (2004) investigated the factors that influence recipients appraisals of hurtful communication, including those contextual relational factors and message-specific factors. The following conclusion emerged:

How a message was stated was pivotal in determining recipients appraisals of it. Comments that were stated harshly, abrasively, or that used extreme language were likely to be viewed more negatively. Research on verbal aggression (Infante and Myers 1994) has found comparable results – interactions characterised by verbal aggression are perceived to be destructive. Like verbally aggressive messages, hurtful comments that are stated intensely may be viewed as particularly detrimental. In short, the cliche 'It's not what you say but how you say it' rings true with regard to recipients' appraisals about hurtful messages. This finding suggests a promising area of enquiry for relationship research, because it implies that how people grapple with negative emotions evoked by their relational partners does not rest solely on perceptions about the relationship or about the other person. Rather, the manner in which the message is communicated impacts how a message will be appraised. . . . this study suggests that it is difficult for recipients to engage in cognitive appraisals to minimise the negativity associated with an intensely stated hurtful comment. (Young 2004: 300)

Young's final sentence reflects the argument I put forward in Sections 2.2.4 and 6.6, namely, that impolite behaviours engulf the perceivers' field and are difficult to minimise. Interestingly, there is a little evidence that the relationship between intensity and offensiveness may not be linear. Greenberg's (1976) study of perceived verbal aggressiveness found that when an utterance reaches the higher levels of aggression the addition of boosters (specifically, frequency qualifiers like 'always') made little difference to how it was perceived. In other words, the relationship between intensity and offensiveness may be curvilinear; above a certain point the addition of further intensity may not produce a proportional increase in offensiveness. I will address a similar issue in Section 5.5.

4.5.2   Lexical and grammatical ways of achieving message intensity

Perhaps not surprisingly, scholars in communication studies and social psychology have been rather vague about what intensity consists of from a linguistic point of view. In practice, much of what they manipulate in their studies relates to what linguists would recognise under such labels as pragmatic/discourse markers, illocutionary force modifiers, hedges/boosters, modality, and so on. Thus they discuss the effects of messages with items such as 'positively/greatly/mostly/definitely/extremely' as opposed to 'perhaps/possibly/some/slightly/somewhat', or 'seems to be/may cause/could' as opposed to 'is/cause/must' (all examples taken from McEwen and Greenberg 1970: 344). Clearly, intensifying modifiers play a role in exacerbating the impoliteness of impoliteness expressions, especially in the context of insults (compare: 'you're stupid' with 'you're so stupid'). However, in my view there are equally clearly other ways in which language conveys 'the strength or degree of emphasis with which a source states his [sic] attitudinal position towards a topic' (McEwen and Greenberg 1970: 340). Foremost among these is the attitudinal meaning associated with a particular lexical item. What I am referring to is what Leech ([1974] 1981: 15) refers to as 'affective meaning', which concerns 'how language reflects the personal feelings of the speaker, including his [sic] attitude to the listener, or his attitude to something he is talking about'. This sort of meaning 'is often explicitly conveyed through the conceptual or connotative content of the words used' (Leech 1981: 15), and 'is largely a parasitic category in the sense that to express our emotions we rely upon the mediation of other categories of meaning – conceptual, connotative, or stylistic' (Leech 1981: 16). Such variation in word meaning would explain, for example, why 'bad/ rubbish/horrendous/crap/shit' in a frame such as 'that's X' seem different, each, I suspect, expressing an increasingly negative attitude towards the thing referred to. My particular choice at the end of these example adjectives of taboo words is not incidental; as Jay (1992: 63) remarks, taboo words 'intensify descriptions'.

   What kind of words are considered to carry strong negative affective meaning? This question could be rephrased as what words are likely to cause strong offence. With regard to British culture, various surveys have been carried out, usually by media bodies concerned about what to censor. For example, a noteworthy piece of research, involving a questionnaire delivered to 1,033 informants, is Millwood-Hargrave (2000). This was commissioned as a joint project by the Advertising Standards Authority, the British Broadcasting Corporation (BBC), the Broadcasting Standards Commission and the Independent

Television Commission. The research investigated people's attitudes to swearing and offensive language, and also examined the role of context.

It needs to be emphasised yet again that there is no claim that these words are equally offensive in all contexts. Indeed, one of the points of the study was to emphasise variation according to context. A 'national culture' is made up of many cultures, as emphasised in Introducing impoliteness. For example, the research found that *bastard* was more likely to be thought 'very severe' in the Midlands and north of England (40% and 39%, respectively) than in the south (26%), and that women were more likely to think it 'very severe' than men (43% and 21% respectively) (2000: 11). It also revealed interesting cultural diachronic shifts. Racially related words, particularly *nigger* and *paki*, have experienced huge shifts up the ranking. Millwood-Hargrave (2000) did not explore the usage of these words in particular situations. However, Jay (1992, 2008), working on North American data, has done precisely that. He demonstrates how people are sensitive to the kind of speaker, location and the specific word used. For example, he provides evidence that people think that it is less appropriate for a dean to swear compared with a student; that it is more appropriate for the dean to swear in the office than anywhere else on campus; and that it is very inappropriate for the student to swear in the Dean's office yet appropriate in the student dorm (Jay and Janschewitz 2008: 283). On the other hand, Jay cautions that 'in all contexts the actual taboo word used greatly affects appropriateness' (Jay and Janschewitz 2008: 283). Moreover, note that the top four items in Table 4.1 remain unchanged. This supports my argument that the more offensive the item the more context-spanning it is likely to be.

The kind of negatively affective words I have been discussing here have also been treated by Allan and Burridge (1991, 2006) under the heading 'dysphemism'. A 'dysphemism' is considered the opposite of a euphemism and defined thus:

A dysphemism is an expression with connotations that are offensive either about the denotatum or to the audience, or both, and it is substituted for a neutral or euphemistic expression for just that reason. (Allan and Burridge 1991: 26)

The notion of connotations is not often defined, but Allan and Burridge (2006: 31) gives the following useful definition:

The connotations of a word or longer expression are semantic effects (nuances of meaning) that arise from encyclopaedic knowledge about the word's denotation and also from experience, beliefs and prejudices about the contexts in which the word is typically used.

This neatly fits my understanding of the contextual meanings associated with conventional impoliteness expressions. In fact, they explicitly state that impolite behaviour is dysphemistic (2006: 32). As I indicated above, an important

Table 4.1 *Words and offensiveness in Britain in the year 2000 (the numbers in brackets indicate the rank order in a parallel study in 1997)*

Rank-ordered 1–14	Rank-ordered 15–28
1. Cunt (1)	15. Spastic (14)
2. Motherfucker (2)	16. Slag (18)
3. Fuck (3)	17. Shit (15)
4. Wanker (4)	18. Dickhead (19)
5. Nigger (11)	19. Pissed off (16)
6. Bastard (5)	20. Arse (20)
7. Prick (7)	21. Bugger (21)
8. Bollocks (6)	22. Balls (22)
9. Arsehole (9)	23. Jew (24)
10. Paki (17)	24. Sodding (23)
11. Shag (8)	25. Jesus Christ (26)
12. Whore (13)	26. Crap (25)
13. Twat (10)	27. Bloody (27)
14. Piss off (12)	28. God (28)

context for negatively affective words or dysphemisms is insults. Allan and Burridge's (2006: 79) comment on insults gives a good sense of the semantic field to which insulting words belong:

Insults are normally intended to wound the addressee or bring a third party into disrepute, or both. They are therefore intrinsically dysphemistic, and so typically taboo and subject to censorship. Insults typically pick on and debase a person's physical appearance, mental ability, character, behaviour, beliefs and/or familial and social relations. Thus insults are sourced in the target's supposed ugliness, skin colour and/or complexion, over- or undersize (too small, too short, too tall, too fat, too thin), perceived physical defects (short-sighted, squint, big nose, sagging breasts, small dick, deformed limb), slovenliness, dirtiness, smelliness, tardiness, stupidity, untruthfulness, unreliability, unpunctuality, incompetence, incontinence, greediness, meanness, sexual laxness or perversion, sexual persuasion, violence towards others (even self), ideological or religious persuasion, social or economic status, and social ineptitude. And additionally, supposed inadequacies on any of the grounds just listed among the target's family, friends and acquaintances.

Of course, this list need not stop here (and indeed Allan and Burridge go on to add detail). What essentially we are dealing with are items that are attributed a low value within a particular culture, items that damage some aspect of face. However, we should not think that what counts as having low value within a particular culture cannot be characterised in terms of typicality. Jay (1992: 169), for example, found that there is 'general agreement that American [adult] taboos are those stemming from terms for body parts, body products, body processes, religious, animal, and ethnic terms, as well as social deviations and ancestral allusions'.

It is worth briefly returning to the classic linguistic items which appear in the studies of intensity, namely, intensifying modifiers. Consider differences among the following expressions: 'you're hopeless', 'you're so hopeless', 'you're shit', 'you're so shit' and 'you're fucking shit'. Not only can nouns and adjectives used to refer to people be loaded with positive or negative affective meaning, but words used as intensifiers can also be thus imbued. An intensifier such as *so* deflates the low value of the item to which it refers yet further. Taboo intensifiers also perform this function by virtue of the fact that they fill the intensifier slot, as for example 'fucking lazy' (=extremely lazy) (also note: 'fuck all' (=nothing at all), and 'what the fuck' (=what on earth)). However, an intensifier such as *fuck* not only performs this deflationary function, but also intensifies the emotional experience for the perceiver (cf. Jay 1992: 11). A taboo intensifier itself can violate the social norms of particular groups about appropriate language. Such intensifiers, then, are an effective way of increasing the intensity of conventional impoliteness expressions.

In concluding this section, let us examine the two word conventional impoliteness formula *shut up*. Frequently, it is not at all impolite, as the following example illustrates:

[3]

> **Fiction** They heard Ashton's teasing voice wafting down the stairwell. 'We'll be home around midnight or one. Just warning you two romantics so we don't catch you by surprise when we come back.'
> '*Shut up* and go get your date you ass,' Brian's voice shot back. (*OEC*)

Of course, this is a written example (posing as speech). We work out from the context that it is unlikely that Brian is using the prosody that usually contributes to this conventional impoliteness formula; he is unlikely to use a raised voice, a sharply falling intonation contour with a high onset, and so on. On the contrary, it is more likely that we are supposed to imagine him avoiding these things in order to signal that he is in fact reciprocating the teasing. After all, he is commanding Ashton to do something of benefit to him ('go get your date'). However, this formula can be modified in other ways, as the following example illustrates:

[4]

> **Law** Shortly thereafter, while the witness and her father were getting into the car to be driven to some friends, she observed her mother from the balcony yelling at her father not to 'even think about bringing my daughter in that car with a gun in there.' Upon hearing this, the father's response was, "*Shut the fuck up*, you stupid bitch." (*OEC*)

The intensifying and taboo infix 'the fuck' exacerbates the offence. Moreover, all the examples of 'shut the fuck up' in their differing contexts given in the

OEC seem to be taken as impolite, and are often followed by an insulting vocative, as here. *Shut up* does have a strong correlation with impoliteness events in the *OEC* data, but does not clearly exceed the 50 per cent level (it can express, for instance, solidarity, as above). In contrast, *shut the fuck up*, has a stronger correlation, clearly exceeding 50 per cent, hence this formula type was included in my list of conventionalised impoliteness formulae in Section 4.4.3.

4.5.3 Prosodic and non-verbal ways of achieving message intensity

Let us start with an example from the quiz show *The Weakest Link*, which evolved on the BBC but is now franchised to many different parts of the world. I will describe this kind of show more thoroughly in Section 7.6.2. Central to the success of the show has been the host, Anne Robinson, and her acerbic style. As the BBC website proclaims, she is well-known for particular 'contemptuous and dismissive' phrases, and has earned the 'title of the Rudest Woman on Television'. The catchphrase I will consider here is 'you leave with nothing' (it can be heard on the web, for example, on the audio page of *The Weakest Link* Depository). This is said at the point when one of the contestants leaves the show because they are designated as having the lowest score in answering the quiz-style questions. In itself 'you leave with nothing' is a conventionalised impoliteness formula: it is a personalised negative assertion, displaying the fact that the target failed to win anything – they are an abject failure. Figure 4.1 displays the results of an instrumental analysis of the prosody.

The figure consists of three tiers. The top tier represents fluctuations in air pressure, providing an indication of relative loudness (intensity) and duration; the middle represents changes in pitch (fundamental frequency expressed in Hertz) over time, providing an indication of the intonation contour of the utterance; the bottom represents the words that were spoken. Note that there is no direct relationship between these representations and meaning. They are cues that may trigger the perception of phonological features, and then those features may in turn be used in an inference process to generate particular meanings. An important feature of this catchphrase is that it forms two distinct tone units, 'you leave with' and 'nothing'. The break here occurs between the preposition 'with' and its complement 'nothing': it is a salient disruption. To understand this break, one needs to remember what happens in standard game shows. When a contestant must leave, they leave with a prize, even if it is only a consolation prize, and the host announces the prize as a surprise: hence, rising intonation on 'you leave with', and then a dramatic pause before the prize is revealed. Anne Robinson's impoliteness here partly feeds off this background knowledge: instead of the expected prize, the contestant gets 'nothing'. Also, note that the second tone unit does not contain the kind of prosody one might

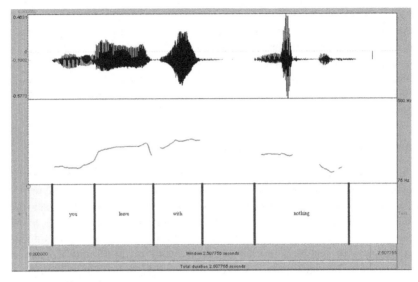

Figure 4.1 Instrumental analysis of 'you leave with nothing'

expect of jubilation. 'Nothing' steps down the pitch range, relative to the proceeding discourse, and contains a falling tone, thereby adding an air of deflation and a sense of finality (cf. Wichmann 2000a: 69–71). The explicit withholding or frustration of reward can be seen as Equity rights impoliteness, as it works by reminding the contestant that a 'benefit' has been withheld (it also has secondary implications for Quality Face, as withholding the benefit implies that the contestant was not good enough to merit it).

Remarkably, the bulk of research on politeness or impoliteness pays woefully little attention to the role of prosody (for an account of prosody, politeness and impoliteness, see Culpeper forthcoming b). The single exception of note is the politeness work of Arndt and Janney (e.g. 1985, 1987), and for that reason I will devote some space to it here. Their notion of politeness involves emotional support conveyed multimodally through verbal, vocal and kinesic cues. According to Arndt and Janney (1987: 248, et passim), 'utterances become "meaningful" – by which we mean interpretable – only through the interaction of verbal, prosodic, and kinesic actions in context'. Consistent with this position, they point out that '[i]t seems that it is not the simple occurrence per se of prosodic effects that is significant in interpersonal communication, but the distribution and intensity of these effects in relation to the acoustic bass line (cf. Crystal and Davy 1969: 108)' (1987: 227–8). The chief merit of Arndt and Janney (1987) is a systematic and detailed discussion of how words and structures, prosody and kinesic features interact and create meaning in communication. Of particular relevance to the concerns of this section is their discussion of attitudinally marked prosody. They argue that it is unexpected prosodies that trigger the search for attitudinal interpretations, including 'interpersonal interpretations, e.g., the customer wants to insult me (he's being arrogant, impolite, dominating, etc. on purpose, who does he think he is?)' (1987: 273). Attitudinally marked intonation contours they define as those that are not clearly motivated by syntactic considerations (1987: 273–4). For example, a declarative has the expectation of a falling intonation contour, and so a rise would be attitudinally marked. They suggest the following set of possibilities:

(1) *rising pitch* together with declarative, imperative or wh- interrogative utterance types would be considered attitudinally marked;

(2) *falling pitch* together with all other interrogative utterance types would be considered attitudinally marked;

(3) *falling-rising* pitch, as a mixed contour, would be considered attitudinally relevant, regardless of the utterance type with which it is combined;

(4) *all remaining combinations* of pitch direction and utterance type – i.e., the so-called 'normal' ones, grammatically speaking, would be considered attitudinally relevant only in conjunction with other types of cues or cue combinations.

Arndt and Janney (1987: 275)

The first three items all involve 'contrastive patterning', which Arndt and Janney view as 'central to emotive communication' (1987: 369). They also discuss 'redundant patterning', but 'redundant patterning amplifies verbal messages', whereas 'contrastive patterning modulates or modifies them' (1987: 369). The use of contrast between what is said and how it is said in the case of irony or sarcasm is an illustration of the latter. I will have much to say about contrastive patterning in the following chapter (an excellent illustration is example [2] of Introducing impoliteness). Here, what concerns me is the intensification of verbal messages through redundant patterning.

The label 'redundant' is open to misinterpretation. Though not spelt out in Arndt and Janney, the technical sence of redundancy here is that of information theory:

The term *redundant*... was given a new technical meaning by Shannon and Weaver (1949), namely, to describe signs or behaviors that serve to reduce the ambiguity of a message. In information theory, redundant acts are not viewed as unnecessary but rather as serving to increase the likelihood of a correct decoding of the meaning. (Bavelas and Chovil 2000: 185)

Rather than redundant, I will use the term matching; and rather than contrastive, I will use the term mismatching. A key issue here is: what exactly is being (mis)matched? Prosodic features can be (mis)matched with various other features in order to achieve markedness, not just syntactic features. Indeed, one of the key aims of analyses in the following chapters is to show how the context, in particular the co-text but also the situation, contribute to establishing a speaker's prosody as marked. One can also match and mismatch at various levels simultaneously. This is particularly relevant to the intensification of conventional impoliteness formulae. By definition, something that is intensified or amplified mismatches attitudinal neutrality. On the other hand, intensifying conventional impoliteness formulae is a matter of making them less equivocal, not actually changing the 'message' being conveyed – and this is why Arndt and Janney (1987) would consider this redundancy (specifically, they are concerned with how cues relate to the emotional message, cf. 1987: 367–9).

The important role prosodic features play in disambiguating messages has been repeatedly demonstrated in research in communication (e.g. Archer and Ackert 1977; DePaulo and Friedman 1998). By intensifying the message in particular ways, the prosody leaves us in no doubt – or at least less doubt – about how to understand that message. One way in which this works is through a link between certain prosodies and certain emotions. A line of research carried out by researchers, often psychologists, on the interface between linguistics and psychology focuses on this link and asks the research question: what are the acoustic correlates of which emotions? Answering this question is fraught with problems on both sides, the acoustics and the emotions. Which features or which combinations of features are the ones that are key in emotional expression and perception? What does the label 'emotion' refer to – the physiological arousal, the subjective feeling or the use of language to express those feelings? Also, emotions are not static but part of a process. A more general methodological difficulty with these studies (see Frick 1985; Scherer 1986; Murray and Arnott 1993, for numerous references), and one that is particularly pertinent to the subject of impoliteness, is that these studies are lab-based and focus on an assumed direct relationship between vocal features and emotional meanings without the messiness of context. Nevertheless, whilst there are methodological problems, a mass of studies have revealed covariation between particular acoustic features and particular emotions. It is a mistake, of course, to assume that such covariation necessarily holds in any particular real-life communication, but we can assume that there are default meanings for some acoustic features or, more accurately, some combinations of acoustic features, based on people's knowledge of these regular covariations.

The default meanings of acoustic emotional displays are an interactional resource that speakers can draw on and exploit in the delivery of conventional impoliteness formulae. The literature in the area of acoustic features and emotions has been regularly reviewed (e.g. Frick 1985; Scherer 1986; Murray and Arnott 1993), and these reviews help identify the more robust patterns of covariation and thus possible default meanings. I shall not supply the detailed surveys that they do, but instead pick out findings from Murray and Arnott (1993) for two emotions particularly relevant to impoliteness events:

Anger (rage): slightly faster, much higher pitch average, wide pitch range, louder, breathy, chest tone, abrupt pitch changes on stressed syllables, tense articulation (Murray and Arnott 1993: 1103–4, 1106).

Disgust (hatred, contempt, scorn): very slow speech rate, much lower pitch average, slightly wider pitch range, quieter, grumbled, chest tone, wide falling terminal contours, normal articulation (Murray and Arnott 1993: 1104–5, 1106).

Of these two emotions, there is considerably more agreement on the acoustic cues of anger than disgust in the literature (Banse and Scherer 1996: 614–6). A swift example from my report data involving the acoustic characteristics of anger is the following:

[5]
> A flatmate at University banged on my door + demanded to come in, but he was drunk and stoned so I refused to let him, because I said no he called me and tried to force entry. He started raising his voice and ended up shouting loud enough that my other flatmates came out and had to hold him back. I probably provoked him slightly by raising my voice back but I was annoyed by his outburst and upset by what he was saying.

It is not simply the fact that an unwanted 'demand' is being made but that the speaker was 'raising his voice' and 'shouting'.

Prosodic intensification, of course, need not be limited to using particular bundles of acoustic features to index particular emotions which, depending on context, then help create or bolster impoliteness. It can interact in many other ways with what is being said, in a more rhetorical fashion as noted at the end of Section 4.4.3, in order to help secure the impoliteness uptake. Example [6] from my report data illustrates the use of stress, both placement and degree, to exacerbate a conventional insult:

[6]
> I was having a conversation with a few of my friends and one of my friends said 'you are so gay'. This comment was said when we were all sitting around the kitchen table and was said in a slightly aggressive way with the word 'gay' being accentuated. The conversation carried on and nobody made a comment.

This informant's comment indicates the key role stress played in arriving at an impoliteness judgement: 'It didn't really bother me that much but it was just the fact that the word "gay" seemed to be used in a negative way towards me.'

The near final sentences of Ofuka *et al.*'s (2000: 215) paper on prosodic cues for politeness in Japanese are worth noting:

People appear to be very sensitive to unnaturalness by their standards and this listener-specific sensitivity may bias politeness judgements. A single extreme value for any acoustic feature (e.g., very fast speech rate) may reduce perceived politeness, but this will differ listener by listener.

Extreme values – that is, extreme in terms of what the participant expects in that context – for any acoustic feature in the delivery of a conventionalised impoliteness formula can exacerbate the offensiveness: they seem to point to extreme attitudes. Of course, extreme acoustic values do not in themselves necessarily lead to a judgement of impoliteness, as the above quotation seems to suggest. Consider this meta-impoliteness comment on 'tone of voice' drawn from a North American weblog:

[7]
> Anyone have any ideas on how to quell the nasty tone of voice? This seems to a constant struggle in our house. Instead of using a polite tone of voice to ask a question or make a request, there is that demanding, whiny voice, especially when my kids talk to each other. I can remember my parents saying to me 'It's not WHAT you said, it's HOW you said it.'
> http://midvalleymoms.com/index.php?q=tone_of_voice

The 'tone of voice' is negatively evaluated, being described at the outset as 'nasty'. Because it is contrasted with 'a polite tone of voice', it is by implication an impolite tone of voice. Moreover, it is impolite in a specific pragmatic context, namely, that of asking a question or making a request. In this context it becomes 'demanding', probably because it conflicts with the normal and/or prescribed social organisation of the family in this culture, namely, that only parents have the power to demand. Even when the 'kids talk to each other', this tone of voice is proscribed in the family context. Regarding the specifics of the voice, we learn that it is 'whiny', an auditory description that suggests the voice is markedly high-pitched and enduring. The point is that the mere presence of a particular 'tone of voice' in a particular context can be enough to act as a cue for impoliteness. Importantly, a very high pitched voice is not in itself impolite – it could, for example, signal happy excitement. As Arntd and Janney (1987: 343) observe of pitch prominence, extremes are 'generally interpreted as sign of emotional involvement', and this could be either positive or negative. In fact, B&L (1987: 268) make the following generalisation that high pitch is associated with negative politeness usage:

> . . . high pitch has natural associations with the voice quality of children: for an adult speaker to use such a feature to another adult may implicate self-humbling and thus deference (B&L 1974). We predict therefore that sustained high pitch (maintained over a number of utterances) will be a feature of negative-politeness usage, and creaky voice a feature of positive-politeness usage, and that a reversal of these associations will not occur in any culture. (B&L 1987: 268)

Of course, they are talking about the specific context of discourse between adults, but note that the rationale for this polite 'self-humbling' is the vocal characteristics of children. Clearly, they did not have whining in mind! To be fair, whining does suggest extremely high pitch sustained over a period of time, which is probably not a characteristic of the kind of scenario that B&L were thinking of. But it is more than this. Whining involves not just extremely high pitch but also, as I pointed out, a particular context, such as the family and more specifically a child requesting something from a parent. It is this tone of voice in this context that is likely to evoke impoliteness.

Non-verbal visual cues, even more than oral/aural cues, are neglected in politeness and impoliteness research. Again, the notable exception is Arndt and Janney (1987: Chapter 7, especially). As with oral/aural aspects, they are an interactional resource that participants can use to boost the impoliteness of a conventionalised impoliteness formula or create impoliteness for an expression where none had been obvious in a particular context. My report data never flagged up visual cues. However, this is probably a consequence of the fact that informants were asked to 'collect records of conversations in which someone *said* something' (my emphasis). Here, I will very briefly overview some relevant features.

Non-verbal visual cues such as gaze, facial expressions, body move-ments/gestures (e.g. with the head, shoulders, hands) and the spatial positioning of the self play a key role in communication (see Bavelas and Chovil 2000: 164, for numerous references). Yet it is still an area that receives relatively little attention in communication and pragmatics studies. As with prosody, it is a mistake to assume that non-verbal cues are separable from other aspects of the communication (with the exception of a few gestural 'emblems', e.g. the thumbs up, the two-fingered gesture). Behaviour is a multimodal stream, with one modality interacting with other modalities to create a whole. Moreover, as I observed in Section 4.3.2, there is a high degree of redundancy, in the technical sense of reducing ambiguities and equivocations of meaning.

Different non-verbal areas have been associated with different socio-emotional aspects. Facial expressions may be described with reference to the state of specific facial components: the forehead, eyebrows, eyes (including eyelids), nose, cheeks, mouth (including lips), and chin. When the face is neu-tral, and thus relatively uninformative, the facial muscles are relaxed. The bulk of empirical research on facial expressions has investigated their correlation with particular emotions, notably surprise, fear, anger, disgust, sadness and happiness (e.g. Ekman *et al.* 1971). According to Ekman *et al.* (1971), anger is associated with such characteristics as the eyebrows being pulled down and inward, the lower eyelids being tensed and raised, and the lips being pressed tightly together or an open, squared mouth with lips raised. How one positions oneself in relation to other people broadly correlates with the degree of social distance that pertains. This has been a well-established research finding since Edward Hall (1966) first comprehensively investigated spatial distance between people. The norm for everyday interactions with friends and acquaintances, for example, is 0.5–1.25 metres. This, of course, will be subject to great cultural variation. Hall introduced the notion of 'personal space'. Transgressions of personal space can leave people feeling uncomfortable or even threatened. Gaze direction and duration has rather complex, context-dependent meanings. However, it is interesting to note that sustained gaze can express dominance or even threat. Ellsworth *et al.* (1972) set up an experiment whereby one of the research team stared at some drivers waiting at a crossroads. Those who were stared at departed more rapidly. As with prosody, non-verbal visual aspects are not confined to indexing socio-emotional meanings, but are designed to interact with the verbal stream of talk. Let us take two examples, eyebrow movements and pointing. Chovil (1991–1992) and Ekman (1979) have discussed how eyebrow movements can act as 'syntactic stressors', in much the same way as intonational stress. Sometimes functions of pointing are more deictic than gestural, though the two cannot be completely separated (consider that the original Greek sense of deixis means to point). A particularly relevant function is that it can make unambiguous the target of an insult. But pointing can also be oriented to the verbal message: a wagging finger can help identify new and important information, again in much the same way as intonational stress.

4.6   Conclusion

Aggressive facework is all too often ignored or given minimal space in the literature. When it is tackled, the main problem is that the connection between aggressivework practices and context is not fully articulated. I noted Tracy and Tracy's (1998) useful scalar distinction between context-dependent and context-spanning aggressive facework. This chapter has focused on relatively context-spanning conventionalised impoliteness formulae. I considered arguments for politeness being wholly inherent in linguistic expressions. In fact, it is very difficult to find mainstream supporters of this position. Discursive scholars who oppose it are, to an extent, shooting at a straw target. Discursive work, perhaps by definition, is focused on dynamic, locally constructed meanings. However, I argued that critics of discursive work have also been shooting at something of a straw target, as such approaches do accommodate local norms. Nevertheless, the impression discursive approaches give is of great instability of meaning and uncertainty in communication. This impression does not square with the intuitions we share with others in our communities about conventionalised meanings even out of context, nor with the evidence for a large amount of informational redundancy in multimodal communication – all of which points towards stability and certainty (though of course these can never be absolute).

My own position might be described as dual: there is a semantics side and a pragmatics side to impoliteness, both being interdependent opposites on a scale, neither guaranteeing an interpretation that something is impolite in context.

A conventionalised impoliteness formula is a form of language in which context-specific impoliteness effects are conventionalised. I approached this issue via conventionalised politeness formulae, reporting the work of Marina Terkourafi, where it is argued that they arise as a result of regularities of co-occurrence between unchallenged expressions and particular types of context. My next step was to take this forward with respect to impoliteness. The problem here is that people have knowledge of impoliteness formulae which far exceeds their direct experience of them. So, frequency cannot be the sole or even dominant factor in their conventionalisation. I argued that indirect experiences play a key role in the conventionalisation of impoliteness formulae, and especially experience of metadiscourse (see Chapter 3). This metadiscourse is the long shadow of impoliteness behaviours. It is partly driven by the salience of any impoliteness behaviour, but also by the fact that that metadiscourse is part of the social dynamic that makes a behaviour count as impolite in the first place. Impoliteness behaviours rupture ideologically embedded social norms – principles of action jointly accepted by members of groups who demonstrate their group membership by upholding those principles in impoliteness metadiscourse.

I proposed two methodologies for investigating conventionalised impoliteness formulae, one being to investigate the expressions to which impoliteness metadiscourse orients, and the other being to focus on regularities of expression in impoliteness contexts. I had already demonstrated the first method in Section 3.9. A limitation here is that whilst good at revealing pragmatic strategies those strategies may or may not have specific linguistic expressions embedded within them. The second methodology involved contexts associated with impoliteness events. I collected utterances accompanied by participant evidence that somebody had construed them as impolite. With Pattern Grammar in mind, I then generated a list of conventionalised impoliteness formulae in English. The fact that my list of conventionalised impoliteness formulae was devised on the basis of frequency in specific types of context is something that it has in common with Terkourafi's account of politeness formulae. I proposed that conventionalised impoliteness formulae vary according to three scales: degree of conventionalisation, the extent to which they are context-dependent or context-spanning, and the degree of offence they are associated with. I hypothesised that these scales are linked: more offensive items are more context-spanning and more conventionalised.

Section 4.5 was devoted to the exacerbation of the offensiveness of conventionalised impoliteness formulae. I argued that the intensification of such formulae is more than an optional extra; it is part of what makes impolite formulae attitudinally extreme, less equivocal and more likely to cause the target to take offence (cf. Young 2004). I proposed that this is achieved primarily in two ways. One is through message intensity, the use of words which are strongly negatively affective, including taboo words, and/or modifiers, some of which can also be strongly negatively affective *per se*. The other is through non-verbal, especially prosodic, intensification. With respect to conventionalised impoliteness formulae, they can be intensified by matching prosody (i.e. by redundant patterning). The prosody can index a relevant emotion (e.g. anger, disgust), or, more rhetorically, an extreme acoustic value can reinforce an extreme attitude and emotional involvement.

5 Non-conventionalised impoliteness: Implicational impoliteness

5.1 Introduction

Needless to say, many impoliteness events do not involve conventionalised impoliteness formulae at all. Fifty-nine of my 100 reported impoliteness events did not involve conventional impoliteness formulae. Instead, informants interpreted what was said (or done) or not said (or done) in a particular context as impolite, despite the fact that what was said (or done) was not 'pre-loaded' for impoliteness. In this chapter, I propose a classification for what I will call implicational impoliteness, derived from analyses of how impoliteness was implied/inferred in my data, both my diary report data and other data sources. This chapter focuses on particular behaviours as triggers for impoliteness attributions in impoliteness events. My use of the term behaviour refers to behaviours in their multimodal fullness. It is more difficult to specify where 'a behaviour' in interaction begins and where it ends. Typically, their upper limit is that they never exceed one conversational turn; their lower limit is that they must consist of some communicative material, be it as little as a single word or gesture; their norm is that they contain one or two clauses (which can be reduced) or gestures; their cohesive principle is that all parts must contribute to the same pragmatic strategy or move. Of course, in interpreting these behaviours I will need to bring in the broader context. As far as my diary report data is concerned, it is worth remembering that what counts as the impolite behaviour and what counts as relevant in understanding it is designated by the informant.

My classification of implicational impoliteness contains three groups, varying according to the way in which the implication might be triggered:

(1) *Form-driven*: the surface form or semantic content of a behaviour is marked.
(2) *Convention-driven*:
    (a) Internal: the context projected by part of a behaviour mismatches that projected by another part; or
    (b) External: the context projected by a behaviour mismatches the context of use.

(3) *Context-driven*:
   (a) *Unmarked behaviour*: an unmarked (with respect to surface form or semantic content) and unconventionalised behaviour mismatches the context; or
   (b) *Absence of behaviour*: the absence of a behaviour mismatches the context.

Convention (and conventionalised) here refers specifically to either politeness or impoliteness conventions of the type discussed in the previous chapter. Regarding marked, there is a general sense in which all impoliteness triggers are marked – they are all abnormal in some way. But my use of the term marked is restricted to aspects of the surface form or semantic content. I have in mind deviations from pragmatic principles governing the exchange of information between participants, most famously formalised by Grice in his Cooperative Principle (1975), though further developed by various Neo-Griceans (e.g. Levinson 2000). All the remaining triggers rely on mismatches with the context of various kinds. With regard to 'context-driven', of course, all impoliteness is influenced by context. Here, I am referring specifically to the occasions where the behaviour *per se* is not in any obvious way the main trigger for the impoliteness implication/inference.

It is possible to characterise these groups in terms of the scale of conventionalisation discussed in Section 4.4.1, running from the more semantic to the more contextual. It runs from group 1, which could include inferencing of the more generalised type (i.e. generalised implicature II), to the more restricted inferencing of group 2 (i.e. generalised implicature I), to the more particularised inferencing of group 3a, and finally to the entirely knowledge-based inferencing of group 3b. However, I have not characterised my groups thus, for two reasons: (1) my discussion of implications and inferencing is not restricted to the production and recovery of implicatures, and (2) group 1 is not restricted to generalised implicatures but also includes particularised implicatures.[1]

The following sections follow the order of the groups proposed above the previous paragraph. In the final section of this chapter, I step back and look at directness (or explicitness, as I prefer) and how that might interact with gravity of offence.

5.2   Implicational impoliteness: Form-driven

By form-driven here I am referring to form-driven triggers for implication/inferential impoliteness except for cases that are conventionally impolite. The impoliteness I am dealing with overlaps with various phenomena to which everyday terms such as 'insinuation', 'innuendo', 'casting aspersions', 'digs', 'snide comments/remarks', and so on refer. Although these terms are far from consistent in their application and refer to a diffuse range of phenomena, they have in common the fact that they refer to implicit messages which are triggered by formal surface or semantic aspects of a behaviour and which have negative consequences for certain individuals. I will also deal with what is often referred to as 'mimicry' here. In some ways, this kind of implicational impoliteness seems to fit B&L's (1987) description of the off-record polite-ness super-strategy, but there are two important differences. Firstly, and most obviously, the inference results in the ascription of impoliteness, involving the conceptual notions discussed in this book, and not politeness. Secondly, and perhaps most importantly, is the degree to which an alternative 'polite' inter-pretation is possible. The possibility of such an alternative is a central part of the definition of off-record politeness (B&L 1987: 211, 212). But with regard to the phenomena under scrutiny here such an alternative is less likely or ludi-crously implausible. The act of having performed the trigger is enough to do the damage; trying to deny responsibility for the damage can make matters worse. With regard to innuendo, Bell (1997: 46–7) highlights the consequences of this for implicature:

Innuendo . . . is a manifestation of the use of implicature in a particular form of social behavior. As such the social properties of innuendo tend to distinguish it from the logical properties of implicature. And this is the case with respect to what has been held to be the most prominent distinguishing characteristic of a conversational impli-cature: cancellability. . . . Whereas cancelling a conversational implicature may involve the articulation of what is already considered to be mutually manifest, the cancellation or denial of an innuendo articulates and so makes more explicit what is considered to be non-mutually manifest. A classic example of the way in which the non-overt message in an innuendo can be made explicit by an act of apparent cancellation occurred in the 1992 Presidential election. During the campaign, President Bush's deputy press officer, Mary Matalin, was criticized for putting out what was described as a 'snarling' press release attacking Bill Clinton. In an interview with the press, Matalin defended herself against accusations of sleaze: 'We've never said to the press that he's a philandering, pot smoking draft dodger.' (*New York Times*, 5 August 1992: A22)

As we shall see from the examples, it is also the case that prosody and other intensifying techniques are used to ensure that we are guided to the 'impolite' interpretation. We should also note that there is one sense perhaps in which the phenomena here do not overlap with the everyday terms above: they are almost always addressed to the person for whom the consequences of the behaviour are negative. In contrast with this, Bell (1997: 51–2) observes that generally the target of innuendo is rarely the addressee, while noting exceptions such as discourse in the courtroom between cross-examiners and witnesses/ defendants.

The examples in this section all rely on some kind of marked surface form or semantic content relative to Gricean Cooperativeness (cf. 1975). Of course, it may seem to be absolute nonsense to apply a 'co-operative' principle to data that are strikingly uncooperative. The solution taken by researchers dealing with uncooperative data (e.g. Thomas 1986; Pavlidou 1991; and, specifically treating impoliteness, Bousfield 2008: chapter 2) is to make a distinction between formal or linguistic cooperation and extralinguistic or social cooperation. By restricting Gricean cooperativeness to the former, we can account for why it is that even when people are being confrontational, impolite, and so on, they can still exchange information sufficiently to perform the confrontation. There are, however, some concerns about how separable formal cooperation is from social, extra-linguistic cooperation (see Sarangi and Slembrouck 1992). But Lumsden (2008: 1903) points out that Grice was aware of problematic cases such as quarrelling, which is why his description of the Cooperative Principle refers not only to 'a common purpose or set of purposes' but adds 'or at least a mutually accepted direction' (Grice 1989: 26). He argues that we need not opt for one kind of cooperation only. Instead, we can opt for a more constrained version of cooperation in the absence of the broader:

where there is cooperation with a broader [extra-linguistic, social] goal it is this goal that appears to determine relevance and so forth in the conversation... where there is no extra-linguistic cooperation we can fall back on merely linguistic cooperation.

Needless to say, the operation of the Cooperative Principle will depend on the context. For example, what counts as a clear and straightforward expression will partly depend on the genre of which it is a part. At the beginning of the following chapter, I will briefly mention the notion of 'activity type', a notion that can help contextualise the workings of the Cooperative Principle (see Mooney 2004: 903–5, for elaboration of this point; see Culpeper 2005a, for how activity types can play a role in inferencing and impoliteness). The first four of the following examples show how a Gricean account can capture some aspects of impoliteness. Each example will illustrate the operation of a particular maxim. The remaining examples and discussion in this section focus on mimicry. Although these could be explained in terms of Grice, such an explanation would be clearly inadequate. Thus, I will deploy the relevance-theoretic account of irony, that is, the echoic mention view (e.g. Sperber and Wilson 1981, 1995 [1986]).

Implicational impoliteness: Examples that fit the Gricean account

[1]
'Uh, Im always tidying this fucking room' – person X
Implied I never tidy the living room (which isn't true!)
Said in the living room, semi-angry, emphasising 'always'.
Said by a housemate. No one else was there.
My response – silent annoyance

The offender's statement flouts the Maxim of Quality, at least from the informant's point of view. It is false to say that he is 'always' tidying the room.

Inferencing needs to be undertaken for the impolite implication to be drawn: if he is 'always' tidying the room, other people, including the informant, are not tidying it. Interestingly, note the role of intensification here. The key word 'always' seems to have been stressed, and the statement is emotionally intensified by the addition of the word 'fucking'.

[2]

> Meeting up in a café with friends in the holiday after all being at different universities for the term.
>
> We were all talking about our various course, one of my friends said something like –
>
> 'It's cool we've got one of each . . . a lawyer, a medic, an economist . . . ' and then everyone looked at me . . . 'and Sue'

Here, the offender flouts the Maxim of Manner, specifically the sub-maxim 'be orderly'. The offender creates regularity by listing three professions, and then she or he breaks that regularity by adding a personal name, Sue. The markedness of this deviation from an internally established regularity seems to be enhanced prosodically by a pause before the final item. The impoliteness implication is that Sue is the odd one out.

[3]

> Sitting with housemates in the lounge and one comes in after finishing making her tea. She sits close to me and my other housemate ie within close earshot and says
>
> 'see I made a curry that doesn't come out of a jar',
>
> Knowing full well that I eat food like that which she clearly looks down upon.

In example [3] the offender supplies more information about the curry than seems to be necessary, thus flouting the Maxim of Quantity, yet clearly has a message to convey (cf. 'see'). Given the context – knowledge that the informant eats curries that 'come out of a jar' and that food from a jar is generally considered inferior to freshly made food – the impolite implication that the informant eats inferior food can be drawn.

[4]

> I was at a Christmas Ball with friends and one friend was telling me about another girls dress and how expensive it was. I, for a fact, knew the girl in question and that her dress wasn't the price the other girl was saying but she still persisted it was. I said 'I know X and she wouldn't spend that amount on a dress' and the girl replied saying something like 'Well you may not, coz well . . . (and points to my dress). This made me feel hurt and upset. I didn't respond to this.

This example involves a more complex web of inferencing. The referents of 'you' and of the deictic pointing need to be inferred (i.e. the informant and the dress). Not only this but the informant reports heavy stress (as presumably indicated by the underlining) on 'you' and a possible pause before the deictic action. These features could be taken as flouts of the Maxim of Manner. In the context of the offender's previous arguments that this girl would buy an expensive dress, the informant can infer the impoliteness implications: in contrast to the girl, the informant in particular would not spend that amount of money on a dress, and evidence that she would not spend that amount of money on a dress is in the kind of dress she is wearing currently. Not spending money on clothes can be associated with negative values such as being poor or miserly (needless to say, this only pertains to some group value systems!).

[5]
> As I walked over to the table to collect the glasses, Sarah said to Tim 'come on Tim lets go outside', implying she didn't want me there. This was at the pub on Sunday night, and I just let the glasses go and walked away.
>
> I didn't particularly feel bad, but angry at the way she had said that straight away when I got there. We aren't particularly friends but she was really rude in front of others.

The interpretation of example [5] partly rests on assumptions about for whom the message is intended. Clearly, the informant assumes that, whilst the addressee is Tim, the target is her, something which seems to be supported by the fact that it was said 'straight away when I got there'. It is possible, of course, that the offender also used non-verbal means to clarify the target, such as looking at her whilst she spoke. Taking the informant as the target, the utterance 'come on Tim lets go outside' seems to have no relevance at all for her: it flouts the Maxim of Relation. The informant draws the implication that going outside entails moving away from where she is, in other words, she is being excluded.

All of the above examples were reported because they caused offence. Off-recordness in contexts where the impoliteness interpretation is clear seems not to mollify the offence; if anything, it might exacerbate it. Note that the impoliteness interpretation can be guided by lexical and prosodic cues, as well as by the co-text. Consider the following example. Apparently, the Republican presidential candidate John McCain was teased by his wife about his thinning hair in front of reporters, to which he nastily retorted: 'At least I don't plaster on make-up like a trollop, you cunt' (*The Week*, 12 July 2008). The first part of his utterance is off record: it is a statement about what *he* does. But of course it implies via the Maxim of Relation that this is what she does. The second part of the utterance is a highly conventionalised and highly impolite formula. It is possible that using such terms between them is some mark of familiarity and closeness (see Section 4.2, for an example of this very formula being used thus), but it seems more likely that the impoliteness uptake of the first part is being reinforced by that of the second.

Implicational impoliteness: Mimicry and echoic mention   Mimicry consists of a caricatured re-presentation. As Goffman (1974: 539) points out, mimicry involves quoting someone, and a quotation in spoken face-to-face interaction will involve features of the original accent and gestural behaviour as well. But if one quotes 'too much' (e.g. all the original speaker's prosodic features) the quoter becomes 'suspect'. This is the kind of mimicry that interests me. What exactly counts as 'too much'? To recognise a 'quotation' as such and to infer the speaker's meaning requires inferential work. One can conceive of impolite mimicry as a special case of Sperber and Wilson's (1986) echoic irony, where the 'echo' is of somebody's behaviour (typically, a characteristic behaviour), rather than only their verbal utterance or thoughts. According to Sperber and Wilson (1986: 240), the recovery of the relevant implicatures depends

first, on a recognition of the utterance as an echo; second, on an identification of the source of the opinion echoed; and third, on a recognition that the speaker's attitude to the opinion echoed is one of rejection or disapproval.

An initial adjustment for mimicry requires broadening the term 'utterance' by replacing it with 'behaviour', the replacement of the abstract term 'opinion' with 'behaviour', and an extra element (the third item):

first, on a recognition of the behaviour as an echo; second, on an identification of the source of the behaviour echoed; third, the recognition that the source behaviour is a characteristic of the identity of the speaker who gave rise to it, and fourthly, on a recognition that the speaker's attitude to the behaviour echoed is one of rejection or disapproval.

With this in mind, let us work through some examples, and then I shall clarify the inferential steps needed for mimicry.

We have already met Anne Robinson and the talent show *The Weakest Link* in the previous chapter. Mimicry is used with great regularity by Anne Robinson. Let us consider the following example (Danny is a contestant on the show and has just been asked by Anne why he moved away from Liverpool):

[6]

Danny: eer
AR: eeh
Danny: [laughter] it's quite a rough place Anne so I wanted to better myself so
            I moved to the Midlands to er give the Brummies a bit of humour

Danny's long pause-filler 'eer' is articulated further to the front of the mouth than would be the case in RP, which would be closer to [ə]. This is a character-istic of his Liverpool accent. To the left of Figure 5.1, the position of Danny's 'eer' relative to other vowel sounds is represented with a star; to the right, Anne Robinson provides 'eeh' as an echo of Danny, again represented by a star.[2]

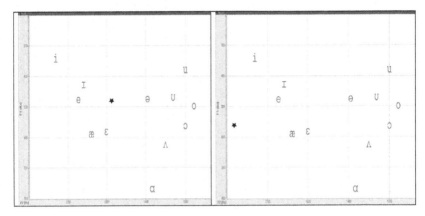

Figure 5.1 Instrumental analysis of 'eer' on the left and 'eeh' on the right

The articulation of Danny's pause-filler is further to the front of the mouth relative to, for example, any southern British accent – it is a feature of his Liverpool accent. Anne Robinson's sound is absurdly fronted. The hearer must recognise (1) Anne Robinson's 'eeh' as an echo, (2) Danny's 'eer' as the source of the echo, and (3) Danny's particular articulation of 'eer' as one of his identity characteristics (i.e. of his Liverpool accent). Then they must work out Anne Robinson's attitude. Regarding the final point, Sperber and Wilson (1986: 241) state: '[g]enuine irony is echoic, and is primarily designed to ridicule the opinion echoed'. Whilst I am not convinced that their sweeping statement applies to all types of irony, it does fit mimicry. Sperber and Wilson (1986) do not offer guidance on how we might work out a speaker's attitude. Anne Robinson clearly has a highly negative attitude towards Danny's accent. There are two reasons why I say 'clearly' here: (1) Anne Robinson's negative attitude towards the contestants is a well-known part of this activity type, and (2) mimicry does not involve any kind of echo but a distortion – a caricature.

Work by Couper-Kuhlen (1996) on prosodic register (i.e. the overall pitch of an utterance) matching suggests that mimicry generally occurs when a speaker attempts an absolute (near perfect) match with another speaker's prosody, rather than a relative match (i.e. if another speaker's speech is x above their norm, then the mimicker's speech will also be x above their own norm). Some cases of absolute matching involve distortion, as when a speaker with a naturally low base tries to mimic a speaker with a much higher base, and so adopts a falsetto voice (Couper-Kuhlen 1996: 389). In my data, the cases of Danny and Shaun (to be discussed below) involve neither relative matching nor absolute matching, but the exaggeration of a pre-existing mismatch – the mismatch between Anne Robinson's accent and that of the contestants. Note that in all these cases the trigger for the mimicry is a marked echo (which is why I discuss it in this section), whether it is marked because it departs from the prosodic norms of the speaker who uttered it or because it is a distortion or exaggeration of a perceived mismatch.

In terms of my impoliteness model, mimicry often involves Social Identity Face, since it implies that an identity characteristic of the speaker, such as regional accent, is odd or unpleasant. But, as with many other politeness and impoliteness strategies, there are other social implications. It generally involves Equity Rights impoliteness, since it casts judgement downwards from a position of power. Observe that Danny's laughter seems to be a counter strategy – an attempt to 'laugh off' the attack. Moreover, the laughter is some evidence of the fact that Danny might have perceived Anne Robinson as being impolite in the first place. How genuine that impoliteness is, of course, is an issue, not least of all because, paradoxically, Anne Robinson herself originally comes from Liverpool and has a working-class background (though this might not be known by the contestants).

I will look at one more example of mimicry, and again one that involves accent (the contestant, Jay, is a fitness instructor, and Anne has just asked him who trained him):

[7]
> 26 Jay: the Australian army trained me
> 27 AR: oh. is that why you go up in all your sentences
> 28 Jay: yes

Jay is Australian. As is clear from the orthographic transcription, Anne Robinson draws attention to a feature of Jay's pronunciation. The high rising tone (or Australian question intonation) is a well-known feature of Australian English (e.g. Guy and Vonwiller 1989), not just in academic circles but also more generally through its discussion in the media. It refers to the use of rising contours, which many speakers of other English accents might expect to correlate with questions, for statements. Although Anne Robinson's *words* draw attention to a characteristic of Jay's speech, there are no obvious implications of unpleasantness, because the mimicry is conveyed by the prosody. Let us first look at Jay's immediately preceding discourse, as represented in Figure 5.2.

Rising intonation is not transparent here. There is just a slight rise on 'me'. But the fact that there are not clear rises is not important for Anne Robinson, since there are other features that are characteristic of the Australian accent. An accent is not perceived on the basis of individual acoustic features but as a collection of acoustic features associated with a collection of social features. For example, Australian English speakers tend to have a narrower range of pitch, and this is quite noticeable in the figure. Also, various segmental features are marked (for some speakers). For example, the first vowel in 'army' is

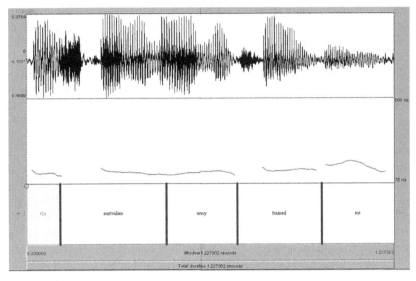

Figure 5.2 An instrumental analysis of 'the Australian army trained me'

closer to the [a:] of broad Australian English than the [ɑ:] of RP (and of Anne Robinson). In sum, Jay sounds Australian, and this affords Anne Robinson the grounds for strongly implying that he has the stereotypical Australian feature of the high rising tone. Anne Robinson's echo is represented in Figure 5.3.

Anne Robinson produces an echoic acoustic caricature of a purported feature of Jay's prosody. She attacks his Social Identity Face. Interestingly, Anne Robinson utters a yes/no question, which would normally carry a rising tone anyway (e.g. Quirk *et al.* 1985: 807). In order to carry off the mimicry of the high rise, she produces two exaggerated rises: one on 'up' and one at the end of her utterance on 'sentences'. The fact that Jay's original prosody bears only the faintest relation to her caricature is not an issue: mimicry can work by attributing a behaviour to the target, regardless of how apparent or real that behaviour is.

Finally, note that Jay's response, 'yes', apparently accepts the face damage. However, as shown in Figure 5.3, it is much lower in pitch. As Wichmann (2000a: 139ff.) points out, speakers can do conflicting things by simultaneously signalling 'disaffiliation' through a marked shift in pitch and loudness, whilst uttering cooperative words. This is an impoliteness counter-strategy that hovers between accepting and blocking the face-attack. It has the advantage that it is difficult to counter, since disaffiliation could be denied.

With the above discussions in mind, I can state that impolite mimicry is a caricatured (re-)presentation involving:

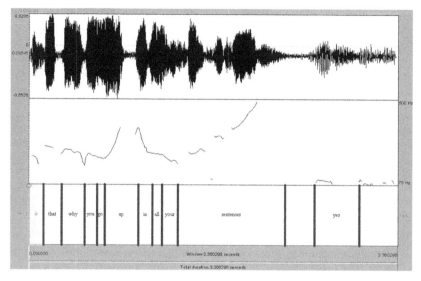

Figure 5.3 An instrumental analysis of 'is that why you go up in all your sentences' and 'yes'

An echoed behaviour. A behaviour referenced by an echo.

An echo. A behaviour which is recognised as referencing an earlier behaviour.

A marked echo and the implied echoed behaviour. The echo is marked (usually involving distortion or exaggeration), thus signalling the need for further inferencing. Moreover, the marked echo implies that the behaviour it echoes is also marked, that is, abnormal in some way. This is the implied echoed behaviour.

An implied echoed behaviour and the echoer. The implied echoed behaviour is attributed to the person who gave rise to it; more specifically, it is typically attributed to an identity characteristic of that person.

The echoer and the echoed. The recognition that the discrepancy between the echoed behaviour and the implied echoed behaviour reflects the negative attitude of the echoer towards the echoed person.

5.3 Implicational impoliteness: Convention-driven

Everyday terms for the kind of phenomena I will be discussing include 'sarcasm', 'teasing' and some labels for humour, such as '[harsh/bitter] jokes/humour'. Although, as in the previous section, we should remember that metadiscoursal terms such as these refer to fairly diffuse phenomena, all have in common the fact that they very often involve mixed messages in some way. More specifically, they mix features that point towards a polite interpretation and features that point towards an impolite interpretation. As far as academic study of these phenomena goes, the same kind of mix appears to be a feature. For example, Keltner *et al.* (2001: 234), having conducted an impressively wide-ranging review of the literature on teasing, including how teasing might be treated in relation to facework and politeness, propose the following definition of teasing:

> We define a tease as an intentional provocation accompanied by playful off-record markers that together comment on something relevant to the target. We refer to the concept of provocation instead of aggression or criticism because, as we detail below, a tease involves an act, either verbal or non-verbal, that is intended to have some effect on the target. Although the provocation itself can be delivered indirectly (as in ironic teasing), what typically makes the tease indirect and less face threatening for both teaser and target is the accompanying off-record markers, which signal that the provocation is to be taken in jest.

The notion of 'off-record' here seems to be some kind of indication (e.g. exaggeration, metaphor, prosodic variation) that the provocation is not to be taken at face value (2001: 233–4). The key point is that we have a mix. Of course, such a mix could lead to confusion or disorientation. However, in many cases the context overrules one of the interpretations. Here, I will focus more on cases where the mixed behavioural trigger plus the context lead to an impolite interpretation. I will have much more to say about the role of context in the next chapter.

This section builds on the kind of conventional formulae discussed in the previous chapter. As Coupland (2007: 84) remarks:

> Even when speakers operate 'within a predictable repertoire', they are not limited to recycling pre-existing symbolic meanings. They can frame the linguistic resources available to them in creative ways, making new meanings from old meanings.

Interpretations involve matching information encoded in the formal features of the utterance with the pragmatic context (e.g. van Dijk and Kintsch 1983; Dascal 1983). The essential feature of the phenomena discussed in this section is that there is a mismatch between the context projected by or associated with the conventionalised formula and either some other aspect of the behaviour performed or the wider context. Here are three short examples: the utterance 'Could you just fuck off?' mixes conventionalised politeness and conventionalised impoliteness formulae ('could you just' versus 'fuck off') (there is an internal mismatch); 'be quiet', whilst it might be considered normal if I said it to my daughter whilst I was trying to speak on the phone, could well cause offence if I said it to a neighbour who had just popped in (there is an external mismatch with context); and 'I'm sorry to trouble you but could you possibly be quiet for a moment' said to my daughter whilst I was trying to speak on the phone, might be taken as offensive (there is an external mismatch with context). An interpretation triggered through mismatching is more implicit and involves more inferencing than one triggered through matching, as targets must spend cognitive effort in resolving internal or external mismatches. How exactly does this inferencing work? Insights can be drawn from the hot debates on the processing of rhetorical figures such as irony, metaphor and idioms.

A useful account of this inferencing is Rachel Giora's (2003) Graded Salience Hypothesis, a hypothesis that is supported by extensive empirical evidence. In this view, comprehension consists of two phases, initial activation followed by subsequent integration processes. The initial phase has two sources of information: the mental lexicon (including of course our conventionalised impoliteness formulae) and contextual information. The order in which things get accessed depends on their salience. More salient meanings are more 'coded meanings foremost on our mind due to *conventionality, frequency, familiarity, or pro-totypicality*' (2003: 10, my emphasis), and they will be 'accessed faster than and reach sufficient levels of activation before less salient ones' (2003: 10). Importantly, Giora (e.g. 2003: 37) argues that even though a salient, predictive context may be accessed early and allow us to guess appropriate aspects of the speaker's meaning, it 'cannot obstruct access of salient information when inappropriate, since contextual and lexical processes do not interact initially but run in parallel' (2003: 40). Note that lexical items and formulae stored in the mental inventory are highly coded items by definition, consequently, their 'salient meanings would always be activated when the linguistic stimulus is encountered' (2003: 70). What we are saying here, then, is that in the case of external mismatches people entertain, at least initially, both the linguistic meaning and the contextual meaning in their heads. Similarly, in the case of internal linguistic mismatches both meanings are entertained: 'when two or more meanings of the word or expression are similarly salient, they are all accessed simultaneously' (2003: 37). During the subsequent integration processes, some salient meanings may be suppressed because they are incompatible with the context, although Giora (2003: 38) notes that some highly salient meanings are difficult to suppress, and that may be relevant to the phenomena I am dealing with here. The importance of these issues will be clear in the following paragraph, where I explain why mixed messages have the impact on impoliteness that they do. A key general point to remember is that both the polite message and the impolite message are likely to be initially entertained in one's head; it is not the case, for example, that one half of the message is never accessed. Of course, this is not to say that the messages are always exactly equal in salience.

There is a lack of definitive empirical evidence as to whether such mismatches make things worse or better in the expression of negative messages. One particular phenomenon involving mismatching is sarcasm. The impact of sarcasm has indeed been researched. Of particular relevance is the research relating to ironic insults such as 'a fine friend you are' (meaning they are not at all a friend). But results are mixed. Colston (1997) and Toplak and Katz (2000) found evidence that irony enhances the criticism conveyed by a more direct insult; Dews *et al.* (1995; Dews and Winner 1995, 1997) found the opposite. Pexman and Olineck (2002) found that the underlying intended message of ironic insults was interpreted as more 'mocking' than their direct counterparts, as long as the context was sufficiently clear to rule out the positive impression created by the surface meaning of the statement itself (see especially p. 215). This is also consistent with Kotthoff (1996) whose qualitative analyses showed that what was of crucial importance were the social relations amongst participants. The upshot is that the use of conventionalised politeness strongly mismatching a context in which a polite interpretation is not sustainable could end up exacerbating the impoliteness of the message. Let us return to Giora (2003), in order to account for how this exacerbation might work. Her comments on the function of irony are relevant here:

> The salient literal meaning of irony functions as a reference point relative to which the ironicized situation is to be assessed and criticised. What irony conveys, then, is frustration with or dissociation from what is referred to, rather than from what is said – that is, from the opinion or thought expressed by what is said. Indeed what is said often alludes to the desired situation/opinion/thought that the criticised state of affairs fails to comply with. The intended meaning is the realisation of the extent to which the state of affairs in question has fallen short of expectations usually made explicit by what is said. (2003: 94)

A conventionalised politeness formula can provide such a reference point against which a conventionalised impoliteness formula or context predicting an impolite interpretation can be assessed. It alludes to a desired politeness context and in doing so provides a measure of the extreme distance by which the message flowing from the conventionalised impoliteness formula or context falls short.

In the following two sections I have grouped the data according to whether the mismatch occurs internally within the behaviour or with some aspect of the context. The groupings in this chapter are there to represent different ways in which impoliteness can be triggered, but the separation between these groups in this section is not always hard and fast. To illustrate this point, consider the following example:

[8]

> A friend that I used to work with came to visit me with his partner (who used to work for me last year). She is pregnant and before she even said hello to me she walked into my house and said 'Yeah mate – I'm 5 months now and I'm no where near as big as you were – you were a monster (laughs) wasn't she Daz' So I replied with 'Oh, hello, come in – very nice to see you again too!'

> After saying this in a sarcastic tone, I looked at my friend Darren (the pregnant girls partner) who cringed + mouthed silently 'sorry' to me and then said 'who's for a nice cup of tea' in a smiley voice.

The utterance 'Oh, hello, come in – very nice to see you again too!' is a conventionalised politeness greeting. This mismatches the context, specifically, the previous utterance which is more consistent with impoliteness (cf. 'you are a monster'). So, there is an external mismatch. But there may well be also an internal mismatch, as the informant reports that she spoke with 'a sarcastic tone'. As with many metapragmatic labels, the notion of a sarcastic tone is not necessarily a coherent, bounded entity but is more likely to refer to a diffuse set of features that tend to accompany a diffuse set of pragmatic effects. I will discuss and illustrate the sound of sarcasm in the following section. One way of conveying sarcasm is to use prosody that undermines the politeness or impoliteness expressed verbally. This may well be the case in this particular example, in which case we also have an internal mismatch.

5.3.1   Internal

Multimodal mismatches   As discussed in Section 4.5.3, impoliteness involves multimodal behaviours. This is the main means by which internal mixed messages can be conveyed: verbal, oral and visual elements can be matched or mismatched. As will be seen in examples in this book, non-verbal elements are not in any way trivial. Cupach (2007: 152) remarks:

[n]on-verbal cues such as the absence of touch, lowered eyebrows, unpleasant facial expression, expansive gestures, indirect bodied orientation, and a loud voice 'communicate greater rudeness or a lack of concern for face' (Trees and Manusov 1998: 578), regardless of how polite criticism is linguistically.

Actually, as argued in the previous section, it is not simply the presence of these non-verbal cues that communicates 'greater rudeness', rather it is the way that these non-verbal cues mismatch verbal politeness cues that creates greater rudeness. I will concentrate on examples involving prosodic mismatches, not least of all because prosody was clearly flagged up as an issue in my report data (visual aspects rarely were). Moreover, Wichmann (2000a: 146) comments that '[m]any intonationally conveyed attitudes . . . , in particular negative ones, are the result of some kind of mismatch'.

Let us examine what is probably Anne Robinson's (the host of the quiz show *The Weakest Link*) most famous catchphrase 'you are the weakest link goodbye'. This is in fact cited on the BBC's *The Weakest Link* website as being one of Anne Robinson's particular 'contemptuous and dismissive' phrases. 'You are the weakest link' is a conventionalised impolite formula – it is a personalised negative assertion. But it is not at all obvious that this alone qualifies it as being 'contemptuous and dismissive'. For this, we must look to the prosody. Figure 5.4 displays the results of an instrumental analysis of this phrase, which can be heard on the web, for example, on the audio page of *The Weakest Link* Depository.

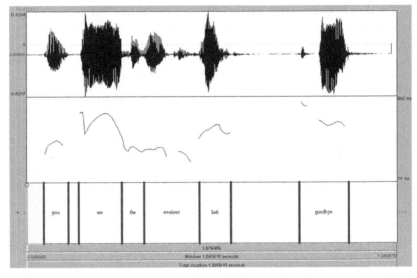

Figure 5.4 Instrumental analysis of 'you are the weakest link goodbye'

As Figure 5.4 makes clear, the catchphrase is made up of two distinct tone units, 'you are the weakest link' and 'goodbye'. Regarding the first, heavy stress falls on 'are'. This can be seen from the pitch prominence, loudness and duration. Notice also that there is a brief pause immediately before 'are', giving the stress even greater perceptual prominence. In terms of Sperber and Wilson's (1986) relevance theory, such heavy stress makes a claim on our attention, and thus guarantees some informational reward. That information might be an interpretation such as: 'the suspicion was that you were the weakest link; I am now confirming that you *really are* the weakest link'. This is a prosodically intensified conventionalised impolite formula orientated to Quality Face. Turning to the second distinct tone group, 'goodbye', we find the mixed message. This lexical item is ostensibly a conventionalised minimally polite farewell, or what Watts (2003) might refer to as a politic farewell, doing what is socially expected in that context. But now consider the prosody. This utterance fits the vocal characteristics of 'anger/frustration', such as slightly faster tempo, tense articulation, and – as is transparent from the figure – much higher pitch average (cf. Murray and Arnott 1993: 1103–4, and references therein). Furthermore, observe the intonation contour is that of a fall with a very high starting point – a pattern that is likely to suggest finality to the hearer (cf. Wichmann 2000a: 69–71). This rapid dismissal of the contestant can be interpreted as an attack on Equity Rights (e.g. the belief that we are entitled to 'fair dismissal'), but also has important secondary implications for Quality Face, as it implies their lack of value. As this analysis shows, it is the prosody of 'you are the weakest link goodbye' that gives the impression of being 'contemptuous and dismissive'. But more than this, it is the use of the conventionalised politeness formula 'goodbye' that puts people in mind of the polite context with which this situation contrasts.

Let us turn to two other examples from Anne Robinson, which appear in an interaction with the contestant Shaun. The first example is actually more of a case of external mismatching, but it helps provide a context for the internal mismatching of the second example, so I will treat it here. Anne notes Shaun's job title, 'traffic management operative', and asks him to explain what he 'actually' does:

[9]
Shaun: er put traffic cones in in the road
AR: you don't
Shaun: I do
AR: well what an interesting person you turned out to be

In this context, even without hearing the prosody, it is clear that 'you don't' is a negative declarative question seeking verification. And, indeed, Shaun provides that verification when he says 'I do'. Actions seeking verification suggest that there is some doubt in the mind of the speaker, as would have been the case had Shaun claimed he worked for MI5 or NASA. But Shaun's job, by any account, is somewhat mundane. Clearly then, Anne Robinson flouts the Maxim of Quality and implicates that Shaun's job is extremely mundane. There is, however, even more going on here. Consider Figure 5.5, showing an analysis of the prosody of 'you don't'.

Given that it is a declarative question, one might expect a rising intonation (cf. Quirk *et al.* 1985: 814). This is not what we get. In fact, Anne Robinson's prosody better fits descriptions of the prosodic characteristics of sarcasm. For example, Fónagy and Magdics (1963: 297, cited in Murray and Arnott 1993: 1105) suggest that the most important feature of sarcasm is the '"portamento" of the stressed syllables gliding to a low level in a "wide arc"', and also noted 'a lengthening of stressed syllables, "restrained" tempo, "tense" articulation leading to "grumbling, purring"' (similar features, but particularly reduction in pitch and changes in vocal quality, were confirmed in a very recent study, Cheang and Pell 2008). As a measure of this 'lengthening', consider the duration of Anne Robinson's utterance. The value for 'you' is 0.279 seconds and for 'don't' it is 0.729 seconds, making a combined total of 1.008 seconds. By way of comparison, Shaun's following utterance 'I do' has a value of 0.343 seconds – roughly a third the length of Anne Robinson's 'you don't'.

There is a problem, however, with the description of the prosodic characteristics of sarcasm. Note that there is some similarity with the characteristics of surprise/astonishment: '"the beginning of the phrase bears a strong stress, the

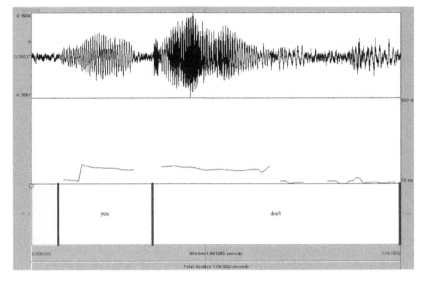

Figure 5.5 An instrumental analysis of 'you don't'

following syllables run down weakly," the "tempo is restrained," and the "voice is breathy"' (Fónagy and Magdics 1963: 297, cited in Murray and Arnott 1993: 1105). In the literature on emotion and prosody, sarcasm is a secondary emotion, it feeds off other emotions such as surprise, and so it is easy to understand why they have characteristics in common. In a study conducted by Bryant and Tree (2005) they failed to find an 'ironic tone of voice' which could be mapped in a one-to-one fashion onto irony or sarcasm. Their nuanced conclusion reflects the approach taken to prosody in this book, and is worth quoting:

> The acoustic analyses and perceptual studies of spontaneous ironic speech presented here provide very little support for the notion of an ironic tone of voice; that is, prosodic consistency across verbal irony utterances. The perception of any such tone appears to be a result of the integration of multiple sources of information (including, we believe, non-acoustic) and thus likely more an illusion than an actual speech production phenomenon. This is not to say that particular vocal characteristics do not accompany categories of language in systematic ways, but rather, extensive discussion and description at that level of analysis may be an exercise in futility. Researchers should examine how language use interacts with prosodic production and perception by breaking up the exploration into more specific problems such as those relating to sentence focus, reference, and emotional communication. (Bryant and Tree 2005: 273–4)

What makes sarcasm sarcasm is a contextual judgement that it is so. Anne Robinson's prosody is consistent with polite surprise or sarcasm. The fact

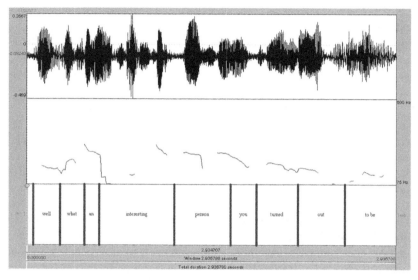

Figure 5.6 An instrumental analysis of 'well what an interesting person you turned out to be'

that she seeks verification with a negative declarative question implies her disbelief, something that reinforces the surprise interpretation. The idea of surprise attending this is more suggestive of politeness: in British culture, informing somebody that you do an impressive job is likely to elicit a polite 'wow', whereas informing somebody that you do a boring, ordinary job is unlikely to receive any particular comment (it may even result in embarrassed silence). But polite surprise conflicts with the mundane job Shaun actually does. The most relevant interpretation in this context is that Anne Robinson's polite surprise is sarcasm: we can infer an implication that Shaun's job is extremely mundane, and this of course attacks his Social Identity Face. Here, the polite surprise provides a reference point from which Anne Robinson dramatically departs.

Anne Robinson's response to Shaun's confirmation 'I do' is 'well what an interesting person you turned out to be'. An instrumental analysis of this utterance is displayed in Figure 5.6. The intonation contour resembles a staircase going down. This downwards pattern seems to signal boredom. In Anne's previous utterance we had the prosody of surprise conflicting with propositions in the previous utterance which suggested something mundane. In contrast, here we have the prosody of boredom conflicting with a proposition stating that something is interesting. So, the potentially polite verbal assertion turns out to be part of sarcasm, whereas in the previous case the potentially polite prosody turned out to be part of sarcasm. Interestingly, some researchers (e.g. Arndt and Janney 1987) seem to assume that it is the verbal content that is 'untrue' in sarcasm not the prosody, which is viewed as some kind of contextual cue as to the real state of affairs. My discussion here demonstrates that it can be otherwise: mixing can work in both directions.

Verbal formula mismatches   In this section, I turn to mismatches created out of a conventionalised politeness formula in the context of either a conventionalised impoliteness formula or a behaviour that otherwise expresses impoliteness. My paradigm example of the former is 'Could you just fuck off?' Let us look at another example which occurs in my army recruit training data (for details and further analysis, see Culpeper 1996). A female recruit has failed to carry out a task, refusing in the end to do it. She is given a 'dressing down' by three non-commissioned officers, lasting about fifteen minutes. One of those non-commissioned officers says: 'you really impress people with your little act, girl'. 'You really impress people' is a conventionalised politeness compliment formula, which then clashes with a conventionalised impoliteness insulting condescension, 'little act', followed by a possible conventionalised impoliteness vocative insult for an adult female 'girl'.

One particularly rich source of this kind of mismatch is Simon Cowell, the famously rude judge of various exploitative talent shows such as *X Factor* and *Britain's Got Talent*. The following are just some examples produced by Cowell during his shows (all quoted from Tony Cowell 2006):[3]

[10]
>   She was amazing, but she is completely and utterly barking mad. (p. 41)
>   I admire Paula for admiring me. (p. 60)
>   You are gorgeous, but your voice isn't. (p. 67)
>   I think you're amazing: amazingly dreadful. (p. 73)
>   That was extraordinary. Unfortunately, extraordinarily bad. (p. 73)

Again, they mix conventionalised politeness with conventionalised impoliteness: the contrast is with contexts projected by the co-texts and not the situation. In some cases, the contrast is formalised by *but*, a word that gives rise to the conventional implicature that there is a contrast between its conjuncts. In other cases, the two parts are held together by repetition. The fact that there are two halves is something that Cowell exploits. By beginning with conventionalised politeness, these utterances construct a 'garden path' pragmatic strategy: the listener is led towards an understanding that Cowell thinks positively of them, and Cowell invariably pauses to allow that understanding to linger. He then completes the rhetorical strategy by violently derailing the polite interpretation.

The book from which the above quotations are taken is called: *I Hate to be Rude but... the Simon Cowell Book of Nasty Comments* (Cowell 2006). Of course, the title of this book is the very rhetorical strategy I identified with Cowell. What is different about 'I hate to be rude [but]' is that, unlike the other Cowell examples discussed above, it has some general currency. The following examples are taken from the *OEC*:

[11]

> **fiction** 'Um, actually **I hate to be rude** but I told Kevin that I would hang out with him all day.
>
> **fiction** But whatever it is, leave me out of you and your little power games because, and **I hate to be rude**, but you're really pissing me off.'
>
> **weblog** **I hate to be rude**, what the hell were folks without motor vehicles supposed to do?
>
> **weblog** Y'know, **I hate to be rude** about your country, Tim, but don't you clean floors in Australia?

A similar expression is 'no offence', as illustrated by the following, again from the *OEC*:

[12]

> **computing** 'Eidos and IO Interactive would like to stress that **no offence** was intended but would like to apologise to the Sikh community and other persons for any offence taken.'
>
> **computing** And so the schools are filled with two-a-penny Biologists (**no offence**, some of them are lovely) who, of course, are all Intelligent Design advocates.
>
> **fiction** 'Because **no offence** but you look like shit.'
>
> **fiction** 'Still leaves you one marksman short,' Matt continued, pushing the concern for Kenny aside, 'and now you want to take me off the team as well – **no offence**, but the rest of you can't shoot worth crap next to me or him.'

What both these expressions have in common is that they express some mitigation of the negative impact of what is just about to be delivered. In this they look like some kind of politeness strategy. More specifically, 'I hate to be rude' standardly implies, via the Maxims of Quality and Quantity, that the speaker will actively try to avoid being rude. 'No offence' seems to have developed from 'no offence was intended', as in the first example above, or a similar clause, into a parenthetical metapragmatic device designed to clarify what the speaker intends the pragmatic effects of the upcoming utterance to be. However, despite this (as implied conventionally by 'but'), in both cases the speakers go ahead with the utterance of something offensive, and sometimes possibly very offensive (e.g. 'you're really pissing me off', 'don't you clean floors in Australia?', 'you look like shit', 'the rest of you can't shoot worth crap next to me or him'). The point is that if the speakers really hated being rude and really intended to avoid causing offence they would not have preceded with the second part of the utterance in the way that they do. Instead, we seem to have blatantly superficial lip-service paid to politeness.

A similar rhetorical device to those mentioned above is 'with respect' in initial position. Unlike the previous examples, it is strongly associated with one particular context, that of the courtroom. The following are some examples from the *OEC*:

[13]
>   **law**   **With respect** I do not believe that you have either the grounds or authority for taking such a step.
>   **law**   **With respect** I suggest you look again at my letter of 9th June 2000.
>   **law**   **With respect** I do not find this a convincing explanation of Antico.
>   **law**   **With respect** I do not agree.

As with previous examples, this expression is followed by an utterance that could point more in the direction of an impoliteness interpretation. For instance: the first example states that the addressee does not have the 'grounds or authority' for the step they propose; the second example implies (via, amongst other things, the iterative presupposition associated with 'again') that the addressee did not properly look at the letter the first time round. What is going on here is very similar to what can also be found in the discourse of the British Parliament. Harris (2001) explored the discourse that takes place in the House of Commons during Prime Minister's Question Time, when Members of Parliament have an opportunity to pose questions (Parliamentary rules require that such questions are addressed to the Speaker of the House of Commons, though they obviously target the Prime Minister or other members of parliament). Harris (2001: 463) observes that:

the Prime Minister's Question Time data are particularly interesting . . . since negative politeness features, i.e. those which attempt to avoid impoliteness, appear to coexist with the performance of deliberate threats to the hearer's positive face, i.e. acts which are clearly intended to be impolite.

On the one hand we see features related to deference, respect, depersonalisation and distancing – features associated with negative politeness (B&L 1987) – conveyed by, for example, terms of deference such as 'the Prime Minister', 'my Right Honourable Friend', 'Honourable (or Right Honourable) Gentleman/Lady (or Friend)' (2001: 464). On the other hand, these are followed by such propositions as:

that the Prime Minister refuses to answer questions (accusation)

that his failure to answer questions is ever more evident (contempt)

that he has signed away the country's legal rights (criticism) that he is not a good lawyer (ridicule)

that his chances are not valid ones (challenge) (Harris 2001: 464)

Harris (2001: 464) adds: '[m]oreover these propositions are intensified by means of deliberately insulting lexical choices, i.e. "dodging questions", "pathetic", "absolutely worthless"'. This is precisely the kind of intensification associated with impoliteness, as I discussed in Section 4.5.2.

When one hears 'I hate to be rude', 'no offence' and 'with respect', there is a strong likelihood that something offensive will follow, though how offensive it will be can vary. One thing that sets 'with respect' and the kind of mixed devices in the British Parliament aside from the other items is that in the institutional context of the courtroom and the Parliament impoliteness is expected and sanctioned, and even rewarded (as Harris 2001: 466 points out of the former). Prosecutors and parliamentarians are doing their jobs in using adversarial discourse to expose the truth. It is not the case, of course, that anything goes. Regarding the courtroom, this is exemplified by William P. Smith (the head of a bankruptcy department), who said the following to Judge Isicoff in the Southern District of Florida, USA:

[14]
>   I suggest to you with respect, your honour, that you're a few French fries short of a Happy Meal in terms of what's likely to take place.

Judge Isicoff responded later by issuing a *sua sponte* Order to Show Cause as to why his license to practice should not be revoked, which cited the Model Rules of Professional Conduct of the American Bar Association and the court Guidelines for Courtroom Decorum. Smith had used both the 'with respect' device and a deferential term of address, 'your honour', but then had followed this with a strikingly creative way of making the point that the judge is out of touch. I will consider the issue of legitimacy in Section 6.2.2 and also institutional impoliteness in 7.6.

One issue that remains is whether the mixed message devices discussed in this section actually cut deeper than non-mixed alternatives, such as simply using a conventionalised impoliteness formula. This clearly is a complex issue that depends on, amongst other things, the salience of the polite message versus the impolite message, and the context. In the case of the courtroom and Parliament, the context is highly salient and perhaps, especially regarding the latter, primes the expectation of impoliteness. Actually, the same point can be made in relation to Simon Cowell: this mixing of messages has now become something of a stock strategy for Cowell; in other words, it is becoming conventionally associated with impolite effects. The 'polite' device is becoming a conventionalised prelude to impoliteness. Some of these regular ways of performing mixed impoliteness are themselves becoming conventionalised to an extent. The interpreter need not work through all the inferential steps that characterise the resolution of mixed messages, but can short-circuit the process by recognising the impolite meaning projected by the conventionalised impolite mixed message. The same is likely to be true of certain familiar forms of sarcasm and banter, or for that matter irony, metaphor and idioms. In Silverstein's (1998: 128–38) thinking, these would be considered second-order indexicals. Note that in becoming thus conventionalised they lose their contrast with the context. On account of this one might hypothesise that they lose some of their impact. However, we need systematic research to test this hypothesis. What I can say is that there are still occasions where the fact that the message was mixed in a superficial way seems to exacerbate the impoliteness. Consider the following example (at which I was present; I also spoke to the participants about it later):

[15]

> [A mother is recounting to her family how, whilst she was invigilating a university exam, there were two interruptions, one by a member of staff who thought, incorrectly, that his own examination students should be in that room and the other involving a fire alarm.]
>
> Mother: Then the fire alarm went off!
> Father: God! What did you do?
> Mother: Fortunately it stopped after a few rings. I went phew [mimes wiping the sweat from her forehead with the back of her hand] to the students.
> Son: No offence but they must have thought you were stupid.
> Mother: What do you mean no offence! That was extremely offensive.

From the mother's point of view the attribution of stupidity to her action was not only face damaging but unwarranted by the context, resulting in the up-take of strong impoliteness. Here, the use of 'no offence' was more than trivial: its usage when strong offence was likely to be caused by the following words was taken to be part of the problem. It was taken as evidence of a bloody-minded disregard for the offence caused.

5.3.2   *External*

In Culpeper *et al.* (2003), we provided a particularly interesting example of 'sarcasm'. I will repeat the example here, but reanalyse it in terms of my category of convention-driven implicational impoliteness, specifically the subcategory involving a mismatch between expressed behaviour and the context. This is taken from the TV series *Clampers*, which involves interactions between traffic wardens (who add clamps to illegally parked cars) and car owners. In the following example, a van driver has returned to his vehicle to find that a clamping official has just finished clamping it. After some heated exchanges, the van driver snatches the penalty ticket and other details away from the clamper and tells him to 'go away'. He then returns to his own vehicle to leave the scene, and as he does so he initiates the following exchange:

[16]
> Driver: [sarcastically] have a good day
> Clamper: I will do
> (adapted from Culpeper *et al.* 2003: 1559)

'Have a good day' is a conventionalised politeness formula associated with the termination of interactions. However, the prosody that accompanies it constitutes an internal mismatch, most likely triggering an ironic or sarcastic interpretation. Furthermore, it is extremely improbable in this context that the driver is terminating interaction with an item designed to achieve politeness. This is an external mismatch. In this context, using a conventionalised politeness formula provides a reference point, a desired politeness context, against which we can perceive the extreme distance by which the message flowing from the context falls short. We should also consider here that the particular choice of salutation, 'have a good day', is one that may for the British be conventionally tinged with insincerity, given echoes of politeness formulae popularised in the UK in tightly-scripted customer-service interactions promoted by American corporations, such as McDonald's.[4] What makes the above example especially interesting is that the Clamper's response is consistent with the literal conventionalised meaning, not the sarcastic meaning derived from a mismatch. It is a explicit way of denying that the sarcastic interpretation has found its mark. The blatant misunderstanding here may further antagonise.

Examples that do not involve multimodal mixes but just mismatches between aspects of what is said and the context in which it is said are easier to find in written discourse, for obvious reasons. The following example is a letter in Lancaster University's electronic staff bulletin:

[17]
> I would just like to say thank you to the person who backed into my car on the perimeter road yesterday. It was a wonderful surprise when I'd finished work and made my way back to my car. ... As a single parent and part-time member of staff on a clerical grade, I look forward to receiving an obscene quote from my local garage and then not eating for a week! Thank you SO VERY MUCH.

Here, a conventionalised polite item is recontextualised so that the projected polite context contrasts with the current impolite communicative context, i.e. a letter of complaint. An everyday label such as sarcasm would be appropriate for the phenomenon here. In fact, I have two other examples from other issues of the same bulletin reacting to the same type of event with sarcasm. One includes 'THANKS!' and the other 'a big THANK YOU'. Of course, *thanks/thank you* are highly conventionalised politeness formulae, occurring both regularly and being a focal point of politeness rules. They are a useful candidate for max-imising the contrast between the projected context and the current context. But more than this, these have become regular ways of doing sarcasm. Rockwell (2004) found 'thanks', in North American data, to be common in sarcastic state-ments. Note that such items are accompanied by typographical features, such as capitalisation and exclamation marks, to help signal the sarcastic context (see Yus 2000, on such written features in ironic interpretation), just as in spoken discourse sarcasm is aided by prosodic features, as discussed in the previous section. An important point about this regularity in performing sarcasm in par-ticular ways is that those ways are themselves becoming conventionalised – we have familiar sarcasm or second-order indexicals (Silverstein 1998: 128–38). The interpreter need not work through all the inferential steps that characterise ironic interpretation, but can short-circuit the process by recognising the sar-castic context projected by the conventionalised impoliteness (sarcastic) mixed device.

5.4   Implicational impoliteness: Context-driven

To reiterate, any behaviour judged to be impolite has involved a contextual judgement to some extent. What I am concerned with here are cases where the trigger is not marked and there is no mismatch involving a conventionalised politeness formula. Instead, impoliteness interpretation is primarily driven by the strong expectations flowing from the context. I will organise my material into two groups, one of which involves unmarked behaviour and the other the total absence of behaviour.

5.4.1   Unmarked behaviour

In fact, very few behaviours can be described as neither marked nor conven-tionalised. This is not surprising: language users rely on regularities to facil-itate the cognitive pressures of real-time language processing, and they also use deviations from regularities to help signal to other users particular prag-matic meanings. Brown and Levinson (1987) bald-on record strategy involves unmarked, in a Gricean sense, utterances. However, the contexts and functions discussed and illustrated for bald on record do not quite match what I have in mind here (see B&L 1987: 94–101). They summarise these thus:

Normally, an FTA will be done in this way only if the speaker does not fear retribution from the addressee, for example in circumstances where (a) S and H both tacitly agree that the relevance of face demands may be suspended in the interest of urgency or efficiency; (b) where the danger of H's face is very small, as in offers, requests, suggestions that are clearly in H's interests and do not require great sacrifices of S (e.g.,

'Come in' or 'Do sit down'); and (c) where S is vastly superior in power to H, or can enlist audience support to destroy H's face without losing his own. (1987: 69)

(a) is a particular usage that is highly unlikely to be interpreted as impolite; similarly, (b) has more to do with reinforcing acts which are likely to be interpreted as polite. However, (c) describes a power asymmetry in which the speaker is at liberty to 'destroy H's face'. This does sound relevant to impoliteness. But is it really? I agree that in a position of power someone can perform face-attacking acts with less fear of retribution. However, if the power is perceived to be socially legitimate, that will make it less likely to be perceived as impolite. It is whether the exercise of power is perceived to be an abuse of power, and not simply whether one has power or not, that heavily determines the judgement of impoliteness in this kind of context. I already noted English informants' sensitivities regarding patronising behaviour in Section 3.6.4. Further evidence that potentially impolite utterances are perceived as less impolite when produced by people exercising perceived legitimate power is given in Section 5.5.3, and I discuss some of the issues in Section 7.3. These issues are also relevant to the two examples below.

The first example of unmarked behaviour is as follows:

[18]
> TO SHOP ASSISTANT: You've not given me the pound.
>
> SHOP ASSISTANT: I think I did [Abruptly]
>
> TO SHOP ASSISTANT: Well it's not there. Look. (opened wallet to show him)
>
> SHOP ASSISTANT: Go like that. [Implied I was trying to con him] (He pointed to his sleeves, gesturing to loosen them)
>
> TO SHOP ASSISTANT: See. [Raised volume] (Opened sleeve to show him) (He handed me a pound)
>
> TO SHOP ASSISTANT: Thank you.

The shop assistant says 'go like that'. On the surface, that appears to be a fully cooperative utterance, although of course the referent of 'that' will need to be inferred and the meaning of 'go' disambiguated. But the customer/informant draws the implication that the shop assistant is implying that he 'was trying to con him'. Our knowledge about hiding things in sleeves, about magicians or pickpockets, is triggered. So, although it is a cooperative utterance in a Gricean sense, in this particular context it may trigger impolite implications. As the informant comments: 'I was embarrassed by being ordered to loosen my sleeves.' Note that the shop assistant is in some position of power – he or she actually has the pound. However, the issue of who has right of ownership over the pound is more debatable; it is difficult to prove one way or the other. The principle of deferring to the customer ('the customer is always right') is clearly ignored by the shop assistant, and this is probably why the informant describes his behaviour as 'rude and unprofessional'. This example also, incidentally, illustrates the kind of phenomenon I will discuss in the following subsection to do with the absence of politeness: the informant reports that he was 'annoyed that he [the shop assistant] didn't apologise for his mistake'.

The second example is as follows:

[19]
> Mum – Hello
> Vikki – Hiya Mum
> . . .
> Mum – Have you sorted your finance
> Vikki – Yea kind of
> Mum – Vikki, you need to do it, you are going to be in trouble. Go tomorrow and go to student finance
> Vikki – Mum stop going on I know
> Mum – Stop leaving things till the last minute
> Vikki – Right I'm going your doing my head in. Love you.

The informant, a student, describes her mother's behaviour as 'irritating and annoying'. Her mother's final three turns are all bald on record: there is a bald yes-no question about the delicate area of finance; an attention-getter ('Vikki') followed by a bald assertion of need, a warning of negative consequences and two imperative requests; and finally a further imperative request (which also contains the change-of-state verb 'stop', thus presupposing that she always is 'leaving things till the last minute'). This behaviour is not untypical of parent–child talk. It is generally legitimated, and thus is less likely to be seen as impolite. However, the problem here is that the power differential is no longer straightforwardly accepted, as the informant comments: '[s]he is very protective but needs to remember I am 20. I am old enough to take responsibility and consequences of my actions.' Thus, the mother is perceived to violate what is socially acceptable, and it is this that makes it impolite.

5.4.2   Absence of behaviour

Bober (1991; cited in Tedeschi and Felson 1994: 216) found that omissions of behaviours were judged equally intentional and blameworthy as commissions of behaviours, when they resulted in harmful consequences. Brown and Levinson (1987: 5) touch on the face-damaging implications of withholding politeness work: 'politeness has to be communicated, and the absence of communicated politeness may, *ceteris paribus*, be taken as the absence of a polite attitude'. Similarly, Watts (2003: 169; see also 131, 182) suggests that if politic behaviour is 'missing', it 'tend[s] to lead to an evaluation of a participant's behaviour as "impolite", "brash", "inconsiderate", "abrupt", "rude", etc.'. The kind of examples I have in mind are ones in which a participant understands a context to require the performance of certain behaviours, as is illustrated in the following examples.

[20]

The teacher had asked a question and I put my hand up to answer it. She pointed at me and said 'yes?', so I gave my answer. I soon realised that my answer was incorrect as, without saying a word, or giving any feedback, the teacher asked another pupil to give their answer. She ignored my attempt and moved to the next person. So, I was just quiet and continued listening to other answers.

The informant was clearly expecting some kind of receipt for her answer, and the absence of this leads to an understanding of impoliteness. She comments:

I felt humiliated in front of the whole class, and that my answer must have been so feeble that it wasn't worth the teacher answering me. I felt it was very unfair. I was trying me best in answering the question, but was completely ignored. I think the teacher should have known better and been more polite. I would label the behaviour 'rude'.

[21]

Jen:	Hi sugar	(on the phone)
Ben:	Hi	

. . .

Ben:	. . . it's a month since Christmas & you still haven't been round with my present that you forgot to bring when we all met up before Christmas to swap presents, you took Sarah's round new years week but –
Jen:	I brought yours to the pub.
Ben:	Yeah, the wrong one. Jenny, I live a 5min bus journey from you, it takes you longer to walk to Sarah's, you're at uni for fecks sake
(silence) Ben:	Oh, go quiet, go and hide in your shell.
(Jen hangs up)	

This conversation, reported by Ben, illustrates the power of the social norm of reciprocity. What made Ben 'angry and fed up' was a classic impoliteness case of a gift being given and then not being reciprocated. Of course, the gift in this case is literal, but it can also be symbolic. What additionally annoys the informant is that 'she seemed to act like nothing was wrong & I was bad for laying everything out for her'. Clearly, the informant thinks that Jen is pretending that nothing is wrong.

5.5 Directness, context and gravity of offence

5.5.1 Directness and (im)politeness

The notion of directness is not at all straightforward. I do not have space to elaborate the issues. Briefly, in my view Searle's (1975) notion of directness, concerning essentially (mis)matchings of syntax and speech act, only captures one aspect, though an important one, of what is going on. Generally, I prefer the notion of pragmatic explicitness, which is based on the transparency of three things: the illocutionary point, the referent(s), and the propositional content. This notion is also testable: implicit meanings should take longer to process. Furthermore, contrary to many studies of directness, I am also mindful of the fact that evidence of, for instance, the illocutionary point, is not solely resident in linguistic form but also the context. Holtgraves (1994), for example, found that knowing that the speaker was of high status was enough to prime a directive interpretation, in advance of any remark having been actually made (see also Ervin-Tripp *et al.* 1987 and Gibbs 1981, for the general importance of social context in speech act interpretation).

The main dimension along which B&L's (1987) super-strategies for performing politeness are ordered is directness, defined in terms of complying with or deviating from Grice's Cooperative Principle. At one end we have bald on record and at the other end we have off record (or even avoiding the face-threatening act altogether), and in between we have negative and positive politeness strategies. Bald on record is supposedly the strategy of choice for situations in which face threat is minimal; and off record is for situations in which face threat is great. Bald on record, then, may be a candidate for impoliteness. However, as elaborated in Culpeper *et al.* (2003: 1547–8), identifying utterances that count as truly bald on record is not easy. Moreover, as I pointed out in Section 5.4.1, with respect to utterances that might be taken as impolite, few are bald on record. Nevertheless, let me formulate on the basis of B&L (1987) an impoliteness hypothesis that can be tested: *Hypothesis 1a: There is a positive linear relationship between gravity of offence and directness; the more indirectly the impoliteness is triggered the less the offence taken.*

Leech's (1983: 108) comments on the relationship between politeness and indirectness are frequently cited. Indirect utterances, such as 'Could you possibly answer the phone', tend to be more polite because they increase optionality for the hearer, whilst decreasing illocutionary force (cf. Leech 1983: 108). This is in tune with hypothesis 1a. Less well known is Leech's idea that indirectness can increase impoliteness:

... in this case obliquity works in the opposite direction: because 'You have something to declare' is an impolite belief, the more indirect kinds of question [e.g. 'Haven't you something to declare'] are progressively more impolite, more threatening, than the ordinary yes–no question. (1983: 171)

To take another example, 'Do you have sawdust for brains?' is clearly more indirect than 'You fool' or 'You're stupid', and Leech's prediction would be that it will be interpreted as more impolite. Of course, Leech would be the first to admit that the bi-directional correlation between indirectness and politeness/impoliteness does not apply in all contexts, and that other factors, aside from indirectness, affect politeness/impoliteness. Most notably, observe that the quotation from Leech above refers to the expressions of an 'impolite belief'; in the case of polite beliefs, increased directness correlates with increased politeness (cf. Leech 1983: 109–10). What is a polite or impolite belief? In Leech's view (1983: 104–5), they are beliefs that somebody has engaged in linguistic or other behaviour in order to pursue competitive or convivial illocutionary goals. 'Competitive goals are those which are essentially discourteous, such as getting someone to lend you money' (Leech 1983: 105) (a footnote refers the reader to B&L's notion of FTAs). Directive speech acts, for example, compete with the 'social goal of establishing and maintaining comity' (1983: 104). Polite beliefs, on the other hand, relate to convivial illocutionary functions, which are 'intrinsically courteous: politeness here takes a more positive form of seeking opportunities for comity' (Leech 1983: 105) (including speech acts such as offering, inviting, greeting, thanking, etc.). I need not rehearse the difficulties of linking (im)politeness to particular speech acts (see Section 4.3.1), and it should be noted that Leech is discussing 'the most general level' (1983: 104), acknowledging that '[d]ifferent kinds and degrees of politeness are called for in different situations' (Leech 1983: 104). However, even after factoring in the role of context in shaping the understanding of an (im)polite belief, the basic idea remains: it is postulated that indirectness increases the impoliteness of impolite beliefs. Leech provides no evidence to support this. Let me reformulate Leech's idea as a hypothesis that can be tested: *Hypothesis 2a: There is a positive linear relationship between gravity of offence and directness; the more indirectly the impoliteness is triggered the greater the offence taken.*

It is worth noting here that these contradictory hypotheses, 1a and 2a, are possible because indirectness or implicitness are not automatically linked to a particular interpretation. In B&L's (1987: 71–4) line of thinking, indirectness or off-recordness is associated with tactfulness, non-coercion and the possible avoidance of accountability. Leech does not give an explanation as to why indirectness or implicitness might exacerbate impoliteness, though we may suppose that it is due not just to the cost of extra processing but by the fact that one is forced to dwell on the impolite expression in order to work it out. Both arguments are plausible. What is likely to be a key factor in separating them, in my view, is the role of context. If the context is weighing heavily towards an impolite interpretation, then the balance tips towards Leech's hypothesis.

Hypothesis 1a does not entirely square with the work of other researchers on politeness. Blum-Kulka's (e.g. 1987) work on requests in various cultures suggested a different picture. Where both Hebrew and English speakers in her 1987 study agreed is that conventional indirect requests are the most polite. Her explanation for this is that the loss of 'pragmatic clarity' accompanying the more indirect strategies is a cost for the target and needs to be factored in. Thus, the politest way of making a request is by 'appearing to be indirect without burdening the hearer with the actual cost of true directness'

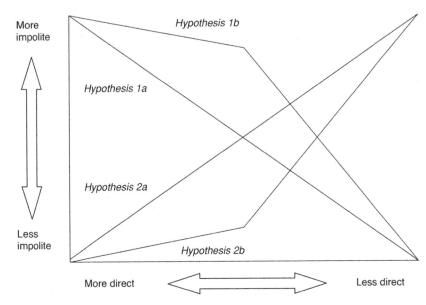

Figure 5.7 Interactions between directness and gravity of offence in the expression of impoliteness

(1987: 143–4). Conventionally indirect strategies short-circuit the necessary inferencing to arrive at the illocutionary point of the utterance. The key point for impoliteness is that conventionally indirect expressions are only marginally more indirect than direct expressions, because hearers can short-circuit the inferential process. This suggests two variants of hypotheses 1 and 2, which accommodate the different status of conventional indirectness. We can formulate these thus:

Hypothesis 1b: Conventionalised impolite expressions are only marginally less direct than fully direct expressions; only fully indirect non-conventional expressions stand apart as being least offensive.

Hypothesis 2b: Conventionalised impolite expressions are only marginally less direct than fully direct expressions; only fully indirect non-conventional expressions stand apart as being most offensive.

The hypotheses discussed thus far are displayed in Figure 5.7.

5.5.2   Investigating the relationship between directness and (im)politeness

Here, I will briefly report on the first of a set of studies that I am undertaking with John Dixon (Department of Psychology, Lancaster University), designed

Table 5.1 *Pragmatic explicitness: Syntactic and prosodic directness*

Pragmatic explicitness	Directness category	Command items	Syntactic realisation	Semantic matching
Explicit	direct	you be quiet	imperative	match
↑	conventionally indirect	could you be quiet	yes-no interrogative	partial match
↓				
Implicit	non-conventionally indirect	you aren't being quiet	negative declarative	mismatch

to test the hypotheses outlined in the previous section. In the first of these, we administered a questionnaire to ninety-five Lancaster University psychology undergraduates. The questionnaire contained three different scenarios which we manipulated for utterances varying in directness. Students read these and then evaluated the utterances in the scenarios on six scales. This kind of informant testing methodology, using written questionnaires and judgement tasks, has been fairly widely used in politeness research. However, we are under no illusions as to the limitations and difficulties in producing instruments that can test highly contextualised and usually spoken phenomena. Nevertheless, we think it can tap into some aspects of schematic knowledge (cf. Holtgraves 2005: 89), and offer findings which can be further investigated using other methodologies.

In order to control our test items, the speech act and propositional content were not varied: they concern commands to be quiet. What we vary is directness, that is, whether the command is matched by an imperative, whether it is partially matched with respect to one of its felicity conditions, or whether there is no match at all. These various options are displayed in Table 5.1.

The three command items in the third column – 'you be quiet', 'could you be quiet' and 'you aren't being quiet' – were the items we used in our scenarios.[5] The following are the three basic scenarios deployed (*x* stands in place of one of the three command items):

Scenario: At a gathering of staff in the factory meeting room, the boss is explaining the work-schedule for that day. An employee is chatting to workmates about what they are going to do that night. The boss says to the employee '*x*'.

Scenario: In the courtroom, the judge is explaining the programme for the trial that day. A defendant is chatting to co-defendants about what they are going to do that night. The judge says to the defendant '*x*'.

Scenario: At a parade ground gathering of army recruits, the sergeant-major is explaining the drill for the day. A recruit is chatting to fellow recruits about what they are going to do that night. The sergeant-major says to the recruit '*x*'.

What is particularly important to note is that we generated a further three scenarios in which the power asymmetry is reversed: the employee commands the boss, the defendant commands the judge and the army recruit commands the sergeant-major. Thus we have three scenarios constituting a 'high-power to low-power' (hereafter H→L power) condition and three scenarios constituting a 'low-power to high-power' (hereafter L→H power) condition. And so we have six scenarios which would be repeated but with the different command items, giving a total of 18 different scenarios. To make this more manageable for our informants, we split them so that roughly half the students looked at scenarios in the H→L power condition and the other half looked at scenarios in the L→H power condition. The scenarios were administered in randomised order. Thirty-eight students completed questionnaires in the H→L power condition and forty-seven students completed questionnaires in the L→H power condition.

How power interacts with both politeness and impoliteness is of great interest (see, for example, Locher 2004; Bousfield and Locher 2008). As we saw in Section 5.4.1, according to B&L (1987) the direct strategy bald on record is appropriate in situations of relative high power. Thus the prediction is that hypotheses 1a and 1b should be more easily confirmed in the L→H power condition. With regard to Leech (1983), using a command in the context of a L→H power condition is likely to be taken as pursuing a competitive goal, that is, expressing an impolite belief. Thus, hypotheses 2a and 2b should be more easily confirmed in that condition.

Our informers were asked to evaluate each scenario on six scales, incorporating the following items: *patronising, rude, aggressive, inappropriate, hurtful* and *impolite*. The first five of these were chosen because they had appeared in the top six metalinguistic labels that my report data informants had selected.[6] This is perhaps an unusual step compared with other studies. With the exception of *impolite*, we used evaluative labels supplied by informants of the same social background. Other studies have tended to use labels which suited and were chosen by researchers. Each label was presented in the context of an assertion, for example 'it was patronising', and informers were asked to indicate the degree to which they agreed with the assertion on a seven-point Likert-type scale, as follows:

$$6 = \text{strongly agree}$$
$$5 = \text{agree}$$
$$4 = \text{agree somewhat}$$
$$3 = \text{neither agree nor disagree}$$
$$2 = \text{disagree somewhat}$$
$$1 = \text{disagree}$$
$$0 = \text{strongly disagree}$$

We used the Cronbach alpha statistical test to give us some indication as to the internal consistency of the informants' evaluations on the scales, that is, how

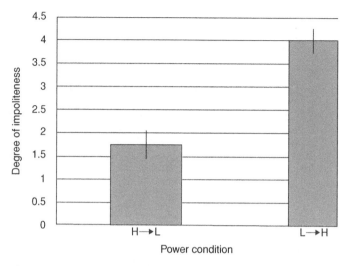

Figure 5.8 Degree of impoliteness: High to low vs Low to high power conditions

well they might function as a single, unidirectional construct. In fact, results indicated that informants gave similar ratings on all scales: all results were above 0.7, most were above 0.8. This suits our purposes here, as we will treat these items collectively as constituting a scale of impoliteness.

Using SPSS, we conducted Analysis of Variance (ANOVA) tests in order to establish whether the means of our results were significantly different from each other. The ANOVA F statistic was used to calculate whether there was more difference between groups than variability within groups. The larger the value of F, the more likely that there are real differences. All differences reported below are highly statistically significant. All of the following figures also include 95 per cent confidence interval bands (marked at the top of the bars). These give an indication of the confidence with which we can assume that a mean (i.e. as represented by the top of the bars) is a true mean; in other words, in 95 per cent of the cases the true mean will fall within the range represented by the bar.

Figure 5.8 displays the degree of impoliteness attributed in the L→H power condition and the H→L power condition. Clearly, there is a huge difference ($F = 113.871$; $p < 0.001$). Power is hugely influential in determining the degree of impoliteness. In the H→L power condition our command items are not quite considered impolite (the mean hovering below 2, i.e. 'disagree somewhat'), whereas in the L→H power condition they are much more likely to be considered impolite (the mean being approximately at 4, i.e. 'agree somewhat').

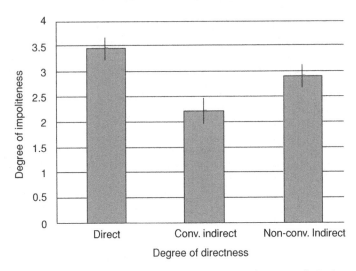

Figure 5.9 Degree of impoliteness and degree of directness (in both power conditions combined)

Figure 5.9 displays the degree of impoliteness attributed to each of the three degrees of directness of the command item (direct, conventionally indirect and non-conventionally indirect) regardless of power condition. Again there are clear differences ($F = 93.701$; $p < 0.001$), although not as striking as those for power. With respect to the hypotheses displayed in Figure 5.7, the pattern we see here, with direct commands rated most impolite but with non-conventionally indirect commands not far behind and then conventional indirectness rated as slightly not impolite (below 2, i.e. 'disagree somewhat'), is not one we see there.

Figure 5.10 displays the degree of impoliteness attributed to each of the three degrees of directness of the command item (direct, conventionally indirect and non-conventionally indirect) in the H→L power condition, and this is followed by Figure 5.11 which displays the same except for the power condition which is the opposite, i.e. L→H. The differences for the degree of impoliteness between the three degrees of directness in a particular power condition are highly significant ($F = 12.094$; $p < 0.001$).

In the H→L condition of Figure 5.10, all three degrees of directness are ranked low on the scale of impoliteness: all well below the neutral three (3, i.e. 'neither agree nor disagree'). There are clear differences between the impoliteness ratings attributed to the different degrees of directness. What is particularly striking is the low score for conventional indirectness: it is below one (1 = disagree). It seems to be not at all impolite to use a conventionally indirect

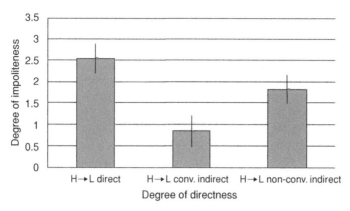

Figure 5.10 Degree of impoliteness and degree of directness in high to low power condition

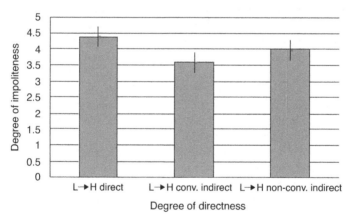

Figure 5.11 Degree of impoliteness and degree of directness in low to high power condition

command when one is in a position of relative power. This overall pattern is not what B&L (1987) or what Leech (1983) predict for differing degrees of directness. We have a U-shaped curve, and this does not match what we see in Figure 5.7. In contrast, in the L→H condition of Figure 5.11, all three degrees of directness are ranked high on the scale of impoliteness: all well above the neutral three (3, i.e. 'neither agree nor disagree') (the direct category has moved beyond 4, 'agree somewhat', towards 5, 'agree'). Again, this is not what B&L (1987) or what Leech (1983) predict. And again we have a U-shaped curve that does not match what we see in Figure 5.7. However, it is important to note the fact that the U-shaped curve is much flatter than that for the H→L condition. In fact, we can see that for the first time the confidence intervals are overlapping: whilst direct and conventionally indirect do not overlap, non-conventionally indirect overlaps with both.

What do these results mean? To get at that fully would require additional investigations and complementary methodologies. What we can do, however, is suggest how what we have found relates to extant hypotheses and findings. Regarding power, what was seen in Figure 5.8 is entirely consistent with B&L's predictions for the power variable (and Leech's are similar): the more the relative power of the speaker, the more politeness – hence less impoliteness – they tend to receive (e.g. Baxter 1984; Brown and Gilman 1989; Holtgraves 1986; Holtgraves and Yang 1990; Lim and Bowers 1991; Leichty and Applegate 1991). The U-shaped curve observed for the three categories of directness in Figures 5.9, 5.10 and 5.11 does not support any of the hypotheses as a whole displayed in Figure 5.8. However, one could say that it supports part of their claims: directness attracts higher evaluations of impoliteness, as does non-conventional indirectness, especially in the L→H power condition (i.e. when impolite beliefs are being expressed). It is conventional indirectness that is the odd one out. The fact that conventional indirectness is not considered impolite in the H→L power condition fits the findings of Blum-Kulka (e.g. 1987). It is also consistent with Terkourafi's (e.g. 2001) frame-based approach to politeness: it is doing what is normal in the frame. Why is there a flatter U-shaped curve displayed for the L→H power condition in Figure 5.11? One way of accounting for this is to say that above a certain impoliteness threshold the linguistic differences between our command items were not sufficiently salient to influence the judgement of impoliteness. Remember that Holtgraves (1994) found that knowing that the speaker was of high status was enough to prime a directive interpretation, in advance of any remark having been actually made. One might argue that knowing that a speaker of relatively low status is making a command is enough to prime an interpretation of high impoliteness. Moreover, as mentioned in Chapter 4, Greenberg's (1976) study of perceived verbal aggressiveness found that when an utterance reaches the higher levels of aggression the addition of boosters made little difference to how it was perceived: above a certain point the addition of further intensity does not produce a proportional increase in offensiveness. One might be puzzled that in the L→H power condition represented in Figure 5.11 that conventional indirectness is not considered the most impolite. Is it not the case that we have a mismatch between the politeness of the formula and the impoliteness of the situated act that exacerbates the overall impoliteness judgement? Recollect the discussion of irony at the beginning of Section 5.3. Dews *et al.* (1995; Dews and Winner 1995, 1997) did not find that irony exacerbated judgements. Consistent with their 'tinge hypothesis', they found that utterances such as 'what a lovely day for a picnic' were judged as less aggressive than their literal counterpart 'what a lousy day for a picnic'; in other words, the positive literal meaning of the first utterance tinged the interpretation, leading to an impression of less aggressiveness (see Giora 2003: 86–9, for additional empirical evidence). However, note my conclusion in Section 5.3 that it is the use of conventionalised politeness *strongly mismatching* a context in which a polite interpretation is not sustainable that could end up exacerbating the impoliteness of the message. As we saw, examples of mismatches that are likely to exacerbate impoliteness tend to exaggerate the conventionalised politeness formula. So, rather than simply writing 'thank you', the author of example [17] wrote 'Thank you SO VERY MUCH.' In Watts's (2003) terms, that is an example of politeness, whereas our test item, 'could you be quiet', is an example of politic behaviour – it is much less marked.

5.6 Conclusion

This chapter examined implicational impoliteness, focusing on its linguistic triggers. Relatively few cases can be captured easily through the Gricean account, the clearest relating to phenomena such as innuendo, insinuations and snide remarks. I discussed the important – because it is common in my data – phenomenon of mimicry, something that is often conveyed by acoustic means, and did this with more efficacy through the theory of echoic irony (Sperber and Wilson 1995). Moving on from the form-driven triggers of Section 5.2, the remaining sections (excluding Section 5.5) all have in common that they work through a mismatch of some kind. Convention-driven linguistic triggers involve the context projected (conventionally) by the behavioural trigger mismatching either the context projected by another part of the behaviour (an internal mismatch) or the context of use (an external mismatch). They cover everyday notions such as sarcasm, and, as with mimicry, multimodality is key. Drawing on the literature on irony, I concluded that the use of conventionalised politeness strongly mismatching a context in which a polite interpretation is not sustainable points towards the exacerbation of the impoliteness of the behaviour. Specifically regarding internal mismatches, I noted the use of mixes such as the ostensibly polite 'I hate to be rude but', 'no offence but' and 'with respect' followed by an (often intensified) impolite utterance. I suggested that the regularity with which these three formulae are followed by impoliteness could in itself be becoming conventionalised, that is to say, they are becoming second-order conventionalised impoliteness. I then turned to context-driven triggers, that is, whether behaviour is either unmarked or altogether absent in contexts where it is clearly expected – it mismatches contextual expectations. This category is somewhat marginal: it is certainly not replete with examples; in fact, the only candidates in my 100 report forms are analysed in this section. Behaviour that really is unmarked in Gricean terms and not conventionalised for a particular context of use is very rare (which in turn hints that it is a suspect category).

The final section of this chapter, 5.5, looked at the topic of directness and more generally explicitness. I reviewed the claims of scholars such as B&L (1987) and Leech (1983). Their hypotheses about (im)politeness and directness turned out not to be entirely supported. My work with John Dixon suggested that power symmetry/asymmetry was the most important factor in determining judgements of impoliteness. We also found that conventional directness was not considered impolite at all in the case of high-power speakers addressing relatively low-power speakers. Generally, with respect to directness, it is departures from the conventional, whether through using directness or non-conventional indirectness, that led to higher evaluations of impoliteness. Regarding low-power speakers commanding high-power addressees, we found that the differences between the different degrees of directness with respect to impoliteness judgements were relatively small. We suggested that the mere fact of commanding someone of relatively high power in a context where they clearly have no special right to do so is enough to lead to the evaluation of strong impoliteness, and at these higher levels of impoliteness the finer linguistic differences amongst our command items gets lost in the 'white noise' of offence. We suggested that the fact that the conventionally indirect 'could you be quiet' uttered in this context does not exacerbate the impoliteness more than the other directness categories may be because of possible leakage from the conventional polite meaning associated with 'could you X' structures and the fact that the mismatch between that conventional meaning and the context is not strong.

6 Impoliteness events: Co-texts and contexts

6.1 Introduction

From the very first sentence of Section 1.2 where I define the notion of impoliteness used in this book, I stressed its context dependence: impoliteness is a negative evaluative attitude towards behaviours in context. Clearly then, I need to consider in more detail the role of context, and this is the job of this chapter. Here, I will also discuss co-text, a distinct category of context defined by the fact that it is constituted by text. In this chapter and the next I am particularly concerned with impoliteness events, a term I use to refer to constellations of behaviours and co-textual/contextual features that co-occur in time and space, have particular functions and outcomes, and are/can be discussed and remembered by participants after the event. Impoliteness events are the fuel of schematic knowledge about impoliteness. Different participants can of course have different understandings of the same impoliteness event, having activated different schemata – different cognitive contexts – in their understandings (see Section 2.4). Needless to say, a context cannot be everything accompanying the text (including all the knowledge we have), otherwise our minds would be overloaded, so there must be a principle by which context is limited. Here, I follow the view of context articulated in Relevance theory (Sperber and Wilson 1986, 1995), where it is stated that:

> The set of premises used in interpreting an utterance . . . constitutes what is generally known as the *context*. A context is a psychological construct, a subset of the hearer's assumptions about the world. (Sperber and Wilson 1986: 15)

A context, in Relevance theory terms, is selected to maximise relevance: essentially, maximising meanings (informational rewards) whilst minimising inferential effort.

It will be clear from other parts of this book that the conceptual background to my approach to impoliteness events largely draws on schema theory (see, for example, Introducing impoliteness and Sections 2.4.1 and 6.3.1). In this, it is not dissimilar to Terkourafi's (e.g. 2001) frame-based approach to politeness (see also, for example, Locher and Watts 2005, who also allude to frames).

Frames, like schemata, can – depending on how they are defined – capture generic bundles of cognitive knowledge. However, schemata are not in themselves obviously connected to interactional matters. This is where the notion of activity type (e.g. Levinson 1992 [1979a]) comes in. Put simply, an activity type, such as a seminar, a family dinner event or a birthday party, is a collection of conversational contributions, including speech acts, that stand in particular pragmatic relationships to each other and have become a relatively conventionalised whole (a comprehensive description, and application involving politeness and cross-cultural issues, can be found in Culpeper *et al.* 2008; for some discussion in relation to impoliteness, see Culpeper 2005). Understanding what activity type is involved will 'help to determine how what one says will be "taken" – that is, what kinds of inferences will be made from what is said' (Levinson 1992: 97) (e.g. 'how are you' is unlikely to be taken as a phatic question in a doctor–patient interaction). Interestingly, the interpretive side of activity types – what Levinson refers to as the 'inferential schemata' (1992: 72) – resembles what Schank and Abelson (1977) label a 'script', a specific kind of schema, consisting of: 'A structure that describes appropriate sequences of events in a particular context. . . . Scripts handle stylised everyday situations. Thus, a script is a predetermined, stereotyped sequence of actions that defines a well-known situation' (1977: 41). It is important to observe that this definition characterises scripts as involving 'appropriate' sequences of events. As mentioned at other points of this book, schema-theoretic notions allow us to tap into empirical norms that contribute to politic behaviour, that is, behaviour which is 'expectable' and 'perceived to be appropriate to the social constraints of the ongoing interaction' (Watts 2003: 19; see also Introducing impoliteness). Scanning Watts's (2003) analyses of data, one can find fairly frequent recourse to the term 'activity type', though it is not spelt out what is meant by this term or whether a particular literature is alluded to. Furthermore and importantly, activity types also have a more interactional side that accommodates the idea that language is not only shaped by context but language also shapes context. Gumperz's notion of 'contextualization cues', which have some affinity with conventionalised impoliteness formulae as described in Chapter 4, are based on the latter idea. He defines them as 'those verbal signs that are indexically associated with specific classes of *communicative activity types* and thus signal the frame of context for the interpretation of constituent messages' (Gumperz 1992a: 307, my emphasis; see also Gumperz 1982a, 1982b, 1992b). Of course, in practice meanings are generated through a dynamic interaction between both context and language (see in particular the papers in Duranti and Goodwin 1992).

The first section of this chapter focuses on the contextual background for impoliteness behaviours in particular, especially contexts in which they are considered normal or legitimate. In Section 6.3, I look at the role of context in priming face components and social norms. The following section turns to co-text. I focus on the role of language in setting (im)politeness thresholds, and the implications this has for subsequent interactants. In the penultimate section, I examine the recontextualisation of conventionally impolite formulae, particularly with the result that they are construed as mock, non-genuine impoliteness. Here, I discuss banter and some types of teasing and humour. Finally, I examine the role of context in neutralising impoliteness effects.

6.2 The backdrop for impoliteness

Some norms are reflected in explicit rules and enforced by legislation and sanctions, as we saw in Section 3.9. Other norms are more implicit. They are the background to everyday life. This is consistent with how norms were described in Section 1.4: they are regular habits and/or agreed social oughts, the stuff that lends a sense of naturalness to occasions and does not draw attention to itself. Garfinkel (1967) investigated such norms using ethnomethodology. His method was to violate these norms in order to draw attention to them. In one study he arranged for his students to act at home for fifteen minutes as if they were boarders. Specifically, they were instructed 'to conduct themselves in a circumspect and polite fashion' and 'to avoid getting personal, to use formal address, and to speak only when spoken to' (1967: 47). The students' reports of family member reactions were full of 'accounts of astonishment, bewilderment, shock, anxiety, embarrassment, and anger, and with charges by various family members that the student was mean, inconsiderate, selfish, nasty, or impolite' (1967: 47). There are two important points of interest here. Firstly, it is behaviour that is not consistent with implicit norms that most clearly makes them explicit. Secondly, the norm-disrupting behaviour was judged impolite, despite the fact that the behaviour consisted of behaviours traditionally labelled polite, that is, behaviours that are positively valenced. This, of course, supports the point that linguistic politeness does not fully determine politeness judgements (see Section 4.3).

In this section I focus on the norms that act as a backdrop for impoliteness. In particular, I am concerned with contexts where, at least in some perspectives, impoliteness is considered normal and/or appropriate.

6.2.1 Experiential norms: when impoliteness is habitual

As I argued in Section 2.4, a cognitive approach such as schema theory can account for subjectivity and variability. Importantly, only schemata that are currently active form expectations. Neisser argues that 'schemata are anticipations, they are the medium by which the past affects the future' (1976: 22). Rumelhart suggests that in a sense 'conceptually-driven processing is *expectation-driven* processing' (1984: 170). Schema theory explains why instances of impoliteness are often better remembered than instances of politeness; as Kasper (1990: 193) observes, politeness often passes unnoticed. Disconfirming or incongruent information requires more effort to process than congruent information – it provides a greater cognitive shock – and so that information may be well remembered (e.g. Fiske and Taylor 1984: 165). This tallies with the idea that people generally better remember impoliteness events than politeness events.

Schema-theoretic approaches have been deployed in the context of research on aggression. Huesmann (1988), for example, proposed that persistent aggressive behaviours should be understood in terms of the schemata that people form of their environments. Discussing the socialisation of children in the context of frequent aggressive behaviours, he also noted that aggressive schemata tend to guide people towards aggressive behaviours when dealing with conflict and predispose them to understanding conflict in terms of aggression, and this in turn contributes to the possibility that aggression may become self-perpetuating and escalate over time. From this, we might hypothesise that familiarity with impoliteness contexts generally predisposes people towards impoliteness and particularly predisposes them to meeting impoliteness with impoliteness. Impoliteness, from their perspective, may be considered both appropriate and normal. The question to ask at this point is: would they still consider their behaviour impolite or is that just an external perspective?

In Culpeper (1996: 355) I suggested that 'impoliteness is very much the parasite of politeness'. Generally, the more salient the politic/politeness behaviour expectations are the more salient the impoliteness (as I will elaborate in Section 6.3). So, according to this, if one is immersed in an event where impoliteness is normal, it can only be weakly impolite at best *in terms of that event*. However, a series of cautions is needed: (a) face is sensitive to attack in any circumstance, (b) face-attack can only be neutralised when the target can adequately factor in the context and people do not automatically do this (see Section 6.6), and (c) although people may be predisposed towards impolite schemata, they may well be able to understand how others might construe the same phenomena (e.g. as impolite). Indeed, to expand on the last point, just because one operates within one value system does not mean one has no awareness of others. Socialisation in schools, moral outrages in the media, police interventions, and so on ensure that other value systems are kept in focus, and in particular value systems underpinned by institutional authorities.

6.2.2   Social norms: when impoliteness has positive cultural values or is ideologically legitimised

In Section 1.3.1, I noted that the notion of face is comprised of 'positive' attributes, but also that those attributes can be evaluated differently by different people. Different cultures have different norms and given values. A good example is provided by Mills (2005: 273), who suggests that:

linguistic features which seem to be stereotypically positively associated with masculinity and hence power are: the use of direct assertions rather than indirectness; swearing; unmitigated statements and expressions of negative opinion; face-threatening acts in general; verbal wit and humour, non-emotional language.

Of course, what Mills is listing here includes the very behaviours that much of the politeness literature would use to exemplify impolite or non-polite behaviours. The point is that such behaviours may be associated with positive values, and it may suit participants – whether male or female – to use such behaviours to project a masculine identity as a face claim. What all this suggests is that we need to take account of the social norms and cultural ideologies mediating the value systems that underpin face claims. Let us note further examples. Vandello and Cohen (2003) studied the 'culture of honour', a culture that ascribes positive values to male violence as a way of restoring social reputation or economic position, and can be found in various parts of the world including some Mediterranean countries, the Middle East, Central and Southern America, and the southern United States. Another cultural ideology, labelled 'subculture of violence' (Toch 1969), concerns a subgroup of society, typically an urban gang, in which a higher level of violence is accepted as a social norm – a 'lifestyle' choice. A related ideology is that of 'machismo', which places a positive value on aggression as a way of dealing with challenges and differences of opinion, and has been studied in various countries including Italy and Latin America. Tomada and Schneider (1997) linked machismo in some of the more traditional areas of Italy to the higher rate of male bullying in school compared with some other countries. Ruggiero and Lattin (2008) provide evidence of the fact that verbal aggressiveness (including obscenties, name-calling, insults and threats) in the cultural context of competitive sports training is seen as positive functional behaviour, driving athletes to perform better. Such ideologies legitimise as positive values values which others may take as negative.

As I argued in Section 4.4.2, Gilbert's (1989) account of social norms (see Section 1.4.2) skates over the unequal influence particular groups have (and individuals in groups have) in reproducing and imposing those social norms and values. Impoliteness rules and punitive sanctions are generally unidirectional: they are imposed by the more powerful on the less (see Section 3.9, for more on rules and sanctions). The issue here is of dominant ideologies, belief systems that can sustain and normalise patterns of behaviour that serve power hierarchies (cf. Barthes 1970). For example, it is generally not considered impolite in British cultures for parents to use direct requests and threats to their children, but extremely impolite for children to use the same to their parents. Insults, particularly those involving social identity face (e.g. racist and sexist insults), can be a means of controlling others as well as maintaining dominant groups in society at the expense of others. Flynn (1977: 66) highlights the motivations for using such insults:

(1) dominant values and norms can be reaffirmed, (2) the insulter might gain status within his own reference group, and (3) the dominant group might have social objects upon which to project their unacceptable feelings and desires.

I will return to the notion of power, especially coercive power, in Section 7.3. What I'm interested in here is the inter-meshing of power, ideology and legitimation, and what that means for the use and understanding of impoliteness. In fact, we have already seen what this means for impoliteness in the investigation I reported in Section 5.5.2. The strongest differences in perceived impoliteness were brought about through changes in the power condition, whether low to high or high to low. When commands, however they are couched, are uttered by an employer to an employee, by a judge to a defendant or by an army sergeant to a recruit they hardly counted as impolite. Institutional power structures underpin these contexts and give rise to dominant ideologies by which impoliteness is legitimated and (typically) unchallenged (for institutional impoliteness, see Section 7.6). Sanctioned, legitimated behaviour is the flipside of social norms (social 'oughts'), as it is unrestricted, legitimate and free from social penalties. Note a deeper issue here: legitimation conceals the dominance of one person/group over another; it licences what otherwise might be construed as impoliteness, and, moreover, impoliteness used for coercive purposes (see Section 7.3). What people frequently react to and label as impoliteness are abuses of power, that is, cases where a person or group exerts power over another person or group beyond what is considered legitimate. Legitimation only goes so far and is always dependant on ideological perspective. This is consistent with my metalinguistic findings in Section 3.6.4, which revealed labels related to patronising as key − in other words, labels relating to perceived abuses of power. We will see examples of this, particularly in Section 7.3. One particular case where legitimation falls short is where it conflicts with the norm of fairness (see Section 1.4.2), and in particular the idea that punishments should be similar for similar others. Singling people out for especially harsh punishment, or impoliteness abuse, will violate the norm of fairness.

There are complex interactions between behaviours, cultural social norms and values, and ideologies. Tetreault's (2009) work is an interesting illustration and discussion of this. She reports an ethnographic study, exploring how the local expressions of identity amongst Muslim French adolescents both reproduce and challenge North African (specifically Algerian) cultural ideologies relating to generation and gender. The study focuses on the practice of what she labels 'parental name calling', that is, the irreverent use by an adolescent of the first name of a peer's parent in public. The avoidance of first names in personal address, particularly if the interlocutor is older or does not have the same gender, is widely prescribed across North Africa and practised by the parents of these adolescents (2009: 66, 70). The adolescents articulate the cultural value of this social norm by referring to it as *le respect* ('respect'). This is a norm of politeness embedded within a particular ideology. It consists not simply of reproduced Arab-Muslim values imported from North Africa but 'a set of moral discourses and practices that emerge in France' (2009: 73). However, the teenagers subvert this norm:

> In parental name-calling, however, teens intentionally do the exact opposite [of following the politeness norm], that is, they publicly voice the name of a peer's parent in order to playfully tease, incite anger, or exercise social control. In this regard, parent name-calling constitutes a particularly important discursive genre for adolescents to articulate cultural ties to both their immigrant origins and their emergent adolescent subculture. Through practising the genre, French adolescents of North African descent construct their peer group both in relation to cultural ideals of *le respect* and in contrast to those ideals. (2009: 70)

What emerges, in complex ways, amongst these adolescents is a distinct norm of 'respect', a distinct morality (particularly concerning sexuality) and a distinct ideology. This study encompasses many of the issues discussed in this book, including face, social norms, morality, attitude schemata and ideology. It also illustrates the role of discourse in creating, maintaining and subverting all these notions.

6.3   Contextual priming: Face components, sensitivity and exposure

When people encounter a situation, they search their memory for similar situations, and use those situations to help them organise and make sense of the new encounter. In other words, they deploy relevant schemata. There is much evidence that behaviours in initial interactions are highly dependent on schematic scripts (Kellerman 1995). But what are the factors that determine which schemata become activated? I have already pointed out that Relevance theory (Sperber and Wilson 1986) argues that context is selected to maximise relevance, but this is a very general principle. Which schemata exactly would be easier to access than others? Scholars have identified the following as being key (further supporting references can be found in Fiske and Neuberg 1990: 9–12):

Context. Fiske and Taylor (1984: 176) suggest that the situational context may influence which schemata are activated. The things are perceived and remembered in context, and so knowing the context can prime a link to the thing. For example, seeing a football pitch makes it more likely that the dimly viewed people on the far side wearing sports kit will be assumed to be footballers. Similarly, coercive, high-emotion situations, for example, are likely to prime knowledge about impoliteness language, making it more likely that a person will 'take' verbal activity as impoliteness.

Frequency. Researchers in social cognition (e.g. Fiske and Taylor 1991: 145–6; Zebrowitz 1990: 50) have also argued that schemata which are frequently activated are more accessible, and thus more likely to spring to mind. This factor is actually related to the previous, as Fiske and Taylor (1991: 197) point out: '[c]onsistent short-term contexts add up to long-term context over time. A child who grows up as the smartest child on the block should be acutely aware of being smart in most day-to-day contexts'. Similarly, someone who is regularly a target of impoliteness would be more likely to interpret verbal activity as impoliteness.

Recency. Researchers in social cognition (e.g. Fiske and Taylor 1991: 145–6; Zebrowitz 1990: 50) have argued that schemata which have been recently activated are more accessible, and thus more likely to spring to mind. This has also been shown for self-schemata (e.g. Markus and Nurius 1986). Similarly, someone who has recently been a target of impoliteness would be more likely to interpret subsequent verbal activity as impoliteness.

Regarding the kinds of cues that activate schemata it is worth stressing the importance of visual context: in many encounters visual cues will trigger schemata about, for example, setting (e.g. an office, a party, the family dinner table) and participants (consider the different dress codes) before a word has been spoken.

The above factors apply to any kind of schema, including, for example, schematic knowledge about appropriate norms, the self and others. This is important because face (and facework) is always understood within such a conceptual context (Penman 1994), and in particular against the value systems discussed in the previous section. Particular components of face are primed in particular contexts. For example, when asking my bank manager for a further overdraft, I wish to be seen as trustworthy; when at work, I wish to be seen as competent; when seeking the help of a doctor, I wish to be seen as ill (implications to the contrary would make me feel a fraud; my face would be assailed). I have noted in Section 1.3.1 that face varies in terms of emotional importance to the self, with the most face sensitive elements at the centre. The context may prime a face component that is highly sensitive. Moreover, context may affect the extent of perceived face exposure. Ensconced in the enclosure of a 'portaloo' in Leicester Square (London) no face is lost on account of my state of undress. Face is not primed in non-social situations; face is not an issue if it has no exposure. But if the sides of the portaloo fell away revealing me to the stares of passers-by, I would suffer acute embarrassment, as I became aware that I was exposed to so many. We can hypothesise that the potential for face damage is related to the degree of sensitivity of the face component at issue and also the perceived degree of exposure, as illustrated in Figure 6.1.

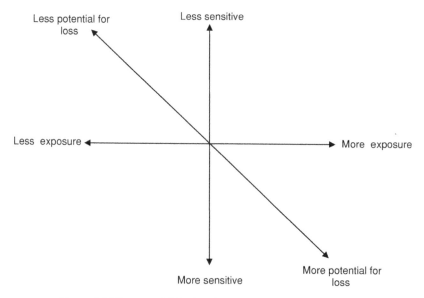

Figure 6.1 The potential for face loss

6.4   Co-textual priming: (Im)politeness thresholds and reciprocity

Once interaction – including talk – starts, that interaction itself becomes a norm against which any potential impoliteness works. Relevant context is not just a matter of accessing relatively static prior knowledge (schemata); it is constantly being updated by the changing perceptual environment, and notably, in the realms of communication, by the co-text.

In classic research on norms, Sherif (1936) conducted a set of experiments which showed that people use norms as a 'frame of reference', just as today people would argue for schemata. Moreover, he showed that when people made perceptual judgements alone in a context free from the influence of previously established norms (the judgement of light movement in a darkened room), their own judgements rapidly became the norm – the frame of reference. However, when they were in the same context but in a group, diverse individual assessments (i.e. judgements articulated in talk) converged to become a common assessment, and people used that as the norm. This is more accurately a social norm, created by group fiat, rather than an experiential norm based largely on regularity. Thus, the norm *emerged* from the interaction between group members, and once created acquired a life of its own (in fact, in a follow-up experiment, individuals continue to use the group norm a year later (Rohrer *et al.* 1954)). The findings of Sherif's work has been confirmed in other studies, such as Bettenhausen and Murnighan (1985), though they also note the important point that acceptance of group norms is not automatic: '[a]lthough [newcomers to an organisation] may willingly modify their interpretations of the situation, they may also raise objections and challenge the groups understanding of what constitutes an appropriate behaviour' (1985: 370). The key point for us here is that norms emerging in interaction are important interpretative touchstones. Moreover, the way in which those norms emerge and solidify or dissolve in talk exerts a powerful influence on how that talk is understood and matched.

There seems to be a tendency for people to match the kinds of social behaviours produced by others. Cialdini *et al.* (1978) investigated the function of norms and people's behaviours in the context of litter dropping. He placed flyers under the windscreen wipers of cars and watched what people did with them. Furthermore, he manipulated the context so that before they got to their cars some owners would see somebody (one of Cialdini's team) pick up a bag from a fast-food restaurant lying on the ground and throw it in the bin. Of the car-owners who did not see this responsible behaviour, over a third threw the flyers on the street; of the car-owners who did see this responsible behaviour, almost none threw them on the street. There are two important points here. One is that social behaviours take place in the context of other behaviours, which exert some influence. Presumably, the observation of socially responsible behaviour heightened the observer's awareness of social norms of the type discussed in Section 1.4.1, and this influenced their behaviour. The other point is that Cialdini and his researchers were able to manipulate the context through actions that they performed. This is precisely what happens in social interactions. People can create certain (im)politeness thresholds that can be matched or mismatched. Moreover, as the interaction progresses so the (im)politeness threshold is being continually up-dated.

Let us illustrate this through an example.

[1]

> [*Graffiti dialogue written on a Lancaster University Library desk; from the handwriting it seems to be the case that each line has a different author*]
>
> Good luck if you are revising for your exams!
> R U fucking gay? Is U Mom a fucking WHORE?
> VERY HARSH TWAT!

There is no strong expectation of a high politeness threshold within graffiti dialogues. Hayes's (2005) quantitative work on graffiti dialogues suggested that approximately 80 per cent (n = 51) contain phenomena that can be construed as impolite. What happens here is that the first turn engineers a high politeness threshold through performing an altruistic act of good wishes. The fact that such an act is not typical of graffiti makes it all the more salient in this context. The following turn strikingly violates that politeness threshold, deploying two intensified conventionalised impoliteness formulae (challenging rhetorical questions). Perhaps it is also worth noting that the first of these attacks the first writer's masculinity. There is, in fact, no evidence as to the gender of the first writer; *gay* could apply equally to a woman. The second writer simply seems to be targeting a stereotypical association between politeness and femininity (this squares with the point made in Section 6.2.2 that impoliteness can project masculine identities). Finally, the third writer responds with an intensified conventionalised insult. Readers may agree with me that this third turn seems far less impolite than the second. Of course, they deploy different impoliteness formulae intensified in different ways, and this may account for some of the difference. But I would argue that in addition the (im)politeness threshold has been reset by the second writer at a much lower negative value.

My description of the graffiti example is consistent with research in social psychology. In fact, an interactional norm here has already been discussed in Section 1.4.1. The reciprocity norm (Gouldner 1960) proposes that behaviour, prosocial, antisocial or of some other kind, should be matched − it is a kind of 'tit-for-tat' prescription.[1] Setting the (im)politeness threshold at a particular point constrains the interlocutor to match it. Reciprocal polite 'thank yous', sometimes repeating themselves over several exchanges, are not uncommon in British culture. Conversely, reciprocal impolite exchanges are also not uncommon. People tend not to 'turn the other cheek', but to retaliate in kind in British and North American cultures. Research in aggression has repeatedly shown that verbal insults and taunts are reciprocated (see the references given in Baron and Richardson 1994: 142). The following interaction is a good illustration:

[2]
> [A man in a compact red car was trying to manoeuvre into a parking spot right next to a crosswalk at a corner in New York City. A woman was crossing the street with her two children as the man attempted to park. She was very thin. He had a big 'beer belly'. The two were arguing over whether she, the pedestrian, or he, the driver, had the right of way. Finally, the woman yelled the following]
>
> Woman: Oh shut up you fat pig
> Man: Go fuck yourself
> Woman: Go on a diet
> Man: Go fuck yourself
> (Beebe 1995: 154, sourced from Wendy Gavis, field notes)

Needless to say, there are other motivations feeding into counter-impoliteness. The intial impoliteness may be part of a strategy to coerce the target, for example, overcoming their resistance by 'taking them down a peg' with insults and so on (and this may part of the woman's strategy in the example) (see Section 7.3). Of course, this involves loss of face on the part of the target. Countering with impoliteness not only restores that face loss but might block the coercive strategy. There is also the fact that impoliteness produces a state of emotional arousal in the target and this increases the likelihood that they will retaliate in kind (Jay 2000: 60) (see Andersson and Pearson 1999, for an excellent analysis and discussion of tit-for-tat phenomena, including causes, and 'incivility' in the context of the workplace). Note that some social contexts constrain the target's ability to reciprocate. For example, in the traffic warden data I examined with Derek Bousfield (cf. Culpeper *et al.* 2003), wardens never responded in kind to irate car owners, presumably, part of the role of their job is not to do so; politicians rarely response in kind to hecklers, presumably, it would damage their image of being calm and in control.

The reciprocity norm also has implications for the perception of impoliteness, and this is particularly pertinent to the graffiti example above. If the threshold is set high on a scale of politeness, behaviour which seems impolite is likely to be perceived as violating the reciprocity norm, and thus is likely to be taken as even more impolite. If the threshold is set high on a scale of impoliteness, then behaviour which in other contexts may be very impolite is likely to be perceived as upholding the reciprocity norm, and thus is likely to be taken as less impolite. The kind of impoliteness of the latter scenario is what Kienpointner (1997: 266) labels 'reactive rudeness'. Research has shown that counter-aggression may be taken as a matter of fair defence (e.g. Brown and Tedeschi 1976). Kienpointner (1997: 271) notes: 'reactive rudeness is considered to be legitimate only because of its position in a speech act sequence, that is, its non-initiating character'. Such factors may play a role in my perception of the third turn of the graffiti example being less impolite. Reactive impoliteness/rudeness is one case where impoliteness might be considered appropriate (hence being inappropriate should not be part of a definition of impoliteness; see Section 1.2). However, note that whilst true in many contexts, counter-impoliteness would not necessarily be perceived as fair defence in contexts where the initial impoliteness is licensed (e.g. in a courtroom interaction between the prosecution and a defendant). And, of course, further orientations to (im)politeness thresholds are possible. For example, if the threshold is set high on a scale of impoliteness, then what happens if we have behaviour which seems to be polite? In fact, I have already treated such cases in Section 5.3. This kind of mixing of impolite co-text and polite behaviour is likely to result in an understanding of sarcasm.

In this section and the previous, I have considered the first steps that might be taken in understanding an impoliteness event (e.g. finding a relevant schema) and the role of co-text in shaping the development of that understanding. However, regarding the latter, I have focused mainly on how the discourse of one participant may influence that of the next. What about cases where one particular participant's talk shifts in terms of how polite or impolite it is. Afifi and Burgoon (2000) have investigated this very issue. The key point they emphasise are the negative consequences if a person starts an interaction in a positive way but then shifts:

If individuals choose to move from initial behaviour that is consistent with the social expectation to behaviour that violates social norms, then uncertainty may increase. Observers are less able to discount the socially violative behaviour, because it appears to be a conscious move away from the socially expected behaviour initially displayed. (Afifi and Burgoon 2000: 226)

Particularly noteworthy is our finding that individuals who are relatively consistent in their negativity (i.e., negative congruent violations) are preferred over individuals who begin the interaction with a pleasant demeanour, then become unpleasant midway through the interaction. (Afifi and Burgoon 2000: 228)

In other words, when an individual's own behaviour creates a politic or politeness threshold from which they later deviate towards impoliteness, they are likely to be perceived as particularly impolite. The first example discussed in this book provides a good illustration of this.

6.5   Recontextualising impoliteness: Genuine vs mock impoliteness

In Section 5.3 I treated phenomena to which everyday terms such as teasing and humour are applied as implicational impoliteness, specifically cases where a conventionalised impoliteness formula mismatches the context. There I focused on cases of teasing and humour that were considered 'harsh', cases where contextual expectations of politeness were not strong – they did not block an overall judgement of impoliteness. Here, I wish to focus on conventionalised impoliteness formulae used in contexts where contextual expectations of politeness are very strong. Consider this example:

[3]

> [*Lawrence Dallaglio, former England Rugby captain, describing the very close family in which he grew up*]
>
> As Francesca and John left the house, she came back to give Mum a kiss and they said goodbye in the way they often did. 'Bye, you bitch,' Francesca said. 'Get out of here, go on, you bitch,' replied Mum.
>
> *It's in the blood: My life* (2007), from an extract given in *The Week*, 10/11/07

Here, in the direct speech, we see a conventionalised insulting vocative, 'you bitch', and also a conventionalised dismissal, 'get out of here'. McEnery (2006: 39, 236) provides corpus evidence that there is a strong tendency in British English for *bitch* to be used between women, as here. Nevertheless, these items project contexts that are dramatically at odds with the situation within which they are uttered. Rather than antagonistic relationships, hate, coercion, and so on, we have a strong loving family unit (note that Francesca has just demonstrated her affection by giving her mother a kiss). The recontextualisation of impoliteness in socially opposite contexts reinforces socially opposite effects, namely, affectionate, intimate bonds amongst individuals and the identity of that group.

The example in the previous paragraph involved mock impoliteness, that is, the opposite of genuine impoliteness (the term 'mock impoliteness' is used in Leech 1983; also see Bernal 2008, for a discussion of genuine vs non-genuine impoliteness). Banter is the key everyday label, though most types of teasing and some jokes also have in common the fact that they involve mock impoliteness. Mock impoliteness consists of impolite forms whose effects are (at least theoretically for the most part) cancelled by the context. Leech (1983) describes mock impoliteness within his Banter Principle:

'In order to show solidarity with *h*, say something which is (i) obviously untrue, and (ii) obviously impolite to *h*' [and the Banter Principle thus expressed will give rise to an interpretation such that] 'what *s* says is impolite to *h* and is clearly untrue. Therefore what *s* really means is polite to *h* and true.' (1983: 144)

The fact that banter is obviously impolite is an important part of flagging the mismatch between the impolite formula and the context that characterises mock impoliteness. Leech also indicates that banter involves saying something which is 'obviously untrue'. As banter often involves insults, one can see how this might work, and it does work for many instances. Thus, saying 'you arsehole' to somebody who is a friend you admire flouts the Maxim of Quality, whether you take the literal or the figurative meaning of 'arsehole'. But not all banter involves neatly analysable insults like this. An example that will come up later in this discussion of banter is: 'Who the fucking hell are you?' This is a conventionalised impoliteness formula, but in what way is it obviously untrue? In particular, the use of taboo intensification exacerbates the impoliteness, but this does not seem to be an issue that obviously involves the Maxim of Quality. I prefer to see cases of banter more broadly in terms of an understanding on the part of a participant that the contextual conditions that sustain genuine impoliteness do not apply; flouting the Maxim of Quality is but one possible signal that those conditions do not apply. Drawing on the idea proposed in previous work (e.g. Terkourafi 2001) that politeness concerns the perlocutionary effects of utterances, we can think of mock impoliteness in theoretical terms as involving the cancelling of impoliteness perlocutionary effects flowing from a conventionalised impoliteness formula when an obvious mismatch emerges with the context it is used in. This fits what Austin ([1962] 1972: 104, my emphasis) writes of joking:

There are aetiolations, parasitic uses, etc., and various 'not serious' and 'not full normal' uses. *The normal conditions of reference may be suspended*, and no attempt made at a standard perlocutionary act, no attempt to make you do anything, as Walt Whitman does not seriously incite the eagle of liberty to soar.

The same, of course, would also apply to the converse phenomenon of sarcasm, where politeness perlocutionary effects are cancelled (see Section 5.3).

Leech (1983) argues that banter reflects and fosters social intimacy (i.e. relative equality in terms of authority and closeness in terms of social distance): the more intimate a relationship, the less necessary and important politeness is, and thus lack of politeness can be associated with intimacy. Some empirical support for this can be found in Kowalski's (2000): in 144 informant accounts of teasing none involved strangers. One of the lacunae in B&L (1987) is that they do not treat banter at all. However, they do very briefly mention joking as a positive politeness strategy, and a subset of jokes involve mock impoliteness (humour and joking can be more comprehensively related to B&L's framework, as is demonstrated in Holmes 2000). According to them, '[s]ince jokes are based on mutual shared background knowledge and values, jokes may be used to stress the shared background or those shared values' (1987: 124). This echoes Leech's point about banter showing solidarity. Furthermore, Holmes (2000: 174), discussing humorous insults used in the workplace, writes:

insults between those who know each other well are also signs of solidarity and markers of in-group membership . . . humour encodes the criticism or insult in an acceptable form; insults can be considered instances of 'doing collegiality' between those who work together closely.

If lack of politeness can be associated, amongst other things, with intimacy (something which both B&L 1987 and Leech 1983 predict), surface impoliteness is theoretically even more likely to be interpreted as part of banter in non-intimate contexts, where it is more clearly at odds with contextual expectations. Some support for this hypothesis can be found in Slugoski and Turnbull's (1988) investigation of the interpretation of ironic compliments and insults. Subjects tended to interpret an insult as polite (i.e. as banter) in conditions of high social distance. More importantly, their study revealed the even stronger influence of affect (liking or disliking) operating as an independent variable. The more people like each other, the more concern they are likely to have for each other's face. Thus, for example, insults are more likely to be interpreted as banter when the interactants like each other.

What about power relations? Consider the advertising slogan used by an Australian meat retailer, displayed in Figure 6.2. One may suppose that the prototypical customer is both socially distant from the retailer and more powerful (in so far as the customer has the power to determine the success or otherwise of the retailer's goals). Clearly, the retailer is not in a position to employ a derogatory term of address, and has nothing to gain from doing so: it is obviously banter. But note that the choice of impoliteness formula is one that is associated with fairly mild impoliteness (as far as British culture is

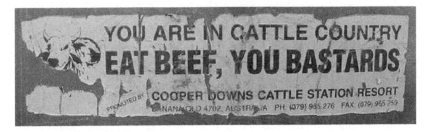

Figure 6.2 Advertisement: 'EAT BEEF, YOU BASTARDS'

concerned, *bastard* is ranked sixth on a scale of offensiveness in Millwood-Hargrave 2000). Keltner *et al.* (1998) found that low-status fraternity members teased high-status fraternity members in more prosocial ways than low-status members, that is, they reduced face threat, by choosing a less offensive insult, and increased redressive action. They clearly lowered the risk in contexts where more is at stake if the mock impoliteness is misunderstood. I shall return to the issue of power towards the end of this section.

The understanding of impoliteness as non-genuine does not rely purely on an evaluation of mismatches with the context. Just as signalling devices, such as taboo words and extreme prosodic features, help secure impoliteness effects (see Section 4.5), so signalling devices are used to help secure politeness effects. Reviewing the literature, Keltner *et al.* (1998: 1233) suggest that devices accompanying the tease that indicate that it is 'off-record, playful, and not be taken seriously' include: 'unusual vocalisations, singsong voice, formulaic utterances, elongated vowels, and unusual facial expressions'. Drew's (1987) study of teasing, deploying Conversation Analysis, also pointed out that politeness was signalled by laughing in an affiliative fashion just before or after the tease (Bernal 2008 has the same finding). There is much more to be said about 'formulaic utterances' in particular, as these are an important feature of the ritualistic character of banter.

Banter exists in a heavily ritualised form as a kind of language game – a specific activity type. In America some forms of this activity are known as 'sounding', 'playing the dozens' or 'signifying', which takes place particularly amongst black adolescents (Abrahams 1962). Labov's (1972) work has been influential in revealing the complexity of the insults used and the well-organised nature of this speech event. Typically, these insults are sexual, directed at a third person related to the target, and couched in rhyming couplets. For example: 'Iron is iron, and steel don't rust, But your momma got a pussy like a Greyhound Bus' (Labov 1972: 302). The key to 'sounding' is that the insult is understood to be non-genuine, an interpretation that comes about on the basis of shared knowledge within the group. The effect is to reinforce in-group solidarity. In fact, the 'parental name calling' identified in a community in France by Tetreault (2009) (see Section 6.2.2) seems similar — which is perhaps an indication that it is not in fact genuine impoliteness. There is a competitive element to ritualised 'sounding'; the winner is the one who has the widest range of ritual insults to hand and can use them most appropriately. Real time improvisation in the creation of ritual insults tends not to occur. A result of the formulaic nature of the insults is that it is easier to recognise that one is engaged in 'sounding' rather than genuine personal insult. Labov also points out that 'weak' insults, ones that are not outrageously bizarre and so obviously untrue, are more dangerous in that they are more likely to be interpreted as genuine insults. Labov illustrates this thus:

Among young adults, to say *I fucked your mother* is not to say something obviously untrue. But it is obviously untrue that 'I fucked your mother from tree to tree' / Your father said, 'Now fuck me!' (1972: 340)

Forms of ritualised banter have been studied extensively in America, but occur in other cultures as well. Thomson (1935) found 'organised' swearing amongst the aborigines of Northern Queensland, and Montagu (2000 [1967]: 13) observed that a similar form of swearing is found amongst the Eskimos. Hughes (1991) points out that 'sounding' is similar to 'flyting'. This was a kind of competitive ritual insult that was common in Old Norse. With the Norse/Danish settlement of England it made its way into English literature, but gradually died out. Vestiges of 'flyting' can be found in Shakespeare's plays (e.g. *Romeo and Juliet* II.iv, *The Taming of the Shrew* II.i). In all these cases ritualised banter seems to act as a societal safety-valve. It is a place where we can be impolite with impunity, since 'in ritual we are freed from personal responsibility for the acts we are engaged in' (Labov 1972: 352–3).

Regarding present-day British culture, it may be thought that the kind of highly ritualised banter being discussed here is not a feature. This is not true. An example of note is the football crowd. Crowley's (2007) description of 'rudeness' amongst football crowds is highly illuminating, and so I will quote at length:

If someone were to shout an insult at a stranger or group of strangers in the street or in a park they would be liable either to a response from that person, or, in given circumstances, an intervention by the forces of the State. Yet the following are all commonplaces inside football grounds: 'You're shit and you know you are', 'Who the fucking hell are you?', 'fuck off X' ... Why would this be offensive in one instance and taken as normal or standard in another? The answer lies precisely in the fact that these are *generic* chants shouted or sung by thousands of people in a specific context. Rather than insults in the familiar sense, these are formulaic expressions in which the particular content is overridden by the nature of acts to which they belong. When a crowd chants 'the referee's a wanker', what is not in question is the private behaviour of a given individual (it's unusual for a referee's name to be used). Instead an illocutionary act is performed whose force is that of a general expression of antagonism. . . . The point about this type of performative is that it needs to be as conventionally offensive as possible. Yet even if these aren't insults in the ordinary sense of the term, they still seem to be expressions of extreme forms of rudeness; but if that were their function then they would have to be taken as clear failures. Given that one of the purposes of intentional rudeness is to inflict harm upon another, then the chanting of football songs at players or the referee seems to be peculiarly ineffective . . . But then the question arises: why, given their practical inefficiency as insults, are such chants sung? The answer lies not in the antagonistic illocutionary force but in the perlocutionary effects of the rude chanting: the function of these songs is not to insult, but to produce a communal bond and identity through repeated performances of empty hostility. (Crowley 2007: 121–2)

Crowley's analysis is consistent with my description of the activity type of ritualised banter. For example, note that he says that the performative needs to be as 'conventionally offensive as possible'; in other words, one needs to select a conventionalised impoliteness formula associated with high offence. Having said that, a feature of banter, as also illustrated in Labov's examples above, is creativity. This is usually achieved through creative adaption of a conventionalised impoliteness formula, rather than something completely non-formulaic. Thereby, a degree of formulaic safety (optimising recognition of mock impoliteness) is maintained along with creative entertainment (for more on creative entertainment, see Sections 7.4 and 7.5). With regard to football, we should note that the chant itself is a creative carriage for an insult: it imposes a particular metrical structure. Further, Crowley (2007: 1–2) observes that

Wittier chants are often responses to insults from opposing fans . . . when Liverpool reached the Champions League final in 2005, held in Istanbul, their fans answer to the condescending 'Champions league? You're having a laugh' was 'Champions league? We're having Kebabs'. In response to the taunt 'you're not famous any more', made by Chelsea fans at Liverpool's ground, the home fans took to chanting 'history, history, you can't buy history'.

The competitive element driving a creative reformulation of the original insult for retaliation was also noted by Labov.

Although I have been discussing highly ritualised mock impoliteness speech activities, it is important to remember that the ritualistic aspects of banter are not confined to a few specialist speech activities but are a feature of much everyday banter, though not necessarily so highly concentrated. Remember in the first example of this section the author observes that the participants 'said goodbye in the way they often did'. In other words, they had developed a particular mock impoliteness local ritual. I have already noted in Section 5.3 how certain familiar forms of impoliteness could become, to use Silverstein's (1998: 128–38) terminology, second-order indexicals. The ritualistic linguistic elements of mock impoliteness are conventionalised impoliteness formulae that have become further conventionalised for the politeness effects of the contexts in which they are regularly recontextualised. The fact that banter, teasing or humorous insults develop ritualistic qualities also points to the fact that these phenomena are sensitive to cultural and social norms (for a review of the literature on teasing, including gender and cultural variation, see Keltner *et al.* 2001).

Thus far, I have concentrated on relatively clear-cut cases, that is, cases where the mismatch between the conventional impoliteness formula and the context is strong, and there are additional signals to secure the relevant non-impolite uptake. Of course, there are many cases where the mismatch is weaker and interpretive ambiguity is stronger. There is also evidence that teased participants tend to have a more negative experience than teasers (Keltner *et al.* 1998); in other words, that participants may not see the same event in the same way. This fits the points made about impoliteness and differences in perspective made in Section 2.2.4. Furthermore, there are cases where participants may exploit mock impoliteness for purposes other than solidarity, and cases where they simply mismanage mock impoliteness. Issues such as these result in the event in question sliding away from mock impoliteness into genuine impoliteness, particularly of the type discussed in Section 5.3 (the type that includes sarcasm). Let us consider some examples from my report data which seem to be somewhere between mock impoliteness and genuine impoliteness. None of these examples involve impolite linguistic items (e.g. insults) that are clearly untrue or ritualistic mock impoliteness − possible signals that the impoliteness remains on the surface, that it is non-genuine. However, they all involve at least in part a joking or humorous contextual frame that, theoretically, could promote an interpretation of mock impoliteness. Having said that, it should be noted that the joking/humour is not reciprocated: this is not the jointly constructed mock-impoliteness activity type that is typical of prototypical banter.

Example [4] takes place in a high school classroom.

[4]
> Results have come from a science test. I've come bottom of the class. A friend hass called me 'thick' and 'stupid'. This may have been said in a jovial way but it alerted the rest of the class who all knew I was bottom, which embarrassed me. I could not reply

Clearly, the fact that intelligence is relevant in the context of the classroom, that it is often a sensitive face claim, and that the comments 'thick' and 'stupid' were said when face was publicly exposed, all maximise face damage. Yet the fact that it was said by a friend and in a 'jovial way', suggests perhaps that the friend did not intend it to be hurtful. But remember, as I argued in Section 2.2.2, the issue of intentionality seems to be backgrounded in intimate relationships, as here: it does not matter so much that it was was not intended to hurt, the fact of the matter is that it was said and it did hurt. Moreover, there is evidence that the informant attributes some kind of responsibility to his friend. The informant comments: 'Careless and petty. Arguable whether this person showed qualities of a friend.' In other words, a friend should have known better than to have caused face loss like this in this context.

Example [5] takes place between the informant and her mother in a car on the way home.

[5]

> M: (recounting a conversation she'd had) I was talking with H today and she said it was so lucky that her daughter had a rich fiancé whose family would pay for the wedding so she wouldn't have to. I said that we'd be okay because you're never going to get married. (laughs)
>
> Me: (annoyed) you'll see, I'll get married to A (a friend) when we're old and crusty.

The informant reports the kind of reaction that could be associated with impoliteness: she felt 'a little sad that my mum had said something like that to a friend = me losing face.' But she also adds 'I think she was joking or maybe trying to get me to rethink my outlook on life.' In fact, the possibility that this was said in a joking contextual frame is supported by the fact that the mother's utterance ends with laughter (cf. Drew 1987). Nevertheless, it does not seem to be the case that the context adequately counterbalances the conventionalised impoliteness insult, 'you're never going to get married'. The consequential face loss of this insult is exacerbated by public exposure, the fact that it had been said to a family friend. Also, note that the function of this mock impoliteness is not to reinforce solidarity; rather, on the mother's part it seems to be (or at least is understood to be) an attempt to get the informant to change her current state in the relative safety of a joking context. It is a matter of cloaked coercion.

The following interaction takes place in the context of a family home; 'P' is the informant's brother, and 'T' is another family member.

[6]

> Me: 'Did you know there's an increase in Chinese in Southampton?'
> P: 'Yeah, they're everywhere . . .'
> Me: 'But these are from China!'
> P: 'Well . . .'
> Me: '. . .'
> (the above conversation was written so that the conversation below is understood)
> T: 'I don't like the new sign for the London Olympics'
> Me: 'Yeah I know . . . what about the Beijing Olympics?'
> P: 'You mean in Southampton?'

The informant labels the other participant's behaviour as 'sarcasm' and reports: 'I felt more embarrassed than bad, because it was a mistake I'd made earlier used against me. I felt stupid, too.' But she also recognised that teasing could be involved: 'it embarrassed me in front of my brother, who enjoys teasing me anyway! . . . They were teasing me with a little sarcasm because they found it funny.' Here, the informant points to two perspectives on the same event: the teased informant may have experienced it as relatively impolite sarcasm, whereas the teasers may have intended it as relatively polite teasing (see Section 2.2.4 for the role of perspective in impoliteness perception). Note again, that the functions involved here are not merely solidarity. On the part of the teasers the function of entertainment seems relevant ('they found it funny'). I will discuss entertainment as a function of genuine impoliteness in Section 7.4.

These examples illustrate the fact that a mock impoliteness event can have a range of functions, can be perceived in different ways by different participants and can be offensive despite the target recognising that it was not (fully) intended to be so. In terms of functions, we have encountered the reinforcement of solidarity, cloaked coercion and exploitative entertainment. Each of these involves rather different contextual characteristics. Usually, mock impoliteness for solidarity reinforcement takes place between equals, typically friends, and is reciprocal; cloaked coercion seems to relate more to power relations; and exploitative entertainment involves pain for the target but pleasure for other participants. Regarding cloaked coercion, Holmes's (2000) findings in her study of workplace interactions are illuminating. When high-status individuals use insults to low-status colleagues, '[h]umour can be used . . . in the service of power to minimally disguise the oppressive intent, i.e. as a repressive discourse strategy' (2000: 176). For those speakers 'humour is one way to "do power" less explicitly – a way that is generally more accessible in a context where informality is valued and status differences are played down' (2000: 176). When low-status individuals use insults to high-status colleagues, 'jocular abuse often functions as a covert strategy for face-attack, a means of registering a veiled protest' (2000: 174). Holmes (2000: 178) notes that humorous insults in the context of non-equals are 'always slightly risky and, however jocular, there is an underlying contestive, challenging or "dark side" to the message which is not adequately analysed with the Politeness Theory framework'. Indeed. Cloaked coercion begins to slide away from mock impoliteness towards genuine impoliteness. Particularly when delivered by a relatively high power participant, cloaked coercion begins to look as if it involves the kind of superficial lip-service to politeness that can actually exacerbate the impoliteness (see Section 5.3). This is one reason why an impoliteness framework is needed.

6.6   Contextual neutralisation of impoliteness

Impoliteness results from a construal of language in context. One theme in this chapter has been contexts which interact with impolite forms and make them in some sense non-impolite. As I have pointed out in Section 6.2.2, such impoliteness contexts can be socially normalised, legitimised or neutralised. Normalisation and legitimation work in a similar way: both rely on an ideology that positively values impoliteness. The difference between normalisation and legitimation is that legitimation relates much more clearly to institutional structures. Those structures create contexts (e.g. army recruit training, parliamentary debates, interrogations) in which (some) impoliteness is licensed and rewarded, at least as far as some participants are concerned. Neutralisation, as in the case of mock impoliteness discussed in the previous section, is rather different. This results from an understanding that the context in which the impolite forms appear is not the requisite context for genuine impoliteness; in other words, the perlocutionary effects of those forms are blocked when you understand the context to indicate that they are not serious, that they were uttered accidentally, that they do not reflect the producer's attitude towards the target, that you are not in fact the target, and so on. In this section, I wish to elaborate briefly on two things: one is the difference between legitimation and neutralisation, and the other is the particular difficulty in neutralising impoliteness.

Watts (2003: 260) refers to a kind of 'impoliteness' which he calls 'sanctioned aggressive facework'. I take 'sanctioned' here to be related to legitimation. According to Watts (2003: 131–2),

certain social interaction types have interaction orders with lines [in Goffman's facework sense] that *sanction or neutralise face-threatening* or *face-damaging acts*, e.g. interaction between family members or among close friends, competitive forms of interaction such as political debate, rigidly hierarchised forms of interaction, e.g. in the military services.

Sanctioned aggressive facework involves the unrestricted and legitimated occurrence of potentially impolite behaviour. However, it is worth briefly mentioning here that not all sanctioned aggressive facework situations involve the sanctioning of impoliteness produced by those with relatively great power targeting those with relatively little power. Sandra Harris (2001), for example, describes the sanctioned impoliteness that takes place in the UK's House of Commons, giving the Opposition MPs opportunities to attack the Government that they might not have had in other contexts; the less powerful are sanctioned to attack the more. As can be seen, Watts gives 'military services' as an example of an impoliteness sanctioning interaction type. In fact, in my earliest published work on impoliteness (1996), I also studied this interaction type. Regarding my analyses of army training discourse, Mills (2002) argues that we need to consider impoliteness as part of a Community of Practice (Wenger 1998). She writes:

I would argue that within that particular CofP, this [the instances of 'impoliteness' identified in the paper] is not classified as impolite, although it would be within almost any other community. The dominant group in the interaction, the officers, has managed to achieve a situation where the seeming excessive impoliteness (barked orders, ritualised insults) is considered to be the norm. Thus, if we simply analyse impoliteness in the apparently decontextualised way that Culpeper does, we will be unable to grasp the way that politeness is only that which is defined by the CofP as such, and even then it is something which may be contested by some community members. Thus, I would suggest that impoliteness only exists when it is classified as such by certain, usually dominant, community members, and/or when it leads to a breakdown in relations. (Mills 2002: 79)

It is not quite true to say that my discussion of the language was 'decontextu-alised' in the way that, for example, Sperber and Wilson (1986) discuss decon-textualised examples (part of my paper discussed the situation, the army training philosophy, and so on). More significantly, Mills's understanding of impolite-ness seems to cut the target out of the equation. In my army training data, there is strong evidence that Private Alves perceived the Non-Commissioned Officers' language to be highly impolite. As I pointed out, she comments to a friend later in the documentary that the 'screaming' of the sergeants and the fact that they come 'up close' can 'get to a person' (1996: 363). Interestingly, in a footnote Mills (2002: 86) reports that a conference participant had stated that in his year's army training 'he found the level of impoliteness personally threatening and offensive', but Mills adds that 'nevertheless he recognized that it was appropriate to the context and did not in fact complain to the authorities about it'. What Watts fails to distinguish adequately and Mills seems to mix-up is the difference between *sanctioning or legitimating* such behaviour and *neu-tralising* it. Much impoliteness in army training is sanctioned, as Mills suggests, by dominant members. I will discuss army training as a case of institutional impoliteness in Section 7.6.1. However, this does not mean to say that any impoliteness is neutralised, i.e. that the target will not take offence at perceived face-attack.

What concerns me is that people can and do still take offence in such situations, even if there are theoretical reasons why they should not. If one understands that in the context of army training impoliteness is legitimated, that it is part of the training philosophy, surely that acts as a neutralising force, as it is clear that the person who produces impoliteness is partly a mouthpiece for this institutional function?[2] But as we saw in the previous paragraph, recruits still take offence. A similar case can be made for the quiz game show *The Weakest Link*. If it is all a game, then why should contestants take offence? But the evidence is that they do take offence. After Danny's pause-filler is mimicked (see Section 5.3), he produces a nervous laugh and looks down; after Chris's job is met with sarcasm (see Section 5.3), he smiles and exhales; and, after Jay's high-rising tone is mimicked (see Section 5.3), he produces a prosodically disaffiliating 'yes' and a smile. These non-verbal features suggest emotional reactions such as embarrassment (see Section 2.3, for a description of such features). In one North American episode when the contestants were children, one participant was clearly tearful. There is also occasional evidence of embarrassment, humiliation and distress in the comments made to the camera by the contestants themselves after they have been voted off.

How do we solve this conundrum? I would argue that generally targets of impoliteness tend not to pay sufficient attention to the context, a point I briefly made in Section 2.2.4. The tendency for people to underestimate the impact of situational factors is a well-established finding in social psychology (e.g. Ross 1977; Tversky and Kahneman 1974; Gilbert and Jones 1986). Additional evidence is in Ruggiero and Lattin's (2008) study of sports training. Despite understanding that verbal aggression was intended as part of the training philosophy, players still felt bad and did not find the verbal strategies motivating. One reason for this is that behaviour tends to be more salient than situational factors; as Heider (1958: 54) puts it: 'it tends to engulf the field rather than be confined to its proper position as a local stimulus whose interpretation requires the additional data of the surrounding field – the situation in social perception'. Impoliteness formulae and impoliteness in general tend to be 'rather marginal to human behaviour in normal circumstances' (Leech 1983: 105), and, consequently, they are even more salient than politeness could be. It is difficult to see the wood for the trees: when experiencing impoliteness, it is difficult to see it *in context*, and so it is still possible for it to cause offence. Pratto and John (2005 [1991]) argue that negative stimuli attract greater attention because of the inherent threat they pose, a prediction they label the 'automatic vigilance hypothesis'. They marshal diverse research to support this claim:

[People] assign relatively more value, importance, and weight to events that have negative, rather than positive, implications for them. In decision-making, potential costs are more influential than potential gains (e.g., Kahneman and Tversky, 1979). In impression formation, negative information is weighted more heavily than positive information (e.g., Anderson, 1974; Fiske, 1980; Hamilton and Zanna, 1972). In non-verbal communication, perceivers are more responsive to negatively toned messages that are positive ones (Frodi, Lamb, Leavitt, and Donovan, 1978). Quite generally, then, 'losses loom larger than gains' (Kahneman and Tversky, 1984: 348).

Negative behaviours, such as conventionalised impoliteness behaviours, engulf the field of perception. To neutralise the impoliteness, the context must compete with the salience of the impoliteness signal. This is exactly what happens with ritualised banter. The formulaicity, flouts of the Maxim of Quality, poetic effects, and so on, compete with the impoliteness to neutralise it (and yet still, on occasion, fail to do so).

6.7   Conclusion

This chapter suggested that impoliteness events can be approached holistically through schema theory, and in particular activity types (e.g. Levinson 1992).

Focusing on the contextual background for impoliteness, I considered event contexts where impoliteness is in some sense habitual or normal. If one is immersed in such contexts, impoliteness can only be weak at best *in terms of that event* (though people can often understand alternative perspectives of the same event). I also considered contexts where the social norms and cultural ideologies (e.g. 'machismo') mediating the value systems that underpin face claims lead to what others would take as impolite behaviours being evaluated positively. Dominant ideologies sustain and normalise – legitimise – patterns of behaviour, including behaviours which from other perspectives and in other contexts are impolite, that serve power hierarchies. Insults in particular can be a means of controlling others, as well as maintaining group dominance. I argued that what people tend to react to and label as impoliteness are abuses of power, that is, cases where a person or group exerts power over another person or group beyond what is considered legitimate (this is consistent with the findings reported in 5.5).

I looked at the role of context in priming face components and social norms. The situational context, and the recency and the frequency with which it is activated in the mind, will influence which component of face or social norm is activated for a particular encounter. I argued that the emotional sensitivity of face components and their degree of public exposure are crucial to understanding the potential for face loss. Further, I focused on the role of language in setting (im)politeness thresholds, and the implications this has for subsequent interactions. In particular, I emphasised the importance of reciprocity in accounting for counter-impoliteness. I also noted research that suggests an individual who starts with talk which is evaluated as polite but then shifts to talk evaluated as impolite is likely to have that impoliteness seen as particularly impolite.

In the penultimate section, I examined the recontextualisation of conventionalised impoliteness formulae, particularly with the result that they are construed as mock, non-genuine impoliteness. I discussed banter and some types of teasing and humour. I argued that mock impoliteness relies on some degree of mismatch between conventionalised impoliteness formulae and the context, along with additional signals (e.g. laughter) that the impoliteness is not genuine. I touched on ritualised banter, observing that ritualisation characterises much banter. I noted that the functions of mock impoliteness extend beyond the reinforcement of solidarity and include cloaked coercion and exploitative entertainment. In the final section, I examined the role of context in neutralising impoliteness effects. Generally speaking, neutralisation by context is difficult to achieve: context in many cases is likely to be overwhelmed by the salience of impoliteness behaviours.

7 Impoliteness events: Functions

7.1 Introduction

My aim in this chapter is to describe the functions of impoliteness, and, more specifically, impoliteness events. As I will be considering rather more extended examples of discourse than hitherto, I will also take the opportunity to cast light on some discoursal patterns associated with impoliteness events. Impoliteness events, as described in Section 6.1, can consist of a single utterance or several utterances building a discourse directed towards certain ends. The kind of impoliteness I focus on is what Beebe (1995: 154) calls 'instrumental': the use of impoliteness 'to serve some instrumental goal'. The notion of instrumental impoliteness echoes the notion of instrumental aggression, long established in the aggression literature (see Buss 1961: 2–4). There have been a few attempts to identify the functions of instrumental impoliteness. Kasper (1990), reviewing linguistic impoliteness, includes a section on rudeness where she proposes that there are three kinds of function for motivated rudeness: (1) rudeness due to lack of affect control, (2) strategic rudeness and (3) ironic rudeness. Beebe (1995), having analysed approximately 600 examples of perceived rudeness, argues that there are two main functions: (1) to get power, and (2) to vent negative feelings. In fact, given that Kasper's discussion of strategic rudeness has much to do with power and that her third category, ironic rudeness, is a subcategory of the second, there is much overlap between these two schemes: both identify the expression of negative feelings and strategic power as key. Although Kasper (1990: 211) briefly mentions banter and solidarity in her discussion of ironic rudeness, neither Kasper nor Beebe dwell on the positive functions that impoliteness behaviour in itself may have for some participants. In my data, impoliteness with a function of entertainment for at least some participants (not necessarily the target) was clearly present. Consequently, I will also discuss this function, and follow that discussion with one on creativity and impoliteness. Finally, I should mention Kienpointner's (1997) more finely nuanced typology of impoliteness (or rudeness, to use his term). Kienpointner is concerned with types of impoliteness as much as functions of impoliteness, and so his categories are not purely functional. Nevertheless, it is worth observing that the category 'strategic rudeness', with its basis in power, is also present in his scheme, only he emphasises much more the role of institutions, as I will do in the final two sections of this chapter. Affective impoliteness is not so obviously present in his scheme, but impoliteness for entertainment is, as it appears in his discussion of sociable rudeness and his discussion of rudeness in literature.

I will organise my discussion around the categories affective impoliteness, coercive impoliteness and entertaining impoliteness. I wish to state at the outset that I do not see these functions as mutually exclusive: it is quite possible to pursue all of them simultaneously. In particular, affective impoliteness leaks into the other categories. This is not surprising, given that impoliteness always involves the expression of strong emotion (see Section 2.5).

7.2 Affective impoliteness

Discussion In the aggression literature, instrumental aggression, aggression as 'a means to some other end' (Geen 2001: 5), is sometimes pitched against affective aggression, although the distinction is acknowledged not to be watertight. In fact, Buss's (1961) highlighting of instrumental aggression was partly a corrective to previous research which has concentrated on 'angry aggression', that is, aggression that is an angry response to frustration and/or provocation. That early research was associated in particular with John Dollard and his colleagues (e.g. Dollard *et al.* 1939) at Yale University. They proposed the frustation–aggression hypothesis, the idea that aggression is always caused by a frustrating event or situation. Road rage is perhaps a particularly pertinent example for contemporary times. Research has been directed towards frustration caused by socio- and economic deprivation (sometimes leading to prejudice and age-group aggression) (e.g. Catalano *et al.* 1997; Dutton *et al.* 2005). However, as an explanation for all kinds of aggression the frustration–aggression hypothesis is overly simplistic. Ultimately, it is a biological, reflexive theory of emotion – we experience emotions, particularly anger, in response to frustration, and give vent to them with aggression – and can thus be rejected for precisely the same reasons articulated in Section 2.3.1. Emotions are not hardwired to behaviours. Emotional states go through a process of cognitive appraisal, whereby the person judges what happened, why it happened, how angry he or she feels, what might be possible courses of action, and so on. A model involving cognition better accounts for the complexities of social encounters. But I also noted that such cognitive appraisal can be more impulsive or more thoughtful (cf. Anderson and Bushman 2002; Anderson *et al.* 1995). In other words, there are times when the frustration–aggression hypothesis is a more adequate account, but other times when it is not. When it is not, then aggression is more instrumental in character.

Exactly the same arguments can be made for affective impoliteness. There are times when it is more strategic, more instrumental and other times when it is more impulsive, more reflexive. But the production of language, as aggression, is never so reflexive as to skip cognitive appraisal (even if that were possible). This point is neatly illustrated by Goffman (1978) in his discussion of response cries. Regarding 'imprecations', which he considers one type of response cry, he points out that 'a man who utters *Fuck!* when he stumbles in a foundry is likely to avoid that particular expletive if he trips in a day nursery' (1978: 799). Contextual monitoring clearly takes place, and this feeds into the choice of an appropriate term. Of course, and this is the point made above, there are times when that contextual monitoring is less thoughtful. This can result in the kind of affective impoliteness discussed by Kasper (1990: 209–10), involving the unrestrained expression of emotion, particularly in contexts where it is not licensed (see also Kochman 1984). As pointed out in Section 2.3.1, people have prescriptive norms about the appropriateness of emotional displays in particular situations. But affective impoliteness can also be much more instrumental than Kasper suggests.

Timothy Jay's (1992, 2000, 2008) work on cursing echoes the argument I have been making. He views cursing as most closely associated with the emotion of anger, but points out that '[a]nger can be viewed as existing along a continuum from reflexive and automatic responses to strategic and controlled expressions' (Jay 2000: 55; see also Montagu 1967). Elaborating on forms of verbal aggression, Jay (2000: 57) writes:

Verbal aggression serves more than one purpose. It generally takes one of two forms: hostile aggression or instrumental aggression. In hostile verbal aggression, the goal of cursing is to harm a person who has hurt the speaker or damaged the speaker's self-esteem. In instrumental verbal aggression, the goal of cursing is to obtain some reward through the use of aggressive speech. Instrumental cursing might result in gaining the admiration of peers for the speaker or, when used to bully or threaten, might result in getting money from a target of the cursing. Hostile and instrumental cursing are strategic, not automatic or reflexive. They unfold in a predictable, stage like fashion . . .

The distinction between hostile and instrumental verbal aggression is not one I make in my work. The key point they have in common is that cursing is used in the pursuit of a particular goal. In fact, in an earlier field study at a summer camp in North America, Jay (1992: 69) found that:

The strong language conveying anger and frustration was targeted towards others 43% [n = 224] of the time and used expletives the remainder of its usage. An example of a targeted usage was, 'what the fuck, Matt?' while expletive usage is exemplified by single word outbursts, such as, 'fuck' or 'damn'.

Targeted anger is strategic, instrumental affective impoliteness. One particular kind of targeted usage identified by Jay concerns retribution, and the 'act of retribution is what swearing, cursing, and insulting is all about' (1992: 106). Retribution or retaliation is, of course, related to reciprocity, as discussed in Section 6.4. As Jay (1992: 107, original emphasis) puts it, 'retribution or retaliation is a *necessary* functional component of human communication because it tells wrongdoers the who, what, where, and when of their offensive acts'. To sum up then, affective impoliteness is the targeted display of heightened emotion, typically anger, with the implication that the target is to blame for producing that negative emotional state. The less targeted affective impoliteness is, the less instrumental it is.

Illustration   The following text is my transcription of an answerphone message attributed to the actor Alec Baldwin. The fact that it is an answerphone message is important, because it means that the speaker received none of the participant co-text that might have shaped his message. It was produced on 11 April 2007, and posted 19 April on the website www.tmz.com. The addressee is apparently Ireland, Baldwin's 11-year-old daughter with Kim Basinger, from whom he had now split. To appreciate this text in full, it is necessary to hear it. The quality of the recording precludes instrumental analysis. However, to convey something of the prosody, I have put in bold any syllables that are exceptionally heavily stressed. Full-stops indicate clear pauses. I have also put in small capitals segments where Baldwin shouts (the term the article on the website used is 'screamed'). The latter was relatively easy to identify, as at these points the recording apparatus was unable to cope and produced some distortion.

[1]
> Hey I want to tell you something okay. I wanna leave a message for you right now cos. again it's 10.30. here in New York on Wednesday. and once again I've made an **ass**. of **my**self. trying to get to a **phone** to call you at a specific **time**. when the **time** comes for me to make that phone call. I stop whatever I'm doing and I go and make that phone call at 11 o'clock in the morning in New York and if you don't pick up the phone at 10 o'clock at night and you don't even have the GODDAMN PHONE TURNED on. I want you to know something okay. er I'm **tired** of playing this game with you. I'm leaving this message with you to tell you. you have insulted me for the **last** time. you have insulted me you don't even have the **brains**. or the **decency**. as a human **being**. I don't give a **damn** that you're 12 years old or 11 years old or that you're a **child** or that your mother was a thoughtless pain in the **ass** who doesn't care about what you do as far as I'm concerned. you have humiliated me for the **last** time on this phone. and when I come out there next week. I'M GOING TO FLY OUT THERE FOR THE **DAY**. just to straighten you OUT. on this issue. I'm going to let you KNOW just how disappointed in you I am. and how **angry** I am with you that you've done this to me again. you've MADE ME FEEL LIKE SHIT. and you've **made me** feel like a **fool** over and over and over [indistinct] again. and this CRAP YOU PULL ON ME. with this GODDAMN PHONE situation that you would never **dream** of doing to your mother and you do it to me. **con**stantly and over and over again. I AM GOING TO GET ON A **PLANE** and I'm gonna come out there for the **day** and I'M GOING TO **STRAIGHTEN** YOU out when I see you. do you understand me. I am going to **really** make sure you get it [indistinct]. I'm gonna turn around and come home. so YOU'D BETTER BE READY Friday the 20th to meet with me so that I'm gonna let you know just how I feel about what a rude little **pig** you really are. you are a rude thoughtless little pig okay

The prosody of this text is a strikingly good match of the characteristics identified for the attitude of hot anger elaborated in Section 4.5.3. The characteristics are slightly faster tempo, much higher pitch average, wide pitch range, louder, breathy, chest tone, abrupt pitch changes on stressed syllables, and tense articulation (Murray and Arnott 1993: 1103–4, 1106). As can be seen, such characteristics intensify during the message. For the first quarter of the message, Baldwin seems to be giving vent to his own frustrations (e.g. 'I've made an ass of myself'). Whether this is considered impolite or not will depend on the norms for expression of emotion in this interpersonal relationship. When he answers 'you don't even have the GODDAMN PHONE TURNED on', we can draw the implicature that he is implying that she should have the phone turned on. It is only with the following series of utterances that it becomes clear that Baldwin is holding the addressee responsible for provoking his anger and we move more clearly towards affective impoliteness:

• you have insulted me for the last time.
• you have insulted me
• you don't even have the brains. or the decency. as a human being.
• your mother was a thoughtless pain in the ass who doesn't care about what you do as far as I'm concerned. you have humiliated me for the last time on this phone.

These are conventionalised impoliteness insults, each deploying a personal second person pronoun and negative assertion by which the addressee (or things she has face invested in, such as her mother) is associated with negative values. They also illustrate rhetorical patterning that is typical of impoliteness events. We have repetition ('you have insulted me' twice), reformulation ('you have humiliated me') and extension ('you don't even have the brains. or the decency. as a human being'). The final utterance listed above contains a veiled threat ('for the last time'). This is followed by more explicit conventionalised impoliteness threats: 'I'M GOING TO FLY OUT THERE FOR THE DAY. just TO STRAIGHTEN YOU OUT. I'M GOING TO LET YOU KNOW just how disappointed in you I am.' In the following sequence, Baldwin makes it clear that his anger is at her for the negative things she has done:

• you've done this to me again.
• you've made me feel like shit.
• you've made me feel like a fool over and over and over [indistinct] again. and
• this crap you pull on me.
• this GODDAMN PHONE situation that you would never dream of doing to your mother and you do it to me. constantly and over and over again

Again, we have conventional impolite insults, and again the use of repetition, reformulation and extension. The words 'MADE ME FEEL LIKE SHIT' are made especially salient through prosody: not only does Baldwin shout, but each word is strongly stressed with a slight pause in between, the result being a staccato-like delivery. He then returns to conventionalised impoliteness threats:

- I AM GOING TO GET ON A PLANE and I'm gonna come out there for the **day** and I'M GOING TO STRAIGHTEN YOU OUT when I see you.
- I am going to **rea**lly make sure you get it [indistinct].
- YOU'D BETTER BE READY Friday the 20th to meet with me.
- I'm gonna let you know just how I feel about what a rude little **pig** you really are.

After the first utterance above he uses a conventionalised impoliteness message enforcer: 'do you understand me'. He concludes his message with a conventionalised insult 'you are a **rude thought**less little pig'. Note that over the course of the message Baldwin has gravitated from more of a focus on the self ('I') to more of a focus on the other ('you'). Attacking the other is more characteristic of instrumental affective impoliteness. He attacks Ireland's Quality face through his insults and Equity rights through his threats.

It may be remembered that in Section 6.2.2 I pointed out that parents are licensed to use more direct language to their children than the reverse. But clearly there are limits on what is considered acceptable. It is reported that the Los Angeles County Superior Court commissioner Maren Nelson heard this tape and temporarily suspended Baldwin's visitation rights. Many of the linguistic features encountered here – for example, the prosodic characteristics, the repetition, the taboo intensifiers (e.g. 'GODDAMN PHONE situation') – are features that linguists have associated with personal affect, a term which in linguistics has been used to encompass people's feelings, emotions, moods and attitudes, as well as personality (Caffi and Janney 1994). Interestingly, it is not the case that anything goes. Other cases I have examined of affective impoliteness have included strongly taboo intensifiers, notably, 'fuck/fucking'. This is lacking here. But we should remember Goffman's (1978) point about avoiding saying 'fuck' in a nursery school; purportedly, Baldwin is addressing a 11-year-old girl.

7.3   Coercive impoliteness

Discussion   Fairclough (e.g. 1989: 43) makes a distinction between power *in* and power *behind* discourse. Power in discourse refers to the exercise of power in the language, whilst power behind discourse concerns the constitution of social institutions and societies through power relations (see Section 6.2.2). Brown and Levinson (1987) and subsequent researchers in that tradition have been generally more concerned with aspects of the power behind an interaction, for example the participant's status. However, Locher points out on a number of occasions that 'people with higher status can refrain from exercising power', whilst 'interactants with low status can decide to exercise power over people with relatively greater status' (2004: 31, see also 208, 218; Watts 1991 and Berger 1994 are cited as making a similar point). In other words, there is no simple match between power in language and power behind it. Moreover, Watts (1991: 56) argues that a notion of power based on status (a person's position in the structure of social relationships) is not very helpful for the analysis of the exercise of power in 'face-to-face verbal interaction, particularly in the absence of overt institutionalised status differences'. Consequently, Watts (1991: 60) deploys the idea of restriction of 'freedom of action' to complement status (which is more oriented to power behind), and Locher (2004) adopts this too. This notion of the restriction of freedom of action, as Locher (2004: Chapter 2) observes, is common to several definitions of power (e.g. van Dijk 1989: 20; Wartenberg 1990: 85, 88), and indeed successfully deployed by Locher in her own analyses. Note that the restriction of a person's action-environment is not in itself enough to warrant the label 'power'. Locher's definition of power also involves a 'latent conflict and clash of interests'. This would seem to rule out more positively oriented types of power. For example, some view coercive impoliteness in the context of sports training as positive (Ruggiero and Lattin 2008). Even so, such types of power are more or less prototypical. As Watts (1991: 58) states: '[t]he central meaning of power surely involves a conflict of interests rather than a consensus'.

We have already briefly met coercive impoliteness in Section 6.5. Coercive impoliteness is impoliteness that seeks a realignment of values between the producer and the target such that the producer benefits or has their current benefits reinforced or protected (the labels producer and target need not refer to individuals, but could refer to groups or institutions). It involves coercive action that is not in the interest of the target, and hence involves both the restriction of a person's action-environment and a clash of interests. This, of course, begs the question of what coercive action is. Here, I shall take a lead from Tedeschi and Felson (1994: 168):

A coercive action is an action taken with the intention of imposing harm on another person or forcing compliance. Actors engaged in coercive actions expect that their behaviour will either harm the target or lead to compliance, and they value one of these proximate outcomes. The value they attach to compliance or harm to the target arises from their belief about the causal relationship between compliance or harm and the terminal values. There are many values that might be pursued through coercive means. For example, actors might value harm to the target because they believe it will result in justice, or they might value the target's compliance because they believe it will lead to tangible benefits.

What is appealing about this definition is that it moves beyond behavioural compliance and includes the imposition of social harm, either of which can lead to beneficial terminal values. Social harm involves 'damage to the social identity of target persons and a lowering of their power or status' (Tedeschi and Felson 1994: 171; social harm was further defined in Introducing impoliteness, and Section 1.1, definition (13)). Whilst compliance may achieve immediate (often material) benefits, social harm is more about symbolic benefits (which may lead in the future to material benefits). It is about using impoliteness to reduce the target's relative symbolic power (Bourdieu 1991). Coercive impoliteness relates to Beebe's (1995) function of 'getting power', and getting power is a matter of exercising power. Beebe (1995) argues that the use of rudeness to get power has the following purposes (summarised from pages 159–63):

(1) To appear superior. Includes 'insults' and 'putdowns'.
(2) To get power over actions (to get someone else to do something or avoid doing something yourself). Includes 'sarcasm' and 'pushy politeness' used to get people to do something, as well as attempts to get people to 'go away or leave us alone or finish their business more quickly'.
(3) To get power in conversation (i.e. to do conversational management) (to make the interlocutor talk, stop talking, shape what they tell you, or to get the floor). Includes saying 'shush!' and rude interruptions.

A striking feature of this list is that each purpose relates, at least at some level, to B&L's (1987) negative face or what Spencer-Oatey (e.g. 2002) would call Equity rights. The close relationship between power and negative face is not surprising, given B&L's (1987: 61) definition of negative face as 'freedom of action and freedom from imposition', words which echo part of the definition of power drawn from Locher (2004) as discussed above. It is clear from B&L (e.g. 1987: 130, 178–9, 209) that power is closely related to negative face, as they define it, particularly with regard to deferential behaviour (see also Holmes 1995: 17). The purpose 'to appear superior' in the above list is obviously related to deference. However, deference is not well handled within B&L's (1987) framework, which is in any case overly categorical. In fact, some of the problems can be seen in the 'to appear superior' purpose above. Insults usually primarily target Quality face or Social identity face, and only secondarily realign the Equity rights pertaining between participants, something more closely associated with deference.

The discourses exercising power referred to in the previous paragraph interact closely with power behind discourses. Thus, for example, the unequal distribution of conversation could reflect an unequal distribution of power behind the conversation. Social structures (e.g. status, roles, institutions) and associated ideologies, of course, shape and are shaped by discourses (see Sections 6.2.2 and 7.6). I would predict that coercive impoliteness is more likely to occur in situations where there is an imbalance of social structural power (see

Kipnis 1976 and Kipnis and Schmidt 1983, both quoted in Tedeschi and Felson 1994: 201, for similar predictions; see also Tedeschi and Felson 1994: 206 on victimization). A powerful participant has more freedom to be impolite, because he or she can (a) reduce the ability of the less powerful participant to retaliate with impoliteness (e.g. through the denial of speaking rights), and (b) threaten more severe retaliation should the less powerful participant be impolite in return. This prediction has been supported by experimental studies, particularly regarding competitive situations (see references in Tedeschi and Felson 1994: 202). It is also consistent with research on the courtroom (e.g. Lakoff 1989; Penman 1990), army recruit training (e.g. Culpeper 1996; Bousfield 2008), sports (especially training, e.g. Kassing and Sanderson 2010) and exploitative TV shows (e.g. Culpeper 2005a). Interestingly, Tedeschi and Felson (1994: 202) point out that the perception that a person with relative coercive power is actually willing to use it plays a role. That perception can be strengthened linguistically. For example, armed robbers use 'an intimidating voice and threatening language to communicate that they mean business (Letkemann 1973)' (Tedeschi and Felson 1994: 202). Of course, coercive impoliteness also occurs in some situations characterised by symmetric social structures, as is the case with much children's discourse (see Cashman's 2006 analyses of strategic impoliteness in children's discourse, and also the references she cites on pages 219–20). In cases such as these, coercive impoliteness may be deployed to engineer a gain in social power. Nevertheless, it is safe to make the prediction that situations characterised by asymmetric social structures are predisposed to coercive impoliteness, and, more specifically, unidirectional impoliteness produced by the more powerful targeting the less.

Power is not the only factor to influence the usage of coercive impoliteness. Whilst coercive impoliteness might be an instrumental means of achieving a realignment of values, it can itself be costly or cheap. Modes of behaviour themselves carry values, that is, procedural values (Tedeschi and Felson 1994: 183–7). The negative cost of the procedure may outweigh the positive values that might be achieved. Just as the procedure of robbery is not in the eyes of many an acceptable way of gaining money, so impolite coercion is often not seen as an acceptable way of achieving a realignment of values (see also the discussion of the face-damaging implications of being perceived to be impolite in Section 1.4.1). Having said that, as highlighted in Section 6.2.2, in some cultural or institutional ideologies impoliteness can even be positively valued as a procedure. Furthermore, coercive impoliteness is risky in that it may achieve a beneficial realignment of values in the short term, but there is a significant risk of the future cost of the target retaliating (see the discussion of counter-impoliteness in Section 6.4). This, of course, is why coercive impoliteness is more likely in asymmetric contexts where the deterrent risk of retaliation is less. Coercive impoliteness may also run the risk of third-party intervention. Alternatively, it may be thought of more as a pre-emptive strike to reduce possible future costs.

Illustration In this section, I analyse an interaction that took place in 2004 between a North American police officer and a suspect, a taxi driver, whom he stops and interrogates. In Section 4.4.4, I briefly described how in police encounters with suspects impoliteness is instrumentally deployed to facilitate coercion. I drew attention to Ainsworth (2008), who argues that swearing is a form of coercion and a demonstration of masculinity that is in tune with the norms and values of police culture. She also notes that, although swearing by police officers is prohibited, it may give the recipient the impression that an officer 'willing to be transgressive about language norms' will 'also be willing to violate other norms, such as the norm against gratuitous physical abuse of citizens' (2008: 11), and this perception of such willingness increases the weight of the symbolic coercive power. These points about swearing can also be made of impoliteness in this context. One particular feature of the interaction discussed in this section is that the suspect has been stopped for a minor traffic infringement. It is not as if the police officer is attempting to arrest an armed robber, something which may characterise the kind of encounters referred to in Section 4.4.4. This interaction, then, is not simply a violation of official rules – that would make it merely part of normal unofficial practices – but is also a violation of normal unofficial practices: it is a striking abuse of power.

The taxi driver had been stopped apparently because the wheels of his taxi touched or crossed the white lines of a pedestrian crossing. The taxi driver (Amanuel Hadis) had left Ethiopia in 1990 on account of the civil war. The police officer (Doug Carr) was working for the Houston Metropolitan Transit Authority. The recording forms the basis of an article in the *Houston Chronicle* (2 November 2004, reported by Steve McVicker), along with information presumably elicited in an interview with Hadis. We learn that Hadis had telephoned his voicemail and thus managed to record the conversation, and had done so because he feared for his safety when Carr 'instantly became abusive, yelling profanities from his patrol car'. The newspaper article describes Carr's initial questions on the recording as being asked 'calmly', but that he 'appears to lose his temper' when Hadis tries to explain that he forgot to bring his insurance card. This may indicate that a degree of affective impoliteness is involved here, although the discourse is very different from the example given in Section 7.2. With the possible exception of his observation that he does not like cabdrivers, Carr does not focus on himself, his feelings and Hadis as a cause of them. The turns of the interaction are numbered for ease of reference.

[2]

(1)	Carr:	This your cab?
(2)	Hadis:	Yes, sir.
(3)	Carr:	It says here it's expired. What else you got?
(4)	Hadis:	My insurance is expired? I didn't get change, but I think I left it at my house.
(5)	Carr:	You didn't get it, or you left it at home?
(6)	Hadis:	I got it . . .
(7)	Carr:	Which lie are you telling me?
(8)	Hadis:	I'm not lying, sir, I'm just . . .
(9)	Carr:	Yes you are. Ran red light, no insurance and not wearing a seat belt. Sign right there. Court date's on the top.
(10)	Hadis:	I did not pass the red light. I was holding the brake.
(11)	Carr:	Let me tell you something, (expletive). You cross that white line out there, that's running the red light. You want to argue with me or you want to go to jail?
(12)	Hadis:	No.
(13)	Carr:	'Cause I'll stick your stinking ass in jail right now, I don't care. I don't like cabdrivers in the first place. I will put you in jail. You pulled out in the middle of the intersection. That's running a red light, whether you backed up or not. I don't know what it's like in your country, but in the United States of America, in the state of Texas, we abide by all the laws. You don't like it here, leave, you got it?
(14)	Hadis:	OK.
(15)	Carr:	You understand me?
(16)	Hadis:	Yes, sir.
(17)	Carr:	Do we understand real good English here?
(18)	Hadis:	Yes, sir. I'm sorry.
(19)	Carr:	We don't need your kind here. You can go back to where you come from if you don't want to abide by our laws. You understand me?
(20)	Hadis:	Yes, sir.
(21)	Carr:	Look at my name. Remember it. Remember C-a-r-r. 'Cause the next time I find you on a city street in Houston, Texas, downtown, and you (expletive) break the law, I will put your ass in jail. Do you understand me?
(22)	Hadis:	Yes, sir.
(23)	Carr:	I'm speaking real straight, slow English.
(24)	Hadis:	All right, sir.

The first six turns match expectations about the activity type taking place: they follow the police–suspect encounter script. Establishing ownership of the offending item through a question is a typical first or early move. Hadis confirms with a politic 'yes, sir', and presumably hands Carr an insurance document as proof of ownership. We then have exchanges concerning the expiry of the insurance document. Hadis, in turn 4, appears to conjoin two contradictory statements: he did not change it versus he left it (where 'it' refers to the new insurance) at his house. At least, this is the way Carr seems to construe the utterance, given that he queries which is true in his following alternative question. But there is an alternative reading that Hadis, somewhat confused and struggling with a non-native language (as evidenced by the lack of subject and past tense marker for 'change'), is attempting to correct a statement that he blurted out. In turn 6, Hadis begins to answer the question with 'I got it', which seems to be the beginning of an assertion that he does in fact have it. The importance of these turns is that they help establish a normative politic context for the impoliteness that follows. As discussed in Section 6.4, an interactant who shifts in a conversation from politeness to impoliteness is likely to have that impoliteness viewed as particularly impolite.

Carr's turn 7 is impolite for two reasons. He interrupts Hadis, denying him the opportunity to defend himself (Equity rights), and does so with a wh-question which presupposes that he is telling a lie either way (Quality face). Both reasons involve conventionalised impoliteness formulae. This turn was also identified as the point when Carr is no longer talking 'calmly', so it would be reasonable to expect some prosodic intensification. Clearly, we have something of a contrast with the context so far established (although we should remember that the newspaper report had indicated that Carr initially got out of his car 'yelling profanities'). In the next turn Hadis issues a defensive move directly contradicting the presupposition, whilst maintaining politic behaviour with 'sir'. Carr counters this defence with another interruption and an impolite assertion: 'yes you are' (Quality face). He then rattles off Hadis's supposed three offences, issues a bald direct imperative command to sign the ticket, followed by a swift reminder of the date of his court appearance. Carr controls the discourse, frames Hadis as guilty and does so in a perfunctory way (note the elliptical clauses). Hadis is denied any rights of defence. This clearly conflicts with his Equity rights, but more than this it conflicts with norms regarding the handling of suspects. Hadis then defends himself with a bald contradiction, 'I did not pass the red light.'

In turn 11, the conversation enters a new phase. Carr's 'let me tell you something' purports, superficially, to be a polite permission request. This conflicts with the context in which an impoliteness interpretation is more likely, something which is also assisted by the expletive. Here we have convention-driven implicational impoliteness (e.g. sarcasm).[1] Carr also uses a type of conventionalised impoliteness question, 'you want to argue with me or you want to go to jail', a highly conducive alternative question which on the face of it constrains the target to either of two unpleasant options (Equity rights). Hadis replies 'no', presumably rejecting both options. Note that from here until the end of the interaction Hadis's responses are minimal, always compliant, mostly politic (cf. the use of 'sir'), and in turn 18 even polite – 'I'm sorry.' He has moved from defence to partial withdrawal and acceptance. Strictly speaking, turn 12 could signal the end of the conversation, as Carr has achieved his apparent objective of making Hadis comply. But impoliteness is not simply about the pursuit of transactional goals; impoliteness can pursue social goals. Carr shifts to using coercive impoliteness for social harm. Flynn's (1977: 66) motivations for using insults not to change behaviours but to maintain dominant groups in society at the expense of others are relevant here, and so I repeat them from Section 6.2.2:

[By using insults] (1) dominant values and norms can be reaffirmed, (2) the insulter might gain status within his own reference group, and (3) the dominant group might have social objects upon which to project their unacceptable feelings and desires.

Carr proceeds to maximise offence. Note that each of his turns contains the same strategy:

(13)   You got it?
(15)   You understand me?
(17)   Do we speak real good English here?
(18)   You understand me?
(21)   Do you understand me?
(23)   I'm speaking real straight, slow English.

'You got it?' is in fact a conventionalised impoliteness formula, but the same cannot be said of the other utterances. The overall effect is achieved through needless repetition across turns, thereby flouting the Maxim of Manner and inviting further inferencing. Possible implications include: Hadis is having difficulty understanding, Hadis is not competent in English, Hadis is not English American, Hadis is not in a position to determine the interpretation of the traffic offence, and Hadis must accept the word of a police officer. There is also an aura of threat, that Carr is beyond reason, capable of doing anything. Regarding the detail, note in turn 17 Carr uses 'we'. 'We' echoes a conventionalised politeness strategy: the directness of 'you' is avoided by a polite fiction that both participants are included. This is convention-driven implicational impoliteness, a sneering, sarcastic mixed message.

Carr also deploys various other tactics. He uses conventionalised impolite threats in turns 13 and 21: ''Cause I'll stick your stinking ass in jail right now'; 'I will put you in jail'; ''Cause the next time I find you on a city street in Houston, Texas, and you (expletive) break the law, I will put your arse in jail.' He uses conventionalised impolite insults in turns 13, 19 and 21. These include the impolite personalised references 'your stinking ass' and 'your ass', an insult that exploits a metonymy in using an entity of low value to refer to a whole person. He also uses a string of strategies to attack Hadis's Social identity face, which create a racist undercurrent. The implication about Hadis's English not being good has already weakly implied that he is not English American. In turn 13, Carr says 'I don't know what it's like in your country'. This standardly implies, via the Maxim of Quality, that he believes that Hadis's country is not the USA. Remember that Hadis has been in the USA for over fourteen years and may well have Social identity face invested in it. Carr then adds: 'but in the United States of America, in the state of Texas, we abide by all the laws. You don't like it here, leave, you got it?' The word 'but' expresses the conventional implicature that the following conjoint contradicts an expectation that arises from the previous; in other words, the expectation that in Hadis's country they do not abide by laws. 'You got it?' is a conventionalised impoliteness message enforcer. Turn 19 is similar. 'We don't need your kind here' violates Association rights: 'we' purports to be the people of America; Hadis is not only excluded but branded – one might say, 'de-faced' – as an unneeded 'kind'. And again with 'You can go back to where you come from if you don't want to abide by our laws' Carr implies, via the Maxim of Quality, that Hadis does not want to abide by American laws, and issues a further message enforcer: 'You understand me?'

Police–suspect interactions are perhaps ripe for coercive impoliteness. Coercive impoliteness is a means of enforcing particular actions. However, such actions are in large part legitimated. What is striking about this particular interaction is that it is far in excess of what might be legitimated (Hadis's offence, after all, was alleged to be touching a white line with the wheel of his taxi). As I suggested above, this interaction, after the first few turns, has more to do with affirming the dominant values and norms of Carr's group and projecting unacceptable feelings upon a minority. It is an abuse of power. We learn from the newspaper article that Hadis was filing a verbal abuse claim, and the police department's professional standards section was investigating the complaint. Carr, upon being told by the newspaper that they had the recording, said that he had no comment and hung up.

7.4   Entertaining impoliteness

Discussion   We briefly encountered the idea that impoliteness can be entertaining in Section 6.5. A more precise description of this impoliteness function is that it involves exploitative entertainment – it involves entertainment at the expense of the target of the impoliteness. Entertaining impoliteness, as with the other functional kinds of impoliteness discussed in this chapter, involves a victim or at least a potential victim. It is not the case that the target is always aware of the impoliteness, that the participants who are entertained are always aware of who the target is, or even that the target is always a 'real' identity. In contexts such as graffiti or weblogs the true identity of the target is not known or is at least uncertain, and in the case of literary fiction the targets are entirely fictional. What is important, however, is that others, aside from the target, can understand the probable impoliteness effects for the target. Without this it would not be entertaining impoliteness.

Why exactly might impoliteness be entertaining? Impoliteness is nasty stuff, people get hurt or angry. Entertainment does not seem to enter the picture. However, the key problem here is that people have focused their discussions on a very narrowly defined interactive frame: it is usually one just involving a dyad comprised of producer and target. This of course is in tune with much research on pragmatics which focuses on a dyad consisting of speaker and hearer. Impoliteness, however, can be designed as much for the over-hearing audience as for the target addressee, and that audience can be entertained. The fact that people can be entertained by symbolic violations to identities and social rights, the stuff of impoliteness, is not surprising when one remembers that people were entertained by gladiatorial shows and are still entertained by boxing matches and rugby. In fact, today's television in the UK, but in many other countries too, is replete with programmes stuffed full of verbal violence. Today's chat shows, quiz shows and talent shows have developed exploitative variants, and I will consider these in Section 7.6.2. Documentaries have seen an explosion in material dealing with aggressive conflicts involving army trainers, traffic wardens, nightclub bouncers, police officers, hotel inspectors, and so on. In fact, consistent with the idea that impoliteness can be entertaining, today the TV genre with the most verbal aggression is comedies/sitcoms (Chory 2010: 182).

Let us examine in more detail the link between impolite interactions and entertainment. I propose that there are five sources of pleasure that can be involved in entertaining impoliteness:

1. *Emotional pleasure.* Observing impoliteness creates a state of arousal in the observer, and that state of arousal can be pleasurable. As Myers puts it, discussing chat shows, '[s]omething is engaging about argument for its own sake' (Myers 2001: 174). Importantly, he adds 'the thrill is in the potential for violence' (Myers 2001: 183). In other words, we don't need actual fisticuffs: the mere suggestion of fisticuffs can cause the thrill.

2. *Aesthetic pleasure.* Outside discussions of banter, little attention has been given in the literature to socially negative uses of verbal creativity. In fact, much impoliteness has elements of creativity, not least of all because of its frequently competitive nature: if one is attacked, one responds in kind or with a superior attack. And to achieve a superior attack requires creative skills. I will have more to say about creativity and impoliteness shortly.

3. *Voyeuristic pleasure.* Observing people reacting to impoliteness often involves the public exposure of private selves, particularly aspects that are emotionally sensitive, and this can lead to voyeuristic pleasure. As Richardson and Meinhoff (1999: 132) point out, talk shows 'trade in the exploitation of human weakness for the sake of voyeuristic pleasure'.

4. *The pleasure of being superior.* 'Superiority theories' (e.g. Bergson 1911 [1900]), developed within humour theory, articulate the idea that there is self-reflexive pleasure in observing someone in a worse state than oneself. Although foreshadowed in Plato and Aristotle, most theorists refer to Hobbes's *Leviathan* (1946 [1651]: Part I, chapter 6):

> *Sudden glory,* is a passion which maketh those *grimaces* called LAUGHTER; and is caused either by some sudden act of their own, that pleaseth them; or by the apprehension of some deformed thing in another, by comparison whereof they suddenly applaud themselves.

Superiority theories have been used to explain the 'butts' of jokes.

5. *The pleasure of feeling secure.* This source overlaps with the previous. Lucretius (1947 [1st century B.C.], *De Rerum Natura,* Book II, 1–4) states it thus:

> It is pleasant, when on the great sea the winds are agitating the waters,
>
> to look from the land on another's great struggle;
>
> not because it is a delectable joy that anyone be distressed,
>
> but because it is pleasant to see what ills you yourself are free from.[2]

Compare, for example, witnessing an actual fight in a pub, in which case you might feel insecure and wish to make hasty exit, with a pub fight represented in a film.

Note that the last three are related to the emotion schadenfreude.

I will consider aesthetic pleasure further in Section 7.5, not least because the aesthetic pleasure is achieved through linguistic creativity, something which some may assume not to be a characteristic of impoliteness.

Illustration The text below is a letter purportedly written by a customer of NTL (a cable company), to complain about the service he had received. The letter has been circulated on many websites. It is claimed that it is a real letter of complaint, and that it won a competition as the complaint letter of the year. We have no way of knowing whether it really is a true letter or not. But that is beside the point. What we do know is that it has been circulated on the Internet for the purpose of entertaining third parties. These are some of the reactions the letter received:

- hahahahha thats just great! ☺ What a guy!
- LOL...:)
- i had to walk out of my cubicle and go outside, this is hysterical even if it's not a real letter, who cares
- hahahaha ☺GREAT choose of words. Really amusing read, thanks for posting

- LOL, This was a funny post, Thanks for the laugh, specially this part.
- Nice read. A total lol 😃😃
- Nearly in tears of laughter, cant agree more with the annoying hold tones tho, and subtle cut offs.
- Nothing more entertaining than overdone criticism.

We should note here that the target is not a single identifiable individual's identity or their rights. It is the group of people associated with the company NTL. It is not the same, then, as observing one person suffering the impoliteness of another. There is also perhaps a sense that some collective identities, and in particular those of corporations, represent legitimate targets.

The letter is as follows (the full text comprises 762 words, but for reasons of space I made a number of cuts; the full text can be found on the Internet by searching on 'NTL customer complaint').

[3]
    Dear Cretins,

    I have been an NTL customer since 9th July 2001, when I signed up for your 3-in-one deal for cable TV, cable modem, and telephone. . . .

    My initial installation was cancelled without warning, resulting in my spending an entire Saturday sitting on my fat arse waiting for your technician to arrive. When he did not arrive, I spent a further 57 minutes listening to your infuriating hold music, and the even more annoying Scottish robot woman telling me to look at your helpful website. . . . HOW?

    I alleviated the boredom by playing with my testicles for a few minutes – an activity at which you are no-doubt both familiar and highly adept. The rescheduled installation then took place some two weeks later, although the technician did forget to bring a number of vital tools – such as a drill-bit, and his cerebrum. Two weeks later, my cable modem had still not arrived. . . .

    Doubtless you are no longer reading this letter, as you have at least a thousand other dissatisfied customers to ignore, and also another one of those crucially important testicle-moments to attend to. Frankly I don't care, it's far more satisfying as a customer to voice my frustration's in print than to shout them at your unending hold music. Forgive me, therefore, if I continue.

    I thought BT were shit, that they had attained the holy piss-pot of godawful customer relations, that no-one, anywhere, ever, could be more disinterested, less helpful or more obstructive to delivering service to anyone else is there? How surprised I therefore was, when I discovered to my considerable dissatisfaction and disappointment what a useless shower of bastards you truly are. You are sputum-filled pieces of distended rectum incompetents of the highest order. British Telecom – wankers though they are – shine like brilliant beacons of success, in the filthy puss-filled mire of your seemingly limitless inadequacy. . . .

    Have a nice day – may it be the last in your miserable short life, you irritatingly incompetent and infuriatingly unhelpful bunch of twats.

Ostensibly, this is a matter of affective impoliteness. The writer sees it an opportunity to 'voice' his 'frustration', and much of the text elaborates his trials and tribulations. However, there is clearly more to it than this. Consider that it is not at all linguistically like the example of affective impoliteness discussed in Section 7.2. In particular, there is an elaborate, sophisticated verbal creativity here that was almost completely lacking in the example of Section 7.2. Of course, this is written text, and it is quite possible that the writer took the time to hone his attacks in this creative way. What matters more, and what is more easily verifiable, is that the linguistic creativity has given pleasure to many readers. Note that one of the reactions I listed above is 'GREAT choose of words' (spelling as per the original). Let us consider some examples of that creativity.

The opening of the letter, 'Dear Cretins', subverts the highly conventional politic beginning of a formal letter by blending the opening formula (e.g. 'Dear Sir/Madam') with an item typical of conventionalised impoliteness insults (e.g. 'You cretins'). In a somewhat similar vein, one of the creative strategies deployed throughout the letter by the writer is to select polysyllabic, relatively rare and/or often Latinate vocabulary (e.g. 'alleviated', 'adept', 'cerebrum', 'attained', 'disinterested', 'considerable dissatisfaction', 'disappointment', 'sputum', 'distended', 'rectum', 'incompetents') that fits the style of a formal letter, but conflicts with the usual monosyllabic, relatively common and/or often Anglo-Saxon vocabulary of strong conventionalised impoliteness or emotional language generally. For example, in the penultimate paragraph the utterance 'you are sputum-filled pieces of distended rectum incompetents of the highest order' appears to echo a conventionalised insult (a personalised negative assertion). However, the formula has been creatively adapted: it is packed with unconventional, as far as impoliteness formulae are concerned, Latinate vocabulary.

In the third paragraph, the writer casts the aspersion that the taboo activity of playing with one's testicles is something at which the target is 'no-doubt both familiar and highly adept'. This of course flouts the Maxim of Quality, as the writer has no real evidence for this claim. It also assumes that the target is male, which may well not be the case. The flaws in the logic of the argument are not the issue – it is more about the emotion of the argument (see Kienpointner 2008, for a discussion of impoliteness and argumentation). The following sentence asserts that 'the technician did forget to bring a number of vital tools – such as his drill-bit, and his cerebrum'. This flouts the Maxim of Manner. Although there is a sense in which the brain is a tool by which things are achieved, it is not usually thought of as a tool. Indeed, the contrast with normal tools is exacerbated by the fact that 'cerebrum' is coordinated with 'drill-bit', which is indeed a prototypical practical, manual tool.

The fourth paragraph has further personalised negative assertions. For example, 'you have at least a thousand other dissatisfied customers to ignore' both asserts that they have dissatisfied customers of that number and also that their action will be to ignore them, and both assertions presumably assail the Social identity face of the customer service representatives at NTL. In the final sentence of the paragraph he writes '[f]orgive me, therefore, if I continue'. This is the stuff of remedial facework (Goffman 1971), which is closely associated with politeness. The writer has just given an account or justification as to why he is writing a letter like this, now he asks for forgiveness for the face damage he is just about to cause. But of course these conventionalised politeness tactics are used in the context of rather extreme impoliteness: there is a clear mismatch. This is convention-driven implicational impoliteness – the conventionalised politeness is merely a sneering veneer.

In the fifth paragraph, what is creative about the personalised negative assertion 'what a useless shower of bastards you truly are' is the collocation of 'shower of' and 'bastards'. In the *OEC* the most frequent collocation of 'shower of' is 'sparks' (231 instances) and the next most frequent is 'rain' (156) (the former item also forms the statistically strongest bond with a Mutual Information score of 15.313). Most of the statistically strongest collocates according to Mutual Information scores fall into the domains of 'sparks' or 'rain' (e.g. 'cinders', 'sparkles', 'embers'; 'hailstones', 'sleet', 'raindrops'), though there are other definite groups too (e.g. 'confetti', 'paper'; 'shards', 'needles'). 'Bastards', then, is statistically and semantically unexpected as a collocate of 'shower of', though it is not unheard of – there are in fact 14 cases in the *OEC*. Finally in this paragaph, we might recognise a conventionalised impoliteness personalised negative reference consisting of 'in the filthy puss-filled mire of your seemingly limitless inadequacy', but this unusually contains a strikingly creative metaphor.

The final paragraph initiates a conclusion with a conventionalised polite salutation, 'have a nice day', but of course this is a conventional trigger for implicational impoliteness – it is sarcasm. The fact that it is sarcasm is made clear by what follows. 'May it be the last in your miserable short life' seems to be a conventionalised impoliteness ill-wish. Note that 'your miserable short life' contains the existential presupposition that the target will have a miserable short life. And finally, we have words that seem to reflect a conventionalised impolite vocative insult 'you irritatingly incompetent and infuriatingly unhelpful bunch of twats'. However, at nine words in length this is a striking departure from the normal length of a conventionalised vocative insult. Vocative insults rarely exceed three words in length. My three-word length claim here is partly based on my impressions, but I have also tested this claim in the *OEC* on specific vocative insults. For example, the frequencies for the formula 'You bastard' and for that formula with up to four pre-head modifiers are displayed in Table 7.1.

Table 7.1 *The frequencies of variants of the formula 'You bastard'*
in the OEC

Formula variant	Frequency	Percentage of errors (clausal cases)
Two-word: You bastard	721	0
Three-word: You # bastard	381	0
Four-word: You # # bastard	156	8
Five-word: You # # # bastard	177	23
Six-word: You # # # # bastard	138	33

(I searched on 'You' with a capital to retrieved examples of the formula in the same syntactic position, namely, at the beginning of the sentence. I analysed the first hundred of each formula variant to discover the percentage that were not genuine vocatives. Cases that were not genuine vocatives were full clauses, such as: 'You can be an ugly bastard like me.')

As can be seen from Table 7.1, the bulk of the examples fall into the first two variants, i.e. within two or three words. The four-word variant accounts for less than half as many as three-word, and we begin to see some errors. Five-word and six-word variants occur with very roughly the same frequency as the four-word variant, but significantly we see the error rate rising rapidly. Hence my claim that vocative insults rarely exceed three words in length, and that a vocative insult of nine words is strikingly unusual. In addition, it contains relatively complex vocabulary – 'irritatingly', 'incompetent' and 'infuriatingly', setting up the background for internal deviation: the final three words here are monosyllabic, and the very final word, 'twats', is a strikingly low-style, informal, non-Latinate (even non-Romance) item, one that is typical of conventionalised impoliteness.[3]

7.5 Creativity and patterns of impoliteness

Creativity clearly is an important feature of entertaining impoliteness. However, creativity is *not* confined to entertaining impoliteness, and this is a particular issue I wish to address in this section. Furthermore, I wish to counter the everyday view that impoliteness, rather like views of slang, is a debased form of language – simplistic, without finesse. I have met this view repeatedly: what is there for a linguist to research if impoliteness is just rotten nasty stuff, screaming, shouting, and so on? The idea that impoliteness is simplistic also tallies with the view that it is merely an emotional reflex, a view that I rejected in Section 2.5.1. My discussion in this section is in large part informed by Ronald Carter's (2004) thought-provoking work on language and creativity, not least of all because it deals with everyday interaction.

Literary genres thrive on verbal creativity and conflict, particularly as a means of furthering plot and characterisation. It all creates dramatic entertainment. Several publications (e.g. Culpeper 1996: 364–6; Kienpointner 1997: 280–2; Culpeper 1998; Rudanko 2006) have highlighted the role of impoliteness in literary texts. However, literariness is not confined to the canon of Literature. Carter articulates the view that many scholars working in the area of stylistics would ascribe to, namely, that there is 'a cline of literariness in language use with some uses of language being marked as more literary than others in certain domains and for certain judges within that domain' (2004: 69). As one might expect, Carter, rightly in my view, argues for a cline of creativity: 'some uses of language are designedly less creative than others' (Carter 2004: 69). Creativity is closely associated with literariness (Carter 2004: 66), although it is not the only feature of literariness: '[w]hether a reader chooses to respond to a text in a literary way is one determinant of its literariness' (Carter 2004: 69).

In order to begin to assess whether and how impoliteness might be creative, we need to have an understanding of creativity. Carter argues that there are two types of creativity:

There are clearly two levels of 'creative' interactions: first, more overt, presentational uses of language, open displays of metaphoric invention, punning, uses of idioms and departures from expected idiomatic formulations (*pattern re-forming*); second, less overt, maybe even subconscious and subliminal parallelisms, echoes and related matchings which regularly result in expressions of affective convergence, in signals of intimacy and in explicit symmetries of feeling (*pattern forming*). (2004: 109)

These two types are illustrated as follows:

(1) Creativity as pattern re-forming

[4]

(*Discussing a stormy marriage and cool relations between the couple*)

<S 01>: He's at it again but he really wants you know just to sit down.

<S 02>: Like they just talk about how they both feel.

<S 01>: Out of the frying pan into the deep freeze this time.

(Carter 2004: 95)

(2) Creativity as pattern forming

[5]

<S 02>: [laughs] Cos you come home.

<S 03>: I come home.

<S 02>: You come home to us.

[6]

<S 03>: Sunday is a really nice day I think.

<S 02>: It certainly is.

<S 03>: It's a really nice relaxing day.

(Carter 2004: 107)

The first kind of creativity discussed by Carter, pattern re-forming, is discussed in the field of stylistics as deviation from some norm (i.e. it is an unexpected irregularity) (e.g. Mukařovský 1970; Leech 1985). Carter's second category seems to be reminiscent of parallelism (i.e. it is an unexpected regularity) (e.g. Leech 1985). However, Carter has in mind 'subconscious and subliminal parallelisms', as illustrated above, rather than the more conscious kinds of parallelism as in, for example, Othello's line 'I kissed thee ere I killed thee', with its tight syntactic and sound parallelisms. It is a moot point whether all the patterns formed across a conversation can be described as creative: some repetition is necessary for reasons of, for example, cohesion. What we can say is that patterns are formed across interactions which vary in creativity. There are, in my view, two other kinds of creativity. Creativity can be achieved through the interaction between language and context. Leech (1969: 182) briefly makes the point, when discussing linguistic deviation in poetry, that 'one special kind of violation . . . arises when a piece of language is somehow at odds with the immediate situation in which it occurs'. The importance of this kind of creativity is acknowledged in sociolinguistics as we already noted in Section 5.3:

Even when speakers operate 'within a predictable repertoire', they are not limited to recycling pre-existing symbolic meanings. They can frame the linguistic resources available to them in creative ways, making new meanings from old meanings. (Coupland 2007: 84)

The other kind of creativity is in fact briefly alluded to by Carter:

The well-known truths expressed by proverbs are usually oblique and implicit rather than direct statements, they often have a metaphorical basis and *their indirectness prompts interpretation and a 'creative' inference of meaning*. (Carter 2004: 134, my emphasis)

With these four types of creativity in mind – pattern-re-forming, pattern-forming, situational deviation and unusual implicitness – my task now is to assess whether impoliteness can be creative. This is something that Carter did not do on account of the limitations of his data:

in CANCODE data generally there are few examples of overtly 'critical' creativity, involving people breaking generic boundaries or resisting norms in order to express rebellion, to underline a negative stance or to conflict with what is expected. Such elements form an important component of creativity but in this corpus creative language use is mainly for convergent purposes. (Carter 2004: 160)

First, let us briefly glance at politeness. Politic behaviour, as defined and exemplified in Introducing impoliteness, is made up of routinised patterns, and it is thus non-creative. In fact, Carter's (1985: 133) comment on less creative language in interaction could equally be a description of politic behaviour: 'in parallel with these creative extensions and reconfigurations is the existence of a range of non-creative, formulaic expressions which, as we have seen, operate primarily to stabilise and routinise the communicative event'.

Politeness, as defined by Watts, is creative in so far as it is perceived to go beyond the expectable social routines of politic behaviour. A glance at my examples in Introducing impoliteness will reinforce the point. There I also argued that politic behaviour and politeness form a cline, and this runs parallel with the idea that they involve a cline of creativity. Now let us turn to impoliteness.

Carter (2004: 41) argues that 'the creative act always requires a background or some relief against which to operate'. Watts (2003) argues that politeness or impoliteness is behaviour which is perceived to go beyond the expectable social routines of politic behaviour. Similarly, I claimed that 'impoliteness is very much the parasite of politeness' (Culpeper 1996: 355). These statements are consistent with my discussion of (im)politeness thresholds in Section 6.4. The higher the politeness threshold the stronger the potential for impoliteness. But is politeness always in the background of impoliteness? I discussed in Section 6.6 interaction types such as army training that '*sanction or neutralise face-threatening* or *face-damaging acts*' (Watts 2003: 260). In my view, face is sensitive to attack and norms to violation in any circumstance. Neutralisation only occurs when the target can adequately factor in the context, and people do not automatically do this (see Section 6.6). Furthermore, impoliteness can be pitched against politeness, even in contexts where face-attack is expected: people can use language to engineer a politeness threshold which they then deviate from (see Section 6.4).

Three of the four types of creativity have already in fact been discussed in relation to impoliteness. Impoliteness can most obviously involve pattern re-forming, as was demonstrated in the analysis in Section 7.4. The fact that conventionally impolite formulae can be creatively re-formed is also proof of their existence. As with all types of creativity, one can find examples inside and outside the prototypical literary canon. Compare the examples below:

[7]
    (*Lancaster University library desk graffiti*)
    [you] [[bitter yorkshire pie munching ale drinking sheep fucking] [poof]]

[8]
    Thou clay-brained guts, thou knotty-pated fool, thou whoreson obscene greasy tallow-catch!
               (Shakespeare, *Henry IV (Part 1)*, Act II, scene iv)

Situationally creative impoliteness was discussed in Section 5.4 as a variety of implicational impoliteness, that which is driven by the context, involving either unmarked behaviours or the absence of behaviours (e.g. not thanking somebody for a gift). Impoliteness involving unusual implicitness attended many of the examples of implicational impoliteness discussed in Chapter 5. I will just repeat one here, namely, William Smith's comment to a Florida judge: 'I suggest to you with respect, your honour, that you're a few French fries short of a Happy Meal in terms of what's likely to take place.'

What about pattern-forming impoliteness? Some aspects of pattern-forming impoliteness were discussed in Section 6.4 in relation to reciprocity and counter-impoliteness. However, Carter (2004: 101) writes that pattern-reinforcement tends to suggest affective connection or convergence. Also, he writes that the absence of pattern-reinforcement appears to suggest disaffection and/or divergence (e.g. Carter 2004: 159). If this is the case, then pattern-forming should not be a characteristic of impoliteness. My analysis of coercive impoliteness in Section 7.3 revealed that there can be a huge amount of pattern-forming in genuine impoliteness, involving repetitions, reformulations, extensions, and so on. However, and importantly, it is not reciprocal pattern-forming – it is not jointly constructed – and it is reciprocal pattern-forming across interactants that Carter seems to have in mind. In asymmetrical situations we tend to see asymmetrical patterns. In contrast, let us consider three examples of pattern-forming across turns in symmetrical situations.

[9]

Repetition

Courtneyde: Get lost.
Silvia: Get lost. Get <unclear>
Courtneyde: You're dirty dog.
Silvia: You're dirty dog. Get lost.
Gwen: <nv>laugh<nv>
        (COLT Corpus, quoted in Stenström *et al.* 2002: 200)

[10]

Escalation

James: I sock you in your nose.
Art: I sock you in the mouth.
James: You gonna have a black eye you keep on.
Art: You gonna have a bloody nose, and a bloody mouth and knocks one of your teeths out. I'm gonna knock 'em down your throat.
        (Lein and Brenneis 1978: 301)

[11]

Oppositions

Lisa: because he treats her like a [whore].
Darlene: excuse me, he treats me like. . . Oh, that's [?]
Lisa: yes he does Darlene.
Darlene: no he does not. You don't [know].
Lisa: yes he does.
Darlene he does not.
        (from the chat show *Jenny Jones*, quoted in Richardson and Meinhof 1999: 137)

All these examples are variants on tit-for-tat patterns. That we have pattern-forming is not in doubt, but the issue is: do we have genuine impoliteness? Examples [9] and [10] actually take place between children. In example [9], Silvia is only two years old; she is learning the activity of doing impoliteness from her sister. Stenström *et al.* (2002: 200) propose that what we see in examples such as these is ritual conflict or banter (see Section 6.5). They suggest the features are as follows:

the opponent *counters* an offensive move by one that is equally or more offensive, eliciting lengthy sequences of insults and counter-insults or challenges with challenges. The oppositional directives, insults, challenges and swear-words mark the sequences as aggravated. (Stenström *et al.* 2002: 200)

So, whilst this *appears* to be jointly constructed impoliteness patterning, it is not supported by the context, which suggests ritualised competition in a pretend, mock frame. Non-verbal and prosodic cues, such as 'exaggerated shouting and laughter', 'a friendly, humorous tone' (Stenström *et al.* 2002: 200–1), help block impoliteness effects. The ritualised nature, particularly in the first example, is also perhaps signalled by obvious flouts of the Maxim of Quality ('you're dirty dog'), which seem to present an alternative fictional world. On the other hand, these elements are missing from example [11] above, and example [2] in Section 6.4, which clearly illustrate pattern-forming repetitions and seem to contain genuine impoliteness (especially in the case of the latter example).

As discussed in Section 6.5, there is no straightforward distinction between genuine and mock impoliteness, or between ritual vs non-ritual activity types. There is a scale between them (cf. Eder 1990, who found speech events halfway between playful and serious). Also, the kind of impoliteness activity one might be engaged in can be perceived differently by different participants (see the example discussed in Culpeper *et al.* 2003: 1567–8). What of the issue that jointly constructed impoliteness pattern-forming always suggests 'affective connection and convergence'? There is good evidence, as given in Section 6.5, that ritualised, non-genuine impoliteness pattern-forming establishes affective connection/convergence, i.e. solidarity. There is also, however, evidence of non-ritualised, genuine impoliteness patterning establishing disaffection and divergence, as mentioned in the previous paragraph. As I argued in Section 6.4, reciprocity and other motivations often call for a riposte, which in turn calls for a further riposte, and so on, leading to pattern-forming. However, there is always the possibility that the competitive activity itself begins to become the motivating factor, and this detracts from genuine, personalised impoliteness. This point is consistent with my argument in Section 6.4 that reactions to initial impoliteness are perceived to be less impolite. Over a sequence of impolite utterances, the initial act recedes and people are driven by reactions, by reciprocity, and so the perceived impoliteness is theoretically reduced.

7.6 Institutional impoliteness

In Section 6.2.2, I discussed the notion of legitimation. I noted how in the study reported in Section 5.5.3 commands uttered by an employer to an employee, by a judge to a defendant or by an army sergeant to a recruit hardly counted as impolite no matter how explicit or direct they were. Institutional power structures underpin all those contexts and give rise to dominant ideologies by which impoliteness is legitimated and (typically) unchallenged. In situations such as the courtroom, as Kasper (1990: 210) points out, the institutional constraints do not licence the target to retaliate, reflecting 'an asymmetric distribution of rights to communicative practice that reflects the unequal power relationship between prosecutor and defendant'. Powerful participants not only do impoliteness but are supported by the social structure – the power behind them – in doing so (e.g. the speaking rights afforded to a judge); in contrast, the less powerful participants are restricted by the social structure from meeting impoliteness with impoliteness – they are more likely to suffer face loss without the ability to counter it. Of course, as pointed out in Section 7.3, this does not mean that impoliteness will never be done by the less powerful participants to the more powerful. Indeed, one possible motivation for doing so may be to gain status within a less powerful group by vigorously challenging somebody with markedly more social institutional power using techniques such as impoliteness (e.g. being impolite to a school teacher, in order to gain status within a particular student peer group). Also, we should bear in mind that institutional power is not always behind instruments with negative purposes. In fact, in my discussion in Section 3.9.1, we saw how institutional rules and policies were designed to protect vulnerable groups.

A particular reason for focusing on institutions in this section is that functions do not pertain to the level of the individual but to the dominant group behind the institution. This is clear in Kaul de Marlangeon's (2008: 738) definition of institutional impoliteness as 'a bounded phenomenon of public nature, performed by individuals that act on behalf of the group sharing the same system of values'. This issue has implications for intentionality in such contexts. Let us briefly consider the notion of institutional racism. Although the notion is often attributed to the black activist Stokely Carmichael, in the UK it is Sir William MacPherson's inquiry report into the murder of Stephen Lawrence in 1999 that brought the notion into clear focus. In that report, institutional racism is defined as (the full report is available at: www.archive.official-documents. co.uk/document/cm42/4262/sli-00.htm):

the collective failure of an organization to provide an appropriate and professional service to people because of their colour, culture or ethnic origin. It can be seen or detected in processes, attitudes and behaviour which amount to discrimination through unwitting prejudice, ignorance, thoughtlessness and racist stereotyping which disadvantage minority ethnic people. (6.34)

At a personal level, racism may appear to be 'unwitting', but at an institutional level there is a sense in which it is the result of collective intentions, which any individual may be less than fully conscious of, leaving the associated ideologies unchallenged (see, for example, Searle 1990 on collective intentions, and more particularly the papers on collective intentionality and social rights in Lagerspetz *et al.* 2001). And so it can be with impoliteness. In the following two sections, I will describe two types of institutionalised impoliteness, one relating to army recruit training and the other to exploitative television.

7.6.1   Institutional mortification: Impoliteness and army recruit training

Institutional mortification refers to institutions, such as mental hospitals, prisons and army recruit training centres, which promote activities with the function of 'killing' some aspect of a person's self so that it can be replaced with an approved self. Goffman (1997 [1958]) referred to such institutions as 'total institutions'; they are institutions to which the entire self is submitted. Consider his description of the arrival of the raw army recruit in a training camp:

> The recruit comes into the establishment with a conception of himself made possible by certain stable social arrangements in his home world. Upon entrance, he is immediately stripped of the support provided by these arrangements in the accurate language of some of our oldest total institutions, he begins a series of debasements, degradations, humiliations, and profanations of self. His self is systematically, if often unintentionally, mortified. He begins some radical shifts in his *moral career*, a career composed of the progressive changes that occur in the beliefs that he has concerning himself and significant others. (1997 [1958]: 55)

'Debasements, degradations, humiliations, and profanations of self' are the stuff of impoliteness. Impoliteness undermines people's sense of identity, as mediated in the concept of face, and their sense of social and moral normality. Flynn (1977: 93–4) argues that there is functional equivalence between the formal rites of passage of some tribal-village and caste-estate societies and the training programmes of modern military institutions:

> Studies of military socialisation in modern societies has shown that insult is one of a number of socialising mechanisms that help break down the recruit's previous bases of identity so that he will be motivated to conform to the norms and embody the values of the military organisation. The overall patterns of insult in the military training programmes are basically similar to the ridicule in which tribal pre-initiates are subjected. In both the modern and the tribal context, the humiliation that is engendered by severe and continuing insult motivates the initiate to escape his lowly status by conforming to expectations that are forcefully imposed upon him. In addition, the recruit is prevented from having any sources of positive reinforcement other than for behaviour which

conforms to the values and expectations of the military organisation. Thus, the insults he receives tear down his pre-military sources of self-esteem and replace them with a positive self-regard that results from his developing capacities to embody military virtues and display fighting prowess.

Breaking down 'bases of identity', tearing down 'sources of self-esteem', getting rid of old norms and values, is the function of coercive impoliteness in this context.

As an illustration, I will revisit an analysis of army recruit training which I published in 1996. The source of the data is the documentary *Soldier Girls* (Broomfield and Churchill 1981), which was filmed at an American recruit training base in 1980. As a 'fly on the wall' study, the documentary, made by the award-winning Nick Broomfield, follows the fortunes of a group of women recruits. My data was drawn from one particular interview lasting approximately six and a half minutes. Although this interview contains a high concentration of impoliteness work, it is not unrepresentative of the kind of linguistic features that occur in army recruit training (see, in particular, Bousfield 2008). In this particular data, the participants are the recruit Private Alves (PA) and three sergeants (S1, S2, S3), one of whom (S3) is a woman. Alves has performed consistently badly in the training programme and proved intractable in the face of repeated attempts by the NCOs to force her to improve. As punishment for her latest failure, she is consigned to digging a hole under the supervision of a squad leader. After digging a substantial hole, she refuses to continue and ends up screaming hysterically whilst the squad leader tries physically to force her to keep digging. The 'interview' takes place in an office shortly after this event. From the point of view of the sergeants, she is not only guilty of failing to try hard enough in the training programme, but also of the far more heinous crime of 'insubordination', i.e. challenging the authority of those above her.

I will not repeat my full analysis here. What I would like to demonstrate is the systematic way in which they use impoliteness to attack aspects of her face. They attack her social roles, including her role as an American citizen

S2:   you don't even deserve to live in the United States

her role as a soldier

S2:   disgrace to the uniform that's what you are Alves a disgrace to be wearing a
       uniform that you're wearing private nothing but a disgrace to that uniform you
       don't even deserve the time to wear it to have it on your little body

her potential role as a mother

S1:   I doubt if you could accept the responsibility of a child
S3:   the baby will cry itself to death before she ever was able to move across the room
       to give her anything to eat

and her role as a human being

SI: you haven't functioned as a human being I doubt since you were about thirteen
        you stopped being a member of the human race

They attack her personal value:

Sl: you are despicable
Sl: you don't deserve to be out there in society

her competence

S2:   can't do anything right

and her self-sufficiency

S2:   what's probably going to end up happening is probably you will find some man
        that will have to end up supporting you for the rest of your life

They attack her mental stability:

S3:   I think she is nutso
S2:   you're nuts you're nuttier than a fruit cake Alves
S2:   you're crazy

and her psychological make-up:

S2:   I think I need to get you evaluated
S2:   let you run around there like a psycho [small laugh] psycho private
S2:   we're going to take you to see a psychiatrist
S3:   you know Alves there's something about you that makes me think that you just
        might be the type that would take a weapon and go up on the top of a building
        and start just picking people off in the street just for the heck of it because you're
        apathetic that sooner or later it's bound to turn to hate and it's got to get out and
        when it gets out it usually manifests itself in a violent manner
S3:   and I would rather you were locked up on that thirteenth floor than out in civilian
        society because you might possibly kill one of my relatives or a member of my
        family

They even attack her genetic make-up (there may be a racist undercurrent here,
since Private Alves is of Mexican origin):

SI: do me a favor don't have any children . . . because unfortunately there is such a
        thing as heredi hereditary genes that I would hate to think that anybody would
        even closely come out like you

Finally, it is worth adding that this kind of systematic face-attacking – this
mortification of the self – is only possible in contexts where certain participants control the discourse. Alves tries to respond to the insults, but is always
interrupted and shouted down.

Table 7.2 *Examples of 'standard' and 'exploitative' chat and quiz shows*

	Standard	Exploitative
Chat show	*The Michael Parkinson Show, Wogan, Donahue*	*The Mrs Merton Show, Dame Edna Experience, Jerry Springer*
Quiz show	*University Challenge, Who Wants to be a Millionaire?*	*The Weakest Link*
Talent show	*Star Search, Stars in their Eyes*	*Pop Idol, X Factor, Britain's Got Talent*

7.6.2   Institutional exploitation: Television shows

Institutional exploitation refers to institutions, especially those relating to the media, which promote and condone activities with the function of attacking some aspect of a person's face or sociality rights in order to entertain others. I will focus on television shows. Table 7.2 gives examples of 'standard' and 'exploitative' chat shows, quiz and talent shows.

There are some *general* similarities between 'standard' chat shows and 'exploitative' variants. They both have: an immediate audience, a remote TV audience, a host, question–answer sequences and participants who are 'ordinary' people (except celebrity show variants). Richardson and Meinhof propose that the following is a general difference: 'A condition of confrontation on screen is that subjects be allowed to talk to one another rather than to the host/audience' (1999: 136). In fact, this particular 'general' difference only applies to the example of Jerry Springer in Table 7.2. What truly separates the exploitative chat shows from the standard shows is that they are all characterised by impoliteness. You may recollect the examples in Chapter 5 of impoliteness produced by Anne Robinson and Simon Cowell, both hosts of exploitative shows. In contrastive, standard chat shows generally treat guests and studio participants with a degree of deference. In fact, there are typically opportunities for a celebration of the achievements of the guests and sympathy for their trials and tribulations. Exploitative chat shows are more intent on humiliating the 'guests' (cf. Montgomery 1999: 105). Exploitative shows have evolved through the subversion of the politeness norms of the standard shows.[4]

Let us focus on one specific type of game show, that is the quiz show. Game shows are based on a competition: identifying either a winner through the elimination of participants from the game, or the amount of money an individual is to be rewarded with. Quiz show competitions are constituted by 'quiz questions', i.e. questions designed to test whether the participants know something. As with chat shows, the exploitative quiz show, of which *The Weakest Link* is the most well known in the UK, has evolved against the backdrop of standard quiz shows, where there are no sustained attempts to

Table 7.3 *The nature of 'chat' in three quiz shows*

	Chat quantity	Chat position	Host's chat orientation
University Challenge	(Very occasional remark)	(After a blatantly wrong answer)	(Non-supportive)
Who Wants to be a Millionaire?	A major part of the discourse	Before the answer is given (and very brief chats after)	Supportive
The Weakest Link	A major part of the discourse	After a round of questions and answers	Non-supportive

humiliate participants. However, to allow greater scope for exploitation, the structure of standard quiz show has undergone some changes. Quiz shows vary according to – amongst other things – the amount and kind of 'chat' that is allowed, chat being 'a clear shift of *register* within the program format where it occurs, such that the primary business of the format is temporarily delayed or suspended' (Tolson 1991: 179). Tolson (1991: 180) identifies three features of chat: (1) topical shift towards the personal/private, (2) displays of wit/humour and (3) the possibility of transgression (e.g. the interviewee putting questions to the interviewer). With quiz shows, the 'primary business of the format' is clearly the question–answer sequences comprising the quiz. But this format does not offer much scope for being impolite to participants. Chat reflecting on the proceedings has much more to offer, not least of all because it can involve a shift towards personal/private matters in which face is invested. In *The Weakest Link*, chat occurs after a round of questions and answers, and has the following structure:

1. The host evaluates the round in general and initiates the discovery of the 'weakest link' (i.e. the person who got most answers wrong).
2. Contestants nominate who they think is the 'weakest link'.
3. The host interacts with each contestant in turn, ostensibly in order to reveal their performance in the quiz.
4. The contestant with the most nominations leaves (a voice-over reveals to the TV audience whether they had in fact got the most questions wrong).

It is in the chat in *The Weakest Link* that impoliteness occurs.

Table 7.3 compares the chat in three quiz shows screened in the UK. *University Challenge* is very much a standard quiz show. Note that chat hardly occurs (hence all cells have entries in brackets). Very occasionally the host, Jeremy Paxman, makes a brief wry remark after an obviously wrong answer. But the suggestion often seems to be that this was a foolish slip, not that the answerer is a complete fool. *Who Wants to be a Millionaire?* deviates from the standard format in having chat as a major part of the programme's discourse, mostly before the answer is given and always supportive in nature. Similarly,

The Weakest Link deviates from the standard format in having a major part of the discourse on the programme as chat, but, importantly, this chat occurs after a round of questions and answers and is non-supportive. In fact, the programme is structured to maximise the potential for face damage. The reasons why *The Weakest Link* has great potential for face damage include:

- Answers are given in public. Face is fundamentally related to what others think. Greater public exposure means that more face is at stake (see Section 6.3).
- Answers are given by individuals, and thus they have complete responsibility for them. Contrast this with *University Challenge*, where some answers are given by the team.
- The easier the question is thought to be, the more foolish the contestant may feel if the answer is wrong. The questions on *The Weakest Link* are considerably easier than those on *University Challenge*. The fact that contestants still get them wrong probably has more to do with the high-pressure situation.
- There is no pre-answer sympathising chat to reduce the impact of an incorrect answer. In contrast, in *Who Wants to Be a Millionaire?*, Chris Tarrant's frequent supportive comment is 'the questions are only easy if you know the answer'.
- The chat allows reflection on the inadequacy of the answers, and thus the answerer. In *University Challenge* chat is minimal, and on *Who Wants to Be a Millionaire?* chat occurs before the answer is given.
- The chat allows a shift towards personal aspects, and thus aspects which may be more face-sensitive (see Section 6.3).

As discussed in Section 6.6, some contexts can neutralise impoliteness effects, at least to an extent. Game shows, like *The Weakest Link*, are constituted by a certain structure and certain conversational acts. They have formulaic elements (e.g. catchphrases and one-liners) and verbal cleverness (e.g. the one-liners), rather like ritualised banter. All this might suggest that the 'impoliteness' is not to be taken seriously. Moreover, the participant responsible for producing most of the potentially 'impolite' utterances is a persona Anne Robinson created for the show – it is a fiction. This means that one cannot straightforwardly attribute face-attacking intentionality to Anne Robinson. A similar point is made by Montgomery (1999: 144) in his discussion of the chat show host Mrs Merton:

> In order for a guest to take issue with a threat to face in the moment by moment conduct of the discourse, would require them to treat Mrs Merton seriously as if she were indeed a real person issuing a real FTA. Instead the rather elaborately contrived persona of Mrs Merton gives a mock or playful quality to the performance of the discourse.

All this means that *theoretically* it is difficult for a hearer to 'take' what the host says as (fully) impolite, since the impoliteness can be seen as a function of the game and not a personal goal. One might argue then that the impoliteness is not only sanctioned by the dominant group (e.g. the people who create, produce and host the show), but neutralised by the nature of the activity type. However, as I argued in Section 6.6, *in practice* things are less straightforward. People can and do still take offence in such situations. There may also be different perspectives on the same event: some people – perhaps including the real Anne Robinson – may see it all as a game and the 'impoliteness' as mock; some others – perhaps the contestants *in situ* – may not pay adequate attention to the context and view the 'impoliteness' as genuine.

7.7   Conclusion

All impoliteness has the general function of reinforcing or opposing specific identities, interpersonal relationships, social norms and/or ideologies. In this chapter I argued that there are three key, specific functional types of impoliteness event: affective impoliteness, coercive impoliteness and entertaining impoliteness. Affective impoliteness may simply involve the unrestrained expression of emotion in contexts where it is not normal or it is prohibited. But a more instrumental variant involves the targeted display of heightened emotion, typically anger, with the implication that the target is to blame for producing that negative emotional state. Coercive impoliteness is impoliteness that seeks a realignment of values between the producer and the target such that the producer benefits or has their current benefits reinforced or protected. I predicted that coercive impoliteness is more likely to occur in situations where there is an imbalance of social structural power, though it can also be used in more equal relationships to engineer a gain in social power. The perception that a person with relative coercive power is actually willing to use it – a perception that can be strengthened linguistically – plays a role in achieving beneficial terminal values. Entertaining impoliteness involves entertainment at the expense of the target of the impoliteness, and is thus always exploitative to a degree. As all genuine impoliteness, it involves a victim or at least a potential victim. I proposed that there are five sources of pleasure that can be involved in entertaining impoliteness: emotional pleasure, aesthetic pleasure, voyeuristic pleasure, the pleasure of feeling superior and the pleasure of feeling safe.

Regarding aesthetic pleasure, I focused on the way it can be achieved through linguistic creativity. Just as all creativity requires a backdrop, I argued that politeness is always in the background of impoliteness, and that the higher the politeness threshold the stronger the potential for impoliteness. I identified four types of creativity – pattern-re-forming, pattern-forming, situational deviation and unusual implicitness – and argued that they all exist in impoliteness. However, Carter (2004) suggests that pattern-forming creativity always involves 'affective connection and convergence'. This is supported by ritualised, non-genuine impoliteness patterning which does indeed tend to establish affective connection and/or convergence, i.e. solidarity. Nevertheless, I pointed to evidence of completely non-ritualised, genuine impoliteness patterning establishing disaffection and divergence. I suggested that this kind of genuine impoliteness pattern-forming is driven by reciprocity and other motivations calling for a riposte (see also Section 6.4). However, I suggested that there is always the possibility that the competitive activity itself begins to become the motivating factor, and this detracts from genuine, personalised impoliteness.

Finally, I addressed the issue of institutional impoliteness. Institutional impoliteness is underpinned by power structures, and has associated dominant ideologies by which the specific kinds of impoliteness associated with an institution are legitimated and (typically) unchallenged. The functions of impoliteness here do not pertain to the level of the individual but the dominant group behind the institution: they serve collective intentions, which an individual may be less than fully conscious of, leaving the institutional ideologies unchallenged. I focused on two specific functions of institutional impoliteness. One is institutional mortification, which promotes activities with the function of 'killing' some aspect of a person's self so that it can be replaced with an approved self. My example was army recruit training. The other is institutional exploitation, which refers to institutions which promote activities with the function of attacking some aspect of a person's face or sociality rights in order to entertain others. Media institutions are often involved in such exploitation – my example of television game shows was but one example. One might think of TV documentaries focusing on events containing verbal conflict (e.g. the police or traffic wardens dealing with offenders), British political interviews which have become increasingly adverserial in recent years, tabloid newspapers, and so on.

8 Conclusions

Let us now revisit and extend the notion of impoliteness given in Section 2.1 thus:

Impoliteness is a negative attitude towards specific behaviours occurring in specific contexts. It is sustained by expectations, desires and/or beliefs about social organisation, including, in particular, how one person's or a group's identities are mediated by others in interaction. Situated behaviours are viewed negatively – considered 'impolite' – when they conflict with how one expects them to be, how one wants them to be and/or how one thinks they ought to be. Such behaviours always have or are presumed to have emotional consequences for at least one participant, that is, they cause or are presumed to cause offence. The degree of offence, and also the quality of offence (the specific negatively valenced emotion experienced), depends in particular on the following factors (some of which overlap):

Attitudinal factors

- which (and the extent to which) expectations, desires and/or beliefs infringed are cognitively active;
- the emotional sensitivity of the expectations, desires and/or beliefs infringed;

Linguistic-pragmatic factors

- the degree of offence conventionally associated with any linguistic formula used;
- the amount and kind of intensifying linguistic work undertaken (the choice of intense lexis, the addition of taboo words or intensifiers, prosodic reinforcement, etc.);
- the amount of inferential work required to understand the behaviour in context;
- the way in which and the extent to which the behaviour matches or mismatches: (1) the other parts of the multimodal behaviour, or (2) the context;

Contextual and co-textual factors

- the extent to which the behaviour is positively or negatively valued in the relevant culture;

- the extent to which face or sociality rights are exposed;
- the extent to which power structures are abused;
- the extent to which the behaviour is legitimised;
- whether the behaviour is in-group or out-group;
- the (im)politeness threshold set, in particular, by the co-text;
- the degree of intentionality ascribed to the actor(s);
- the kind of person the communicator is understood to be; and
- the perspective of the person taking offence.

A symptom of offence being taken is a negative emotional reaction in, particularly, any target of the behaviour, whether that symptom is articulated verbally or non-verbally. An impoliteness attitude may be referred to (and also partly shaped) by particular impoliteness-related labels (e.g. *impolite, rude, discourteous, ill-mannered, aggressive*), which collectively constitute an impoliteness metalanguage embedded in impoliteness metadiscourse. Each label refers to a slightly different domain of impoliteness, domains which vary according to degree of symbolic violence and the in-group/out-group dimension.

Of course, I cannot claim to have presented conclusive evidence for every part of the above; rather, I have some evidence for every part. It awaits future research to test further my proposals.

My previous work (e.g. 1996) was much more focused on impoliteness 'strategies'. Although these have not been the main focus of this book, they have not been overlooked. Table 8.1 displays a summary of data-driven strategies and formulae discussed in this book. The lists of strategies and formulae are restricted to groups of items that arose from my data; they do not purport to be lists of all possible strategies or formula. However, they do have the merit that the items that form all groups are brought into consideration because participants judged them as impolite rather than me the researcher. This is an important point of departure from my previous work. Readers will note some similarities between labels for strategies and labels for formulae. This is not at all surprising as one way of performing a strategy is to use a relevant formula. The groups of formulae could be made more distinct from the groups of strategies by including the structural detail that characterises them. As I showed in Section 4.4.3, each formula consists of particular sets of words which are semantically congruent in some way and which have particular grammatically patterned co-texts. It is important to remember that the expression of impoliteness and/or its understanding is not restricted to the usage of conventionalised formulae or even strategies. Implicational impoliteness is frequently the mechanism by which impoliteness occurs, which is why I devoted a chapter to it. This is where we find phenomena such as mimicry, innuendo and sarcasm, which, although they do not occur in the impoliteness manuals from which I derived my strategy list, denote relatively conventionalised strategies for performing impoliteness. Of course, any formula or strategy is not an island

Table 8.1 *Conventionalised impoliteness strategies and formulae discussed in this book*

Conceptual orientation	Some impoliteness strategies (derived from impoliteness manuals; for details and examples, see Section 3.9.2)	Some impoliteness formulae (derived from my data sets; for details and examples see Section 4.4.3)
Face (any type)	*Insults*: Producing or perceiving a display of low values for some target *Pointed criticism/complaint*: Producing or perceiving a display of low values for some target	• Insults (personalized negative vocatives, personalised negative assertions, personalised negative references, personalised third-person negative references in the hearing of the target) • Pointed criticisms/complaints • Negative expressives (e.g. curses, ill-wishes) • Unpalatable questions and/or presuppositions
Association rights	*Exclusion* (including failure to include and disassociation): Producing or perceiving a display of infringement of inclusion	
Equity rights	*Patronising behaviour*: Producing or perceiving a display of power that infringes an understood power hierarchy *Failure to reciprocate*: Producing or perceiving a display of infringement of the reciprocity norm *Encroachment*: Producing or perceiving a display of infringement of personal space (literal or metaphorical) *Taboo behaviours*: Producing or perceiving a display of behaviours considered emotionally repugnant	• Condescensions • Message enforcers • Dismissals • Silencers • Threats

unto itself, but contextualises and is contextualised in impoliteness events. This ultimately determines its meanings and functions. Regarding the functions of impoliteness events, I argued that they perform one or more of three functions, which I labelled affective impoliteness, coercive impoliteness and entertaining impoliteness.

As I near the close of this book, I would like to flag one area that has not, largely for lack of space, received the attention it deserved. This is the diachronic dimension, both the history of impoliteness for each individual and the history of impoliteness for communities. There is no problem in accommodating the diachronic dimension of impoliteness within the model I have laid out in this book. Schema theory is a theory based on the accummluation of experiences: it is fundamentally historical. And accommodating changes in impoliteness for communities is not a problem, as I, following van Dijk, took a schema-theoretic view of ideology, taking it to be constituted by shared evaluative beliefs (attitude schemata). Community judgements about impoliteness are part of ideologies. However, I paid little attention to the specifics. So, here I will briefly give the flavour of some important issues, first focusing more on the individual, then the community.

Impoliteness overlaps with the notion of bullying (for a recent review of classroom bullying and aggressive communication, see Myers and Rittenour 2010). Why I mention bullying here is that research on bullying often stresses a diachronic dimension. Consider its definition in an authoritative study:

The definition of bullying is widely agreed on in literature on bullying. Bullying is a specific type of aggression in which (1) the behaviour is intended to harm or disturb, (2) the behaviour occurs repeatedly over time, and (3) there is an imbalance of power, with a more powerful person or group attacking a less powerful one. (Nansel *et al.* 2001: 2094)

Repeated behaviours, barely significant in themselves, have a corrosive effect, as they eat through to the core of a person. Repetition is in fact a pattern I noted in my discussion of coercive impoliteness, and this is where bullying fits. However, I only noted repetition within a single impoliteness event. But impoliteness, as in bullying, can take place over a number of temporally separated events, each one forming a pattern with the previous ones. It is this historical pattern that can make a new impoliteness behaviour much more significant than it seems.

Turning to communities, attitudes and ideologies of impoliteness are continually changing. Many British people have the *impression* of a massive explosion in the use of impolite language. However, if we go back over 1,000 years to the Old English text *Beowulf*, we will find jaw-dropping – from a modern British perspective – brusqueness. In Culpeper and Archer (2008), we examined over 1,000 requests in the period 1640–1760 and discovered that approximately half were produced with a direct imperative (e.g. '*Give* me water', '*Get* thee to bed') and, moreover, no other device to soften the request or signal politeness. In contrast, studies of present-day direct requests suggest that they are rather rare – fewer than ten per cent (cf. Blum-Kulka and House 1989). Impoliteness is perceived to be a big deal today because perceptions of what counts as impolite usage are changing, and not because some fixed gold standard has become tarnished. What is driving this change? The sociolinguist, Deborah Cameron (2007) suggests that it is two factors. One is the rise of popular psychotherapy advocating the expression of emotions rather than suppression; the other is the rise of corporate culture advocating direct expression amongst employees rather than indirect. These factors have helped create conditions in which the free expression of emotions and direct talk are positively valued. The problem is that this new cultural ideology flies in the face of the traditional one, by which positive values are ascribed to the control of emotions and circumspect talk. One might say that the new 'let it all hang out culture' is clashing with the 'beat about the bush' culture. A consequence of this ideological clash is a sense amongst traditionalists that their values are under attack.

Notes

INTRODUCING IMPOLITENESS

1 This year also saw the publication of another journal special issue, which, although it is not exclusively devoted to impoliteness, contains a significant number of papers focusing on impoliteness: '(Im)politeness in Spanish-speaking Socio-cultural Contexts' (*Pragmatics* 18 (4), edited by Diana Bravo).
2 In order to reduce the possibility of an interaction effect, the intentionality question and rating scale was separated from the gravity of offence question and rating scale and also placed on a different page.

CHAPTER 1

1 I use the labels *speaker* and *hearer* for convenient reference to elements of a basic communicative stituation. There are, of course, other discourse roles participants can inhabit. I will touch on these where relevant, but in particular in Section 7.4.
2 'Relational face' was added to her scheme in later publications (cf. Spencer-Oatey 2007, 2008).
3 My thanks to Leyla Marti for alerting me to this feature of the Turkish data.
4 I am indebted to Meilian Mei for providing me with both of these explanations.

CHAPTER 2

1 Perhaps it should be noted that many of the concepts that constitute their model are by no means exclusive to this model.
2 It seems likely that van Dijk and Kintsch's (1983) situation model was inspired by Johnson-Laird's (1983) work on 'mental models'.

CHAPTER 3

1 In the remainder of this paragraph, all information and quotations concerning the contents and structure of the *OEC* are sourced from www.askoxford.com/oec, unless stated otherwise.
2 The totals in Tables 3.1 and 3.2 refer to total number of documents indexed for the search term in the top row, not just the total of the top-five subject categories.
3 'Verbally rude' occurred once and 'verbally impolite' occurs twice.
4 Of course, there are yet further ways in which *polite* can be negated (e.g. 'scarcely polite'), but they are less central to my concerns here.

5 *Aggro* has 382 instances in the *OEC*. However, many if not most of these cases are not metalinguistic. Many refer to unnecessary effort or hassle endured by an individual.

6 'Errors' in the above analyses included: (1) tagging errors (e.g. *a little bit rude* or *a tad rude*, where *bit* and *tad* are treated as independent nouns), (2) erroneous repetition of the same example and its source (e.g. four of the seven instances of *polite* as a collocate of *impolite* in a coordinated relationship are all from exactly the same source) and (3) natural repetition of the same example (e.g. 'speak' as an infinitival complement). This final case is illustrated in Table 3.6. Seven of the fourteen instances of this particular example emanate from a single instance in President Bush's West Point speech in June 2002: 'it is somehow undiplomatic and and impolite to speak the language of right and wrong'. This speech was quoted by various news agencies, and thus 'speak' as an infinitival complement emerges as a pattern. Still, overall there are not a large number of errors.

7 It is worth noting that the notion of symbolic aggression is well established in the aggression literature (e.g. Infante and Wigley 1986), where it refers to an attack on an individual's self-concept and contrasts with physical attacks.

8 Of course, giving precise figures for the share of particular languages of the whole Internet is impossible. The figure of 80 per cent English is given in the *Humanising Language Teaching* journal at: www.hltmag.co.uk/may00/idea.htm.

9 In common with the way I represent other data, the typos, grammatical errors and other infelicities that appear in the examples quoted from the Web in this chapter are as per the original.

10 I have inserted punctuation between the two parts of most entries so they make sense when presented as continuous lines.

11 Patronising behaviour is perhaps more usually associated with cases where the producer has a more obvious claim to relative power. However, people can enginer a power relationship that suggests that the interlocutor has less power than they think they have. Talking back to a parent implies that the word of the other is far from decisive; it challenges a power hierarchy – it is patronising.

CHAPTER 4

1 To elaborate, at one end, semantic minimalists (e.g. Borg 2004; Cappelen and Lapore 2005) accord a limited role to pragmatic processes; at the other end, contextualists, notably Recanati (e.g. 2004), and relevance theorists (e.g. Sperber and Wilson 1995; Carston 2002) argue that minimal meanings are not possible – pragmatic processes determine even the truth conditions of utterances. In the light of arguments made by the latter scholars, the notion of 'what is said' becomes problematic; a case is made for more pragmatic intrusion into what is said than Grice had envisaged.

CHAPTER 5

1 It would be theoretically possible to separate out instances that fall into group 1 into those that involve particularised implicatures and those that involve generalised implicatures. Whilst it is possible to identify clear examples at the extremes of the particularised–generalised scale, there is much fuzziness around the middle, and for that reason I have not attempted to make this kind of separation.

2 Figure 5.1 was produced with *Speech Analyzer 2.4* (2001). A vowel sound is comprised of various formants (resonances) produced in the vocal tract. F1, on the vertical axis of the figure, can provide an indication of vowel height, such that the lower the F1 value the higher the vowel; F2, on the horizontal axis of the figure, can provide an indication of tongue advancement, such that the higher the F2 value the further to the front the vowel. The algorithms used to capture formant values are complex and not always reliable. To ensure that Figure 5.1 represents a true picture, I also sampled individual formant values for confirmation.

3 Tony Cowell is Simon's older brother.

4 The variant 'have a nice day' is more frequently used in the polite termination frame 'have a X day' in the context of, for example, McDonald's restaurants. A further example of this kind of McDonald's politeness would be the polite wish 'enjoy' which accompanies the service of food.

5 Our non-conventionally indirect item is perhaps not the best examplar of this category. One could say that it orients to a preparatory condition of the request to be quiet, namely, that one is not being quiet in the first place. This is a characteristic of Searle's (1975) understanding of indirect speeach acts. The problem for us was that we needed to unambiguously maintain the propositional content across the board, manipulating just directness. This rules out non-conventionally indirect examples like 'I can't hear myself think'. Nevertheless, there is no doubt that 'you aren't being quiet' is less conventional than 'could you be quiet', especially in terms of the notion of conventionalisation discussed in this book. Some evidence supporting this is in Aijmer's (1996) corpus work. She found that 'could you' is the most frequent request marker in hearer-oriented questions, whereas 'you aren't' fails to appear in her extensive list of assertion-based request markers.

6 In fact, as can be seen from Section 3.6.4, the label *inconsiderate* was the second most frequent label, but was not used here. The reason *inconsiderate* was not chosen was because it was not revealed in the pilot metalinguistic label study, which originally informed the study discussed here. Given that inconsiderateness is a very broad notion and that ratings on all scales were very similar, the absence of the label *inconsiderate* is of no consequence to the results.

CHAPTER 6

1 As with all norms, this is culturally specific. See Tedeschi and Felson (1994: 214 and 262), for useful references.

2 As far as the British Army is concerned, impoliteness is less part of any training philosophy now. I am informed that 'beasting' is not now used in any form, and the emphasis now is on 'encouragement'.

CHAPTER 7

1 One may wonder whether this formula has become conventionalised for impoliteness, i.e. it is more of a second-order indexical. I checked examples in the *OEC*. Whilst some accompany what might be construed as impoliteness contexts, in the main there is no strong correlation with such a context.

2 My translation of:

> Suave, mari magno turbantibus aequora ventis,
> e terra magnum alterius spectare laborem;
> non quia vexari quemquamst iucunda voluptas,
> sed quibus ipse malis careas quia cernere suave est.

3 The origin of 'twat' is uncertain. There seems to be a case for arguing that it is derived from the Old Norse item 'þveit', referring to a piece of land, a clearing or cut in a forest.

4 Of course, now the norm of the exploitative show is well-established. The dynamic of the backdrop of the standard show is receding.

References

Abrahams, Roger D. (1962) Playing the dozens. *Journal of American Folklore* 75: 209–20.

Adams, James S. (1965) Inequity in social exchange. In: Leonard Berkowitz (ed.) *Advances in Experimental Social Psychology, Vol. II*. London and New York: Academic Press, pp. 267–99.

Afifi, Walid. A. and Judee K. Burgoon (2000) Behavioral violations in interactions: The combined consequences of valence and change in uncertainty on interaction outcomes. *Human Communication Research* 26: 203–33.

Aijmer, Karin (1996) *Conversational Routines in English*. London: Longman.

Ainsworth, Janet (2008) Linguistic features of police culture and the coercive impact of police officer swearing in police-citizen street interaction. *Register and Context* 1 (downloaded 10 January 2009 from www.registerandcontext.de/ainsworth1.html).

Alexander, C. Norman and Gordon W. Knight (1971) Situated identities and social psychological experimentation. *Sociometry* 34: 65–82.

Allan, Keith and Kate Burridge (1991) *Euphemism and Dysphemism: Language Used as Shield and Weapon*. New York and Oxford: Oxford University Press.

 (2006) *Forbidden words: Taboo and the Censoring of Language*. Cambridge: Cambridge University Press.

Allwood, Jens S. (1976) *Linguistic Communication as Action and Cooperation: A Study In Pragmatics*. Göteborg University: Department of Linguistics.

Andersen, Susan M., Roberta L. Klatsky and John Murray (1990) Traits and social stereotypes: Efficiency differences in social information processing. *Journal of Personality and Social Psychology* 59 (2): 192–201.

Anderson, Craig A. and Brad J. Bushman (2002) Human aggression. *Annual Review of Psychology* 53: 27–51.

Anderson, Craig A., William E. Deuser and Kristina M. DeNeve (1995) Hot temperatures, hostile affect, hostile cognition, and arousal: Tests of a general model of affective aggression. *Personality and Social Psychology Bulletin* 21: 434–48.

Anderson, Elizabeth (2000) Beyond homo economicus: New developments in theories of social norms. *Philosophy and Public Affairs* 29 (2): 170–200.

Anderson, Lynne and Christine Pearson (1999) Tit for tat? The spiraling effect of incivility in the workplace. *Academy of Management Review* 24 (3): 452–71.

Archer, Dane and Robin M. Akert (1977) Words and everything else: Verbal and nonverbal cues in social interpretation. *Journal of Personality and Social Psychology* 35: 443–9.

(1980) The encoding of meaning: A test of three theories of social interaction. *Sociological Inquiry* 50 (3–4): 393–419.

Archer, Dawn E. (2008) Verbal aggression in the historical courtroom: Sanctioned but not necessarily impolite? In: Derek Bousfield and Miriam Locher (eds.) *Impoliteness in Language: Studies on its Interplay with Power in Theory and Practice.* Berlin and New York: Mouton de Gruyter.

Arndt, Horst and Richard Wayne Janney (1985) Politeness revisited: Cross-modal supportive strategies. *International Review of Applied Linguistics in Language Teaching* 23 (4): 281–300.

(1987) *Intergrammar: Toward an Integrative Model of Verbal, Prosodic and Kinesic Choices in Speech.* Berlin: De Gruyter.

Arundale, Robert B. (1999) An alternative model and ideology of communication for an alternative to politeness theory. *Pragmatics* 9 (1): 119–53.

(2006) Face as relational and interactional: A communication framework for research on face, facework, and politeness. *Journal of Politeness Research: Language, Behaviour, Culture* 2 (2): 193–217.

(2008) Against (Gricean) intentions at the heart of human interaction. *Intercultural Pragmatics* 5 (2): 229–58.

Asch, Soloman E. (1946) Forming impressions of personality. *Journal of Abnormal and Social Psychology* 41: 1230–40.

Augoustinos, Martha and Iain Walker (1995) *Social Cognition: An Integrated Perspective.* London: Sage.

Austin, J. Paddy M. (1987) The Dark Side of Politeness: A Pragmatic Analysis of Non-cooperative Communication. Unpublished Ph.D. dissertation. Christchurch: University of Canterbury.

(1990) Politeness revisited – the dark side. In: Alan Bell and Janet Holmes (eds.) *New Zealand Ways of Speaking English.* Clevedon and Philadelphia: Multilingual Matters, pp. 277–93.

Austin, John L. (1962) *How to Do Things with Words.* Oxford University Press.

Bach, Kent (1975) Performatives are statements too. *Philosophical Studies* 28: 229–36.

(1995) Standardization vs. conventionalization. *Linguistics and Philosophy* 18: 677–86.

(1998) Standardisation revisited. In: Asa Kasher (ed.) *Pragmatics: Critical Concepts.* London: Routledge, pp. 712–22.

Bach, Kent and Robert M. Harnish (1979) *Linguistic Communication and Speech Acts.* Cambridge, MA: MIT Press.

Bakhtin, Mikhail (1986) *Speech Genres and Other Late Essays.* Translated by Vern W. McGee; edited by Caryl Emerson and Michael Holquist. Austin: University of Texas Press.

Banse, Rainer and Klaus Scherer (1996) Acoustic profiles in vocal emotion expression. *Journal of Personality and Social Psychology* 70 (3): 14–636.

Bargiela-Chiappini, Francesca (2003) Face and politeness: New (insights) for old (concepts). *Journal of Pragmatics* 35 (10–11): 1453–69.

Bargh, John A. (1982) Attention and automaticity in the processing of self-relevant information. *Journal of Personality and Social Psychology.* 43 (3): 425–36.

Barker, Chris (2000) *Cultural Studies: Theory and Practice.* London: Sage.

Baron, Robert A. and Deborah R. Richardson (1994) *Human Aggression*. New York: Plenum.

Barthes, Roland (1970) *Mythologies*. Paris: Seuil.

Bartlett, Frederic C. (1995 [1932]) *Remembering: A Study in Experimental and Social Psychology*. Cambridge University Press.

Batchelor, Susan, Michele Burman and Jane Brown (2001) Discussing violence: Let's hear it from the girls. *Probation Journal* 48: 125–34.

Bavelas, Janet B. and Nicole Chovil (2000) Visible acts of meaning: An integrated message model of language in face-to-face dialogue. *Journal of Language and Social Psychology* 19 (2): 163–94.

Baxter, Leslie A. (1984) An investigation of compliance-gaining as politeness. *Human Communication Research* 10: 427–56.

Beatty, Michael J. and Michelle E. Pence (2010) Verbal aggressiveness as an expression of selected biological influences. In: Theodore A. Avtgis and Andrew S. Rancer (eds.) *Arguments, Aggression, and Conflict: New Directions in Theory and Research*, pp. 3–25. London and New York: Routledge.

Beebe, Leslie M. (1995) Polite fictions: Instrumental rudeness as pragmatic competence. In: James E. Alatis, Carolyn A. Straehle, Brent Gallenberger and Maggie Ronkin (eds.) *Linguistics and the Education of Language Teachers: Ethnolinguistic, Psycholinguistics and Sociolinguistic Aspects. Georgetown University Round Table on Languages and Linguistics*. Georgetown: Georgetown University Press, pp. 154–68.

Bell, David M. (1997) Innuendo. *Journal of Pragmatics* 27 (1): 35–59.

Bell, Eugene C. and Roger N. Blakeney (1977) Personality correlates of conflicts modes. *Human Relations*, 30 (9): 849–57.

Berger, Charles R. (1994) Power, dominance, and social interaction. In: Mark L. Knapp and Gerald R. Miller (eds.) *Handbook of Interpersonal Communication*. Thousand Oaks, CA: Sage, pp. 450–507.

Bergson, Henri (1911 [1900]) *Laughter: An Essay on the Meaning of the Comic*. London: Macmillan.

Berkowitz, Leonard (1984) *Advances in Experimental Social Psychology, Vol. 17: Theorizing in Social Psychology: Special Topics*. London and New York: Academic Press.

(1993) *Aggression: Its Causes, Consequences, and Control*. Philadelphia: Temple University Press.

Bernal, Maria (2008) Do insults always insult? Genuine politeness versus non-genuine politeness in colloquial Spanish [¿Insultan los insultos? Descortesía auténtica vs. descortesía no auténtica en el español coloquial]. *Pragmatics* 18 (4): 775–802.

Bettenhausen, Kenneth and J. Keith Murnighan (1985) The emergence of norms in competitive decision-making groups. *Administrative Science Quarterly* 30 (3): 350–72.

Biber, Douglas, Susan Conrad and Randi Reppen (1998) *Corpus Linguistics: Investigating Language Structure and Use*. Cambridge University Press.

Biber, Douglas (2009) A corpus-driven approach to formulaic language in English: Multi-word patterns in speech and writing. *International Journal of Corpus Linguistics* 14 (3): 275–311.

Blakemore, Diane (1987) *Semantic Constraints on Relevance*. Oxford: Blackwell.

Blasko, Dawn G. and Cynthia M. Connine (1993) Effects of familiarity and aptness on metaphor processing. *Journal of Experimental Psychology: Learning, Memory, and Cognition* 19 (2): 295–308.

Blum-Kulka, Shoshana (1987) Indirectness and politeness in requests: Same or different? *Journal of Pragmatics* 11: 131–46.

(1990) You don't touch lettuce with your fingers: Parental politeness in family discourse. *Journal of Pragmatics* 14 (2): 259–87.

Blum-Kulka, Shoshana and Juliane House (1989) Cross-cultural and situational variation in requesting behavior. In: Shoshana Blum-Kulka, Juliane House and Gabriele Kasper (eds.) *Cross-Cultural Pragmatics: Requests and Apologies.* Vol. XXXI: Advances in Discourse Processes. Norwood, NJ: Ablex, pp. 123–54.

Borg, Emma (2004) *Minimal Semantics*. Oxford University Press.

Bourdieu, Pierre (1991) *Language and Symbolic Power*. Cambridge: Polity Press.

Bousfield, Derek (2007a) Impoliteness, preference organization and conducivity. *Multilingua* 26 (1–2): 1–33.

(2007b) Beginnings, middles, and ends: A biopsy of the dynamics of impolite exchanges. *Journal of Pragmatics* 39 (12): 2185–216.

(2008) *Impoliteness in Interaction*. Philadelphia and Amsterdam: John Benjamins.

Bousfield, Derek and Miriam Locher (eds.) (2008) *Impoliteness in Language: Studies on its Interplay with Power in Theory and Practice*. Berlin and New York: Mouton de Gruyter.

Bowers, John W. (1963) Language intensity, social introversion, and attitude change. *Speech Monographs* 30: 345–52.

Bradac, James J., Aaron Castelan Cargile and Jennifer S. Hallett (2001) Language Attitudes: Retrospect, Conspect, and Prospect. In: W. Peter Robinson and Howard Giles (eds.) *The New Handbook of Language and Social Psychology*. Chichester: John Wiley, pp. 137–55.

Brenneis, Donald and Laura Lein (1977) 'You fruithead': A sociolinguistic approach to children's dispute settlement. In: Susan Ervin-Tripp and Claudia Mitchell-Kernan (eds.) *Child Discourse*. London and New York: Academic Press, pp. 49–65.

Brewer, Marilynn B. and Wendi Gardner (1996) Who is this 'we'? Levels of collective identity and self representations. *Journal of Personality and Social Psychology* 71 (1): 83–93.

Brockner, Joel, Batia M. Wiesenfeld and Christopher Martin (1995) Decision frame, procedural justice, and survivors' reactions to job layoffs. *Organizational Behavior and Human Decision Processes* 63 (1): 59–68.

Broomfield, Nicholas and Joan Churchill (1981) *Soldier Girls*. Channel 4 Television.

Brown, Bert R. (1970) Face-saving following experimentally induced embarrassment. *Journal of Experimental Social Psychology* 6: 255–71.

Brown, Penelope (1995) Politeness strategies and the attribution of intentions: The case of Tzeltal irony. In: Esther N. Goody (ed.) *Social Intelligence and Interaction: Expressions and Implications of the Social Bias in Human Intelligence*. Cambridge University Press, pp. 153–74.

Brown, Penelope and Stephen C. Levinson (1987) *Politeness: Some Universals in Language Usage*. Cambridge University Press.

Brown, Robert C. and James T. Tedeschi (1976) Determinants of perceived aggression. *Journal of Social Psychology* 100: 77–87.

Brown, Roger and Albert Gilman (1989) Politeness theory and Shakespeare's four major tragedies. *Language in Society* 18: 159–212.

Bruckner, Elke and Karin Knaup (1993) Women's and men's friendships in a comparative perspective. *European Sociological Review* 9 (3): 249–66.

Bryant, Gregory A. and Jean E. Fox Tree (2005) Is there an ironic tone of voice? *Language and Speech* 48: 257–77.

Burman, Michele, Jane Brown, Kay Tisdall and Susan Batchelor (2002) *A View from the Girls: Exploring Violence and Violent Behaviour*. British Economic and Social Research Council Research Report.

Buss, Arnold H. (1961) *The Psychology of Aggression*. New York: Wiley.

(1980) *Self-consciousness and Social Anxiety*. San Francisco, CA: W. H. Freeman.

Buss, David M. (1990) The evolution of anxiety and social exclusion. *Journal of Social and Clinical Psychology* 9: 196–201.

(1999) Evolutionary psychology: A new paradigm for psychological science. In: David H. Rosen and Michael C. Luebbert (eds.) *Evolution of the Psyche*. Westport, CT: Praeger, pp. 1–33.

Caffi, Claudia and Richard Wayne Janney (1994) The pragmatics of emotive communication. *Journal of Pragmatics* 22: 325–73.

Cahn, Dudley D. (1997) Conflict communication: An emerging communication theory of interpersonal conflict. In: Branislov Kovacic (ed.) *Emerging Theories of Human Communication*. New York: State University Press, pp. 45–64.

Cameron, Deborah (2004) Out of the bottle: The social life of metalanguage. In: Adam Jaworski, Nikolas Coupland and Dariusz Galasiński (eds.) *Metalanguage: Social and Ideological Perspectives*. Berlin and New York: Mouton de Gruyter, pp. 311–21.

(2007) Redefining rudeness: From polite social intercourse to 'good communication'. In: Mina Gorji (ed.) *Rude Britannia*. London: Routledge, pp. 127–38.

Cappelen, Herman and Ernie Lepore (2005) *Insensitive Semantics: A Defense of Semantic Minimalism and Speech Act Pluralism*. Oxford: Blackwell.

Carston, Robyn (2002) *Thoughts and Utterances: The Pragmatics of Explicit Communication*. Oxford: Blackwell.

Carlson, Michael, Amy Marcus-Newhall and Norman Miller (1989) Evidence for a general construct of aggression. *Personality and Social Psychology Bulletin* 15: 377–89.

Carter, Ronald (2004) *Language and Creativity: The Art of Common Talk*. London and New York: Routledge.

Carver, Charles S. and David C. Glass (1978) Coronary-prone behavior pattern and interpersonal aggression. *Journal of Personality and Social Psychology* 36: 361–66.

Catalano, Ralph, Raymond Novaco and William McConnell (1997) A model of the net effect of job loss on violence. *Journal of Personality and Social Psychology* 72: 1440–7.

Cashman, Holly (2006) Impoliteness in children's interactions in a Spanish/English bilingual community of practice. *Journal of Politeness Research: Language, Behaviour, Culture* 2 (2): 217–46.

Cheang, Henry S. and Marc D. Pell (2008) The sound of sarcasm. *Speech Communication* 50: 366–81.

Chen, Serena, Helen C. Boucher and Molly Parker Tapias (2006) The relational self revealed: Integrative conceptualization and implications for interpersonal life. *Psychological Bulletin* 132 (2): 151–79.

Chomsky Noam (1962) Paper given at *Third Texas Conference on Problems of Linguistic Analysis in English*, 1958. Austin: University of Texas.

Chory, Rebecca M. (2010) Media entertainment and verbal aggression: Contents, effects, and correlates. In: Theodore A. Avtgis and Andrew S. Rancer (eds.) *Arguments, Aggression, and Conflict: New Directions in Theory and Research*. London and New York: Routledge, pp. 176–97.

Chovil, Nicole (1991–1992) Discourse-oriented facial displays in conversation. *Research on Language and Social Interaction* 25: 163–94.

Christie, Chris (2005) Editorial. *Journal of Politeness Research: Language, Behaviour, Culture* 1 (1): 1–7.

Cialdini, Robert B., John T. Cacioppo, Rodney Bassett and John A. Miller (1978) Low-ball procedure for producing compliance: Commitment then cost. *Journal of Personality and Social Psychology* 36: 463–73.

Clark, Herbert H. (1996) *Using Language*. Cambridge University Press.

Collins Cobuild English Language Dictionary (1987) [1st edn.] Edited by John Sinclair, Patrick Hanks, Gwyneth Fox, Rosamund Moon and Penny Stock. London and Glasgow: Collins.

Colston, Herbert L. (1997) I've never heard anything like it: Overstatement, understatement, and irony. *Metaphor and Symbol* 12 (1): 43–58.

Conway, Martin A. and Debra A. Bekerian (1987) Situational knowledge and emotions. *Cognition and Emotion* 1: 145–91.

Couper-Kuhlen, Elizabeth (1996) The prosody of repetition: On quoting and mimicry. In: Elizabeth Couper-Kuhlen and Margaret Selting (eds.) *Prosody in Conversation*. Cambridge University Press.

Coupland, Nikolas (2007) *Style: Language Variation and Identity*. Cambridge University Press.

Coupland, Nikolas and Adam Jaworski (2004) Sociolinguistic perspectives on metalanguage: Reflexivity, evaluation and ideology. *Language, Power and Social Process* 11: 15–52.

Cowell, Tony (2006) *I Hate to be Rude, but . . . Simon Cowell's Book of Nasty Comments*. London: Blake Publishing.

Craig, Robert, Karen Tracy and Frances Spisak (1986) The discourse of requests: Assessment of a politeness approach. *Human Communication Research* 12: 437–68.

Crowley, Tony (2007) When Saturday comes: The boundaries of football rudeness. In: Mina Gorji (ed.) *Rude Britannia*. London and New York: Routledge, pp. 115–26.

Cruse, Alan D. (2000) *Meaning in Language: An Introduction to Semantics and Pragmatics*. Oxford University Press.

Culpeper, Jonathan (1996) Towards an anatomy of impoliteness. *Journal of Pragmatics* 25: 349–67.

(1998) (Im)politeness in drama. In: Jonathan Culpeper, Mick Short and Peter Verdonk (eds.) *Studying Drama: From Text to Context*. London: Routledge, pp. 83–95.

(2001) *Language and Characterisation: People in Plays and other Texts*. London: Longman.

(2005) Impoliteness and entertainment in the television quiz show: The Weakest Link. *Journal of Politeness Research: Language, Behaviour, Culture* 1: 35–72.

(2008) Reflections on impoliteness, relational work and power. In: Derek Bousfield and Miriam Locher (eds.) *Impoliteness in Language: Studies on its Interplay with Power in Theory and Practice*. Berlin and New York: Mouton de Gruyter, pp. 17–44.

(2009) The metalanguage of impoliteness: Explorations in the Oxford English Corpus. In: Paul Baker (ed.) *Contemporary Corpus Linguistics*. London: Continuum.

(forthcoming a) Conventionalised impoliteness formulae. *Journal of Pragmatics*.

(forthcoming b) 'It's not what he said, it's how he said it!': Prosody and impoliteness. In: Members of the Linguistic Politeness Research Group (eds.) *Politeness Now: A Collection of Essays by the Linguistic Politeness Research Group*. Berlin: Mouton de Gruyter.

Culpeper, Jonathan, Derek Bousfield and Anne Wichmann (2003) Impoliteness revisited: With special reference to dynamic and prosodic aspects. *Journal of Pragmatics* 35: 1545–79.

Culpeper, Jonathan, Robert Crawshaw and Julia Davies (2008) 'Activity types' and 'discourse types': Mediating 'advice' in interactions between foreign language assistants and their supervisors in schools in France and England. *Multilingua* 27: 297–324.

Culpeper, Jonathan, Leyla Marti, Minna Nevala, Meilian Mei and Gila Schauer (forthcoming) The cross-cultural variation of impoliteness: A study of face-attack in impoliteness events reported by students in Britain, China, Finland, Germany and Turkey. *Intercultural Pragmatics*.

Cupach, William R. (2007) 'You're bugging me!': Complaints and criticism from a partner. In: Brian H. Spitzburg and William R. Cupach (eds.) *The Dark Side of Interpersonal Communication* (2nd edn). New Jersey and London: Lawrence Erlbaum, pp. 143–68.

Cupach, William R. and Sandra Metts (1994) *Facework*. London: Sage.

Cupach, William R. and Brian H. Spitzberg (eds.) (1994) *The Dark Side of Interpersonal Communication* (1st edn). New Jersey and London: Lawrence Erlbaum.

Dailey, René, Carmen M. Lee and Brian H. Spitzberg (2007) Communicative aggression: Toward a more interactional view of psychological abuse. In: Brian H. Spitzburg and William R. Cupach (eds.) *The Dark Side of Interpersonal Communication* (2nd edn). New Jersey and London: Lawrence Erlbaum, pp. 297–326.

Daly, Nicola, Janet Holmes, Jonathan Newton and Maria Stubbe (2004) Expletives as solidarity signals in FTAs on the factory floor. *Journal of Pragmatics* 36: 945–64.

Darwin, Charles R. (1872) *Origin of Species*. London: John Murray.

Dascal, Marcelo (1983) *Pragmatics and the Philosophy of Mind, Vol. I: Thought in Language*. Amsterdam and Philadelphia: Benjamins.

DePaulo, Bella M. and Howard S. Friedman (1998) Nonverbal communication. In: Daniel T. Gilbert, Susan T. Fiske and Gardner Lindzey (eds.) *The Handbook of Social Psychology, Vol. II* (4th edn). Berkshire and New York: McGraw-Hill, pp. 3–40.

Deutsch, Morton (1975) Equity, equality, and need: What determines which values will be used as a basis of distributive justice? *Journal of Social Issues* 31: 137–50.

Dews, Shelly, Joan Kaplan and Ellen Winner (1995) Why not say it directly? The social functions of irony. *Discourse Processes* 19: 347–67.

Dews, Shelly and Ellen Winner (1995) Muting the meaning: A social function of irony. *Metaphor and Symbolic Activity* 10: 3–19.

  (1997) Attributing meaning to deliberately false utterances. In: Charlotte Mandell and Allyssa McCabe (eds.) *The Problem of Meaning: Behavioral and Cognitive Perspectives*. Amsterdam, Netherlands: Elsevier Science, pp. 377–414.

Dollard, John, Leonard W. Doob, Neal E. Miller, Orval Hobart Mowrer and Robert R. Sears (1939) *Frustration and Aggression*. New Haven, CT: Yale University Press.

Domenici, Kathy and Stephen W. Littlejohn (2006) *Facework*. London: Sage.

Drew, Paul (1987) Po-faced receipts of teases. *Linguistics* 25: 219–53.

Duranti, Alessandro (2006) The social ontology of intentions. *Discourse Studies* 8 (31): 31–40.

Duranti, Alessandro and Charles Goodwin (eds.) (1992) *Rethinking Context: Language as an Interactive Phenomenon*. Cambridge University Press.

Dutton, Donald G., Ehor O. Boyanowsky and Michael Harris Bond (2005) Extreme mass homicide: From military massacre to genocide. *Aggression and Violent Behaviour* 10: 437–73.

Eder, Donna (1990) Serious and playful disputes: Variation in conflict talk among female adolescents. In: Allen D. Grimshaw (ed.) *Conflict Talk: Sociolinguistic Investigations of Arguments and Conversations*. Cambridge University Press, pp. 67–84.

Edwards, Derek and Jonathan Potter (1992) *Discursive Psychology*. London: Sage.

Eelen, Gino (2001) *A Critique of Politeness Theories*. Manchester: St Jerome Publishing.

Ekman, Paul (1979) About brows: Emotional and conversational signals. In: Mario von Carnach, Klaus Foppa, Wolf Lepenies and Detlev Plogg (eds.) *Human Ethology*. Cambridge University Press, pp. 169–202.

Ekman, Paul, Wallace V. Friesen and Silvan S. Tomkins (1971) Facial affect scoring technique: A first validity study. *Semiotica* 3: 37–58.

Ellsworth, Phoebe C., Merrill J. Carlsmith and Alexander Henson (1972) The stare as a stimulus to flight in human subjects: A series of field experiments. *Journal of Personality and Social Psychology* 19: 302–11.

Ervin-Tripp, Susan M., Nancy Bell, Martin Lampert and Amy Strage (1987) Understanding requests. *Linguistics* 25 (1): 107–43.

Eysenck, Michael W. and Mark T. Keane (2010) *Cognitive Psychology: A Student's Handbook*. (6th edn). Hove and New York: Psychology Press.

Fairclough, Norman (1989) *Language and Power* (1st edn). London: Longman.

Feeney, Judith A. (2004) Hurt feelings in couple relationships: Towards integrative models of the negative effects of hurtful events. *Journal of Social and Personal Relationships* 21: 487–508.

Fehr, Ernst, Urs Fischbacher and Simon Gachter (2002) Strong reciprocity, human cooperation and the enforcement of social norms. *Human Nature* 13: 1–25.

Ferguson, Tamara J. and Brendan G. Rule (1983) An attributional perspective on anger and aggression. In: Russell G. Geen and Edward I. Donnerstein (eds.) *Aggression: Theoretical and Empirical Reviews, Vol. I*. London and New York: Academic Press, pp. 41–74.

Fiske, Susan T. and Steven L. Neuberg (1990) A continuum of impression formation, from category-based to individuating processes: Influences of information and motivation on attention and interpretation. In: Mark P. Zanna (ed.) *Advances in Experimental Social Psychology*, Vol. 23. London and New York: Academic Press, pp. 1–74.

Fiske, Susan T. and Shelley E. Taylor (1984) *Social Cognition* (1st edn). New York: Random House.

(1991) *Social Cognition* (2nd edn). Berkshire and New York: McGraw-Hill.

Flynn, Charles P. (1977) *Insult and Society: Patterns of Comparative Action*. London and New York: Kennikat Press.

Fónagy, Iván and Klara Magdics (1963) Emotional patterns in intonation and music. *Zeitschrift für Phonetik* 16: 293–326.

Francis, Gill, Susan Hunston and Elizabeth Manning (eds.) (1996) *Collins COBUILD Grammar Patterns 1: Verbs*. London: HarperCollins.

(1998) *Collins COBUILD Grammar Patterns 2: Nouns and Adjectives*. London: HarperCollins.

Fraser, Bruce (1990) Perspectives on politeness. *Journal of Pragmatics* 14: 219–36.

(1999) Wither politeness. Plenory lecture. International Symposium for Linguistic Politeness, Bangkok, Thailand.

Fraser, Bruce and William Nolen (1981) The association of deference with linguistic form. *International Journal of the Sociology of Language* 27: 93–109.

Frick, Robert W. (1985) Communicating emotion: The role of prosodic features. *Psychological Bulletin* 97 (4): 412–29.

Gabriel, Yiannis (1998) An introduction to the social psychology of insults in organizations. *Human Relations* 51 (11): 1329–54.

Gard, Stephen W. (1980) Fighting words as free speech. *Washington University Law Quarterly* 58 (3): 531–81.

Garfinkel, Harold (1967) *Studies in Ethnomethodology*. Englewood Cliffs, NJ: Prentice Hall.

Gee, James Paul (2008 [1999]) *Social Linguistics and Literacies: Ideology on Discourses* (3rd edn). London and New York: Routledge.

Geen, Russel G. (2001) *Human Aggression*. Buckingham: Open University Press.

Gernsbacher, Morton Ann (1984) Resolving 20 years of inconsistent interactions between lexical familiarity and orthography, concreteness, and polysemy. *Journal of Experimental Psychology: General* 113 (2): 256–81.

Gibbs, Raymond W. (1981) Your wish is my command: Convention and context in interpreting indirect requests. *Journal of Verbal Learning and Verbal Behavior* 20: 431–44.

(1983) Do people always process the literal meanings of indirect requests? *Journal of Experimental Psychology: Learning, Memory, and Cognition* 9: 524–33.

(1999) *Intentions in the Experience of Meaning*. Cambridge University Press.

Gilbert, Daniel T. and Edward E. Jones (1986) Perceiver-induced constraint: Interpretations of self-generated reality. *Journal of Personality and Social Psychology* 50: 269–80.

Gilbert, Margaret (1989) *On Social Facts*. Princeton, NJ: Princeton University Press.

Giora, Rachel (2003) *On Our Mind: Salience, Context, and Figurative Language*. Oxford University Press.

Goffman, Erving (1956) Embarrassment and social organization. *American Journal of Sociology* 62 (3): 264–71.

(1997 [1958]) The characteristics of total institutions. Extracts in: Charles Lemert and Ann Branaman (eds.) *The Goffman Reader*. Massachusetts and Oxford: Blackwell, pp. 55–71.

(1967) *Interactional Ritual: Essays on Face-to-face Behavior*. Garden City, NY: Anchor Books.

(1971) *Relations in Public: Microstudies of the Public Order*. New York: Basic Books.

(1974) *Frame Analysis: An Essay on the Organization of Experience*. New York: Harper and Row.

(1978) Response cries. *Language* 54 (4): 787–815.

Goldberg, Adele E. (1995) *Constructions: A Construction Grammar Approach to Argument Structure*. University of Chicago Press.

Gorji, Mina (2007) *Rude Britannia*. London and New York: Routledge.

Gouldner, Alvin W. (1960) The norm of reciprocity: A preliminary statement. *American Sociological Review* 25 (2): 161–78.

Greenberg, Bradley S. (1976) The effects of language intensity modification on perceived verbal aggressiveness. *Communication Monographs* 43: 130–39.

Greenwell, J. and Harold A. Dengerink (1973) The role of perceived versus actual attack in human physical aggression. *Journal of Personality and Social Psychology* 26: 66–71.

Grice, H. Paul (1957) Meaning. *The Philosophical Review* 66: 377–88.

(1969) Utterer's Meaning and Intentions. *The Philosophical Review* 68: 147–77.

(1975) Logic and conversation. In: Peter Cole and Jerry Morgan (eds.) *Syntax and Semantics 3: Speech Acts*. London and New York: Academic Press, pp. 41–58.

(1989) *Studies in the Way of Words*. Cambridge, MA: Harvard University Press.

Gu, Yueguo (1990) Politeness phenomena in modern Chinese. *Journal of Pragmatics* 14 (2): 237–57.

Gudykunst, William B. and Young Y. Kim (2003) *Communicating with Strangers* (4th edn). Berkshire and New York: McGraw-Hill.

Gumperz, John J. (1982a) *Discourse Strategies*. Cambridge University Press.

(1982b) *Language and Social Identity*. Cambridge University Press.

(1992a) Interviewing in intercultural situations. In: Paul Drew and John Heritage (eds.) *Talk at Work: Interaction in Institutional Settings*. Cambridge University Press, pp. 302–27.

(1992b) Contextualization and understanding. In: Alessandro Duranti and Charles Goodwin (eds.) *Rethinking Context: Language as an Interactive Phenomenon*. Cambridge University Press, pp. 229–52.

Guy, Gregory and Julie Vonwiller (1989) *The High Rise Tones*. In: Peter Collins and David Blair (eds.) *Australian English: The Language of a New Society*. St Lucia: University of Queensland Press.

Haidt, Jonathan (2003) The moral emotion. In: Richard J. Davidson, Klaus R. Scherer and H. Hill Goldsmith (eds.) *Handbook of Affective Sciences*. Oxford University Press, pp. 852–70.

Hamilton, David L. and Jeffrey W. Sherman (1994) Stereotypes. In: Robert S. Wyer and Thomas K. Srull (eds.) *Handbook of Social Cognition, Volume II: Applications* (2nd edn). New Jersey: Lawrence Erlbaum Associates, pp. 1–68.

Hall, Edward T. (1966) *The Hidden Dimension*. Garden City, NY: Doubleday.

Harris, Christine R. (2001) Cardiovascular responses of embarrassment and effects of emotional suppression in a social setting. *Journal of Personality and Social Psychology* 81 (5): 886–97.

Harris, Mary B. (1993) How provoking! What makes men and women angry? *Aggressive Behavior* 19: 199–211.

Harris, Sandra (2001) Being politically impolite: Extending politeness theory to adversarial political discourse. *Discourse and Society* 12 (4): 451–72.

Haugh, Michael (2007) The co-constitution of politeness implicature in conversation. *Journal of Pragmatics* 39 (1): 84–110.

(2008) Intention in pragmatics. *Intercultural Pragmatics* 5 (2): 99–110.

Haugh, Michael and Carl Hinze (2003) A metalinguistics approach to deconstructing the concepts of 'face' and 'politeness' in Chinese, English and Japanese. *Journal of Pragmatics* 35: 1581–611.

Hayes, Christopher (2005) '*Why the fuck do people write on desks?*': *Exploring impoliteness in the social event of a graffiti dialogue*. Unpublished MA dissertation. Lancaster University.

Hecht, Michael L. (1993) 2002 – A research odyssey: Toward the development of a communication theory of identity. *Communication Monographs* 60: 76–80.

Hecht, Michael, Jennifer R. Warren, Eura Jung and Janice L. Krieger (2005) A communication theory of identity. In: William B. Gudykunst (ed.) *Theorizing About Intercultural Communication*. Thousand Oaks, CA: Sage, pp. 257–78.

Heider, Fritz (1958) *The Psychology of Interpersonal Relations*. New York: Wiley & Sons.

Heise, David R. and Cassandra Calhan (1995) Emotion norms in interpersonal events. *Social Psychology Quarterly* 58 (4): 223–40.

Heisel, Alan D. (2010) Verbal aggression and prefrontal cortex asymmetry: Verbal aggressiveness as an expression of selected biological influences. In: Theodore A. Avtgis and Andrew S. Rancer (eds.) *Arguments, Aggression, and Conflict: New Directions in Theory and Research*. London and New York: Routledge, pp. 26–43.

Ho, David Yau-fai (1976) On the concept of face. *American Journal of Sociology* 81: 867–84.

Hobbes, Thomas (1946 [1651]) *Leviathan: or the Matter, Forme and Power of a Commonwealth Ecclesiastical and Civil*. Oxford: Basil Blackwell.

Hoey, Michael (2005) *Lexical Priming: A New Theory of Words and Language*. London and New York: Routledge.

Hofstede, Geert (1991) *Cultures and Organizations: Software of the Mind*. Berkshire and New York: McGraw-Hill.

(1994) *Cultures and Organizations: Intercultural Cooperation and its Importance for Survival*. London: Harper Collins.

Holmes, Janet (1995) *Women, Men and Politeness*. London: Longman.

(1996) Women's role in language change: A place for quantification. In: Natasha Warner, Jocelyn Ahlers, Leela Bilmes, Monica Oliver, Suzanne Wertheim and Melinda Chen (eds.) *Gender and Belief Systems: Proceedings of the Fourth*

Berkeley Women and Language Conference. University of California, Berkeley: Berkeley Women and Language Group, pp. 313–30.

(2000) Politeness, power and provocation: How humour functions in the workplace. *Discourse Studies* 2 (2): 159–85.

(2005) Politeness and postmodernism – an appropriate approach to the analysis of language and gender? *Journal of Sociolinguistics* 9 (1): 108–17.

Holmes, Janet, Meredith Marra and Stephanie Schnurr (2008) Impoliteness and ethnicity: Māori and Pākehā discourse in New Zealand workplaces. *Journal of Politeness Research: Language, Behaviour, Culture* 4 (2): 193–219.

Holmes, Janet and Stephanie Schnurr (2005) Politeness, humor and gender in the workplace: Negotiating norms and identifying contestation. *Journal of Politeness Research: Language, Behaviour, Culture* 1 (1): 121–49.

Holtgraves, Thomas (1986) Language structure in social interaction: Perceptions of direct and indirect speech acts and interactants who use them. *Journal of Personality and Social Psychology* 51: 305–14.

Holtgraves, Thomas (1994) Communication in context: The effects of speaker status on the comprehension of indirect requests. *Journal of Experimental Psychology: Learning, Memory and Cognition* 20: 1205–18.

(1997) Politeness and memory for the wording of remarks. *Memory and Cognition* 25: 106–16.

(2005) Social psychology, cognitive psychology, and linguistic politeness. *Journal of Politeness Research: Language, Behaviour, Culture* 1: 73–93.

Holtgraves, Thomas and Joong-Nam Yang (1990) Politeness as universal: Cross-cultural perceptions of request strategies and inferences based on their use. *Journal of Personality and Social Psychology* 59: 719–29.

Hu, Hsien Chin (1944) The Chinese concepts of 'face'. *American Anthropologist* 46: 45–64.

Huesmann, L. Rowell (1988) An information processing model for the development of aggression. *Aggressive Behavior* 14: 13–24.

Hughes, Geoffrey (1998 [1991]) *Swearing: A Social History of Foul Language, Oaths and Profanity in English.* London: Penguin Books.

(2006) *An Encyclopedia of Swearing: The Social History of Oaths, Profanity, Foul Language, and Ethnic Slurs in the English-speaking World.* Armonk, NY: M.E. Sharpe.

Hummert, Mary L. and Ellen B. Ryan (2001) *Patronizing communication.* In: William P. Robinson and Howard Giles (eds.) *The New Handbook of Language and Social Psychology.* Chichester: John Wiley & Sons, pp. 253–69.

Hunston, Susan and Gill Francis (2000) *Pattern Grammar: A Corpus-driven Approach to the Lexical Grammar of English.* Amsterdam: Benjamins.

Hutchby, Ian (2008) Participants' orientations to interruptions, rudeness and other impolite acts in talk-in-interaction. *Journal of Politeness Research: Language, Behaviour, Culture* 4 (3): 221–41.

Hwang, Kuang-kuo (1987) Face and favor: The Chinese power game. *The American Journal of Sociology* 92 (4): 944–74.

Ide, Sachiko, Beverly Hill, Yukiko M. Carnes, Tsunao Ogino and Akiko Kawasaki (1992) The concept of politeness: An empirical study of American English and Japanese. In: Richard J. Watts, Sachiko Ide and Konrad Ehlich (eds.) *Politeness in Language: Studies in its History, Theory and Practice.* Berlin and New York: Mouton de Gruyter, pp. 281–98.

Infante Dominic A. and Charles J. Wigley (1986) Verbal aggressiveness: An interpersonal model and measure. *Communications Monographs* 53: 61–9.

Jakobson, Roman (1960) Closing statement: Linguistics and poetics. In: Thomas A. Sebeok (ed.) *Style and Language.* Cambridge, MA: MIT Press, pp. 350–77.

Jaszczolt, Katarzyna M. (forthcoming) Semantics and pragmatics: The boundary issue. In: Klaus von Heusinger, Paul Portner and Claudia Maienborn (eds.) *Semantics: An International Handbook of Natural Language Meaning.* Berlin: Mouton de Gruyter.

Jaworski, Adam, Nikolas Coupland and Dariusz Galasiński (eds.) (2004a) *Metalanguage: Social and Ideological Perspectives.* Berlin and New York: Mouton de Gruyter.

(2004b) Metalanguage: Why now? In: Adam Jaworski, Nikolas Coupland and Dariusz Galasiński (eds.) *Metalanguage: Social and Ideological Perspectives.* Berlin and New York: Mouton de Gruyter, pp. 3–8.

Jay, Timothy (1992) *Cursing in America: a Psycholinguistic Study of Dirty Language in the Courts, in the Movies, in the Schoolyards and on the Streets.* Philadelphia: John Benjamins.

(2000) *Why We Curse: A Neuro-psycho-social Theory of Speech.* Philadelphia and Amsterdam: John Benjamins.

Jay, Timothy and Kristin Janschewitz (2008) The pragmatics of swearing. *Journal of Politeness Research: Language, Behaviour, Culture* 4: 267–88.

Johnson-Laird, Philip N. (1983) *Mental Models: Towards a Cognitive Science of Language, Inference, and Consciousness.* Cambridge, MA: Harvard University Press.

Jones, Edward E. (1990) *Interpersonal Perception.* New York: W.H. Freeman.

Jones, Edward E. and Richard E. Nisbett (1972) The actor and the observer: Divergent perceptions of the causes of behavior. In: Edward E. Jones, David E. Kanouse, Harold H. Kelley, Richard E. Nisbett, Stuart Valins and Bernard Weiner (eds.) *Attribution: Perceiving the Causes of Behavior.* Morristown, NJ: General Learning Press Jones, pp. 79–94.

Kakavá, Christina (2003 [2001]) Discourse and conflict. In: Deborah Schiffrin, Deborah Tannen and Heidi E. Hamilton (eds.) *The Handbook of Discourse Analysis.* London: Blackwell, pp. 650–70.

Kachru, Yamuna (1999) Culture, context and writing. In: Eli Hinkel (ed.) *Culture in Second Language Teaching and Learning.* Cambridge University Press, pp. 75–89.

Kasper, Gabriele (1990) Linguistic politeness: Current research issues. *Journal of Pragmatics* 14 (2): 193–218.

Kasper, Gabriele (2008) Data collection in pragmatics research. In: Helen D. M. Spencer-Oatey (ed.) *Culturally Speaking: Culture, Communication and Politeness Theory* (2nd edn). London: Continuum, pp. 279–303.

Kassing, Jeffrey W. and Jimmy Sanderson (2010) Trash talk and beyond: Aggressive communication in the context of sports. In: Theodore A. Avtgis and Andrew S. Rancer (eds.) *Arguments, Aggression, and Conflict: New Directions in Theory and Research.* London and New York: Routledge, pp. 253–66.

Kaul de Marlangeon, Silvia (2008) Impoliteness in institutional and non-institutional contexts. *Pragmatics* 18(4): 735–49.

Kellerman, Eric (1995) Crosslinguistic influence: Transfer to nowhere? *Annual Review of Applied Linguistics* 15: 125–50.

Kellerman, Kathy and Rodney Reynolds (1990) When ignorance is bliss: The role of motivation to reduce uncertainty in Uncertainty Reduction Theory. *Human Communication Research* 17: 5–75.

Kelley, Harold H. (1973) The processes of causal attribution. *American Psychologist* 28: 107–28.

Keltner, Dacher, Lisa Capps, Ann M. Kring, Randall C. Young and Erin A. Heerey (2001) Just teasing: A conceptual analysis and empirical review. *Psychological Bulletin* 127 (2): 229–48.

Keltner, Dacher, Randall C. Young, Erin A. Heerey, Carmen Oemig and Natalie D. Monarch (1998) Teasing in hierarchical and intimate relations. *Journal of Personality and Social Psychology* 75 (5): 1231–47.

Kempson, Ruth M. (1977) *Semantic Theory*. Cambridge University Press.

Kienpointner, Manfred (1997) Varieties of rudeness: Types and functions of impolite utterances. *Functions of Language* 4 (2): 251–87.

    (2008) Impoliteness and emotional arguments. *Journal of Politeness Research: Language, Behaviour, Culture* 4 (2): 243–65.

Kihlstrom, John F. and Nancy Cantor (1984) Mental representations of the self. In: Leonard Berkowitz (ed.) *Advances in Experimental Social Psychology, Vol. 17: Theorizing in Social Psychology: Special Topics*. London and New York: Academic Press, pp. 1–47.

Kilgarriff, Adam, Pavel Rychly, Pavel Smrz and David Tugwell (2004) The Sketch Engine. Proceedings of the *EURALEX* conference. Lorient, France, pp. 105–16.

Kipnis, David (1976) *The Powerholders*. University of Chicago Press.

Kipnis, David and Stuart M. Schmidt (1983) An influence perspective on bargaining within organizations. In: Max H. Bazerman and Roy J. Lewicki (eds.) *Negotiating in Organizations*. Beverly Hills: Sage, pp. 179–210.

Kirkpatrick, Betty (1998) *Roget's Thesaurus*. New Edition. London: Penguin.

Knowles, Gerald (1984) Variable strategies in intonation. In: Dafydd Gibbon and Helmut Richter (eds.) *Intonation, Accent and Rhythm: Studies in Discourse Phonology*. Berlin and New York: de Gruyter, pp. 226–42.

Kochman, Thomas (1983) The boundary between play and nonplay in black verbal duelling. *Language in Society* 12: 329–37.

    (1984) The politics of niceness: Social warrants in mainstream American public etiquette. In: Deborah Schiffrin (ed.) *Georgetown University Round Table on Languages and Linguistics 1984*. Washington, DC: Georgetown University Press, pp. 200–9.

Kotthoff, Helga (1996) Impoliteness and conversational joking: On relational politics. *Folia Linguistica* 30 (3–4): 299–327.

Kowalski, Zobin M. (2000) 'I was only kidding!': Victims' and perpetrators' perceptions of teasing. *Personality and Social Psycholosy Bulletin* 26: 231–41.

Kroeber, Alfred L. and Clyde Kluckhohn (1952) *A Critical View of Concepts and Definitions*. Cambridge, MA: Harvard University Press.

Labov, William (1972) *Language in the Inner City: Studies in the Black English Vernacular*. Oxford: Blackwell.

Lachenicht, Lance G. (1980) Aggravating language: A study of abusive and insulting language. *International Journal of Human Communication* 13 (4): 607–88.

Lagerspetz, E. Heikki Ikaheimo and Jussi Kotkavirta (eds.) (2001) *On the Nature of Social and Institutional Reality*. Finland: SoPhi.

Lakoff, Robin Tolmach (1973) The logic of politeness, or minding your p's and q's. *Papers from the Ninth Regional Meeting of the Chicago Linguistic Society*: 292–305.

(1989) The limits of politeness: Therapeutic and courtroom discourse. *Multilingua* 8 (2–3): 101–29.

Leary, Mark R., Carrie Springer, Laura Negel, Emily Ansell and Kelly Evans (1998) The causes, phenomenology, and consequences of hurt feelings. *Journal of Personality and Social Psychology* 74: 1225–37.

Leech, Geoffrey N. (1969) *A Guide to English Poetry*. London: Longman.

(1981 [1974]) *Semantics: The Study of Meaning* (2nd edn). Harmondsworth: Penguin Books.

(1983) *Principles of Pragmatics*. London: Longman.

(1985) Stylistics. In: Teun A. van Dijk (ed.) *Discourse and Literature*. Amsterdam and Philadelphia: John Benjamins, pp. 39–57.

(2003) Towards an Anatomy of Politeness in Communication. *International Journal of Pragmatics* 14: 101–23.

(2007) Politeness: Is there an East-West divide? *Journal of Politeness Research: Language, Behaviour, Culture* 3 (2): 167–206.

Leichty, Greg and James L. Applegate (1991) Social cognitive and situational influences on the use of face-saving persuasive strategies. *Human Communication Research* 17 (3): 451–84.

Lein, Laura and Donald Brenneis (1978) Children's disputes in three speech communities. *Language in Society* 7: 299–323.

Le Page, Robert B. and Andree Tabouret-Keller (1985) *Acts of Identity: Creole-based Approaches to Language and Ethnicity*. Cambridge University Press.

Lerner, Melvin J. (1980) *The Belief in a Just World*. New York: Plenum Press.

Levinson, Stephen C. (1992 [1979a]) Activity types and language. In: Paul Drew and John Heritage (eds.) *Talk at Work: Interaction in Institutional Settings*. Cambridge University Press, pp. 66–100.

(1979b) Activity types and language. *Linguistics* 17 (5–6): 356–99.

(1995) Interactional biases in human thinking. In: Esther N. Goody (ed.) *Social Intelligence and Interaction: Expressions and Implications of the Social Bias in Human Intelligence*. Cambridge University Press, pp. 221–60.

(2000) *Presumptive Meanings: The Theory of Generalised Conversational Implicature*. Cambridge, MA: MIT Press.

(2002) Contextualizing 'contextualization cues'. In: Susan Eerdmans, Carlo Prevignano and Paul J. Thibault (eds.) *Language and Interaction: Discussions with John Gumperz*. Amsterdam: John Benjamins, pp. 31–9.

Lewis, David K. (1969) *Convention: A Philosophical Study*. Cambridge, MA: Harvard University Press.

Lim, Tae-Seop and John Waite Bowers (1991) Facework: Solidarity, approbation and tact. *Human Communication Research* 17 (3): 415–50.

Lin, Dekang (1998) Automatic retrieval and clustering of similar words. *COLING-ACL.* Montreal, pp. 768–74.

Liu, Runquig (1986) The Politeness Principle and 'A Dream of Red Mansions'. Unpublished M.Phil. dissertation. Lancaster University.

Locher, Miriam A. (2004) *Power and Politeness in Action: Disagreements in Oral Communication.* Berlin and New York: Mouton de Gruyter.

(2006) Polite behaviour within relational work: The discursive approach to politeness. *Multilingua* 25 (3): 249–67.

Locher, Miriam A. and Derek Bousfield (2008) Introduction: Impoliteness and power in language. In: Derek Bousfield and Miriam A. Locher (eds.) *Impoliteness in Language: Studies on its Interplay with Power in Theory and Practice.* Berlin and New York: Mouton de Gruyter, pp. 1–13.

Locher, Miriam A. and Richard J. Watts (2005) Politeness theory and relational work. *Journal of Politeness Research: Language, Behaviour, Culture* 1 (1): 9–33.

(2008) Relational work and impoliteness: Negotiating norms of linguistic behaviour. In: Derek Bousfield and Miriam A. Locher (eds.) *Impoliteness in Language: Studies on its Interplay with Power in Theory and Practice.* Berlin and New York: Mouton de Gruyter, pp. 77–99.

Lorenz, Konrad (1966) *On Aggression.* London: Methuen & Co.

Lucretius, Titus Carus (1947 [1st century B.C.]) *De Rerum Natura.* Oxford University Press.

Lucy, John A. (1992) *Language Diversity and Thought: A Reformulation of the Linguistic Relativity Hypothesis.* Cambridge University Press.

(1993) Reflexive language and the human disciplines. In: John A. Lucy (ed.) *Reflexive Language: Reported Speech and Metapragmatics.* Cambridge University Press, pp. 9–32.

Lumsden, David (2008) Kinds of conversational cooperation. *Journal of Pragmatics* 40 (11): 1896–1908.

Malle, Bertram F. and Joshua Knobe (1997) The folk concept of intentionality. *Journal of Experimental Social Psychology* 3: 101–27.

Mao, LuMing Robert (1994) Beyond politeness theory: 'Face' revisited and renewed. *Journal of Pragmatics* 21 (5): 451–86.

Markus, Hazel and Paula S. Nurius (1986) Possible selves. *American Psychologist* 41 (9): 954–69.

Matsumoto, Yoshiko (1988) Reexamination of the universality of face: Politeness phenomena in Japanese. *Journal of Pragmatics* 12 (4): 403–26.

Matthews, Gordon (2000) *Global Culture/Individual Identity: Searching for Home in the Cultural Supermarket.* London: Routledge.

McEnery, Anthony M. (2006) *Swearing in English: Bad Language, Purity and Power from 1586 to the Present.* London: Routledge.

McEwen, William J. and Bradley S. Greenberg (1970) The effects of message intensity on receiver evaluations of source, message, and topic. *Journal of Communication* 20: 340–50.

Meier, Ardith J. (1995) Defining politeness: Universality in appropriateness. *Language Sciences,* 17 (4): 345–56.

Merriam-Webster Thesaurus, The (1991) Springfield, MA: Merriam-Webster Incorporated.

Merriam-Webster's Online Thesaurus (2009) Merriam-Webster, Incorporated. See: www.merriam-webster.com/

Mertz, Elizabeth (1998) Linguistic ideology and praxis in U.S. law school classrooms. In: Bambi B. Schieffelin, Kathryn A. Woolard and Paul V. Kroskrity (eds.) *Language Ideologies: Practices and Theory*. New York and Oxford: Oxford University Press, pp. 149–62.

Mills, Sara (2002) Rethinking politeness, impoliteness and gender identity. In: Lia Litoselliti and Jane Sunderland (eds.) *Gender Identity and Discourse Analysis*. Amsterdam and Philadelphia: John Benjamins, pp. 69–89.

(2003) *Gender and Politeness*. Cambridge University Press.

(2005) Gender and impoliteness. *Journal of Politeness Research: Language, Behaviour, Culture* 1 (2): 263–80.

(2008) Language and Sexism. Cambridge University Press.

(2009) Politeness and culture. *Journal of Pragmatics* 41: 1047–60.

Millwood-Hargrave, Andrea (2000) *Delete expletives?: Research undertaken jointly by the Advertising Standards Authority, British Broadcasting Corporation, Broadcasting Standards Commission and the Independent Television Commission*. London: ASA, BBC, BSC and ITC.

Minsky, Marvin (1975) A framework for representing knowledge. In: Patrick H. Winston (ed.) *The Psychology of Computer Vision*. Berkshire and New York: McGraw-Hill, 211–77.

Montagu, Ashley (2001 [1967]) *Anatomy of Swearing*. University of Pennsylvania Press.

Montgomery, Martin (1999) Talk as entertainment: The case of The Mrs Merton Show. In: Louann Haarman (ed.) *Talk about Shows: La Parola e lo Spettacolo*. Bologna: CLUEB, pp. 101–50.

Montry, Jill A. (2002) *How To Be Rude! A Training Manual for Mastering the Art of Rudeness* (2nd edn). Irving, TX: Rapid Random, Ltd.

Mooney, Annabelle (2004) Co-operation, Violation and Making Sense. *Journal of Pragmatics* 33: 1601–23.

Morris, Desmond J. (1967) *The Naked Ape*. London: Bantam Books.

Mukařovský, Jan (1970) Standard language and poetic language, ed. and trans. by Paul L. Garvin. In: Donald C. Freeman (ed.) *Linguistics and Literary Style*. New York: Holt, Rinehart and Winston, pp. 40–56.

Mummenday, Amélie and Sabine Otten (2001) Aggressive behaviour. In: Miles Hewstone and Wolfgang Stroebe (eds.) *Introduction to Social Psychology*. Oxford: Blackwell, pp. 315–40.

Murray, Iain R. and John L. Arnott (1993) Toward the simulation of emotion in synthetic speech: A review of the literature on human vocal emotion. *Journal of the Acoustical Society of America* 93 (2): 1097–108.

Myers, Greg (2001) 'I'm out of it; you guys argue': Making an issue of it on The Jerry Springer Show. In: Andrew Tolson (ed.) *Television Talk Shows: Discourse, Performance, Spectacle*. Mahwah, NJ: Lawrence Erlbaum, pp. 173–91.

Myers, Scott A. and Christine E. Rittenour (2010) Student aggressive communication in the K-12 classroom. In: Theodore A. Avtgis and Andrew S. Rancer (eds.) *Arguments, Aggression, and Conflict: New Directions in Theory and Research*. London and New York: Routledge, pp. 139–58.

Nansel, Tonja R., Mary Overpeck, Ramani S. Pilla, June W. Ruan, Bruce Simons-Morton and Peter Scheidt (2001) Bullying behaviors among US youth: Prevalence and association with psychological adjustment. *Journal of the American Medical Association* 285(16): 2094–100.

Neisser, Ulric (1976) *Cognition and Reality: Principles and Implications of Cognitive Psychology.* San Francisco: W. H. Freeman.

Nwoye, Onuigbo G. (1992) Linguistic politeness and socio-cultural variations of the notion of face. *Journal of Pragmatics* 18 (4): 309–28.

O'Driscoll, Jim (2007) What's in an FTA? Reflections on a chance meeting with Claudine. *Journal of Politeness Research: Language, Behaviour, Culture* 3 (2): 243–68.

Ofuka, Etsuko, J. Denis McKeown, Mitch G. Waterman and Peter J. Roach (2000) Prosodic cues for rated politeness in Japanese speech. *Speech Communication* 32 (3): 199–217.

Ohbuchi, Kennichi and Toshihiro Kambara (1985) Attacker's intent and awareness of outcome, impression management and retaliation. *Journal of Experimental Social Psychology* 21: 321–30.

Opp, Karl-Dieter (1982) The evolutionary emergence of norms. *British Journal of Social Psychology* 21: 139–49.

Ortony, Andrew, Gerald Clore and Allan Collins (1988) *The Cognitive Structure of the Emotions.* Cambridge and New York: Cambridge University Press.

Osgood, Charles E. (1962) Studies on the generality of affective meaning systems. *American Psychologist* 17 (1): 10–28.

Osgood, Charles E., George J. Suci and Percy H. Tannenbaum (1957) *The Measurement of Meaning.* Urbana: University of Illinois Press.

Palmer, Frank R. (1981 [1976]) *Semantics* (2nd edn). Cambridge University Press.

Pavlidou, Theodossia (1991) Cooperation and the Choice of Linguistic Means: Some evidence from the use of the subjunctive in modern Greek. *Journal of Pragmatics* 15: 11–42.

Pearce, W. Barnett (1989) *Communication and the Human Condition.* Carbondale: University of Southern Illinois Press.

Pearce, W. Barnett and Vernon E. Cronen (1980) *Communication, Action, and Meaning: The Creation of Social Realities.* New York: Praeger.

Pearce, W. Barnett and Stephen W. Littlejohn (1997) *Moral Conflict.* Thousand Oaks, CA: Sage.

Perry, David G., Louise C. Perry and Janet P. Boldizar (1990) Learning of aggression. In: Michael Lewis and Suzanne M. Miller (eds.) *Handbook of Developmental Psychopathology.* New York: Plenum, pp. 135–46.

Penman, Robyn (1990) Facework and politeness: Multiple goals in courtroom discourse. *Journal of Language and Social Psychology* 9: 15–38.

   (1994) Facework in communication: Conceptual and moral challenges. In: Stella W. C. Ting-Toomey (ed.) *The Challenge of Facework.* Albany: State University of New York Press, pp. 15–46.

Pexman, Penny M. and Kara M. Olineck (2002) Does Sarcasm Always Sting? Investigating the Impact of Ironic Insults and Ironic Compliments. *Discourse Processes* 33 (3): 199–217.

Piirainen-Marsh, Arja (2005) Managing adversarial questions in broadcast interviews. *Journal of Politeness Research: Language, Behaviour, Culture* 1 (2): 193–217.

Pratto, Felicia and Oliver P. John (1991) Automatic vigilance: The attention-grabbing power of negative social information. *Journal of Personality and Social Psychology* 61: 380–91.

Pratto, Felicia and Oliver P. John (2005 [1991]) Automatic vigilance: The attention-grabbing power of negative social information. In: David L. Hamilton (ed.) *Social Cognition*. London: Taylor & Francis, pp. 250–65.

Quirk, Randolph, Sidney Greenbaum, Geoffrey Leech and Jan Svartvik (1985) *A Comprehensive Grammar of the English Language*. London and New York: Longman.

Rancer, Andrew S., Yang Lin, James M. Durbin and Emily C. Faulkner (2010) Nonverbal 'verbal' aggression: Its forms and its relation to trait verbal aggressiveness. In: Theodore A. Avtgis and Andrew S. Rancer (eds.) *Arguments, Aggression, and Conflict: New Directions in Theory and Research*. London and New York: Routledge, pp. 267–84.

Recanati, François (2004) *Literal Meaning*. Cambridge University Press.

Richardson, Kay and Ulrike Hanna Meinhof (1999) *Worlds in Common? Television Discourse in a Changing Europe*. London: Routledge.

Rockwell, Patricia (2004) The sarcastic: A linguistic and paralinguistic analysis. *Language and Social Interaction Division, International Communication Association Annual Convention*, May 2004. New Orleans, Louisiana.

Roget's 21st Century Thesaurus (3rd edn) (2008) Philip Lief Group. See: http://dictionary.reference.com/ or http://thesaurus.reference.com/

Rohrer, John H., Seymour H. Baron, E. L. Hoffman and D. V. Swander (1954) The stability of autokinetic judgments. *Journal of Abnormal and Social Psychology* 49: 595–7.

Rondina, Catherine and Dan Workman (2005) *Rudeness: Deal With It If You Please*. Toronto, Ontario: Lorimer.

Rosch, Eleanor (1973) Natural categories. *Cognitive Psychology* 4: 328–50.

(1978) Principles of categorization. In: Eleanor Rosch and Barbara B. Lloyd (eds.) *Cognition and Categorization*. New Jersey and London: Lawrence Erlbaum, pp. 27–48.

Rosch, Eleanor, Carolyn B. Mervis, Wayne D. Gray, David M. Johnson and Penny Boyes-Braem (1976) Basic objects in natural categories. *Cognitive Psychology* 8: 382–439.

Rosenbaum, Ray H. and Meyer Friedman (1974) Neurogenic factors in pathogenesis of coronary heart disease. *Medical Clinics of North America* 58: 269–79.

Ross, Lee (1977) The intuitive psychologist and his shortcomings: Distortions in the attribution process. In: Leonard Berkowitz (ed.) *Advances in Experimental Social Psychology, Vol. 10*. London and New York: Academic Press, pp. 173–220.

Rozin, Paul, Laura Lowery, Sumio Imada and Jonathan Haidt (1999) The CAD triad hypothesis: A mapping between three moral emotions (contempt, anger, disgust) and three moral codes (community, autonomy, divinity). *Journal of Personality and Social Psychology* 76 (4): 574–86.

Rudanko, Juhani (2006) Aggravated impoliteness and two types of speaker intention in an episode in Shakespeare's Timon of Athens. *Journal of Pragmatics* 38 (6): 829–41.

Ruggiero, Thomas E. and Kristi S. Lattin (2008) Intercollegiate female coaches' use of verbally aggressive communication toward African American female athletes. *The Howard Journal of Communications* 19: 105–24.

Ruhi, Şükriye (2008) Intentionality, communicative intentions and the implication of politeness. *Intercultural Pragmatics* 5 (3): 287–314.

Rumelhart, David E. (1984) Schemata and the cognitive system. In: Robert S. Wyer and Thomas K. Srull (eds.) *Handbook of Social Cognition*. New Jersey and London: Lawrence Erlbaum, pp. 161–88.

Russell, James A. (1991) In defense of a prototype approach to emotion concepts. *Journal of Personality and Social Psychology* 60 (1): 37–47.

Sarangi, Srikant and Stefaun Slembrouck (1992) Non-cooperation in communication: A reassessment of Gricean pragmatics. *Journal of Pragmatics* 17(2): 117–54.

(1997) Confrontational asymmetries in institutional discourse: A socio-pragmatic view of information exchange and face management. In: Jan Blommaert and Chris Bulcaen (eds.) *Political Linguistics*. Amsterdam: John Benjamins, pp. 255–75.

Schank, Roger C. and Robert P. Abelson (1977) *Scripts, Plans, Goals, and Understanding: An Inquiry into Human Knowledge Structures*. New Jersey and London: Lawrence Erlbaum.

Scherer, Klaus R. (1986) Vocal affect expression: A review and a model for future research. *Psychological Bulletin* 99 (2): 143–65.

Scollon, Ron and Suzanne W. Scollon (2001) *Intercultural Communication: A Discourse Approach* (2nd edn). Oxford: Blackwell.

Searle, John R. (1975) A Taxonomy of Illocutionary Acts. In: Keith Gunderson (ed.) *Language, Mind, and Knowledge*. Minneapolis: University of Minnesota Press, pp. 344–69.

Searle, John R. (1990) Collective intentions and actions. In: Philip R. Cohen, Jerry L. Morgan and Martha E. Pollack (eds.) *Intentions in Communication*. Cambridge, MA: Bradford Books, pp. 401–15.

Sedikides, Constantine and Marilynn B. Brewer (2001) *Individual Self, Relational Self, Collective Self*. Philadelphia: Psychological Press.

Shaver, Phillip, Judith Schwartz, Donald Kirson and Cary O'Connor (1987) Emotion knowledge: Further exploration of a prototype approach. *Journal of Personality and Social Psychology* 52 (6): 1061–86.

Sherif, Muzafer (1936) *The Psychology of Social Norms*. New York: Harper & Brothers.

Shisanjing zhushu (Qing Ruanyuan jiaokeban) (1998) *Hangzhou: Zhejiang Guji Chubanshe*. Explanations of Thirteen Lections (The version published under Ruanyuan's direction in Qing dynasty). Hangzhou: Zhejiang Ancient Books Publishing House.

Silverstein, Michael (1993) Metapragmatic discourse and metapragmatic function. In: John A. Lucy (ed.) *Reflexive language: Reported Speech and Metapragmatics*. Cambridge University Press, pp. 33–58.

(1998) The uses and utility of ideology: A commentary. In: Bambi B. Schieffelin, Kathryn A. Woolard and Paul V. Kroskrity (eds.) *Language Ideologies: Practices and Theory*. New York and Oxford: Oxford University Press, pp. 123–45.

Simpson, Jeffry A. and Douglas T. Kenrick (eds.) (1997) *Evolutionary Social Psychology*. New Jersey and London: Lawrence Erlbaum.

Simpson, Paul (1994) 'Nothing new under the sun': Can stylistics be radical? *Paper presented at the Poetics and Linguistics Association conference.* Sheffield Hallam University, April 1994.

Sinclair, John McH. (2004) *Trust the Text: Language Corpus and Discourse.* London: Routledge.

Slugoski, Ben and William Turnbull (1988) Cruel to be kind and kind to be cruel: Sarcasm, banter and social relations. *Journal of Language and Social Psychology* 7: 101–21.

Spencer-Oatey, Helen D. M. (2000) Rapport management: A framework for analysis. In: Helen D. M. Spencer-Oatey (ed.) *Culturally Speaking: Managing Rapport Through Talk Across Cultures.* London and New York: Continuum, pp. 11–46.

(2002) Managing rapport in talk: Using rapport sensitive incidents to explore the motivational concerns underlying the management of relations. *Journal of Pragmatics* 34 (5): 529–45.

(2005) (Im)Politeness, face and perceptions of rapport: Unpackaging their bases and interrelationships. *Journal of Politeness Research: Language, Behaviour, Culture* 1 (1): 95–119.

(2007) Theories of identity and the analysis of face. *Journal of Pragmatics* 39 (4): 639–56.

(2008) *Culturally Speaking: Managing Rapport through Talk across Cultures* (2nd edn). London and New York: Continuum.

Spencer-Oatey, Helen D. M. and Wenying Jiang (2003) Explaining cross-cultural pragmatic findings: Moving from politeness maxims to sociopragmatic interactional principles (SIPs). *Journal of Pragmatics* 35: 1633–50.

Sperber, Dan and Deirdre Wilson (1981) Irony and the use-mention distinction. In: Peter Cole (ed.) *Radical Pragmatics.* London and New York: Academic Press, pp. 295–318.

(1995 [1986]) *Relevance: Communication and Cognition* (2nd edn). Oxford and Cambridge, MA: Blackwell.

Spitzburg, Brian H. and William R. Cupach (eds.) (2007) *The Dark Side of Interpersonal Communication* (2nd edn). New Jersey and London: Lawrence Erlbaum.

Stamp, Glen H. and Mark L. Knapp (1990) The construct of intention in interpersonal communication. *Quarterly Journal of Speech* 76: 282–99.

Steffensen, Margaret S., Chitra Joag-Dev and Richard C. Andersen (1979) A cross-cultural perspective on reading comprehension. *Reading Research Quarterly* 15: 10–29.

Stenström, Anne-Brita, Gisle Andersen and Kristine Hasund (2002) *Trends in Teenage Talk.* Amsterdam: Benjamins.

Storms, Michael D. (1973) Videotape and the attribution process: Reversing actors' and observers' points of view. *Journal of Personality and Social Psychology* 27: 165–75.

Strube, Michael J., Charles W. Turner, Dan Cerro, John Stevens and Frances Hinchley (1984) Interpersonal aggression and the Type A coronary-prone behavior pattern: A theoretical distinctiona and practical implications. *Journal of Personality and Social Psychology* 47: 839–47.

Stubbs, Michael (2001) On inference theories and code theories: Corpus evidence for semantic schemas. *Text* 21 (3): 437–65.

Sunstein, Cass R. (1995) Problems with rules. *California Law Review* 83: 953–1030.

Tangney, June Price, Jeff Stuewig and Debra J. Mashek (2007) Moral emotions and moral behaviour. *Annual Review of Psychology* 58: 345–72.

Taylor, Shelley E., and Susan J. Fiske (1975) Point-of-view and perceptions of causality. *Journal of Personality and Social Psychology* 32: 439–45.

Tedeschi, James T. and Richard B. Felson (1994) *Violence, Aggression, and Coercive Actions*. Washington DC: American Psychological Association.

Terkourafi, Marina (2001) Politeness in Cypriot Greek: A frame-based approach. Unpublished Ph.D. dissertation. University of Cambridge.

— (2002) Politeness and formulaicity: Evidence from Cypriot Greek. *Journal of Greek Linguistics* 3: 179–201.

— (2003) Generalised and particularised implicatures of politeness. In: Peter Kühnlein, Hannes Rieser and Henk Zeevat (eds.) *Perspectives on Dialogue in the New Millennium*. Amsterdam: John Benjamins, pp. 151–66.

— (2005a) Beyond the micro-level in politeness research. *Journal of Politeness Research: Language, Behaviour, Culture* 1 (2): 237–62.

— (2005b) Pragmatic correlates of frequency of use: The case for a notion of 'minimal context'. In: Sophia Marmaridou, Kiki Nikiforidou and Eleni Antonopoulou (eds.) *Reviewing Linguistic Thought: Converging Trends for the 21st Century*. Berlin: Mouton de Gruyter, pp. 209–33.

— (2005c) Identity and semantic change: Aspects of T/V usage in Cyprus. *Journal of Historical Pragmatics* 6(2): 283–306.

— (2008) Towards a unified theory of politeness, impoliteness, and rudeness. In: Derek Bousfield and Miriam Locher (eds.) *Impoliteness in Language: Studies on its Interplay with Power in Theory and Practice*. Berlin and New York: Mouton de Gruyter, pp. 45–74.

Tetreault, Chantal (2009) Reflecting respect: Transcultural communicative practices of Muslim French youth. *Pragmatics* 19 (1): 65–84.

Thibaut, John and Laurens Walker (1975) *Procedural Justice: A Psychological Analysis*. New Jersey and London: Lawrence Erlbaum.

Thomas, Jenny (1986) The dynamics of discourse: A pragmatic analysis of confrontational interaction. Unpublished Ph.D. dissertation. Lancaster University.

— (1995) *Meaning in Interaction: An Introduction to Pragmatics*. London and New York: Longman.

Thomson, Donald F. (1935) The joking relationship and organised obscenity in North Queensland. *American Anthropologist* 37 (3): 460–90.

Ting-Toomey, Stella W. C. (1985) Toward a theory of conflict and culture. In: William B. Gudykunst, Leah P. Stewart and Stella W. C. Ting-Toomey (eds.) *Communication, Culture and Organizational Processes*. New York: Sage, pp. 71–87.

— (1988a) Intercultural conflicts: A face-negotiation theory. In: Young Y. Kim and William B. Gudykunst (eds.) *Theories In Intercultural Communication*. Newbury Park, CA: Sage, pp. 213–35.

— (1988b) Rhetorical sensitivity style in three cultures: France, Japan and the United States. *Central States Speech Communication Journal* 38: 28–36.

— (1988c) Intergroup communication and intergroup simulation in low context and high context cultures. In: David Crookall and Danny Saunders (eds.) *Communication and Simulation: From Two Fields to One Theme.* Clevedon: Multilingual Matters, pp. 169–76.

Ting-Toomey, Stella W. C. and Atsuko Kurogi (1998) Facework competence in intercultural conflict: An updated face-negotiation theory. *International Journal of Intercultural Relations* 22: 187–226.

Toch, Hans H. (1969) *Violent Men: An Inquiry Into The Psychology of Violence.* Chicago: Aldine.

Tolson, Andrew (1991) Televised chat and the synthetic personality. In: Paul Scannel (ed.) *Broadcast Talk.* London: Sage, pp. 178–200.

Tomada, Giovanna and Barry H. Schneider (1997) Relational aggression, gender, and peer acceptance: Invariance across culture, stability over time, and concordance among informants. *Developmental Psychology* 33: 601–09.

Toplak, Maggie and Albert Katz (2000) On the uses of sarcastic irony. *Journal of Pragmatics* 32: 1467–88.

Tracy, Karen (1990) The many faces of facework. In: Howard Giles and William P. Robinson (eds.) *Handbook of Language and Social Psychology.* Chichester: Wiley, pp. 209–26.

(2008) 'Reasonable Hostility': Situation-appropriate face-attack. *Journal of Politeness Research: Language, Behaviour, Culture* 4 (2): 169–91.

Tracy, Karen and Sarah J. Tracy (1998) Rudeness at 911: Reconceptualizing Face and Face Attack. *Human Communication Research* 25 (2): 225–51.

Traugott, Elizabeth C. (1999) The role of pragmatics in a theory of semantic change. In: Jef Verschueren (ed.) *Pragmatics in 1998: Selected Papers from the 6th International Pragmatics Conference, Vol. 2.* Antwerp: International Pragmatics Association, pp. 93–102.

(2004) Historical pragmatics. In: Lawrence R. Horn and Gregory Ward (eds.) *The Handbook of Pragmatics.* Oxford: Blackwell, pp. 538–61.

Truss, Lynne (2005) *Talk to the Hand: The Utter Bloody Rudeness of Everyday Life (or Six Good Reasons to Stay Home and Bolt the Door).* London: Profile Books.

Tulving, Endeland (1972) Episodic and semantic memory. In: Endeland Tulving and Wayne Donaldson (eds.) *Organisation of Memory.* London and New York: Academic Press, pp. 382–403.

Tversky, Amos and Daniel Kahneman (1974) Judgment under uncertainty: Heuristics and biases. *Science* 185: 1124–31.

Urdang, Laurence (1991) *The Oxford Thesaurus.* Oxford University Press.

(1995) *The Macmillan Dictionary of Synonyms and Antonyms.* London and Basingstoke: Macmillan.

Vaillancourt, Tracy, Patricia McDougall, Shelley Hymel, Amanda Krygsman, Jessie Miller, Kelley Stiver and David Clinton (2008) Bullying: Are researchers children/youth talking about the same thing? *International Journal of Behavioural Development* 32: 486–95.

Vandello, Joseph A. and Dov Cohen (2003) Male honour and female fidelity: Implicit cultural scripts that perpetuate domestic violence. *Journal of Personality and Social Psychology* 84: 997–1010.

van Dijk, Teun A. (1987) *Communicating Racism: Ethnic Prejudice in Thought and Talk.* Newbury Park, CA: Sage.

(1988a) *News as Discourse*. New Jersey and London: Lawrence Erlbaum.

(1988b) *News Analysis: Case Studies of International and National News in the Press.* New Jersey and London: Lawrence Erlbaum.

(1989) Structures of discourse and structures of power. In: James A. Anderson (ed.) *Communication Yearbook 12*. Newbury Park, CA: Sage, pp. 18–59.

(1990) Discourse & Society: A new journal for a new research focus. *Discourse & Society* 1: 5–16.

(2008) *Discourse and Context: A Sociocognitive Approach.* Cambridge University Press.

(2009) *Society and Discourse: How Context Controls Text and Talk.* Cambridge University Press.

van Dijk, Teun A. and Walter Kintsch (1983) *Strategies of Discourse Comprehension.* London and New York: Academic Press.

Vangelisti, Anita L. (1994) Messages that hurt. In: William R. Cupach and Brian H. Spitzberg (eds.) *The Dark Side of Interpersonal Communication* (1st edn). New Jersey and London: Lawrence Erlbaum, pp. 53–82.

(2001) Making sense of hurtful interactions in close relationships: When hurt feelings create distance. In: Valerie L. Manusov and John H. Harvey (eds.) *Attribution, Communication Behavior, and Close Relationships*. New York: Cambridge University Press, pp. 38–58.

(2007) Communicating hurt. In: Brian H. Spitzberg and William R. Cupach (eds.) *The Dark Side of Interpersonal Communication* (2nd edn). New Jersey and London: Lawrence Erlbaum, pp. 121–42.

Vangelisti, Anita L. and Stacy L. Young (2000) When words hurt: The effects of perceived intentionality on interpersonal relationships. *Journal of Social and Personal Relationships* 17: 393–424.

Verschueren, Jef (1999) *Understanding Pragmatics*. London: Arnold.

Verschueren, Jef (2004) Identity as denial of diversity. In: Frank Brisard, Michael Meeuwis and Bart Vandenabeele (eds.) *Seduction, Community, Speech*. Amsterdam: Benjamins, pp. 171–81.

Waite, Maurice (ed.) (2001) *The Oxford Paperback Thesaurus* (2nd edn). Oxford University Press.

Wartenberg, Thomas E. (1990) *The Forms of Power: From Domination to Transformation*. Philadelphia: Temple University Press.

Watts, Richard J. (1989) Relevance and relational work: Linguistic politeness as politic behaviour. *Multilingua* 8: 131–66.

(1991) *Power in Family Discourse*. Berlin and New York: Mouton de Gruyter.

(2003) *Politeness*. Cambridge University Press.

(2005) Linguistic politeness research: Quo vadis? In: Richard J. Watts, Sachiko Ide and Konrad Ehlich (eds.) (2005) *Politeness in Language: Studies in its History, Theory and Practice* (2nd edn). Berlin and New York: Mouton de Gruyter, pp. xi–xlvii.

(2008) Rudeness, conceptual blending theory and relational work. *Journal of Politeness Research: Language, Behaviour, Culture* 4 (2): 289–317.

Watts, Richard J., Sachiko Ide and Konrad Ehlich (eds.) (2005) *Politeness in Language: Studies in its History, Theory and Practice* (2nd edn). Berlin and New York: Mouton de Gruyter.

Weizman, Elda (1985) Towards an analysis of opaque utterances: Hints as a request strategy. *Theoretical Linguistics* 12 (1): 153–63.

(1989) Requestive hints. In: Shoshana Blum-Kulka, Gabriele Kasper and Juliane House (eds.) *Cross Cultural Pragmatics: Requests and Apologies*. Norwood, NJ: Ablex, pp. 71–95.

Wenger, Etienne (1998) *Communities of Practice*. Cambridge University Press.

Wichmann, Anne (2000a) *Intonation in Text and Discourse: Beginnings, Middles and Ends*. London: (Longman) Pearson Education.

(2000b) The attitudinal effects of prosody, and how they relate to emotion. In: *Proceedings of the ISCA workshop on Speech and Emotion*. Newcastle, N. Ireland.

Wierzbicka, Anna (2003) *Cross-Cultural Pragmatics: The Semantics of Human Interaction* (2nd edn). Berlin and London: Mouton de Gruyter.

Wittgenstein, Ludwig (1958) *Philosophical Investigations*. Oxford: Blackwell.

Wodak, Ruth (1996) *Disorders of Discourse*. London: Longman.

Young, Stacy L. (2004) Factors that influence recipients' appraisals of hurtful communication. *Journal of Social and Personal Relationships* 21: 291–303.

Yus, Francisco (2000) On reaching the intended ironic interpretation. *International Journal of Communication* 10 (1–2): 22–78.

Zebrowitz, Leslie A. (1990) *Social Perception*. Buckingham: Open University Press.

Zipf, Goerge K. (1965 [1935]) *The Psycho-Biology of Language*. Cambridge, MA: MIT Press.

Index

abuse
  verbal, 4–5, 55, 232–3
accent
  mimicry of, 161–4
activity type, 196
aggravating language. *See* swearing
aggression, 3–4, 20
  and intentionality, 50
  and Type-A Personality, 54
  general aggression model, 56
  verbal, 140, 222–3
Allan, Keith and Kate Burridge, 142–3
Anderson, Craig A., 56
Archer, Dane and Robin M. Akert, 123–4
Aristotle, 61
Arndt, Horst and Richard Wayne Janney, 146–8
Arundale, Robert B., 27–8

bald on record strategy, 180–1, 184
banter, 12, 57, 209
  Banter Principle, 208
  ritualised, 211, 244
Baron and Richardson, 3, 20, 205
Beebe, Leslie M., 19, 220
behaviour, anti-social
  definition of, 21
behaviours
  conventionalised impolite, 136
  in impoliteness events, 155
behaviours, absence of
  as implicational impoliteness trigger, 182–3
Bousfield, Derek, 7, 19, 20
Brown and Levinson, 6, 118–19, 180–1, 184
  definition of face, 25
  difficulties accounting for impoliteness, 7
bullying, 257
Burman, Michelle, xii, 4

Carter, Ronald, 240–4
Chomsky, Noam, 75

cognitive stereotypes, 14
communication studies, 5
Community of Practice, 216
conflict studies, 5
  and discourse, 5
  interpersonal, 5
context, 21, 125
  contextual priming, 201–2
  definition, 195
  model. *See* situation model
contextualisation cues, 125, 129, 196
contrastive patterning. *See* mismatching
Cooperative Principle
  in implicational impoliteness, 157–8
  Maxim of Manner, 159, 160
  Maxim of Quality, 158, 208
  Maxim of Quantity, 159
  Maxim of Relation, 160
co-text, 11–12
  co-textual priming, 203–7
Coupland, Nikolas, 74
Cowell, Simon, 174–5, 177
Craig, Robert, 6–7
creativity
  pattern forming, 240–1
  pattern re-forming, 240–1
  types of, 240–1
Culpeper, Jonathan, 6, 19
  previous work on impoliteness, 7
culture
  cross-cultural studies, 21
  definition of, 12
  individualist vs collectivist, 26
  national, 13–14
cursing, 222–3

data analysis
  criteria for, 11–12
datasets, 8–11
  diary reports collection of, 9–11
diary reports
  emotional reactions, 62–5

288

Made in the USA
Coppell, TX
11 September 2022